UTRECHT:
BRITAIN AND THE CONTINENT
ARCHAEOLOGY, ART AND ARCHITECTURE

Edited by
Elisabeth de Bièvre

THE BRITISH ARCHAEOLOGICAL ASSOCIATION
CONFERENCE TRANSACTIONS XVIII

The Association is especially grateful to

The British Academy
Gemeente Utrecht, Sector Monumenten
Historic Scotland

for generous grants towards the publication of this volume

ISBN Hardback 0 901286 72 9
Paperback 0 901286 73 7

British Library Cataloguing in Publication Data
A catalogue record of this book is available from the British Library

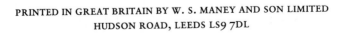

PRINTED IN GREAT BRITAIN BY W. S. MANEY AND SON LIMITED
HUDSON ROAD, LEEDS LS9 7DL

CONTENTS

CONTENTS

PREFACE

The Association celebrated its 150th anniversary in 1993, having survived a variety of vicissitudes and changes in its fortunes. The reason for holding the annual conference abroad was the determination that the BAA's European interests should be reflected. The choice of Utrecht as the centre for the conference and the anniversary celebrations was a natural result of the city's well-known art-historical and architectural links with Britain and the long-established friendships with many archaeologists and other scholars.

The conference would have been impossible had not the Association been fortunate in securing the services of Tarquinius J. Hoekstra of the Department of Ancient Monuments and Historic Buildings of the Municipality of Utrecht as Conference Convenor: we are greatly indebted to him for organizing the programme, receptions and excursions and particularly for compiling and producing a booklet for the visits and excursions.

Attended by 91 delegates from Britain, Germany, France, The Netherlands, Ireland, and the United States of America, of whom eight had been awarded scholarships by the Association, the conference took place between 23 and 27 July. Residential accommodation was at the medieval castle of Beverweerd, Werkhoven, a few miles south of Utrecht, and lectures were held in the Municipal Music School, Domplein 4, Utrecht.

Of all recent conferences this one was memorable in the scale and quality of the receptions afforded to us. We were honoured on 24 July by lunch in the University Library, where we were welcomed by the Director, Peter Bongers, and by the privilege of being shown the Utrecht Psalter by Koert van der Horst. Later, in the Centraal Museum, Eveline Reeskamp, on behalf of the Director, K. M. T. Ex, received us. In the evening we were the guests of Paul Hoogervorst in the bookshop Broese Keminck. The next day Mr Van Tetterode kindly received us for lunch in the canteen of the Municipal Transport Company, and Paul Dirkse, on behalf of the Director, H. L. M. Defoer, introduced us to the collections of the Museum Catherijneconvent. In the evening we were offered a splendid buffet supper in St Peter's church hosted by Jan Seyffert. The following day, the Queen's Commissioner for the Province of Utrecht, P. A. C. Beelaerts van Blokland, invited us to the elegant apartments of the Pope's House for lunch.

On the final day (27 July) an excursion took us into Germany to see the churches of St Martin at Emmerich and of St Clement at Wissel, both formerly in the diocese of Utrecht. In Deventer, Alderman N. van der Plas welcomed us for lunch in the Town Hall. This was followed by visits to the church of St Lebuïnus and the medieval town, guided by Dr Dirk J. de Vries and Mr J. R. M. Magdelijns. The conference concluded with a reception and dinner in the medieval hospital of St Bartholomew, hosted by Dr Ger Mik, Alderman and Deputy Mayor of Utrecht.

Our debt to Tarquinius Hoekstra is acknowledged above. To this must be added our special thanks to Miss Ann Hilder (Conference Secretary) and Dr Richard Morris (Conference Organizer). Gratitude is extended also to Professor Dr Ir. C. L. Temminck Groll, our guide at St Peter's, to Mr A. de Groot for his presentation at the cathedral and to Mr A. F. E. Kipp who guided us up the cathedral tower.

This volume differs from the usual format of the *Transactions* in that, while seven of the conference speakers have articles printed here, because the majority of academic publications is available only in Dutch, the other papers have been specially commissioned. The Association is especially indebted to Dr Elisabeth de Bièvre who has so skilfully compiled and edited the volume. To Dr Martin Henig warmest thanks are due for his never failing support, while editorial assistance was happily received from Koos Gils, Matthew Moran and Julian Munby. In the production of the volume we are especially grateful to Mr B. G. Maney and Mrs Jackie Maidment, of our printers W. S. Maney and Son Ltd., who, as always, have been of enormous assistance with wise counsel and practical help.

This volume is a fitting reminder of a very special conference. It will surely stand for no little time as the only work in English on the archaeology, art and architectural history of the diocese of Utrecht, to the greater benefit of scholarly research.

Laurence Keen, *President*
August 1996

PLATES

The copyright of the photographs belongs to the individuals and organizations identified.

IA.   Utrecht. Tufa fragment of the archway to the *principia*. The largest part has a height of *c.* 0,85 m. The width of the arch would have been between *c.* 3,20 and *c.* 3,80 m
C. Schokker, Amsterdam

B.   Utrecht. Excavations Domplein 1993. The *principia*, showing the atrium surrounded by a portico. The bases are put on a foundation of tufa and cobblestones.
Fotodienst Gemeente Utrecht

C.   Utrecht. Fragment of a Roman rooftile with inscription of the second cohort of the Spanish infantery: COH II HISP PED PF
Rijksdienst Oudheidkundig Bodemonderzoek, Amersfoort

IIA.   The chancel of St Martin's/Holy Cross-chapel, from the north.
R. Rijntjes 1993

B.   South annex with rectangular niche, from the south-east
R. Rijntjes 1993

C.   Chancel and south annex, from the north-east
R. Rijntjes 1993

IIIA.   Detail of the junction of nave (right) and south annex (left) from the east
R. Rijntjes 1993

B.   The junction of south annex and nave; on the foreground: remains of the Roman *principia*
R. Rijntjes 1993

C.   Foundation of church at Elst.

IVA.   The Church of the Saviour at Utrecht. Pen and ink drawing of groundplan by Arnout van Buchel in his historical work *Monumenta passim in templis ac monasteriis Trajectinae urbis*

B.   Model of the early medieval group of churches at Eichstätt. The grand hall in the background was the cathedral, dedicated to the Saviour and Maria. Source: Arnold Angenendt, *Das Frühmittelalter. Die aberländische Christenheit von 400 bis 900* (Stuttgart, Berlin, Cologne, 1990) 278

VA.   The discovery of the medieval Utrecht boat. *Centraal Museum*

B.   The Utrecht boat on arrival in the museum. *Centraal Museum*

C.   The Utrecht boat on display in the museum now. *Centraal Museum*

VIA.   The funeral crown of Emperor Conrad II, Speyer cathedral, from P. E. Schramm and F. Mütherich, *Denkmale der deutschen Könige und Kaiser* München 1980), I, Pl. 149)

B.   Emperor Henry III offers his patron saints, Simon and Jude, the 'Evangeliarium of Goslar' (Echternach, 1050–56), fol. 4^r (P. E. Schramm

TEXT ILLUSTRATIONS

GLOSSARY

Alteratie: the change of religious adherence of the members of the town-council from Catholic to Protestant. In Utrecht this took place in 1577, followed in 1580 with a ban on Catholic practices, through the latter was not accepted by the Provincial States of Utrecht.

Beeldenstorm: iconoclast riots mainly in 1566; in Utrecht also in 1580.

Buurkerk: first parish church in Utrecht (ecclesia civilis or ecclesia civilium -church of the burghers-).

Dom: cathedral

Domplein: cathedral square

Geertekerk: church originally dedicated to St Gertrude

Jacobikerk: church originally dedicated to St James

Janskerk: church originally dedicated to St John

Klaaskerk: church originally dedicated to St Nicholas

Mariakerk: church originally dedicated to the Virgin Mary

Oudmunster: old monastery — old monastery church

Pauluskerk: church originally dedicated to St Paul

Pieterskerk: church originally dedicated to St Peter

Salvatorkerk: church originally dedicated to Christ the Saviour

Zadelmakers gilde: saddlers guild to which the painters and sculptors belonged until 1611

The Beginnings of Utrecht:
Roman Fort and *Vicus**

by Marjo Montforts

IN SEARCH OF ROMAN UTRECHT

The people of Utrecht realized early on that the city had an ancient origin. Already during the Middle Ages, following the discovery of several 'Romeinsche oudheden (Roman antiquities)', her Roman past had become the subject of speculation. It was, however, only during the nineteenth century that research resulted in regular publications dealing with different aspects of Utrecht's possible Roman past. Digging in the centre of town, which was associated with urban redevelopment, brought Roman remains to light; these in their turn encouraged theories about the lay-out and the character of Medieval Utrecht's Roman predecessor.[1]

A series of excavations directed by A. E. van Giffen with the collaboration of C. W. Vollgraf and G. von Hoorn started on the Domplein in 1929 and continued until 1949.[2] The investigation introduced a different level of insight into the Roman past (Fig. 1) revealing an army camp for Roman auxiliaries, a *castellum*, dating between AD 47 and AD 275. The fort had been part of a defensive system on the northern frontier of the Roman empire, the Lower German *limes*.[3] During the reign of the emperor Claudius this frontier was partially constituted by the river Rhine, where it flows East–West through the middle of the Netherlands, reaching the North Sea at Katwijk (Fig. 2). According to a third-century travel guide, the Antonine Itinerary (*Itinerarium Antonini*), this *castellum* was called *Traiectum*, indicating that it was situated on the crossing of a river, namely the Rhine.[4]

Besides the finds from the Domplein, Roman remains have been discovered in other parts of the city. During the 1930s and 1940s further limited excavations beyond the area of the Domplein demonstrated beyond doubt that habitation extended beyond the *castellum*. Although a fuller archaeological survey was possible between 1950 and 1970, when large parts of the town were redeveloped, it was only with the installation of a local archaeological department by the Utrecht council in the year 1972 that more professional and systematic recording was introduced. Instead of being an occasional activity archaeological research then became an integral part of all urban development necessitating interference with the soil. Several sites near the Domplein could now be analysed using modern archaeological methods and techniques.[5]

A *CASTELLUM* UNDER THE DOMPLEIN

The excavations

The excavations of 1929–49 had confirmed the supposition that a Roman *castellum* was hidden under the Domplein. Ironically the initial decision to dig was not in order to explore the Roman past, but to determine the precise location of the early medieval church of St Salvator and the chapel of the Holy Cross. The Roman remains, which

---

*Translated from the Dutch.

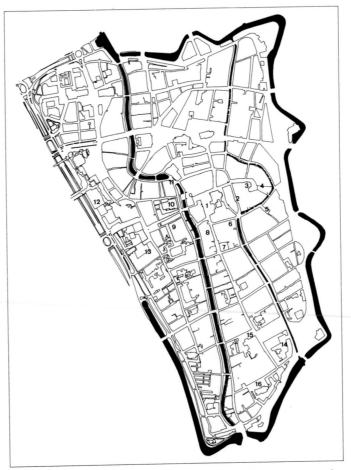

FIG. 1.   Survey of Roman finds in the centre of Utrecht: 1. Domplein; 2. Achter St Pieter;
3. Pieterskerk; 4. Pieterskerkhof; 5. Jeruzalemstraat; 6. Trans; 7. Hamburgerstraat; 8. Korte
Nieuwstraat; 9. Boterstraat; 10. Buurkerk; 11. Stadhuisbrug; 12. Achter Clarenburg; 13. Walsteeg;
14. Nieuwe Gracht; 15. Vrouwjuttenstraat; 16. Nicolaaskerkhof

turned up by chance shortly after the excavation had started, soon became the major
focus of the whole exercise. The team of researchers concentrated on questions of the
size, the number of building phases and the dating of the Roman *castellum*. Much
attention was given to the defenses around the fort: the ramparts, the ditches, the stone-
wall and the gates. Another point of interest was the discovery of the headquarters
building, the *principia*. After 1949 only sporadic excavations could take place, mainly
in connection with building and drainage works (1956, 1975, 1980, 1987, and 1991).
More data were collected, particularly relating to the construction and the layout of the
stone-wall around the fort. Finally, in 1993, while excavating the site of the Holy Cross
chapel, further details of the *principia* were revealed.

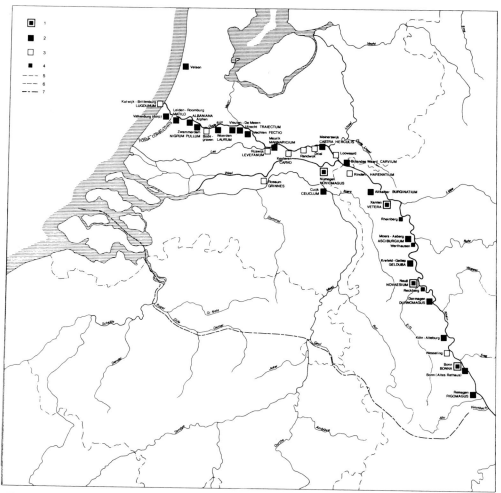

FIG. 2.   The line of forts along the Lower German limes *c.* 47–275: 1. legionary fortress (*castra*);
2. auxiliary fort (*castellum*); 3. possible fort; 4. small fort; 5. border; 6. canal; 7. probable border of
the province of Germania Inferior (Willems 1988)

The results

Although in total only ten percent of the surface of the fort has been excavated, it is
nevertheless possible to sketch the general layout. In a two metre thick layer, between
1.35 and 3.25 m above sea level (NAP), are the remains of five forts built directly on
top of each other during the period AD 47 to AD 175. They are all constructed on a
rectangular plan with rounded corners facing the Rhine. This type of *castellum*, with a
long front, is characteristic of the forts in the delta region of the Rhine. The shape is
known from Valkenburg (South Holland), Zwammerdam and Vechten as well. The
first four *castella* in Utrecht were constructed from timber and earth. They covered a
surface of about 1.3 ha (*c.* 145 × 88/89 m). Utrecht thus belongs to the group of small
forts along the Lower German *limes*.

THE TIMBER FORTS

The first *castellum* was built on the south bank of the river Rhine in the middle of the first century. Arriving from the south the river made a wide loop around what is now the Domplein and continued westward. The natural foundation of that area is made up of river deposits consisting of sand and clay. In order to construct the *castellum* the surface was raised by means of clay sods. The second *castellum*, replacing the first between the years AD 47 and AD 69, was destroyed in the summer of AD 70 during the Batavian revolt of Julius Civilis, as witnessed by the heavy black layer full of carbon and burnt lime. Buried beneath it a gold treasure was found, consisting of fifty *aurei*, most of them dating from Nero's reign, but with the most recent ones being struck during the civil war of AD 68.[6] It is possible that these coins were the property of a soldier, perhaps a centurion, who tried to safeguard his savings by hiding them shortly before the outbreak of violence. Soon after AD 70 the fort was reconstructed for the third time and remained intact until AD 125. The fourth *castellum* seems to have lasted throughout the second century with some repair works probably being executed around AD 180, as can be concluded from the find of roof tiles with stamps of the consul Didius Julianus (SUB DIDO IUL COS) and also those of the Lower German armies (EX GER INF or VEX EX GER INF). These tiles are from the military tile-kilns at Holdeurn near Nijmegen, where, from about AD 175, the roof-tiles for the forts along the *limes* were fired. The end of the fourth *castellum* can be dated around AD 210 late in the reign of Septimius Severus.

The materials used for the foundation and construction of the first four camps were timber and earth. The defenses of the fort consisted of an earthen rampart with timber breastwork and two V-shaped ditches (spitsgrachten), each about two metres wide. The rampart was laid on small tree trunks, about three metres long, and built up with alternating layers of clay sods and beams. This construction was strengthened at the front by a palisade of stakes or boards. A similar rampart is found in the fort of Valkenburg. Of the four entrance gates, which are usually placed in the middle of each side, only two have been found in Utrecht: the East gate (*porta principalis dextra*) and the South gate (*porta decumana*). The position of the other two can be reconstructed, based upon the ground-plan. West of the South gate four post-holes were found, probably belonging to a square tower on the corner. Within the camp the four gates were connected by a cross of roads. Traces of roads have been found in a few places near the South and East Gates and north of the *principia*. Parts of the *via praetoria* and its connection with the *via principalis* have been particularly well examined. From these explorations it emerged that until *c.* AD 200 the roads were constructed with a surface of tree trunks (knuppelwegen) with gutters on each side — sometimes even with a third gutter in the middle to drain torrential rainwater. Very little can be rediscovered of the built-up area within the walls. Only the headquarters building of the fort near the crossing of the *via praetoria* and the *via principalis* has been well investigated. Slight remains of wooden barracks have been found east and west of the headquarters.

THE STONE FORT (Fig. 3)

A stone wall was erected around the camp about AD 210 at the same time that the old timber gates and the *principia* were also reconstructed in stone. It is not clear if other buildings were transformed as well. Only foundations in stone have been found on top

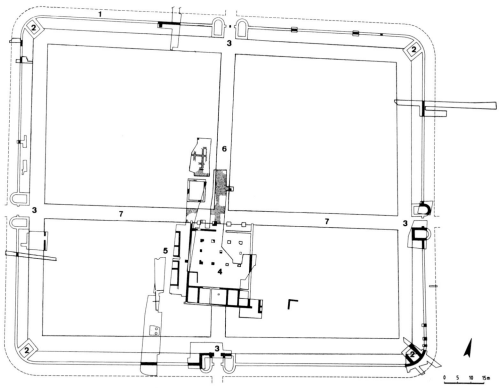

FIG. 3.   Ground-plan of the fifth Roman *castellum*, early third century

of which wooden walls were probably (though not certainly) erected. The new stone perimeter wall was built on the south-, east- and west-ditches of the earlier forts. Only the north wall was moved about 37 m northwards. It is not clear why the fort was extended in this way. Possibly to accommodate a growth in the size of the garrison of the fort, perhaps following a change of unit. The walls were built with properly mortared blocks of tufa and carboniferous limestone on broad foundations made out of rough tufa and slate. In the middle of each side there were again four entrance gates. The South and East Gate each had semicircular towers jutting outward. While towers were mainly square or rectangular during the second century these semicircular towers are a new element in the Roman fortification system. So far Utrecht is the only example of a *castellum* with round towers along the Rhine. The surface of the main roads in the fort was also changed during the third century from wood into stone. This could be observed north of the main building where the *via principalis* crosses the *via praetoria* and also in the continuation of the *via praetoria* towards the North. It is possible that this road was lined on the east side with a row of columns, a *porticus*.

The headquarters building (PRINCIPIA)

Investigation of the *principia* was one of the most important tasks of the excavation. Remains of this building dating from all periods have been recognized. During the first four of these the building was constructed out of timber but in the fifth it was rebuilt in stone at the same time as the rampart, in and around AD 210. It is noteworthy that the *principia* is not at right angles to the *via principalis*. So far no explanation has been advanced to clarify this phenomenon. The building has a rectangular ground-plan (23.30 × 28 m) and its façade looks towards the main gate. In the centre of the north side of the building was the main entrance, a monumental archway constructed of tufa blocks (Pl. IA). Parts of this archway were discovered in 1929 in a well, situated in the inner courtyard of the *principia*. The decoration of the arch is similar to that of the northern entrance gate of Cologne (*Colonia Claudia Ara Agrippinensium*).

Immediately behind the monumental entrance was a rectangular *atrium* surrounded by a portico (Pl. IB). In the middle of the *atrium* the base for an altar was found while in the north western corner the aforementioned well was situated. Behind the *atrium* was a large rectangular hall (*basilica*) with, on the west side, a small L-shaped wall, probably the remains of a speaker's podium (*suggestus*). The *principia* was closed on the south side with a row of about five small rooms, of which the central one was specially designed to house the insignia (*aedes* or *sacellum*). Here the standards and images of the unit were displayed, but it functioned also as its treasury. In the other rooms, which probably fulfilled different administrative functions, some vestiges of a hypocaust for floor heating have been discovered and also fragments of wall-paintings.

Occupation of the CASTELLUM

With the help of the fragments of roof-tiles bearing military stamps we can identify one of the units stationed in Traiectum. It appears that after the year AD 70 (and possibly well into the third century) the *castellum* was home to an infantry division (*cohors peditata*) of about five hundred auxiliaries originally raised in Spain. This is based on tile-stamps so far only found in Utrecht, which read: 'cohors II Hispanorum peditata pia fidelis' (COH II HISP PED PF (Pl. Ic)). The other half of this unit, the 'cohors II Hispanorum equitata', made up of infantry and cavalry, was probably then stationed in Maurik.[7]

Late Roman habitation in the CASTELLUM?

It is not clear what *Traiectum* looked like during the period between AD 275 and AD 450. No archaeological evidence is available to testify to a military occupation of the fort in that period. Domestic artefacts such as sherds from coarse earthenware pots, plates and bowls, dating from the fourth and the fifth centuries and mainly originating from the German Eiffel region as well as a fragment of a decorated bronze hairpin and a bone hair-comb decorated with circular motifs, have been excavated inside the *castellum* indicating that *Traiectum* was not (completely) deserted during this time. Due to the lack of signs of habitation connected with these finds, it is impossible to speculate in precise detail although it is quite easy to imagine a small scale occupation within the fort. Even outside the Domplein area some late Roman finds have come to light. In the east and the north of the present town some fourth-century coins have been found, which may have originated from an earlier bed of the river Vecht. More significant, however, are two complete rough-walled jars, found in the neighbourhood of the Nicolaaskerk. Although we cannot reconstruct the context, we know from similar finds found elsewhere that this sort of vessel is usually associated with funerary contexts. These instances point to, but do not prove, the possible existence of a

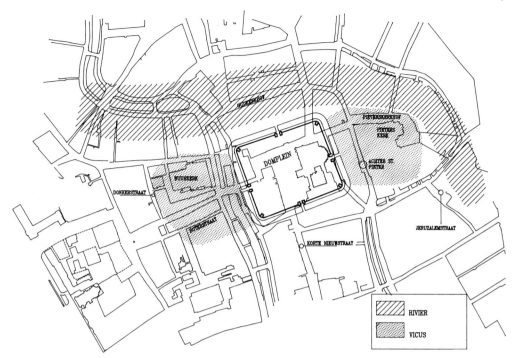

FIG. 4.   The situation of the Utrecht *castellum* with the *vicus* and the possible course of the Rhine, early third century. (Archeologisch en Bouwhistorisch Centrum, Utrecht)

cemetery on the south side of the *castellum*. Hard evidence for the presence of burials is, however, available for the area east of the Domplein, the present day Pieterskerkhof. Here there was a cemetery during the fifth century, of which three burials have been excavated. Two of these are wealthy child-graves dating between AD 410 and AD 443.

HABITATION OUTSIDE THE *CASTELLUM*: THE CIVIL SETTLEMENT (Fig. 4)

The situation of the VICUS

On each side of the Utrecht *castellum* a civil settlement (*vicus*) developed, on the east side around the later Pieterskerk and on the west side round the later Buurkerk. The choice of terrain for the development of the civic quarter was — in the same way as it was for the *castellum* — determined by its relatively high position on the bank of the river. The river bank, about 150 m wide and at its highest 1.20 to 1.30 m above sea level (NAP), followed a line from Pieterskerkhof via Domplein and the Boter/Zadelstraat towards the West. South of the river bank was probably a low-lying area. Although no signs of roads have been found outside the *castellum*, it is probable that the civil population was concentrated along the continuation of the *via principalis* which, in its turn, was part of the road connecting the different forts on the Rhine, parallel to the *limes*. Most *vici* along the *limes* were similarly sited. There was probably no regular occupation south of the *castellum*. No excavations in this area of town have revealed any dwellings from the Roman period, although some pits and ditches have come to

light. The situation is more understandable if one realises that the Rhine in that period
flowed north of the *castellum*.

The area of habitation on the east side presumably stretched from Achter St Pieter
up to and including Pieterskerkhof, ending in the north by the Rhine. The southern
border of the *vicus* was possibly in the area of the Jeruzalemstraat. The surface area of
the eastern *vicus* is estimated at about 2.2 ha. On the west side of the *castellum* it is
now assumed that habitation spread out at least 125 metres to the Donkerstraat. The
southern border was just south of the Boterstraat. Taking these data into account the
surface area can be estimated at about 1.6 ha.

Origins and development of the VICUS

It is likely that at the beginning of the Roman occupation of Utrecht the *vicus* only grew
on a limited scale to the east of the *castellum*. The oldest sherds found outside the
castellum originate from the area of Achter St Pieter, dating from the middle of the first
century, the Claudio-Neronian period. During the Flavian age, in the last part of the
first century, the population expanded. This can be inferred from the growing size of
the area of finds. On the east side expansion took place towards the river near
Pieterskerkhof, while in that period habitation seems to start on the west side as well.
The final phase of civic habitation seems to coincide with the desertion of the *castellum*
around AD 275. In the *vicus* hardly any find dates from the fourth century. The finds of
sherds of this period from within the *castellum* presumably indicate that there was
occupation inside the walls, albeit on a small scale. We know very little in detail about
this period and are reliant on general analogies derived from the situations in Germany
and Britain. The deficiency in our knowledge of the Utrecht *vicus* is partially a result of
the limited and small scale excavations in this part of Utrecht. Moreover, considering
the Utrecht situation one always has to keep in mind that many vestiges of the Roman
and early medieval period have disappeared due to the vagaries of the river, mainly in
the twelfth century.

Traces of habitation

A few material traces bear witness to the three phases of habitation: post-holes (Achter
St Pieter and the 'pandhof' (Chapter Close) of the Pieterskerk), two wells (Achter St
Pieter and Buurkerk) and a few ditches and pits (Korte Nieuwstraat and Boterstraat).
These traces are too restricted at the moment to be used as the basis for further
hypotheses. Only in two cases, in the 'pandhof' of the Pieterskerk and in the Boterstraat
can we begin to reconstruct possible ground-plans of houses. One significant aspect of
the post-holes and ditches east and west of the *castellum* is that their orientation,
although it changes over time, is shared in successive periods. Before the middle of the
second century they were aligned in a south-west–north-east direction or at right angles
to this. This orientation seems to be influenced in part by natural circumstances. By the
second half of the second century these remains are differently orientated, acquiring an
east–west alignment. This alteration may be connected with the flooding of rivers
around the middle of that century, when the area just outside the *castellum* was raised.
In the neighbourhood of Pieterskerkhof, the Trans, the Korte Nieuwstraat and the
Boterstraat particular layers of 0.50 to 1 m thick, have been found, which indicate the
process of raising the ground level.

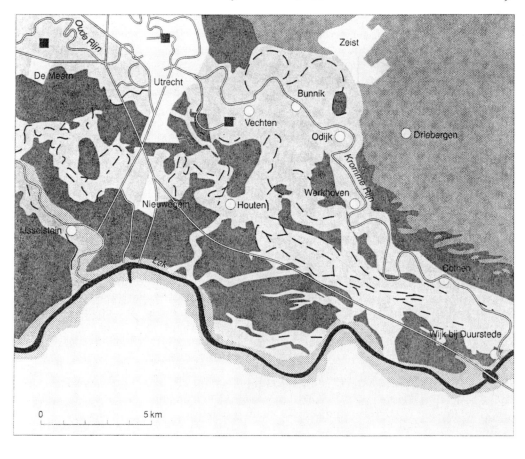

FIG. 5. The surroundings of Utrecht with the course of the most important rivers and the location of the Roman forts at De Meern, Utrecht and Vechten. (ROB, Amersfoort)

The increasing threat of flooding was a problem — and not only for Utrecht. Around AD 200 western parts of the Netherlands, near Katwijk and in the delta of the Maas, began to suffer from floods which, in this area, came from the sea. It is a generally held opinion that problems related to the increasing flooding prevented or at least limited human habitation in the western part of the river areas of the Netherlands from the second half of the third century.

ROMAN UTRECHT AND ITS ENVIRONMENT (Fig. 5)

For a better understanding of Roman Utrecht some attention has to be given to the direct environment of the settlement. At a distance of about five kilometres from the

Domplein there are two more Roman forts, one on the west side in De Meern (Vleuten) and one on the east side near Vechten (Bunnik). In the same way as Utrecht, they are positioned on the left bank of, respectively, the Old and the Crooked Rhine. It is generally assumed that the fort of Vechten (*Fectio*) was constructed near the division of the Rhine and Vecht during the reign of the emperor Augustus, *c.* AD 5. It served as a base from which, using the Vecht and the Oer-IJ near Velsen, territories in the North towards Germany could be conquered. It was only later that this fort was integrated in the defence line along the Rhine.[8]

The fort near De Meern was probably built in the same period as that of Utrecht, around AD 47, at a point where a side stream branches off from the Rhine.[9] The importance of the transport routes to the North via the Vecht explains the strategic significance of the Utrecht area, as is reflected in the construction of the three forts at only one hours walk from each other. The river constituted the border between extensive and impenetrable marsh areas north and west of Utrecht (the Utrecht–Holland peat area) and slightly higher grounds towards the East (the Utrecht Ridge).

These forts were not self-sufficient. For their provisioning the troops depended on the hinterland. Native settlements of agrarian character were ready to supply food. Several of these have been discovered by field survey and some have been explored archaeologically. They seem to have consisted of farms and outbuildings constructed of wood. Habitation was concentrated at the stream ridges, where agriculture was possible. The lower and wetter river basins were not suitable for settlement and could only be used for grazing and hunting. Many of these settlements date from between the middle Iron Age (*c.* 350 BC) and the second half of the third century AD. The Roman settlements are built on the same stream ridges as the ones dating to the Iron Age. In Nieuwegein and Houten, south and south-east of Utrecht, several native settlements have been found,[10] while in the centre of Houten remains of Roman stone construction may point to a Roman villa.[11] The dense web of settlements on the south-east and south-west side of Utrecht indicates a high population density during the Roman period. Even within the boundaries of Utrecht some remains of such settlements have recently been found. They were situated at a distance of about 500 or 600 metres south of the *castellum*, near the Nieuwe Gracht, the Vrouwjuttenstraat and the Catharijnesingel. The character of these native settlements in and around Utrecht and their relations with the Roman forts in this territory require further study.

ABBREVIATIONS

BROB	Berichten van de Rijksdienst voor het Oudheidkundig Bodemonderzoek
JBOU	Jaarboek Oud Utrecht
OMROL	Oudheidkundige Mededelingen uit het Rijksmuseum van Oudheden te Leiden
OVMH	Officieel Orgaan van de Historische Vereeniging Vleuten, de Meern en Haarzuilen

REFERENCES

1. H. M. A. J. van Asch van Wijck, *Geschiedkundige beschouwing van het oude handelsverkeer der stad Utrecht van de vroegste tijden tot aan de veertiende eeuw* (Utrecht 1838), 24; J. J. de Geer van Oudegein, *Het oude Trecht als oorsprong der stad Utrecht* (Utrecht 1875), 14.
2. A. E. van Giffen was director of the former Biological Archeological Institute (BAI) in Groningen, C. W. Vollgraff was professor of Classics at the university of Utrecht and G. van Hoorn was keeper of the

Society of Arts and Sciences of the province of Utrecht (PUG). The excavations of 1929, 1933 and 1935 were published between 1934–38: A. E. van Giffen, C. W. Vollgraff and G. van Hoorn, *Opgravingen op het Domplein te Utrecht*, Wetenschappelijke Verslagen I-V (Haarlem, 1934–1938). The excavations of 1936, 1938, 1943/44 and 1949 were only published in 1989: ed. by L. R. P. Ozinga et al., *Het Romeinse castellum te Utrecht* (Utrecht 1989).

3. For recent research about the Lower German limes: *De Romeinse rijksgrens tussen Moezel en Noordzee kust*, ed. T. Bechert and W. J. H. Willems (Utrecht 1995).

4. O. Curtz, ed., *Itineraria Romana* (Leipzig 1929), 56.

5. A survey of archeological research outside the Domplein can be found in M. J. G. T. Montforts, 'De topografie van Utrecht in de Romeinse tijd', *JBOU* (1991), 7–38.

6. A. C. Haak and A. N. Zadoks-Josephus Jitta, 'De Romeinse muntvondts van het Domplein te Utrecht', *Jaarboek voor Munt- en Penningkunde*, XLVII (1960), 1–6.

7. J. E. Bogaers, 'Thracische hulptroepen in Germania Inferior', *OMROL*, LV (1974), 204–05.

8. A survey of archeological work in Vechten can be found in M. Polak and S. L. Wynia, 'The Roman Forts in Vechten. A survey of the Excavations 1829–1989', *OMROL*, LXXIII (1991), 125–83.

9. See for a survey of the excavation results until 1983, C. A. Kalee, 'De archeologische opgraving op de Hoge Woerd in de Meern in 1982–1983', *OVMH*, IV (1984), 180–83.

10. W. A. van Es and W. A. M. Hessing, ed., *Romeinen, Friezen en Franken in het hart van Nederland: van Traiectum tot Dorestad, 50v.C.–900n.C.* (Utrecht 1994).

11. S. G. van Dockum, 'Houten in the Roman period, Part I: a stone Building in Burgermeester Wallerweg', *BROB*, XL (1990), 297–321.

Utrecht and Dorestad: Fifteen Miles apart, a world of difference*

by Huib L. de Groot

INTRODUCTION

The city of Utrecht is situated at the heart of the Netherlands, in the delta-area of the rivers Rhine and Vecht. With 230,000 inhabitants it is the country's fourth town. Twenty kilometres upstream on the Rhine is former Dorestad, nowadays Wijk bij Duurstede, with an estimated population of more than 20,000.

In describing the origins and development of the two towns scholars have tried to deal with the widely divergent functions of the two urban centres, but so far no completely satisfactory hypothesis has been advanced to explain their inherent differences. Comparisons with two British towns, Winchester and Hamwich, modern Southampton, are frequently proposed. These towns also lie in close proximity to each other. Winchester was an inland administrative and ecclesiastical centre and Hamwich its commercial, coastal satellite. In addition they were both — and still are — situated on the river Itchen. But again no convincing theory has so far been advanced to take their different functions into account.

In this essay I propose to use archaeological material and method in order to analyse and to illuminate the different characters of Utrecht and Dorestad and their interrelationship during the early Middle Ages.

Utrecht's origins are hidden beneath the Domplein. Deep below the level of the modern street lie the remains of the Roman *castellum* (47–*c.* 260 AD). The *castellum* was built to safeguard the northern frontiers of the Roman Empire. For the Netherlands the frontier corresponds with the course of the river Rhine, and nowadays divided into the so-called Crooked- and Old Rhine (Kromme- and Oude Rijn). The Utrecht *castellum* is one of a number defining the lower German *Limes*.

From the sixth century on Utrecht, on the northern edge of the Frankish empire, was hemmed in by Frisian territories to the west and north. The Franks, who saw themselves as the natural heirs to the Roman emperors, systematically reclaimed the former Roman territory, reoccupying abandoned Roman fortifications. Utrecht, where for centuries the walls and probably some of the buildings of the *castellum* had remained intact, was among them. We will see that Frankish influence in Utrecht may have however been introduced much earlier than previously believed. In the border territory of the Frankish empire the Frisians and the Franks jostled for power right into the eighth century. It is well known that during the same period Utrecht became the ecclesiastical and administrative centre from which first Willibrord and later Boniface undertook their missions to the Frisians.

At the same time, towards the end of the seventh century, a trading centre was developing some twenty kilometres upstream on the Rhine. Dorestad became one of the emporia of the Frankish empire, alongside Quentovic on the mouth of the river Canche in north-west France, and Ad Clusas, a major toll-site and pass across the Alps. Dorestad grew where the Rhine branches to form a channel called The Lek. The Lek,

*Translated from the Dutch.

which had been known to the Romans, continued to grow in importance and to surpass this stretch of the Rhine. Another *castellum* may have lain in the immediate vicinity of Dorestad: Levefanum. Although it is well-known that Dorestad was a major centre of overseas trade, recent archaeological discoveries show that it was also a focus of regional markets. The regions around Utrecht and Dorestad were both hit by the Viking raids in the ninth and tenth centuries, and as a result the bishop's see was moved temporarily from Utrecht to Deventer.

SIMILARITIES AND DIFFERENCES

As THE early medieval trading forum in the Low Countries par excellence, Dorestad has long attracted the attention of archaeologists. In 1930 J. H. Holwerda, the first to conduct a serious archaeological investigation of Dorestad, proposed a Roman origin for Dorestad but not for Utrecht.[1] From the results of the excavations carried out by Vollgraff and Van Griffen between 1929 and 1949 it is clear that the Romans built a *castellum* in Utrecht.[2] For Dorestad, too, a Roman *castellum* has been suggested, all remains of which were lost by the change of the course of the Rhine and Lek. The argument for a fort at Dorestad is not based on primary evidence but on finds of two bronze Roman helmets and other items of a military character in the Lek, south-east of Dorestad.[3] When the *castellum* itself disappeared is not known.

Both places thus seem to have been part of a line of defences along the northern frontier of the Roman Empire. Utrecht's *castellum* formed part of a conglomeration of three forts: the *castellum* of De Meern five kilometres to the west and to the east the *castellum* of Vechten (Fig. 2). In general scholars agree that these Roman forts were reoccupied during the Merovingian period.

A second similarity between Utrecht and Dorestad is that they are both situated on the confluence of two rivers. Near Dorestad the Rhine flows towards the north and the Lek to the west. Near Utrecht the Rhine turns westwards and the Vecht to the north. These stretches were the most important transport corridors into the extensive Utrecht-Holland marshes. Both Utrecht and Dorestad were thus situated on important waterways, the most important trading routes at the time. Each of the towns could easily send ships to the west, to England and to the north, to Scandinavia and the Eastsea, via Almere 'within the dunes'. They also enjoyed convenient access to Cologne and its hinterland. Besides, both towns are situated close to the Utrecht Ridge, though originally separated from it by the marshes east of the Vecht, which from Westbroek and Oostbroek extend towards the marshes of Langbroek (Fig. 1)

One difference is that Dorestad is situated more or less centrally in among the network of Netherlandish river-deltas, while Utrecht lies towards its periphery, close to the vast Utrecht-Holland marsh territory. But what do we now know about Utrecht and Dorestad themselves following several decades of archaeological research?

DORESTAD

In each of Van Es' and Verwers' publications of their excavations in Dorestad, a geographical tripartition is introduced (Fig. 3). The most southern part of Dorestad is occupied by the Roman *castellum*, which on account of the change in the course of Rhine and Lek, has disappeared. In the latest publication the existence of a small church is not merely proposed but rather presented almost as fact.[4] In the absence of any material evidence however, the existence of this little church should for the moment

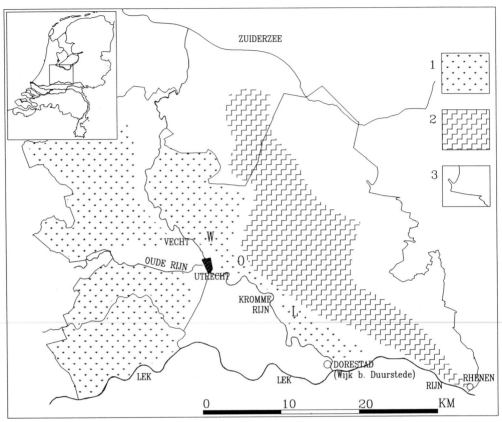

FIG. 1.   Schematic map of the province of Utrecht. Legend: 1: peat bogs; 2: glacial ridge
('Utrechtse Heuvelrug'); 3: boundary of the province of Utrecht

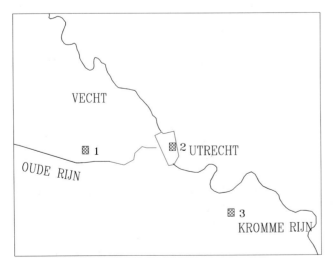

FIG. 2.   The Roman forts.
1: De Meern; 2: Utrecht
(Traiectum); 3: Vechten
(Fectio)

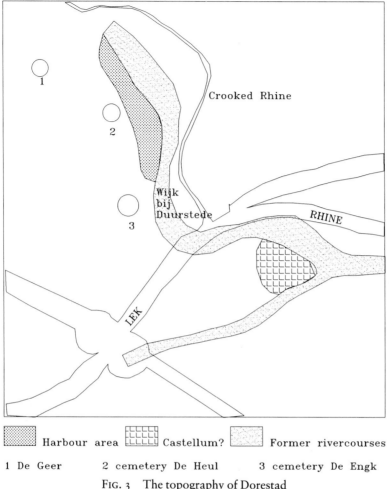

1 De Geer 2 cemetery De Heul 3 cemetery De Engk

FIG. 3 The topography of Dorestad

remain hypothetical. Neither is there any documentary evidence for the existence of ecclesiastical buildings within the fort at Dorestad, as there is for Utrecht. Van Es and Verwers also assume that during the seventh century the coinmaster Madelinus worked within the walls of the Roman *castellum*. His last coins can be dated to shortly before the middle of the seventh century. No continuity in coinage can be observed.

Very little is known of the assumed central area of Dorestad, which may have extended over an area of about six hundred metres. So far excavations have been carried out on a rather small scale. The most important discovery is the cemetery of De Engk, which probably dates from the sixth to the eighth century. As far as we can say anything about the type of habitation, it seems, though the evidence is limited, that the settlement appears to have been supported by an agrarian economy.

Large-scale excavations in the northern part of Dorestad have revealed an extensive harbour area on the left bank of the Rhine. It was established that the river moved eastwards. The harbour consists of a system of wharfs built from wood and earth. The

FIG. 4   Impression of the old town of Bergen (Bryggen). The houses are aligned along narrow alleys, leading from the land to the quays. Drawing after A. Herteig, *The medieval Harbour of Bergen*

harbour was possibly run as a private enterprise. The wharfs were located in front of the (trading) houses, which stood on the riverbank. As the river moved the wharfs were lengthened: they may have reached a length of some 140 metres. If this is indeed so, merchandise unloaded from vessels moored at one end of the platforms had to be carried along the length of the quay to warehouses on the riverbank. It is perhaps more logical to presume that the harbour buildings were relocated as the course of the river changed. Such is the situation at Bryggen, the commercial centre of medieval Bergen in Norway, though in this case the harbour was reconstructed to take account of changes in sea level, not the migration of a river bed. In Bergen both quays and dwellings moved across the shifting shore between land and water. New structures were built in front of existing ones. Raised wooden platforms connected rows of dwellings (Fig. 4).[5] Verwers suggests instead that possibly only warehouses and *no* dwellings were constructed on the quays at Dorestad.[6] His argument is based on the supposition that the quays were flooded during the winter. But I would think that a merchant's first concern is to safeguard his investment: his trading stock. It is even questionable if the quays were built so low that they were flooded by high water. I can therefore see no particular reason to assume that these structures were used simply as stores, and not as both residences and commercial premises. Detailed new research into the lay-out of the harbour and its post-built structures may throw further light on these questions. The possibility remains that some structures which have been identified as quays or jetties may in fact represent buildings. It is to its harbour that Dorestad owes its fame. The port came into existence towards the close of the seventh century, nearly half a century after Madelinus struck his last coins. To the west of the commercial centre a large cemetery has been excavated; the cemetery is known as De Heul. Within the cemetery the remains of a small wooden building with later additions in stone have been identified. The excavators suggest that the building may be a church which was partially rebuilt in stone in a secondary, tenth-century phase. The basis of this interpretation is by no means sound, and depends more on the location of the building than on its structure. However, the cemetery may in fact predate the construction of the building.

West of the cemetery and around 500 metres from the harbour is the settlement of De Geer, which probably has a continuity of occupation from the late Roman period.

Generally our understanding of the archaeology of the northern area of Dorestad has improved during the last decades.

UTRECHT

In Utrecht the remains of the Roman *castellum* lie directly below and around the Domplein. To the east and to the west is a *vicus*, the civilian settlement. North of this area the Rhine flows east to west (see Montforts in this volume Fig. 4). Stretches of the outer wall of the *castellum* have been excavated in several areas together with two entrance gates. An extraordinary find was made east of the Domplein in 1982. A rich burial containing a child was excavated under the square, which is now called the Pieterskerkhof (the cemetery of St Peter). Dated between 410 and 440, and with two other graves, one of which also contained grave goods, may they form part of an early Frankish cemetery in this area. Although part of this cemetery was probably lost following the change of the river's course, it is clear that settlement continued in the *vicus* after the Roman period. Together with new interpretations of late Roman and early medieval levels beneath the Domplein, the Pieterskerkhof tombs provide further evidence of the continuity of occupation in Utrecht, though its population is clearly in decline in these periods. The western *vicus* became the merchants' quarter, Stathe, the origins of which were previously assumed to belong to the tenth century.[8] A recently published find made near the Buurkerk, the oldest parish church in the heart of the former Stathe, gives further reason to place the development of this neighbourhood as early as the middle of the eighth century. The extent of the settlement in its earliest phase is unclear, though it was probably considerably smaller than the Roman *vicus*.[9] The early medieval finds recovered in 1992 from the cellars of houses on the Oude Gracht support an early date for the post-Roman settlement.[10] Post-holes indicate the presence of a number of timber-framed structures. Archaeology has so far yielded no precise information about post-Roman settlement trade and industry on the east-side of the *castellum*. A charter states that the Frankish king Dagobert built a small church within the walls of the *castellum* around 630. This church became the centre of the episcopal see of Utrecht to which Willibrord was first appointed archbishop in 695.[11]

A HYPOTHESIS TO EXPLAIN THE DIFFERENT CHARACTERS

What factors could have caused the two cities to assume such different complexions? One possibility is that the Merovingians considered Utrecht to be too close to the hostile Frisians to function as a commercial centre. By the same consideration the reason for the presence there of the oldest church may be due to the fact that from the Merovingians point of view Utrecht was ideally situated to act as headquarters of the Frisian mission. For it is worth remembering Vecht had long been an important artery into the Frisian territory. Though Dorestad was also positioned on the same trading route, it lay deeper inside Frankish territory. Thus Dorestad may have been a safer place to do trade, despite the on-going struggle for control of the Crooked Rhine between the Frisians and the Franks. Other factors must be brought into consideration. The concept of *nuclear region* was introduced for the early Middle Ages by H. A. Heidinga.[12] A *nuclear region* is an area with administrative status and cultural identity. A group of such *nuclear regions* lay at the basis of the later *gouwen*, although the frontiers and sizes almost certainly were changed. Though their boundaries and size

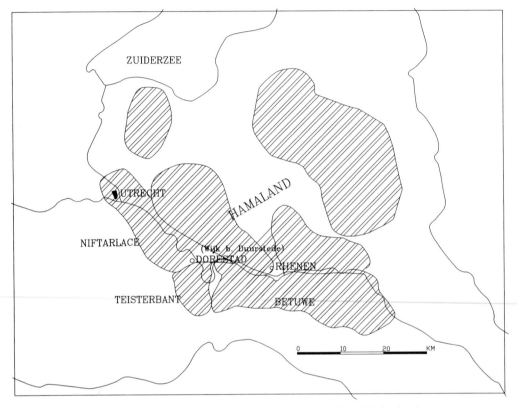

FIG. 5   The 'old habitation areas' in the centre of the Netherlands

changed in time these regions may have been further distinguished by their topographical setting. Rivers can act as natural boundaries as well as arteries of communication
and exchange. Similar borders may also have been provided by expanses of untravers-
able marshland. The marshes east of the Vecht and those of Langbroek probably
constituted such a frontier.

For practical reasons the later names of the *gouwen* will be used here in reference to
the *nuclear regions* (Fig. 5). Heidinga places a Hamaland, the land of the Chamaves, on
the Utrecht ridge and the Veluwe, and argues that Rhenen was the regional capital.
Several early medieval graveyards have been excavated in and around Rhenen; analysis
of the burials indicates that the population enjoyed a high living standard in this period.
These findings are supported by the discovery here of high-status objects, such as the
gold treasure of Remmerden. Heidinga advances the thesis that Utrecht was a port of
exchange on the edge of Hamaland.[13]

If we look at the environment of Utrecht and Dorestad several other important
aspects of the topography of this region become clear. First, the *nuclear region*
Niftarlakce situated between the shores of the Crooked Rhine and the Vecht, and which
probably extended from Wijk bij Duurstede to beyond Utrecht. A long continuity of
occupation is attested on the watersheds and riverbanks of this region. Downstream
from Utrecht the currents of both the Vecht and the Old Rhine diminish considerably,
and thus by contrast occupation here is limited. The existence of settlements in the

Rhine-Vecht watershed is attested by the lists of donations preserved in the *Cartularium* of Radbod.[14] Therefore I wish to propose Utrecht as capital of Niftarlake, as Heidinga identifies Rhenen as the capital of Hamaland. Much archaeological work done in Utrecht over the last twenty-three years has put in evidence the extent and continuity of settlement there. The extraordinarily rich child-burials from the Pieterskerkhof dating from the first half of the fifth century are particularly important. They not only indicate a much earlier Frankish influence than had been thought, but they also suggest an unexpected level of prosperity. The fact that Frisian kings settled in Utrecht during the seventh century can be a further indication of the special position of this town.[15] All factors point to the possibility that Utrecht was the site of an important (administrative?) centre.

Dorestad, on the other hand, is surrounded by several *nuclear regions*: besides Hamaland and Niftarlakce, there is the Betuwe towards the south-east and Teisterband to the south-west, which extends still further west during the period (Fig. 5). The central position of Dorestad in relation to the old centres of habitation is fundamental. This situation, together with Dorestad's position on the branching of the Rhine and Lek, may explain why the town developed as an important centre of regional trade.[16] Despite this Dorestad did not grow simultaneously into an administrative and ecclesiastical centre. The reason for this may lie in the topography of the area. To the south lay the Roman *castellum*, probably reoccupied by the Merovingians. Madelinus may have struck his coins here until 640. The centre of Dorestad is not well known, while the northern side with the harbour area has been extensively studied. This commercial quarter only starts to develop at the end of the seventh century and had its main phase of development in the eighth century. A noteable hiatus seems to exist between the time when Madelinus stopped producing coinage and the development of the harbour, though occupation seems to have continued at De Geer, about five hundred metres to the west. Is it possible that the old *castellum* of Levefanum and its proposed church had already disappeared in the second half of the seventh century due to the change in the course of the river? If so, then it is clear why Dorestad did not become an administrative or ecclesiastical centre. The *castellum*, which functioned both as an actual defensive fortification and symbol of power simply did not exist anymore. In Utrecht the situation is rather different, not only was the *castellum* still intact along with its church, founded by Dagobert, which stood till around 650, when it was destroyed by the Frisians. These observations may also explain why the Frisian kings setttled in Utrecht rather than in Dorestad.

Nevertheless, one written source refers to the *castrum* Dorestad, where the last Frisian king, Radbod, was defeated by Pepin II in 695. The fact that the *castellum* itself had disappeared does not necessarily mean that the name 'Castrum Duristate' was no longer in use. However, reference to this name is only known from one source, the 'Continuatio Fredegardii', of around 636.[17] In this context it is possible that the term is being used to refer to the former territory of the *castellum*, and not to the newly acquired commercial properties of Dorestad. Without archaeological evidence what is implied by the concept *castrum* in this period is unclear.

In a fifth-century text copied in the ninth century Bishop Theutbert is referred to as 'bishop of Dorestad'.[18] However, this does not necessarily imply that Dorestad had its own episcopal seat at this time. The relationship between Utrecht, Dorestad and the bishop's see, may be explained by the analogous case of the see of the bishop of 'the tribe of the Tungri', which 'silently' moved from Tongeren to Luik via Maastricht. In a similar way the earliest bishops of Utrecht may have moved around; the foundation of permanent seats in this period may have been unsettled by the threat of Norman invasions. Considering all this, it is perhaps not so strange that a monastery founded by Willibrord is mentioned — albeit in a sixteenth-century source — in Vechten. Dorestad, Vechten and Utrecht may have been served by a travelling bishop.

It is significant that Utrecht and Dorestad are frequently portrayed as heroic protagonists, so much so that the archaeologist Van Es detects a struggle for hegemony between them, from which 'Utrecht ultimately came out victoriously'.[19] But the rôle of Vechten in this historical drama should not be overlooked. Vechten had its own Roman *castellum*, which still survives, though no further light can be shed upon this at the present stage of archaeological research. As the course of the Rhine shifted during the second century, Vechten, which once stood on its bank, lost access to direct contact with Utrecht and Dorestad formerly provided by the river.

As far as Utrecht and Dorestad are concerned my hypothesis — allowing for other interpretations of the harbour area in Dorestad — may be summarized as follows. Firstly, the development of Dorestad as an important trading centre may chiefly be attributed to its central position in relation to a group of so-called *nuclear regions*. In the same period Utrecht was situated on the border of the area of habitation and was thus less suited to become a regional trading centre. Secondly, the loss of the supposed *castellum* of Dorestad in the second half of the seventh century to the rivers Rhine and Lek may have prevented the town from growing into a more active administrative and ecclesiastical centre. Utrecht, on the other hand, may have been an important early administrative centre. This suggestion is supported by the discovery of rich, fifth-century burials and by the fact that the Frisian kings chose to settle in Utrecht. Why Utrecht proved so attractive to the Frisian élite remains to be explained precisely.

SHORTENED TITLES USED

Van Es and Hessing (1994), ed. by W. A. van Es and W. A. M. Hessing, *Romeinene, Friezen en Franken in het hart van Nederland* (Utrecht/Amersfoort 1994).
ABKGU 1991–92 *Archaeologische en Bouwhistorische Kroniek van de Gemeente Utrecht*, ed. by T. J. Hoekstra.

REFERENCES

1. J. H. Holwerda, *Dorestad en onze vroegste Middeleeuwen* (Leiden 1930).
2. For a survey of the Roman period see *Het Romeinse Castellum in Utrecht*, ed. L. R. P. Ozinga *et al.* (Utrecht 1989).
3. W. A. van Es, 'Dorestad Centred' *Medieval Archaeology in the Netherlands, studies presented to H. H. van Regteren Altena*, ed. J. C. Besteman *et al.* (Assen/Maastricht), 151–82.
4. W. A. van Es, 'Friezen, Franken en Vikingen', Van Es and Hessing (1994), 98–100, and W. H. J. Verwers, 'Wijk bij Duurstede — Dorestad', *idem*, 235–38.
5. A. E. Herteig, 'The medieval harbour of Bergen', *Waterfront archaeology in Britain and northern Europe*, Gustav Milne and Brian Hobley (London 1981), 80–87.
6. W. H. J. Verwers, 'Wijk bij Duurstede-Dorestad', Van Es and Hessing (1994), 235–38.
7. *Ozinga* (1989).
8. Stathe is to be equated with the English Staith, a place where ships can 'stand'; a sloping riverbank.
9. C. A. M. van Rooijen, 'Buurkerk', *ABKGU 1991–1992* (Utrecht 1994).
10. C. A. M. van Rooijen and Bart Klück 'Oude Gracht 137–167'. *ABKGU 1991–1992* (Utrecht 1994), 173–76.

11. See M. van Winter in this volume.

12. H. A. Heidinga, *Medieval Settlement and Economy North of the Lower Rhine* (Assen/Maastrucht 1989) 174–92.

13. W. A. van Es, 'Utrechse Heuvelrug en Zuidwest Veluwerand', van Es and Hessing (1994), 224–46.

14. D. P. Blok, 'Het goederenregister van de St. Maartenskerk te Utrecht', *Mededelingen Naamkunde*, XXXIII (1957), 89–104.

15. H. Halbertsma, *Frieslands Oudheid*, unpublished thesis (Groningen 1982).

16. Van Es (1994), 104.

17. 'Pippinus contra Radbodem ducem gentilem Frigionum gentis adversus alterutrum bellum intulerunt castro Duristate, illinc belligantes invicem.' 'Continuatio Fredegardii', ed. B. Krusch, *Monumenta Germaniae Historia* SS. rer. Merov., II. (Hannover 1888), 172.

18. Marieke van Vlierden, *Willibrord en het begin van Nederland* (Utrecht 1995), 35–36.

19. Van Es (1994), 115–16.

The first centuries of the episcopal see at Utrecht

by Johanna Maria van Winter

Around the year 690 Willibrord transferred his attention to Zeeland and the environs of Antwerp following the failure of his mission to the Frisians north of the rivers Rhine and Leck. Though he initially worked as a priest, not a consecrated bishop, his activities were blessed by the papacy. Only in 695 Willibrord received the dignity of archbishop (with *pallium*) under the Frisians from the hand of the Pope and from the major-domo Pippin a see[1] in Utrecht. He did not become by this act, however, bishop or archbishop *of* Utrecht, which was something which he, just like Boniface, never did become. The latter cooperated with him as a missionary among the Frisians in the years 719–22 and functioned, after Willibrord's death in 739, as custodian (*custos*)[2] of the Utrecht see, being, at that time, archbishop with see in Mainz. In his capacity as custodian, he appointed one or more *chorepiscopi* (= auxiliary bishops), of whom we only know the name of Eoban who was murdered with him at Dokkum in 754. Boniface also appointed an abbot of the clerical community that served the Utrecht *monasterium* which had been founded by Willibrord on the banks of the Rhine[3] and where his see had also been, a see vacant since 739. This abbot, Gregory, was a disciple of Boniface and a grandson of Adela of Pfalzel (titled after an abbey near Treves where she, as widow, was the abbess) and therefore related to the Carolingians.[4]

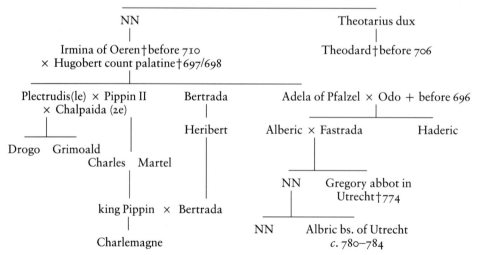

The first person who can be considered as bishop *of* Utrecht was Albric (*c.* 780–*c.* 784), a nephew of Abbot Gregory and, after *c.* 775, his successor as leader of the monastery. Like Abbot Gregory, Bishop Albric was also related to the Carolingians which was, probably, also the case with his successor Theodard (*c.* 784–*c.* 790). That name can be found among the ancestors of Adela of Pfalzel.

The bishops Albric and Theodard should not be confused with the priests Alubert and Thiatbraht, the former being an Englishman (*de gente Anglorum*) who assisted Abbot Gregory as a *chorepiscopus*, according to Gregory's disciple Liudger in his *Vita S.Gregorii*.[5] The latter (Thiatbraht) was a teacher at the school of the Utrecht monastery who, in Bishop Albric's time, used to teach there especially during the winter term, as Altfrid, Liudger's biographer,[6] has told us. Bishop Albric taught there in the spring, the priest Adalger in the summer and Liudger in the autumn. It is possible, however, that this Thiatbraht was the same person as *Theutbertus episcopus de Dorostat*, who, with an eighth-century hand, had written his owner's mark in a sixth-century Livius-codex which is now kept in Vienna.[7] This 'bishop of Dorestad' was presumably also a *chorepiscopus* during the vacancy of Willibrord's see and, therefore, before Albric became bishop.

Albric was consecrated bishop, *c.* 780, in Cologne[8] and so implicitly recognized Utrecht as a suffragan bishopric of that metropolitan see. Boniface's efforts to prevent exactly this dependency (more about which later on) and to keep a direct link with the papacy had failed.

Another effort of Boniface's, that of having bishops nominated because of vocation and capacity instead of nepotism, also failed in Utrecht in the ninth century. The episcopal see, until the arrival of the Normans, was dominated by a clan that is recognizable by the element -ric- in its name, like Ricfried (806–*c.* 815), Frederic (after 815–835/37) and his brother Alberic (*c.* 838–44).[9] Bishop Liudger (*c.* 850–54) must have also belonged to it, for he was related to a layman, Baldric, who, in 850, wanted to found a chapter at Wadenoyen (on the river Linge, in the region called Tielerwaard), endowed with lands from himself and from the church of Utrecht, which should be governed successively by his kinsmen: first bishop Liudger and, after him, Kraft and then Immo, followed by Baldric's grandson, Baldric if he would accept the tonsure.[10]

The aforementioned Kraft should have succeeded Bishop Liudger not only as the leader of this chapter but also as bishop but, although he was the provost of the church of Utrecht and very rich, he refused because of the imminent Norman danger. The priest Odulph, who did not belong to this clan and more or less functioned as the conscience of the Utrecht church, severely reproached him, in vain, for doing so. On Odulph's instruction the deformed canon Hunger was then elected as bishop (854–66),[11] who, shortly afterwards, had to flee from the Normans and take refuge at St Odiliënberg near Roermond, in the diocese of Liege. His successors migrated from there to Deventer which, at least, lay within the diocese of Utrecht; the most important of them being Odilbald (867/69–898) and Radbod (899–917). Not before the tenth century was another member of the -ric-clan able to return to Utrecht: Bishop Balderic (917–75), son of Ricfried.

One might suppose that the Utrecht -ric-clan was related to the Carolingians and to Bishop Albric from the eighth century but this cannot be proved by hard evidence. The kinship of the ninth-century -ric-clan probably extended into the north of France, the Meuse- and the Rhine-regions, but did not belong to the imperial aristocracy, the upper layer of the Frankish nobility. This, at least, is the impression one gets when investigating a list of names from *c.* 935 in the *Liber Memorialis* of the Reichenau abbey that is headed by the royal prince Otto (I), his wife Edith and their little son Liudolf, followed by Balderic, Irimfried, Ricfried and many others, 128 in all.[12] Irimfried was the eldest brother of Bishop Balderic, who had two other brothers, Rudolf and Nevelung. The names of these four brothers are repeated several times in this list, probably as deceased members of older generations. Also the name Robert appears several times and, from the combination of the names Robert and Rudolf, one involuntarily thinks of the early Capetians as counts of Paris. A lineage with the name Nevelung, related to the Pippin-family, was active in the eighth and ninth centuries in Vexin and Autun. But if there would have been a link between this genealogy and the

-ric- clan, then in the Reichenau list we should also come across names like Hildebrand, Bernhard, Theodoric and Heribert, which, however, does not happen.[13]

It has often been that Bishop Ansfried of Utrecht (995–1010) should also be counted among this kinship, some researchers going as far as making Bishop Balderic an uncle of Bishop Ansfried. This certainly was not the case as, I hope, I have satisfactorily proved elsewhere.[14] It is just possible, via a long roundabout route in which the repeated name Robert in the Reichenau list plays a role, that Ansfried could be related to the Balderic-clan as a great grand nephew. Ansfried is presumed to be a great grandson of Robert, count of the Lomme-*pagus* in 887, and he certainly had an uncle Robert who was archbishop of Treves (931–56). The name Ansfried does not, however, appear in the list of names from the Reichenau abbey.

The ancestors of Bishop Balderic had surely been owners of much land in the central Dutch river region, as is testified by the proposed foundation of a chapter at Wadenoyen and the wealth of the provost Kraft. In addition, they must have possessed estates in the present-day province of Drenthe, as this is evident from a gift to the abbey of Werden on the river Ruhr in 820: Theodgrim, son of Aldgrim, bestowed his whole *hereditas* in Arlo (now the hamlet Tinaarlo near Vries), which he had got from Ricfried, to this abbey which, at this time, was lead by Bishop Hildigrim, the brother of the missionary and founder Liudger.[15] It is not known if this Ricfried was the same person as the Utrecht bishop of that name from about 810 or another man but his name indicates that he must have belonged to the -ric-clan. Theodgrim was a grand-nephew of Liudger, and it is interesting to note that Liudger's biographer and relative Altfrid had a name that was a combination of Aldgrim and Ricfried. The Liudgerids and the ric-clan must have already inter-married in the eighth century.

After his return from Deventer, Bishop Balderic enjoyed the royal support of the Saxon House, as can be concluded from the fact that King Henry I entrusted him with the education of his son Bruno, later archbishop of Cologne (953–65). Between the ages of four and fourteen (929–39) Bruno attended the school of the Utrecht monastery which, obviously, still enjoyed some fame.[16] It is quite possible that the Kings Henry I and Otto I, as a kind of a school fee, gave material support to Bishop Balderic for the restoration of the devastated churches on the Domsquare. In addition, he had been endowed with rights of coinage and toll levying by king Otto I as well as fishery rights and lands for his church.[17]

The bishops of Utrecht from the -ric-clan had themselves buried in the church of St Salvator or Oldminster on the Domsquare that also functioned as their family shrine. This church had been founded by Willibrord[18] on the banks of the river Rhine within the remains of the Roman *castellum* where he had also placed his *cathedra*. In about 753, this seat had, however, been transferred to another church within this former fortress, which had been rebuilt by Willibrord, from the foundations upwards, on the ruins of a little church of king Dagobert. This small church, originally dating from the first half of the seventh century with an unknown patron saint (possibly St Thomas), was dedicated by Willibrord, after its rebuilding, to St Martin. We know these things from two documents which give, however, rather diverging versions of events. The first one is a letter from Boniface to pope Stephan II in 753 in which the church of St Martin is called an *ecclesiola*, a little church that, after being put under the supervision of the archbishop of Cologne as a mission centre, had been totally neglected by him and fallen into ruin in contrast with the St Salvator's church of Willibrord and its missionary activities.[19] The other document is a charter from King Pippin of the Franks, from *c.* 753, which tells us that Boniface had shown this king some charters from his

Merovingian predecessors in which the church of St Martin in Utrecht had been endowed with immunity, a gift that was now reconfirmed.[20]

On reading these two documents one cannot avoid the impression that Boniface had either spoken with a double tongue (being at the same time tormented by feelings of guilt, as was continuously the case with him)[21] or that he had been forced by King Pippin's chancery to accept a vision which was not his own.[22] In my opinion, which I defended long ago and to which I still adhere, the first possibility has to be taken: Boniface, out of political considerations, has placed a different emphasis towards the Pope than towards the King.[23] From the Pope he wanted the church of Utrecht to be free of the pretensions of Cologne and to be directly subordinate to the Holy See which was what the St Salvator's patronate referred to. The King, on the other hand, who venerated St Martin as the patron saint of his house, should continue with the actual, if necessary armed, support of the church of Utrecht that his predecessors had provided. To this end, Boniface, in my opinion, had fakes made of some Merovingian charters using existing formularies which he then included in an authentic charter. In fact, no immunity charter had yet been given to the Utrecht church, neither to St Martin's nor to Willibrord's St Salvator's; this so-called reconfirmation was, in fact, the first bestowal.

With this, the church of St Martin became the main church and the location of the see in Utrecht i.e. the cathedral, a role previously fulfilled by St Salvator's. The support of King Pippin must have counterbalanced, in Boniface's eyes, the change of seat and patron saint, although this St Martin's church was probably much smaller in size than St Salvator's. It did not get a chapter of its own at this time: that presumably happened under Bishop Balderic, for we hear, for the first time, about two monasteries in Utrecht in a charter of King Otto I in 944.[24]

In the current debate in Utrecht about the site of the oldest churches on the Domsquare I now share the view that King Dagobert's little church and, therefore, Willibrord's St Martin's as well, will not be found under the choir of today's Dom,[25] but under the Holy Cross-chapel. St Salvator's or Oldminster, in my opinion, was founded by Willibrord on the same site where it was demolished in the sixteenth century, i.e. on the Domsquare southwest of the Holy Cross Chapel and south of the present-day Dom.[26]

I observe a striking analogy with the situation in Münster (Westphalia) at the time of Liudger's death in 809: there was a large monastery church (Münster means minster = monastery) behind which, almost hidden, stood a small cathedral.[27] In that large minster, dedicated to Our Lady and situated under the nave of the present-day's Dom, Liudger was layed in state, as his biographer Altfrid tells us.[28] The then small Dom that, later, after the construction of Bishop Dodo's pre-Norman new Dom (c. 980), was to be called 'der alte Dom' (the old Dom), was possibly unfinished when Liudger died.[29] It is plausible, however, that he himself had ordered its erection after he had been consecrated bishop in 805 and that he also chose St Paul as its patron saint, the saint to which we can prove that the Dom in Münster had already been dedicated in 819.[30] St Paul and Boniface were Liudger's great models as apostles, respectively, of the Peoples and of Germany.

The situation in Münster which puzzles the archeologists and historians working there, becomes clear as soon as we recognize that Liudger copied this grouping from Utrecht where he had been educated by his venerated teacher Gregory at the school of Oldminster: the Utrecht disposition of a large monastery church with a school and public functions alongside a small church for the episcopal see was considered, by him, as the rule. In the second half of the tenth century, as this situation no longer satisfied needs, a western part to the church, dedicated to St Paul, was added to the existing monastery church by Bishop Dodo; the episcopal see being transferred to this new building. The old Dom remained almost without function but, at that time, was not demolished. After a century the cathedral canons even returned to it because of unease about their new house.[31]

In Utrecht, in the tenth century, people will also have been thinking about a new and larger Dom which, because of the topographical situation, could not be realized as a western part of the existing St Salvator's but had to be erected as a new building at another place. In 1023, under Bishop Adelbold, the new St Martin's church was consecrated on the present site.[32] The Holy Cross-chapel that, in my opinion, until that time had functioned as St Martin's cathedral, was not demolished but ceded to the chapter of Oldminster, its neighbour.

Bishop Balderic, on his return from exile in Deventer after the depart of the Normans, found the churches on the Domsquare severely damaged. He restored them as well as he could but did not build a new Dom. If he had done so, this exploit certainly would have been incorporated with the medieval tradition concerning this famous bishop.[33] If the new structure had already been started in the tenth century, then perhaps it could have begun under Bishop Folcmar or Poppo (976–90), who was the uncle of another church builder, Bishop Bernward of Hildesheim (993–1022). The indications, however, of a start to the church building on the site of today's Dom before the eleventh century are very weak indeed. It is more probable, therefore, that Bishop Adelbold had 'all at once' allowed this new cathedral to rise, as a letter from a contemporary observer tells us.[34]

Adelbold's predecessor, Bishop Ansfried, did not build a church in Utrecht but founded a *cellula* or hermitage on the Hohorst near Amersfoort, where he used to retire and where he also died. Bishop Adelbold reshaped this cell into a Benedictine monastery, dedicated to St Paul and other saints, that had to serve as an example for the secular canons of the Dom and Oldminster. This monastery, under Adelbold's successor Bishop Bernold (1027–54), got a stone church in the city of Utrecht that served as the south end of the cross of churches. By finishing three of the four churches of this great enterprise, Bishop Bernold gave this city a whole new face.

ABBREVIATIONS

AASS	*Acta Sanctorum* quotquot toto orbe coluntur, ed. Joannes Bollandus S. J. and Godefridus Henschenius, editio novissima (Brussels-Paris-Rome 1863–1940)
KNOB	Koninklijke Nederlandse Oudheidkundige Bond
MGH	Monumenta Germaniae Historica
MGH SS	MGH Scriptores in folio
OSU I	*Oorkondenboek van het Sticht Utrecht tot 1301*, I, ed. S. Muller Fzn. en A. C. Bouman (Utrecht 1920)
Bonifatius *Briefe*	*Bonifatii epistulae, Willibaldi Vita Bonifatii, Briefe des Bonifatius, Willibalds Leben des Bonifatius*, ed. & transl. Reinhold Rau (Freiherr vom Stein-Gedächtnisausgabe IVb, Darmstadt 1968)
Chronographia	*Chronographia* Johannis de Beke, ed. H. Bruch ('s-Gravenhage 1973, Rijks Geschiedkundige Publicatiën, Grote Serie 143)
Diplomata Belgica	*Diplomata Belgica ante annum millesimum centesimum scripta*, ed. M. Gysseling & A. C. F. Koch (Brussels 1950)
Series Episcoporum	*Series Episcoporum ecclesiae catholicae occidentalis*, Series V, *Germania*, Tomus I, *Archiepiscopatus Coloniensis*, ed. Stefan Weinfurter et Odilo Engels (Stuttgart 1982)

REFERENCES

1. The expression 'sedes episcopalis' that Boniface in his letter to pope Stephan uses in connection with the mandate for Willibrord to convert the Frisians (Bonifatius *Briefe*, 340, Brief nr. 109, anno 753), should not, in my opinion, be considered as a tendentious invention of Boniface's who, with it, wrongly should have suggested that Willibrord had founded the see of Utrecht, as argued, among others, by P. Leupen, 'Sint Salvator en Sint Maarten, Willibrord en Bonifatius', in: *Willibrord, zijn wereld en zijn werk* (Nijmegen 1990), 317–27, especially 322. If this reproach was correct, we should not be entitled to use this expression for the period in which a regular and official bishopric of Utrecht did not yet exist, nor be allowed to speak about Willibrord's Utrecht cathedral, *kathedra* being the same as *sedes*. Thinking further along these lines, Broer and De Bruijn argue that the church of St Martin did indeed become the main church under Boniface *c.* 753 but became the cathedral only in the last quarter of the eighth century: C. J. C. Broer en M. W. J. de Bruijn, *De eerste kerken in Utrecht: Sint-Thomas, Sint-Salvator, Sint-Maarten* (Utrecht 1995), 42, 47.

   For me, it is an anachronistic projection of later canonistic definitions on the Merovingian-Carolingian period, if one exclusively connects the words *sedes* and *kathedra* with a regular bishopric. In addition, a priest being consecrated bishop, with or without the *pallium*, in a still unlimited missionary region must have a seat, a *sedes* or *kathedra*; the church where this see stands may be called his cathedral.

2. He is called this in the charter of May 23, 723 with which the St Martin's church in Utrecht is reconfirmed in the possession of its fiscal tithes, *Diplomata Belgica* nr 175.

3. This description of the site comes from Abbot Theofrid of Echternach, at the beginning of the twelfth century, in Thiofridi Epternacensis *Vita Willibrordi metrica*, ed. Konrad Rossberg (Leipzig, Teubner, 1883), 18–19.

4. Data for the genealogical tree in Eduard Hlawitschka, 'Zu den Grundlagen des Aufstiegs der Karolinger', in *Rheinische Vierteljahrsblätter* 49 (1985), 1–61, with tree on p. 58.

5. *Vita S.Gregorii* auctore Liudgero, ed. O. Holder-Egger, MGH SS XV (Hannover 1887), 63–79, especially 75, caput 10: '- - beatus Gregorius - -. - simul cum chorepiscopo et adiutore suo Aluberhto, qui de Britannia et gente Anglorum veniebat, - -'.

6. *Vita S.Liudgeri* auctore Altfrido, ed. G. H. Pertz, MGH SS II (Hannover 1829), 403–19, especially 409, caput 15.

7. Titus Livius, *Codex Vindobonensis Lat.15 phototypice editus*, praefatus est Carolus Wessely (Lugduni Batavorum 1907; Codices Graeci et Latini photographice depicti, ed. S. de Vries, tomus XI), Praefatio p. LXXXIX 2nd column, facsimile fol. 193 verso 'iste codex est theutberti episcopi de dorostat'.

8. *Vita S.Liudgeri*, 408, caput 15 'Albricus autem cum in Colonia civitate gradum accepisset episcopalem, fecit et Liutgerum secum presbyterii percipere gradum, - -'. The year is not known. For the calculation, see *Series Episcoporum*, pp. 173–74.

9. For information about all these bishops of Utrecht, see *Series Episcoporum*, pp. 175–83.

10. *Diplomata Belgica* nr 184, 850 August 12.

11. 'Vita Odulfi presbyteri', in: *AASS*, Junii tomus III (Paris-Roma 1867), 89–92 (12 June); fragments in: MGH SS XV (Hannover 1887), pp. 356–58.

12. *Libri confraternitatum Sancti Galli, Augiensis, Fabariensis*, ed. Paulus Piper (MGH Antiquitates, Berlin 1884), pp. 184–186. Facsimile in *Das Verbrüderungsbuch der Abtei Reichenau* (Einleitung, Register, Faksimile), ed. Johanne Autenrieth, Dieter Geuenich und Karl Schmid (MGH Libri Memoriales et Necrologia, Nova Series I, Hannover 1979), pp. 24–25. See about this list also: Karl Schmid, 'Unerforschte Quellen aus quellenarmer Zeit (II): Wer waren die *fratres* von Halberstadt aus der Zeit König Heinrichs I.?', in: *Festschrift für Berent Schwineköper Zu seinem siebzigsten Geburtstag* (Sigmaringen 1982), pp. 117–40, especially pp. 131–33.

13. L. Levillain, 'Les Nibelungen historiques et leurs alliances de famille', in: *Annales du Midi* 49 (1937), pp. 337–408, & 50 (1938) 5–66; and Karl Ferdinand Werner, 'Untersuchungen zur Frühzeit des französischen Fürstentums (9.-10. Jahrhundert), V, Zur Geschichte des Hauses Vermandois', in *Die Welt als Geschichte* 20 (1960), pp. 87–119.

14. Johanna Maria van Winter, 'Ansfried en Dirk, twee namen uit de Nederlandse geschiedenis van de 10e en 11e eeuw', in: *Naamkunde* 13 (1981), pp. 39–74.

15. *OSU*, I nr 57, 820 June 18; D. P. Blok, *De oudste particuliere oorkonden van het klooster Werden* (Assen 1960), pp. 198–99, nr 42. See about the Liudgerids: Karl Schmid, 'Die Liudgeriden', in *Geschichtsschreibung und geistiges Leben im Mittelalter. Festschrift für Heinz Löwe* (Köln-Wien 1978), pp. 71–101, with genealogical tree on p. 93.

16. Ruotgeri Vita S. Brunonis archiepiscopi Coloniensis, Leben des hl.Bruno, Erzbischofs von Köln, verfaßt von Ruotger, ed.& transl. Hatto Kallfelz, in *Vitae quorundam episcoporum saeculorum X, XI, XII* (Darmstadt 1973, Freiherr vom Stein-Gedächtnisausgabe Band 22), pp. 169–261, especially pp. 184–87.

17. e.g. domains in Lek-en-IJssel, 944 July 17, *OSU* I, nr 106; fishery at Muiden and in the Almere, 949 June 30, *OSU* I nr. 113;fishery in the Almere plus toll and domain at Muiden and fiscal property on both sides of the river Vecht, 953 April 21 and 975 June 6, *OSU*, I, nrs 120 and 134; right of coinage given by Otto I, 936, *OSU*, I, nr 101, reconfirmed by Otto II, 975 June 6, *OSU*,I nr 134, 136; right to transfer the toll at Muiden fully or partially to Utrecht, 975 June 6, *OSU*, I, nr 135.

18. See below in annotation 26 the debate about Willibrord or Boniface as the founder of this church.

19. Bonifatius *Briefe*, nr 109, pp. 338–43.

20. *Diplomata Belgica*, nr 176, *OSU*, I nr. 40, pp. 751–54, perhaps 753.

21. Mayke de Jong, 'Bonifatius. De cultuur van een Angelsaksische priester-monnik', in *Utrecht tussen kerk en staat*, ed. R. E. V. Stuip and C. Vellekoop (Hilversum 1991; Utrechtse Bijdragen tot de Mediëvistiek, 10), pp. 51–69, especially pp. 60–61, 64–65.

22. Broer and De Bruijn, *De eerste kerken in Utrecht*, 17–18, 30, 32, 40, 42. According to them Boniface has been forced against his wish to accept the change of patron saint: he had offered an authentic immunity charter for St Salvator's for reconfirmation by the King but received a charter for St Martin's in return. The chancery afterwards consciously made the original charter for St Salvator's 'disappear' (p. 32). I should have expected a huge quarrel between Boniface and Pippin in this case, given the fact that Boniface was not a meek lamb; nothing of the kind, however, is known to us.

23. Johanna Maria van Winter, 'Utrecht aan de Rijn. Middeleeuwse Rijnloop en wordingsgeschiedenis van de stad Utrecht', in *Jaarboek Oud-Utrecht* 1975, 44–72, especially 69–71.

24. *OSU*, I, nr 106, 944 July 17.

25. In my article 'Utrecht aan de Rijn', p. 71, I still supposed that the oldest St Martin's church would be found under the present day Dom and, in addition, that this church, after the transfer of the see by Boniface in *c*. 753, had immediately been enlarged so that, in 754, when his corpse was brought to Utrecht from Dokkum, the church was larger than St Salvator's. Now I share the opinion that Dagobert's church and Willibrord's St Martin's church built on top of it must have stood on the site of the Holy Cross Chapel. This, then, must have been the 'ecclesia minor' in the report of Eigil in his *Vita Sturmi* (ed. G. H. Pertz, MGH SS II (Hannover, 1829), pp. 365–77, especially 372, caput 15), where Boniface lay in state waiting for a sepulchre 'in basilica maiore'. Therefore, the latter church must have been St Salvator's.

    That the church of Dagobert must have been situated on the site of the Holy Cross Chapel has been argued by the archeologist H. L. de Groot, 'De Heilige Kruiskapel te Utrecht', in *Bulletin KNOB*, 93 (1994), pp. 135–49, and the art historian Raphaël Rijntjes, 'De *ecclesiola* in het Utrechtse castellum. Bouwhistorische interpretatie van de resten van de Heilig-Kruiskapel', in *Bulletin KNOB*, 93 (1994), pp. 150–61. Especially Rijntjes's remark that the foundations of this chapel show two building periods (not noticed by De Groot) has convinced me of the truth of this hypothesis.

    Recently still another site of Willibrord's St Martin's church has been proposed, i.e. under the present day street called 'Oudkerkhof' (Old Churchyard), where Carolingian graves have been found: L. A. van der Tuuk, 'Waar bevond zich de Sint-Maartenskerk van Willibrord?', in *Oud-Utrecht*, 68 (1995), pp. 52–59. My objections to this theory are twofold: 1) at excavations at this place no foundations of a church have ever been found, nor does any tradition exist about a sacred building on that site; and 2) this place, in the Middle Ages, did not form a part of the immunity of the Dome or Oldminster but was the property of the town from which the canons, in order to expand their claustral areas, took it into hereditary tenure; see M. W. J. de Bruijn, *Husinghe ende Hofstede* (Utrecht 1994), pp. 131–33. In my opinion the graves point to a cemetery for laymen from the period when they still had no parish church of their own.

26. Charlotte J. C. Broer and Martin W. J. de Bruijn, 'De Heilig-Kruiskapel in Utrecht: Sint-Maarten of Sint-Salvator?', in: *Bulletin KNOB* 93 (1994), 162–68, and *De eerste kerken in Utrecht* (Utrecht 1995) argue that two St Salvator's churches existed in Utrecht, the first founded by Willibrord on the site of the later Holy Cross-chapel and the second founded by Boniface at its later well-known place, bordering on the first one. They base this opinion on the description by Johannes de Beke in his *Chronographia* (*c*. 1350), which, as they are well aware, has been adapted to the situation of the fourteenth century but, yet, still considered by them to be useful for their own theory. They, in turn, however, without appearing to notice it, adapt Beke's text to their own opinion which results in a double adaptation. Beke does not write, as they say, that Boniface built a second St Salvator's, bordering on the first one but that Boniface built a chapter church ('cenobitalium canonicorum ecclesiam'), bordering on an oratory ('oratorium') of Willibrord which was dedicated to St Salvator (p. 25, caput 15b); that chapter church, in Beke's eyes, had several patron saints (not mentioned by him), but was called Oldminster because it had kept its old building structure up until his time. Willibrord's oratory is also described by Beke as being dedicated to the Holy Cross (p. 15, caput 9), so that you may consider St Salvator and the Holy Cross to be interchangeable patron saints in his eyes. This oratory, however, was, from his point of view, not a

monastery church and in this respect differed from Boniface's new church which, moreover, was never called St Salvator's by Beke.

Beke's error lays in his opinion that Willibrord's St Salvator's was not a monastery or chapter church, but only an oratory. For this reason no new theory should be built upon his version.

27. *Der Paulus-Dom zu Münster*. Eine Dokumentation zum Stand der neuen Grabungen und Forschungen, hg.von Thomas Sternberg (Münster 1990). On 6–14: Rudolf Schieffer, 'Die Anfänge des Domstifts in Münster', and 15–27: Uwe Lobbedey, 'Die jüngsten Ausgrabungen zur Baugeschichte des Domes zu Münster'. See also Uwe Lobbedey, Herbert Scholz and Sigrid Vestring-Buchholz, *Der Dom zu Münster 793–1945–1993*, Band I (Bonn 1993, Denkmalpflege und Forschung in Westfalen, 26). I only remark that my interpretation of the given facts partially differs from those of these authors.

28. *Vita Liudgeri*, 414, liber II caput 8.

29. Lobbedey, 'Die jüngsten Ausgrabungen', 25 sub D.

30. Schieffer, 'Die Anfänge', 7. To me, it is uncomprehensible that he argues, on p.8, that Our Lady's church where Liudger lay in state, was the real Dom and St Paul's church the place of the divine service of the clergy of the already existing monastery. As strange to me is Lobbedey's conclusion in 'Die jüngsten Ausgrabungen', 25–26, that the small church should have been a 'jüngere Annexkirche' to the main church. How could such an annex church later be titled 'der alte Dom'? Certainly it was a younger church than Our Lady's monastery church, started only after Liudger had been consecrated bishop in 805. But compared to bishop Dodo's new western building it was the old Dom.

31. Schieffer, 'Die Anfänge', 12.

32. Beke, *Chronographia*, 79, caput 42c.

33. No mention of his building a new Dom is even made in an unauthentic charter, so-called from 940 July 1, *OSU* I nr. 104, but probably faked in the twelfth century. In this charter Bishop Balderic depicts the deplorable situation in which he found Utrecht after the Normans and describes his restoration efforts of the churches and erection of town walls, gates and a bridge.

34. *OSU* I nr. 177, *c.* 1022, report to Bishop Adelbold about the miracles of St Walburgis, as told by the custodian of the church at Tiel.

England and the Low Countries at the time of St Willibrord

by David Parsons

INTRODUCTION

The period from the late sixth to the mid-eighth century is one in which the British Isles were heavily involved in the development of Christianity on the western European mainland. Before the conversion of the Anglo-Saxons the Irish dominated the scene, with St Columbanus, who left Ireland for the continent in AD 590, as the principal figure. Exactly one hundred years later the departure of St Willibrord for Frisia marked the third attempt by monks and clerics of Northumbrian origin to establish a mission in the Low Countries. Earlier attempts to Christianize the area had been made by the Franks in parallel with the military expansion of their empire to the east. Two sites in particular are recorded as being provided with churches at this period, one of them associated with the Aquitanian missionary bishop St Amandus (c. 584–c. 675). At Antwerp, close to Frankish territory proper, he erected in the castle a church dedicated to St Peter and St Paul, which was later transferred to Willibrord.[1] The date of this foundation is not known, and there is some doubt about the date of its donation to Willibrord: there is a surviving charter of 726, but a later chronicler ascribes the donation to 694.[2] Further to the north-east, deep in Frisian territory, there was a church before 612 in Utrecht, likewise sited in the former Roman fort; the castle with its church passed by royal gift to the bishops of Cologne, who were charged with the conversion of the Frisians. No progress was made, and pagans destroyed the church down to the foundations.[3]

The first of the Northumbrians to carry out missionary work in Frisia was St Wilfrid (c. 633–709). In 678 he left England to appeal to the pope against the partition of his York see. For complex political reasons his route to Rome took him to the Rhine delta, and no doubt to the port of Dorestad. He continued up the Rhine, meeting Dagobert II, possibly at Strasbourg, where he was offered the episcopal see. Meanwhile, he had spent the winter of 678–79 in Frisia, where he successfully preached the Gospel: 'all the chiefs were baptized . . . as well as many thousands of the common people'.[4] Here as elsewhere, however, Wilfrid's principal motive was not dedication to the missionary cause; rather, he capitalized opportunistically on the circumstances of his exile. His cause won, he returned to his Northumbrian see rather than to the Frisian mission field.

The cause was taken up by another Northumbrian, Bishop Ecgbert, living in voluntary exile in Ireland, where he was head of the expatriate monastic community of Rath Melsigi.[5] According to Bede's account, Ecgbert was aware of the continental Germanic tribes related to the Anglo-Saxons, who were still pagan.[6] Frustrated in his own attempts to become an active missionary, he dispatched another monk, Wihtberht, to Frisia. After two unsuccessful seasons Wihtberht returned to Rath Melsigi.

Ecgbert then turned to Willibrord, who had entered Wilfrid's monastery at Ripon, but later transferred to Rath Melsigi. At the third attempt a successful and longer-lasting missionary enterprise was established in the present-day Netherlands, despite the initial hostility of the local ruler, Radbod, and the temporary collapse of Frankish authority in the area. Willibrord left Ireland in 690 and was consecrated archbishop of the Frisians in November 695, with his episcopal see in Utrecht.

ENGLAND AND THE LOW COUNTRIES UP TO AD 690

Ecgberht's perception of the pagan Germanic tribes as 'cousins' of the Anglo-Saxons is a reminder of the close connections between the Flanders–Frisia region and England in the migration period. Groups of people which included Franks and Frisians, as well as the Angles, Saxons and Jutes mentioned by Bede in the oft-quoted passage, passed through the Low Countries *en route* to England. The material evidence for this includes metalwork, some of which has recently been subjected to detailed scrutiny.[7] Similarities in form indicate the importation of brooches into Anglo-Saxon England in the early fifth century, with Frisia and north Germany as the principal sources. Stylistic parallels continue in the later part of the century, but by the sixth century independent production seems to have begun in England.[8] Further evidence of early contacts between England and the Low Countries is provided by the so-called Anglo-Frisian pottery, which is found on both sides of the North Sea (Fig. 1). This was identified many years ago by the late Dr J. N. L. Myres,[9] whose more recent synthesis of the pottery evidence makes clear the links between the two areas. Myres leaves open the question of whether the evidence implies 'any massive influx of Frisians' into England or whether it merely indicates people moving through the Low Countries on their way to the coast and thence across the North Sea.[10] He identifies specific features of pots from the Lackford/Eye workshop, which occur at Rijnsburg and Wageningen in the Netherlands as well as in Cambridge and East Anglia, while another direct link seems to exist between Northamptonshire and Belgium, with examples at Saint-Gilles-les-Termonde echoing pieces at Desborough and Rothwell. The last site is of particular interest, since the place name contains the Old Frisian element *rothe-*. The significance of this is considered by Myres in a lengthy footnote[11] though the implication that the connection was between Belgium and Northamptonshire alone is modified by the occurrence of the same place-name element in counties as widely spread as Essex, Hertfordshire, Leicestershire, Yorkshire and Northumberland.[12] Further pots in the Netherlands that parallel Anglo-Saxon forms are recorded at Midlaren in Drenthe, Ezinge, Groningen, Hogebeintum, Oosterbeintum, Rhenen and Wijster.[13] To this list of sites taken from the *Corpus* can be added Beetgum, Kimswerd and Raard, all on the Dutch coast, and all like Ezinge and Hogebeintum *terp* sites.[14] A cremation urn from Hogebeintum, displayed at the Willibrord exhibition in 1995, is regarded as Anglo-Saxon and dated 460 × 550, but the earlier interpretation of such vessels as indicating Anglo-Saxon colonization has been abandoned.[15] There is, however, a strong hint that migration occurred in the opposite direction in Procopius's reference to *Frissones* as one of the constituent 'nations' making up the Anglo-Saxon confederation.[16] A recent survey of a related type of pottery, chaff-tempered ware, makes it clear that there must have been close connections between southern England and the coastal region of Flanders, but does not attempt to define their nature.[17]

Whatever the precise meaning of these pottery finds, they are hand-made wares belonging to the phase of migration and settlement, during which the situation on both sides of the North Sea was fluid. In the more stable conditions of the sixth and seventh centuries evidence for trade begins to emerge, and pottery is once again one of the key commodities. Wheel-thrown vessels — bottles, jugs and pitchers — found in Kentish

4

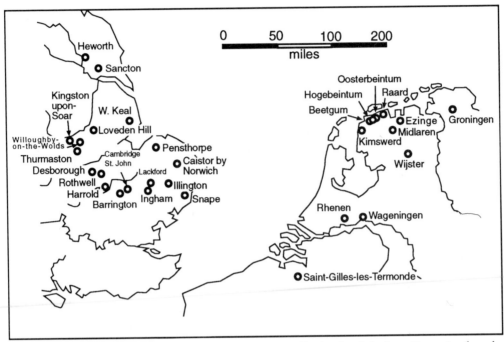

FIG. 1.   Distribution of 'Anglo-Frisian' pottery in eastern England and the Low Countries (based
on Myres, *Anglo-Saxon Pottery and the Settlement of England* (1969), fig. 7, with additions)

graves are an indication of trade, presumably in wine, from north-eastern France and
Belgium.[18] This pottery is only one class of material of Frankish origin found in graves
in Kent and, to a smaller extent, in Essex, East Anglia and elsewhere.[19] The gold-and-
garnet jewellery is notable, at first imported and then manufactured in England itself.
There is so much of this material that an actual invasion or migration of Frankish
people has been postulated.[20] This seems unlikely for a variety of reasons,[21] although
there is evidence that the Franks claimed some sort of hegemony over south-eastern
England in the mid-sixth century.[22] The archaeological evidence points to contacts with
north-west France as much as to the Rhine/Maas delta, and the best known political
event, the marriage in the seventh century of King Æthelbert of Kent to the Frankish
princess, Bertha, is evidence of a dynastic connection with the Paris branch of the
Merovingian family. Nevertheless, there is evidence which points more strongly to the
Low Countries as a trade route. Long distance trade came up through Italy, over the
Alps and down the Rhine, as Martin Welch's distribution map of 'Coptic' bronze
vessels makes clear,[23] while the famous lava quernstones from Niedermendig in the
Eifel region of Germany would naturally have followed the Rhine route on their way to
such English sites as West Stow.[24] It should be noted, however, that the Niedermendig
material found at West Stow consisted entirely of quern fragments, so the correct
interpretation may be that the querns had been imported at an earlier period, broken in
use and the fragments re-employed by the Anglo-Saxons, perhaps as hones for small
hand tools. The author of the report found no evidence to suggest how the fragments
reached the site. Nearer to the Netherlands, the sites manufacturing vessel glass, which
had continued in production since the late Roman period, were located on the lower

Rhine, and material, possibly from these workshops, found its way, first into Kent, and then in smaller quantities into the interior of Anglo-Saxon England.[25] Harden makes it clear, however, that glass was also produced in Belgium and northern France (citing an excavated Belgian site), so that vessels could have reached England in the same way as the wheel-thrown pottery, without passing through the ports of the Rhine–Maas delta.

This and other material makes it clear that there were close contacts between Anglo-Saxon England and the Low Countries in the sixth and seventh centuries, though whether these connections were still current at the time of Willibrord it is difficult to assess. However, Bede's mention of a Frisian merchant living in London in 679 suggests that they were, which is corroborated by the finds of Anglo-Saxon coins on sites in the Netherlands,[26] and Frisian coins in England. The old certainties about the places of origin of these early coins have been challenged, however, by recent research. It has been suggested that certain coin types previously regarded as imports from England into Frisia are in fact of Frisian manufacture, so that their appearance in continental finds can no longer be taken to indicate trade from England to the Low Countries and elsewhere.[27] Conversely, however, their appearance in England supports the interpretation of outward trade from Frisia. Chronologically, these issues belong to the first two decades of the eighth century,[28] while the occurrence of Anglo-Saxon sceattas in hoards in the Low Countries begins only c. 710 (Escharen) to 720 (Hallum and possibly Föhr).[29] This period is regarded as the heyday of the sceatta coinage, and neatly coincides with the middle years of Willibrord's mission, which must therefore be viewed in the context of sustained secular contacts between Anglo-Saxon England and the Low Countries.

THE SETTLEMENT PATTERN IN THE MISSION AREA (see Fig. 2)

The archaeological evidence for settlement in the Netherlands during the post-Roman period is both sparse and difficult to interpret. Most surveys of the period emphasize the scarcity of finds and the difficulties of dating in the absence of diagnostic imported pottery. In the sixth and seventh centuries burials with grave goods provide points of reference, but at one of the key sites (at Lent near Nijmegen), discussed in a recent summary of archaeological evidence at the time of Willibrord, one of two cemeteries was abandoned around 680, while at the other the practice of burying grave goods ceased at about the same time.[30] So about a decade before the arrival of Willibrord this point of reference disappears. Nevertheless, the cemeteries, along with the few excavated settlements and chance finds, afford a general picture of the area inhabited shortly before the missionaries' arrival (Fig. 2). Much of the population was apparently concentrated in the valleys of the major rivers, notably the Rhine and the Maas, and their immediate hinterlands. There was also a concentration in the north-eastern coastal area, where *terp* settlements were relatively common. Areas such as Brabant and Limburg appear to have been settled again after a period of depopulation, though this 'fallow' period is thought to be more apparent than real. However, the sandy areas in the east and north east, the fenland areas, and parts of the south-west coast do seem to have remained unsettled.[31]

Detailed studies of particular areas give a clearer picture of the settlement pattern. In the Rhine–Maas delta the potential depopulation following the southward migration of Frankish settlers during the first half of the fifth century seems to be confirmed by the small number of finds datable to this period, but place-name evidence suggests more continuity than is apparent from the archaeology; settlements with archaic names

FIG. 2.   Merovingian settlement in the Netherlands: circles represent direct
archaeological evidence for settlement sites, triangles indicate cemetery evidence.
The present coastline is shown in broken line, the reconstructed early medieval coastline
in solid (after *Archeologie in Nederland: de rijkdom van het bodemarchief*,
ed. W. A. van Es, H. Sarfatij and P. J. Woltering (Amsterdam/Amersfoort 1988), p. 95)

continue into the seventh and eighth centuries, as written sources demonstrate.[32] In
general Henderikx demonstrates how a combination of different forms of evidence can
be used to illustrate the settlement pattern more fully. Nevertheless there remains a lack
of evidence for areas of peat soil or peat overlain by clay.[33] Further north, the Overijssel
region can also be shown to have supported a population in the Merovingian period.[34]
It is difficult to be precise, but finds dated not later than the eighth century can be
demonstrated at eight sites, mainly located in the valleys of the IJssel and the Dinkel,
and at the confluence of the Regge and the Overijsselse Vecht. A further thirteen
possible sites extend this distribution, but the riverine pattern remains. For large areas

of this region there is no archaeological evidence at all. The overall impression of the spread of population at the time of the mission is that density was greatest in the Rhine–Maas area and close to the north-east coast, while settlement elsewhere existed, but was relatively sparse.

WILLIBRORD'S MISSION AND HIS PRINCIPAL CHURCHES

Between Wilfrid's visit in 678–79 and the failed mission of Wihtberht in the 680s the Franks lost control of Frisia to the pagan local ruler, Radbod. Missionary activity, which frequently went hand in hand with political and military advance, ceased for the time being. It is probably no coincidence that Willibrord's arrival in Frisia in 690 coincided with the re-establishment of Frankish power in its more westerly parts. Even so, the area beyond the old Rhine frontier remained in Radbod's hands until 719, and there was still sufficient hostility to Christianity as late as 754 to lead to St Boniface's murder at Dokkum. Van Es emphasizes Willibrord's restricted area of operations in the early years and his dependence on his first base at Antwerp, which lies well away from Frisia and just outside the present-day Netherlands.[35] Unfortunately there is no archaeological evidence for an early church there.

Utrecht

For both Willibrord and the Frankish kingdom the former Roman fort at Utrecht was a frontier post. In missionary terms it was well placed for advances into Radbod's territory when circumstances should become more favourable; meanwhile Utrecht could serve as a base for consolidation in west Frisia (*citerior Fresia*).[36] As a mission centre it fulfilled the criteria which I have discussed elsewhere in relation to the Bonifacian sites in central Germany in the second quarter of the eighth century.[37] It had the added advantage that as a quasi-urban enclosure it could properly become the seat of a bishop. A formal espiscopal centre became a necessity with Willibrord's elevation to the archbishopric of the Frisians in 695. According to Bede, the site given to him for this purpose was Wiltaburg, which in itself would be credible, since it was the native name for Fectio, also a Roman site.[38] Bede goes on to say, however, that the site was also known as *Traiectum*, which is the Latin origin of the name Utrecht. How the confusion arose is not clear, but it is well explained by Henderikx. Confirmation that the place intended was in fact Utrecht is given by the careful and detailed account in the letter of St Boniface to the pope in 753.

Boniface also records the foundation of two churches in the Roman fort, one of which, dedicated to St Saviour, was to act as the cathedral. The other, 'a certain little church', was discovered by the archbishop razed to the ground; he rebuilt it and dedicated it to St Martin. The only ancient place of worship surviving above ground level on the Domplein in Utrecht is the Gothic cathedral, and that only in part. This is confusingly dedicated to St Martin, the church of Holy Saviour having been demolished in 1587. Also confusing is the term 'Old Minster', applied to St Saviour's, in view of the apparent seniority of St Martin's as the successor to the early Frankish church in the fort. The present cathedral stands slightly to the north of centre in the Domplein, while St Saviour's occupied the south-west corner of the interior of the fort. Between the two was a third church, dedicated to Holy Cross. This is known both from illustrations and

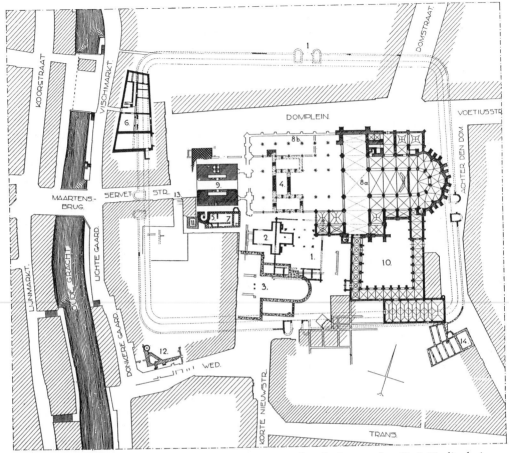

FIG. 3.   Utrecht: early medieval and later churches within the Roman fort (E. J. Haslinghuis,
Nederlandse Monumenten van Geschiedenis en Kunst: geïllustreerde Beschrijving, 2.1.1
('s Gravenhage 1956), p. 12)

from excavations. Its site has recently been re-examined, and it is now suggested in
some quarters that it may have been Willibrord's church of St Martin. The exact
interpretation of the churches in the fort is not at all straightforward, however, and has
given rise to a great deal of debate in recent years.[39] Some of the discussion has failed
sufficiently to emphasize the position of the Holy Cross church. Its small size and its
location between the major churches of St Saviour and St Martin have perhaps obscured
its original significance. In relation to the layout of the interior of the Roman fort its
position was highly important. The eastern half of the church was built over the
northern part of the *principia* of the fort (see Fig. 3); the Roman well in the north-east
corner of the chancel was presumably a deliberate inclusion for ritual purposes. This or
an analogous position was often adopted for the earliest churches in late Roman and
early medieval contexts. A notable example is the church of St Paul in the Bail, Lincoln,
which was built across the courtyard of the forum in the Roman city centre. In Leicester
the potentially early church of St Nicholas was built in the *palaestra* adjacent to the

forum in the town centre. In York the first Norman cathedral was built across the end of the *principia* of the Roman legionary fortress, and is the most closely comparable English example to the Utrecht complex of churches. I argue elsewhere that early date rather than cathedral status is the significant factor in the choice of this type of site.[40]

Echternach

Although Willibrord had Utrecht allocated to him as his archiepiscopal centre and as his forward position for missionary activity, he also had a 'home base' well away from the frontier zone. It was here that he chose to be buried, a wish that was carried out at his death in 739. Echternach had been granted to him in 698 by the Abbess of Oeren and the property enlarged through further grants by Pippin II, Austrasian Mayor of the Palace, and his wife Plectrudis, in 706. A small monastery already existed on the site, but was probably developed after the 706 grant. Twenty years later Willibrord himself donated other property in his possession to Echternach, rather than to his episcopal church in Utrecht, and the question arises whether he was more attached to his monastic retreat than to his see. In this and other documents he is described simply as *episcopus*, or *pontifex*, without any reference to the location of his see.[41] In Pippin's privilege of 706 he is actually designated *Willibrord[us] episcop[us] de monasterio Epternaco*.[42] This parallels the references to his younger compatriot Willibald as 'bishop of the monastery of Eichstätt', rather than of Erfurt, for which see he appears to have been consecrated, but where he never resided.[43] Schroeder attempts to reconcile Willibald's potentially contradictory rôles as missionary pastor and as monk – a contradiction inherent in all monastic involvement in missionary activity – by comparing the Lives of the saint written by Alcuin and Thiofrid respectively.

Excavation has revealed what is thought to be Willibrord's church, dating from immediately after the donation of the property in 706 (see Fig. 4). It was stone-built and consisted of a long rectangular nave with a narrower rectangular chancel; to the south of this was an annexe with a door to the chancel, and to the north-east of the chancel was an earlier building on a different alignment. A further east–west wall joined the east wall of the chancel slightly to the north of the axis line. There was evidence for raised floor levels at the east end of the nave and in the chancel; in the first phase there was a vaulted tomb to the east of the altar, but this was abandoned in one of two reorderings of the east end of the church.[44] The excavator, Jean Dumont, whose discoveries were published posthumously by Cüppers, contributed a brief report to the catalogue of the 1958 Willibrord exhibition. His account mentions remains of a screen to the west of the altar, in the vicinity of which fragments of green marble were discovered. These he interpreted as belonging to a tomb structure into which the body from the grave were translated. He believed that occupant of the grave must have been St Willibrord himself.[45]

OTHER EARLY CHURCHES IN THE LOW COUNTRIES

There are unfortunately relatively few churches of early date surviving above ground in the Low Countries and only a limited amount of archaeological evidence that points clearly to places of worship in existence before, during, or immediately after the period of Willibrord's mission. Those which have so far been identified are conveniently listed

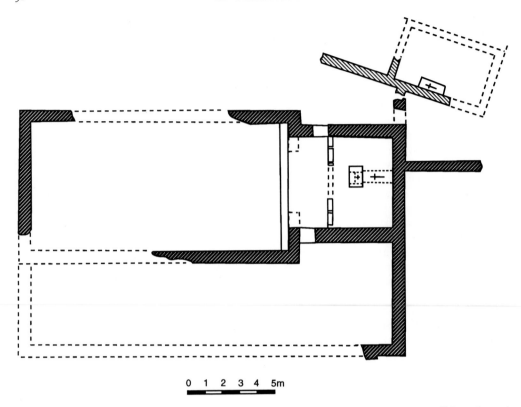

0 1 2 3 4 5m

FIG. 4.   Echternach: plan of the early church; the light shading represents a pre-Willibrordian
building (after H. Cüppers, 'Die Basilica des heiligen Willibrord zu Echternach . . .',
as no. 44, figs 3 and 5)

with summary descriptions in the Munich corpus.[46] In many cases they have been uncovered in the course of excavation during the last fifty years, and frequently the earliest church on any given site has proved to be a simple timber one. Wooden churches have also been listed country by country for the whole of northern Europe.[47] Churches which seem relevant to the mission of Willibrord are described below; that is to say, those churches which already existed at the time of his mission, and those which might be reasonably be ascribed to his activity or its immediate aftermath.

At *Arlon*, Luxemburg (B),[48] the earliest phase of the church was stone-built and was stratigraphically earlier than grave X, whose furnishings dated to approximately 535–50. It therefore belongs to the late Roman or sub-Roman period. It was a rectangular building two squares long and with a narrow space at the east end screened off from the nave. The chancel was narrower than the nave, and tapered to the east with an apsidal end.[49]

Only a small part of the church at *Bovigny*, Luxemburg (B), was encountered in the 1968 excavations, but it appeared to indicate a tiny building with a nave and narrower chancel. The excavator suggested a date in the eighth to ninth century, but the editors of the corpus proposed an earlier date on account of the dedication to St Martin and of topographical considerations.[50]

Traces of a timber building were found at *Dorestad*, Utrecht (NL), in an apparently Christian cemetery. This structure was dated to 'before the Viking incursions, probably eighth–ninth century', but there is doubt whether it was actually a church.[51]

The earliest church at *Echternach* (L), thought to be of early eighth-century date, has been discussed above.

At *Elst*, Gelderland (NL), the earliest church is represented by fragmentary remains of walls discovered by excavation in 1947. They appear to indicate a fairly large single-celled nave with a much narrower square chancel. This building was erected over the remains of two Roman temples, though Stoepker has cast doubt on any symbolic relationship between the two phases of use of the site. The church is usually regarded as a foundation of Willibrord himself, but Stoepker suggests that the date may be as late as the ninth century.[52]

Excavations in 1960 in the former Romanesque two-celled church at *Erpekom*, Limburg (B), revealed two earlier timber structures, the first of which was represented by only a few posts, so that it was not possible to establish the overall plan. Its position in a graveyard led to the interpretation as a church or *cella memoriae*. The excavator suggested a date in the eighth to ninth centuries, but Ahrens regards it as ninth–tenth century.[53]

Documentary evidence indicates a timber church at *Floyon*, dating from the seventh century, but this is not so far confirmed by any archaeological evidence.[54]

A timber predecessor was also revealed by excavation at *Gemonde*, Nord-Brabant (NL), in 1950, but the original interpretation of two separate timber phases has been questioned by Stoepker, whose views have found favour with the compilers of the Munich corpus supplement. A single-phase building with side aisles is now proposed, while the finds do not allow a date earlier than the tenth century. However, a land grant in favour of Echternach in 698–99 seems to include Gemonde, and makes it likely that there was a church here at a relatively early date, though Stoepker thinks the Carolingian settlement has to be sought elsewhere.[55]

Genk, Limburg (B), also had a timber church, of which only traces remained in the excavations of 1956, though many burials in wooden coffins were encountered. The plan of the church could not be determined. The date proposed is eighth–ninth century.[56]

At *Grobbendonk*, Antwerp (B), successive timber churches were built in a Merovingian cemetery. The earlier of these was a simple rectangular building. According to the dating of the furnished burials, this church was in existence by the seventh century.[57]

Another post-built church in a graveyard at *Heiloo* (NL), excavated in 1965 and 1967, appears to date from the period eighth–tenth century, but there were traces of an earlier predecessor of unknown ground plan. Ahrens does not recognize this earlier phase. The place was an early possession of Echternach, and a church may have been founded by Willibrord.[58]

At *Landen*, Brabant (B), two large post-holes are interpreted as the remains of a nave-and-chancel church earlier than the eighth century. It was probably begun along with the graveyard in the seventh.[59] The timber church at *Lovenjoul*, Brabant (B), is recorded in the literature as having been founded by St Lambert, and therefore before his death in 698.[60]

The foundations of a small church were excavated at *Lorcy*, Luxembourg (B), in 1970. The nave was an irregular square and the narrower chancel rectangular, but shorter than it was wide. The excavator assumed a date around 700, but doubt has been cast on this.[61]

In *Liège* (B) two churches need to be considered. The first is St Lambert, dedicated in 717–18 and raised to cathedral status in 722. Traces of this building were found in archaeological investigations between 1977 and 1984. They indicated a church 22.5 m wide, but it was not clear whether it was an aisled or an aisleless structure, and its length was not determined. There was evidence for only about 14 m of its west end, including the crown of a broad apse.[62] The second church, St Martin's, was discovered in the course of rescue excavations in 1980. The evidence consists only of a narrow wall representing the south-west angle of an otherwise indeterminate building. It preceded another excavated structure thought to be the church founded around 963, but is not more closely datable. The dedication to St Martin might indicate an original foundation in the Frankish period.[63]

In *Maastricht* (NL) there are likewise two sites to consider. Excavations in St Servatius, most recently an extensive programme in the 1980s, have revealed three pre-Romanesque phases. The last of these may belong to the early ninth century. It was preceded by a building, parts of whose west, north and south walls survive, though not sufficiently to determine its length or character. It is provisionally dated to around 580. It was subsequently extended to the west to incorporate a *cella memoriae*, which is associated with St Servatius himself, who died in 380.[64] This sequence of structures omits the wooden oratory referred to by Gregory of Tours, and the dating of the various phases may have to be adjusted to take account of that.[65] Another timber structure, close to the church Our Lady, was thought to be the original bishop's church, but is now interpreted as a secular building.[66]

In the ninth century the original timber church of Sts Harlindis and Relindis at *Maaseik* (*Maeseyck*), Limburg (B), of mid eighth-century date, was replaced in stone and the saints were translated into the new church, according to a contemporary biographer. There is no archaeological evidence.[67]

A small timber building was excavated in 1959 on the site of the demolished parish church at *Neder-Heembeek*, Brabant (B), near Brussels. Post-holes indicated a short nave with narrower chancel, but no further details were forthcoming. The excavator proposed a date in the eighth/ninth century.[68]

Under the church of St Gertrude in *Nivelles* (*Nijvel*), Brabant (B), a complex sequence of buildings has been revealed by excavation. The earliest of these, regarded as a cemetery chapel, was a long rectangular building, which is dated to the seventh century. This was replaced on a slightly different axis by a rather larger church with a square chamber to its east, into which the remains of St Gertrude were translated. A date in the period 669–92 is thought likely. The third church, with an eastern ring crypt has been dated to the late ninth century, but a date in the third quarter of the eighth is now proposed.[69]

Near Bruges there was a timber church at *Oudenburg*, West Flanders (B), in the first half of the seventh century, according to documentary evidence. There is no archaeological confirmation.[70]

At *Ronse*, East Flanders (B), a monastery was founded *c.* 630 by St Amandus and dedicated to St Peter. Inside and outside the present church of Saint Hermes evidence has been found for what is currently regarded on typological grounds as the original abbey church. It had a rectangular nave with length to width proportions of 3:2, an almost square side chamber at the north-east corner, and what appears to have been a very narrow chancel.[71]

A church with a comparable plan was excavated at *St-Truiden*, Limburg (B), but here the nave was much longer and the apse was polygonal externally. Evidence for a side chamber was found at the south-east corner. This is considered to be the original building of 657. Probably in the eighth century it was extended to the west, and a south wall was added in line with the south wall of the side chamber. This is interpreted as a conversion to basilican plan, but the addition to the south could have taken the form of a series of chambers, as at Reculver, Kent.[72]

A small two-celled building was excavated in 1978–83 in the church at *Theux*, Liège (B). The length of the nave as published gives a plan which seems hardly credible except as an oratory or *memoria*. It is regarded as the church first mentioned in documents in 814. The excavator proposed dates of fifth and sixth/seventh centuries for the chancel and nave respectively.[73]

At *Tiel*, Gelderland (NL), a church was constructed in a cemetery of not earlier than eighth-century date. It consisted of a square chancel and a long nave of equal width. The wall dividing the two cells was continued to north and south outside the building, giving buttress-like projections which may have been intended to take the thrust of a chancel arch. It may be, however, that the side aisles added at a later date were planned from the start, since their east walls neatly abut these projecting stretches of wall. The excavator proposed a date in the eighth/ninth century.[74]

The churches in *Utrecht* have been discussed above. In 1965 excavations at *Velsen*, North Holland (NL), located numerous post-holes of timber building in the Carolingian graveyard beneath the eleventh-century stone church. The origins of this church go back to its foundation by Willibrord.[75]

Finally, at *Vieux-Virton*, Luxembourg (B), excavation in 1980–83 revealed a rectangular chamber with thick walls, possibly indicating a vaulted *cella memoriae*, set in a graveyard in the ruins of a Roman *vicus*. A *terminus ante quem* is given by a furnished late Merovingian burial lying alongside the west wall.[76]

Discussion

The catalogue above summarizes the evidence, both archaeological and documentary, for a total of 29 distinct sites. A systematic survey of the primary literature would doubtless increase the number but might not alter the overall picture. Of the 29 churches listed, 17 were stone-built in their earliest phase, and 12 were of timber. A maximum of 4 date from the fifth or sixth centuries, 9 are positively assigned to the seventh and 7 to the eighth/ninth. Very few for which there is good archaeological evidence can be ascribed with certainty to the missionary activity of Willibrord or to the period immediately following his death. Only at Echternach and Elst are there churches with long rectangular naves and square chancels that might be considered to have been influenced by the Northumbrian model represented by the church at Escomb in County Durham. This church has long been regarded by continental scholars as the point of reference for putative Anglo-Saxon architectural influence in the context of the eighth-century missions led by Willibrord in the Low Countries and by Boniface in Germany. This notion was given overt expression by Boekelmann forty years ago, but while he saw other plan types as being transmitted by specific groups and families, he recognized the rectangular nave with square chancel as being a pan-European form whose origin it was impossible to localize.[77] More recently Peeters resurrected the idea of this plan form having been imported into the Netherlands from Northumbria, only to be taken to task by Stoepker, who emphasizes the possible contribution of local timber building traditions.[78] Serious consideration must be given to this proposition in view of recent research in England into the origins of Anglo-Saxon secular timber

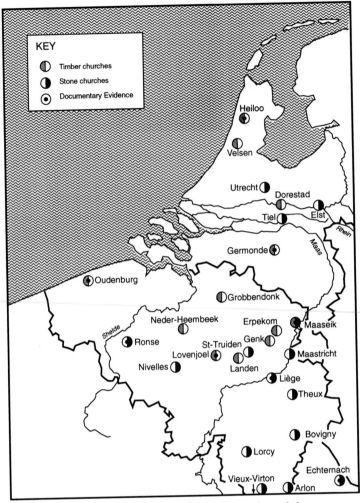

FIG. 5. Churches in the Low Countries up to the eighth century:
archaeological and documentary evidence

buildings, which has drawn attention to the frequent occurrence of the long rectangular plan with end annexes.[79] Meanwhile, Peeters sees no need to look to Northumbria for the source of this plan form, and speaks of 'a general north-European type.[80]

The distribution of the earliest churches, shown in Fig. 5, sheds some light on the missionary activities of Willibrord. The sites are concentrated in the areas between the Schelde and the Maas and between the Maas and the Mosel, and in the Rhine–Maas delta. These areas are within the *limes* of the Roman empire, and had been partly Christianized before the arrival of the Anglo-Saxon missionaries, though the destruction of the early church in Utrecht shows the vulnerability of the frontier zone. Some of the sites are clearly related to the earlier activities of Frankish saints, such as Lambert and Amandus. The addition to the map of other places where we have knowledge of early Christian activity, e.g. Tongeren,[81] merely serves to emphasize this. Other sites west of the *limes* may represent consolidation or reconversion by Willibrord's mission, and the map confirms that his activity was restricted for much of the period to the relatively safe area which had formerly been under Roman occupation. Only at Heiloo and Velsen are there early churches in the clearly pagan territory beyond the Rhine, and from the archaeological point of view Heiloo's claims to be regarded as a church of the missionary period are doubtful in the extreme. There is also no clear evidence that the church was founded by Willibrord himself. Velsen was, but the archaeological evidence is undatable, though possibly Carolingian. The distribution of early church sites therefore emphasizes the relatively modest achievement of the mission, at least in territorial terms, particularly when it is compared with the settlement pattern shown in Fig. 2.

ARTEFACTUAL EVIDENCE FOR INSULAR ACTIVITY

In the absence of any conclusive archaeological evidence for the effects of the mission it is necessary to turn to the portable objects which might have a bearing on the subject. There are in particular two items whose current location in the Low Countries invite comment. The first of these is the diptych, or pair of ivory panels, from Genoels-Elderen in Belgium, now in the Musées Royaux d'Art et d'Histoire in Brussels. They seem to have been part of an elaborate book cover and are carved in low relief in a rather flat style. One panel shows Christ Triumphant trampling the beasts that represent Evil; the other, divided in two horizontally, has the Annunciation above and the Salutation below. There are differences of opinion over the date and provenance of the panels, and these are discussed in some detail in the catalogue of the 1991 London exhibition.[82] The provisional conclusion is that the ivories date from the eighth century, and were made in a continental workshop under Insular influence. The suggestion that the workshop may have been in Bavaria appears to be contradicted by the lack of similarity between these panels and other pieces ascribed to Bavarian Insular production centres. The presence of the Genoels-Elderen panels in Belgium might be taken to imply manufacture at a workshop in the area, where there was clearly the appropriate Insular background.[83]

The other item consists of a number of panels of embroidery, which had been at the monastery of Aldeneik before 1577, when they were moved to Maaseik (both places in Belgium). They are of Anglo-Saxon origin and date to around 800. On both counts they appear not to be the work of the aristocratic sisters who founded the monastery at Aldeneik in the first half of the eighth century, and who are said in their ninth-century Life to have made certain decorative *palliola*.[84] Both the provenance and the date depend upon comparisons with Anglo-Saxon material in other media. Similar decorative roundels can be found both in stone sculpture and on metalwork in the Trewhiddle style, while the arcaded panels filled with vinescroll ornament resemble motifs on the Gandersheim casket and the 'Hedda' stone in Peterborough Cathedral.

Most of these features occur in the Tiberius Bede (BL Cotton Tiberius C II) and related manuscripts, which were produced in southern England in the first half of the ninth century. The Maaseik embroideries cannot therefore be associated with the mission of Willibrord, but they do attest the continuing Anglo-Saxon influence in the Low Countries a century after his death.

A further rare fabric survival is the so-called relic of Lebuinus, a fragment of a silk vestment thought to be part of a liturgical vestment. Because of its attribution to Lebuinus (Liafwine), an Anglo-Saxon active on the continent in the second half of the eighth century, an Anglo-Saxon origin for this piece has been assumed, but it is now thought that it may have been manufactured in Spain, south Germany or Asia.[85] Its association with Lebuinus is at best secondary, since it appears to date from before the eighth century.

More convincing than any of these artefacts are the manuscripts which were produced at the time of Willibrord himself and at places that can be identified. They included such imported pieces as the well-known Echternach Gospels, which despite their name were probably written in Northumbria,[86] or the fragments of two Northumbrian gospel books at Maaseik.[87] Considerable debate has taken place about the origin of the Echternach Gospels, with some commentators emphasizing similarities with the Book of Durrow and suggesting a connection with Ecgbert, Willibrord's mentor. Of the two Maaseik fragments, the first shows a classicism comparable with that of the Ruthwell and Bewcastle crosses, though there are grounds for not assigning it to any of the major Northumbrian centres. The suggestion that it may have been produced in York and be associated with St Wilfrid is an attractive one in the context of the present paper. The provenance of the other Maaseik fragment is uncertain, but it has some characteristics in common with the previous manuscript and with the Trier Gospels (see below), so that it may have been produced at a continental centre under Northumbrian influence.

There are several manuscripts which were certainly produced in the Low Countries, but under strong Insular influence, mainly at the scriptorium of Echternach, which has recently been the subject of intensive study.[88] One of these is the Calendar of St Willibrord, in which the saint's own handwriting is recognizable at a date when he was clearly living in the Low Countries.[89] The script of this manuscript is closely related to that of the Schloss Harburg Gospels, another early eighth-century Echternach book.[90] There are also the Trier gospel book, written by two scribes, one of them an Anglo-Saxon called Thomas, and the Stuttgart psalter.[91] Among the various models for the Trier Gospels, the Book of Echternach and other Northumbrian manuscripts can be identified. The Stuttgart psalter is of great interest because it shows the results of an Anglo-Saxon artist converting traditional Merovingian zoomorphic initial letters to a more Insular style. If not produced at Echternach, this manuscript was probably in use there at some stage. Finally, a somewhat later manuscript, which may have been written at Liège in the early ninth century, reflects an Anglo-Saxon, possibly Northumbrian, manuscript of the eighth century, and this must have been available in the Low Countries to act as a model for it.[92]

CONCLUSION

It is clear that the mission of St Willibrord has to be seen in the context of the extensive archaeological evidence for the close relations between England and the Low Countries from the Migration Period onward. It must also be regarded as an aspect of the military and political development of the Frankish kingdom, as it coincides significantly with the Frankish attempts to impose control over Frisia in the late seventh and early eighth centuries. This was achieved only towards the end of Willibrord's career, and it is noticeable that the archaeological evidence for churches dating from the eighth century or earlier is mainly confined to the area south and west of the Rhine–Maas delta. This area was within the former Roman *limes* and had passed into Frankish control long before the advent of the Anglo-Saxon missionaries.

The archaeological record does not contain any firm evidence for specifically Anglo-Saxon influence in church design, although there are obvious similarities in the plans of small churches consisting of nave and chancel with or without side annexes. Opinion now favours a general European building tradition in which this plan form could emerge at any place without the implication of influence from elsewhere. Evidence for direct Anglo-Saxon influence in the mission area is therefore restricted to the field of artefacts, in particular manuscripts, where the adoption of the Hiberno-Saxon style of decoration and of Insular forms of handwriting, together with the occurrence of English names, make clear the degree to which the continental scriptoria were indebted to Anglo-Saxon models, to Anglo-Saxon scribes on their staff, and to Anglo-Saxon masters instructing their oblates in the Insular manner.

ACKNOWLEDGEMENT

I am most grateful to Drs J. L. Wynia-Gils for her invaluable bibliographical help and for hunting down and sending me copies of important Dutch publications not easily available in Great Britain. Without her this paper would have been vastly inferior.

SHORTENED TITLES USED

Bede, *HE*	*Bede's Ecclesiastical History of the English People*, ed. B. Colgrave and R. A. B. Mynors (Oxford 1969).
Coinage	P. Grierson and M. Blackburn, *Medieval European coinage*, I: *The early Middle Ages* (Cambridge 1986).
Henderikx (1986)	P. A. Henderikx, 'The lower delta of the Rhine and the Maas: landscape and habitation from the Roman period to c.1000', *Berichten van de Rijksdienst voor het Oudheidkundig Bodemonderzoek*, XXXVI (1986), 445–582.
Holzkirchen	C. Ahrens, *Frühe Holzkirchen im nördlichen Europa*, Helms-Museum, Hamburg, publication 39 (Hamburg 1981).
Insular manuscripts	J. J. G. Alexander, *Insular manuscripts: 6th to the 9th century* (London 1978).
Kirchenbauten, I	*Vorromanische Kirchenbauten: Katalog der Denkmäler bis zum Ausgang der Ottonen*, ed. F. Oswald, L. Schaefer and H. R. Sennhauser (Munich 1966–71).
Kirchenbauten, II	*Vorromanische Kirchenbauten: Katalog der Denkmäler bis zum Ausgang der Ottonen. Nachtragsband*, ed. W. Jacobsen, L. Schaefer, and H. R. Sennhauser (Munich 1991).
Levison (1946)	W. Levison, *England and the Continent in the Eighth Century* (Oxford 1946).
Making of England	*The Making of England: Anglo-Saxon art and culture, AD600–900*, ed. L. Webster and J. Backhouse (London 1991).
Myres (1986)	J. N. L. Myres, *The English Settlements* (Oxford 1986).
Myres, *Corpus*	J. N. L. Myres, *A corpus of Anglo-Saxon Pottery of the pagan period* (Cambridge 1977).
Parsons (1983)	D. Parsons, 'Sites and monuments of the Anglo-Saxon mission in central Germany', *Archaeological Journal*, CXL (1983), 284–320.
Peeters (1990)	C. Peeters, 'Kerk- en kloosterbouw in de missiegebieden van Willibrord', *Willibrord: zijn wereld en zijn werk*, ed. P. Bange and A. G. Weiler (Nijmegen 1990), 361–73.
Stenton (1971)	F. M. Stenton, *Anglo-Saxon England*, 3rd edition (Oxford 1971).

Stoepker (1990)   H. Stoepker, 'Church archaeology in the Netherlands: problems, prospects, proposals', *Medieval Archaeology in the Netherlands*, ed. J. C. Besteman, J. M. Bos and H. A. Heidinga (Assen/Maastricht 1990), 199–218.

Van Es (1990)   W. A. van Es, 'Het Nederland van Willibrord: enkele archeologische kanttekeningen', *Willibrord: zijn wereld en zijn werk*, ed. P. Bange and A. G. Weiler (Nijmegen 1990), 67–81.

Van Vlierden (1995)   M. van Vlierden, *Willibrord en het begin van Nederland* (Utrecht 1995).

REFERENCES

1. Levison (1946), 48; for the significance of churches founded on fortified sites see Parsons (1983), 284–320, and J. Blair, 'Anglo-Saxon minster: a topographical review', *Pastoral Care before the Parish*, ed. J. Blair and R. Sharpe (Leicester 1992), 226–66, here 227–31 and 235–41.
2. A. G. Weiler, *Willibrords Missie: christendom en cultuur in de zevende en achtste eeuw* (Hilversum 1989), 96.
3. Levison (1946), 48.
4. *The Life of Bishop Wilfrid by Eddius Stephanus*, ed. B. Colgrave (Cambridge 1927), 53, §xxvi, & 55, §xxviii.
5. The location of this monastery is discussed in D. Ó Cróinín, 'Rath Melsigi, Willibrord and the earliest Echternach manuscripts', *Peritia*, III (1984), 17–42.
6. A detailed account of the beginnings and early progress of the Northumbrian mission to Frisia is given by Bede, *HE*, v, 9–11, ed. Colgrave and Mynors, 474–87; see also Alcuin's account in his *Life of St Willibrord*, English translation in *The Anglo-Saxon Missionaries in Germany*, ed. C. H. Talbot (London 1954), 3–22, here 5–7.
7. C. Mortimer, 'Some aspects of early medieval copper alloy technology, as illustrated by a study of the Anglian cruciform brooch'. Unpublished D. Phil. thesis, Oxford, 1990; see *Aslib Index to Theses*, XLI, pt. 4, p. 1449, no. 41–6845.
8. Note also early 7th-century material from the Netherlands for which an English origin is claimed, for example the Hogebeintum brooch displayed at the Willibrord exhibition: Van Vlierden (1995), pp. 71–72, no. 31.
9. J. N. L. Myres, 'Some English parallels to the Anglo-Saxon pottery of Holland and Belgium in the migration period', *L'Antiquité Classique*, XVII (1948), 453–72.
10. Myres, *Corpus*, 116–17.
11. Myres (1986), 48 n. 2.
12. E. Ekwall, *Concise Oxford Dictionary of Place-Names*, 4th edn. (Oxford 1960), 393.
13. Myres, *Corpus*, 9, 35–36, 40, 41, 55, etc.
14. J. N. L. Myres, *Anglo-Saxon Pottery and the Settlement of England* (Oxford 1969), 95 n. 2 and Map 7.
15. Van Vlierden (1995), p. 69, no. 29.
16. Stenton (1971), 5–6.
17. H. Hamerow, Y. Hollefoet and A. Vince, 'Migration period settlements and 'Anglo-Saxon' pottery from Flanders', *Medieval Archaeology*, XXXVIII (1994), 1–18.
18. V. I. Evison, *A Corpus of wheel-thrown Pottery in Anglo-Saxon Graves* (London 1979).
19. Note also an annular brooch from a cremation at Hogebeintum, whose closest parallel is one from Leicester; Van Vlierden (1955), p. 75, no. 37, considers that it may have been imported into Frisia.
20. V. I. Evison, *The fifth-century Invasions south of the Thames* (London 1965).
21. The arguments are summed up by Myres (1986), 127–28.
22. I. Wood, *The Merovingian Kingdoms, 450–751* (London 1994), 176–79.
23. M. Welch, *English Heritage Book of Anglo-Saxon England* (London 1992), fig. 84 on 117.
24. S. West, *West Stow: the Anglo-Saxon village*, East Anglian Archaeology, XXIV (Ipswich 1985), I, 128.
25. D. B. Harden, 'Ancient glass, III: Post-Roman', *Archaeological Journal*, CXXVIII (1971), 78–117, here 87–93; this overview unfortunately lacks distribution maps, for which see *idem*, in *Dark Age Britain: studies presented to E. T. Leeds* (London 1956), 132–67.
26. Stenton (1971), 221.
27. *Coinage*, 153; S. Lebecq, *Marchands et Navigateurs Frisons du haut moyen âge* (Lille 1983), I, 54–60.

28. For example the 140 sceattas in the hoard from Remmerden near Rhenen: van Vlierden (1955), p. 68, no. 28; note also the slightly later sceatta found in Utrecht: *ibid.*, p. 79, [no. 44] (catalogue entry lacks heading and exhibit number).

29. *Coinage*, 150, 185.

30. Van Es (1990), 67–81.

31. *Archeologie in Nederland: de rijkdom van het bodemarchief*, ed. W. A. van Es, H. Sarfatij and P. J. Woltering (Amsterdam/Amersfoort 1988), 94–96.

32. Henderikx (1986), 483.

33. Henderikx (1986), 491.

34. W. A. van Es and A. D. Verlinde, 'Overijssel in Roman and early-medieval times', *Berichten van de Rijksdienst voor het Oudheidkundig Bodemonderzoek*, XXVII (1977), 7–89.

35. Van Es (1990), 73; see also n. 81 below.

36. Bede, *HE*, v, 10; ed. Colgrave and Mynors, 480–81.

37. Parsons (1983), 284–85.

38. Bede, *HE*, v, 11; ed. Colgrave and Mynors, 486–87.

39. See the contributions elsewhere in this volume by de Groot, Rijntjes and Stöver. The recent literature on this subject is extensive, but many of the opposing views are brought together in the special issue (nos 4/5) of *Bulletin van de Koninklijke Nederlandse Oudheidkundige Bond*, XCIII (1994), 133–96.

40. D. Parsons, 'The Northumbrian Mission to Frisia and its churches', paper prepared for the Golden Age of Northumbria conference at Newcastle upon Tyne, 22–26 July 1996 (publication forthcoming).

41. *Kirchenbauten*, II, 102.

42. J. Schroeder, 'Willibrord — Erzbischof von Utrecht oder Abt von Echternach?', *Willibrord, zijn wereld en zijn werk*, ed. P. Bange and A. G. Weiler (Nijmegen 1990), 348–57, here 348.

43. See my forthcoming discussion of Willibald in *Early Medieval Europe*.

44. *Kirchenbauten*, II, 102–03; H. Cüppers, 'Die Basilica des heiligen Willibrord zu Echternach und ihre Vorgängerbauten', *Hémecht*, XXVII (1975), 228–67: on the church of St Willibrord, see 233–49 and figs 3 and 5.

45. *Exposition Saint-Willibrord: XIIIe centenaire de la naissance de Saint Willibrord 658–1958*. Echternach 24 Mai–24 Août 1958 (Luxembourg n.d.), 135–36.

46. *Kirchenbauten*, II; this supplementary volume has references to the entries in the first three fascicules of the corpus (*Kirchenbauten*, I).

47. *Holzkirchen*.

48. B signifies churches in Belgium, NL those in the Netherlands, and L those in the Grand Duchy of Luxembourg.

49. *Kirchenbauten*, II, 28–29.

50. *Kirchenbauten*, II, 64.

51. *Kirchenbauten*, II, 96–97; *Holzkirchen*, 551.

52. *Kirchenbauten*, I, 69–71; Stoepker (1990), 213–15; see also R. Rijntjes in this volume.

53. *Kirchenbauten*, II, 117–18; *Holzkirchen*, 546.

54. *Holzkirchen*, 546; Ahrens gives the site name as Flogon and lists it under Belgium. However, it is actually in France and was correctly located in Département Nord by G. Kurth, *Notker de Liège et la civilisation au Xe siècle* (Paris/Brussel/Liège, 1905), 302–03, n. 4. Floyon has therefore not been included in Fig. 5.

55. *Holzkirchen*, 553; Stoepker (1990), 203–05; *Kirchenbauten*, II, 136–37.

56. *Kirchenbauten*, I, 96; *Holzkirchen*, 546.

57. *Kirchenbauten*, II, 154–55; *Holzkirchen*, 546.

58. *Kirchenbauten*, II, 172; *Holzkirchen*, 554.

59. *Kirchenbauten*, II, 239–40.

60. *Holzkirchen*, 547.

61. *Kirchenbauten*, II, 251.

62. *Kirchenbauten*, II, 253–55.

63. *Kirchenbauten*, II, 256.

64. *Kirchenbauten*, II, 257–60.

65. *Holzkirchen*, 556.

66. *Holzkirchen*, 556; *Kirchenbauten*, II, 257.

67. *Holzkirchen*, 547.

68. *Kirchenbauten*, II, 303.

69. *Kirchenbauten*, II, 309.

70. *Holzkirchen*, 548.

71. *Kirchenbauten*, II, 352.

72. *Kirchenbauten*, II, 368–69.
73. *Kirchenbauten*, II, 409–10.
74. *Kirchenbauten*, I, 333–35.
75. *Holzkirchen*, 558
76. *Kirchenbauten*, II, 437.
77. W. Boeckelmann, 'Grundformen im frühkarolingischen Kirchenbau des östlichen Frankenreiches', *Wallraf-Richartz-Jahrbuch*, XVIII (1956), 27–69, esp. 31–37 & 57–58.
78. Stoepker (1990), 215.
79. S. James, A. Marshall and M. Millett, 'An early medieval building tradition', *Archaeological Journal*, CXLI (1984), 182–215.
80. Peeters (1990).
81. H. Halbertsma, 'St Willibrord en het bisdom Tongeren', *Munsters in de Maasgouw* (Maastricht 1986), 125–38; note the title of the second section: 'Antwerp as Willibrord's springboard'.
82. *Making of England*, no. 141, pp. 180–83, with colour illustrations.
83. The Utrecht exhibition catalogue gives a lucid brief description of the panels, but does not forward the argument about date and origin: Van Vlierden (1995), p. 90, no. 66. A further exhibit may be briefly mentioned, a small house-shaped reliquary from Andenne (Van Vlierden (1995), p. 90, no. 67); this is decorated with an angular form of interlace, whose widespread use on the continent derives from the Anglo-Saxon manuscript tradition.
84. *Making of England*, no. 143, pp. 184–85.
85. Van Vlierden (1995), pp. 88–89, no. 63 (with colour illustration on 98).
86. *Insular manuscripts*, no. 11.
87. *Insular manuscripts*, nos 22 & 23.
88. N. Netzer, 'Willibrord's scriptorium at Echternach . . .', *St Cuthbert: his cult and his community to AD1200*, ed. G. Bonner, D. Rollason and C. Stancliffe (Woodbridge 1989), 203–12; see also in the same volume D. Ó. Cróinín, 'Is the Augsburg Gospel Book a Northumbrian manuscript?', 189–201, and R. Bruce-Mitford, 'The Durham–Echternach calligrapher', 175–88; see also Netzer's and Ó. Cróinín's contributions to *Willibrord: Apostel der Niederlande, Gründer der Abtei Echternach*, ed. G. Kiesel and J. Schroeder (Luxembourg 1989), 127–34 and 135–43. The Echternach scriptorium is also considered by Rosamond McKitterick in 'The diffusion of insular culture in Neustria between 650 and 850: the implications of the manuscript evidence', *La Neustrie: les pays au nord de la Loire de 650 à 850*, ed. H. Atsma (Sigmaringen 1989), II, 395–432, here 421–29.
89. *Making of England*, no. 123, pp. 159–60; Van Vlierden (1995), pp. 81–82, no. 47.
90. *Insular Manuscripts*, no. 24.
91. *Insular Manuscripts*, nos 26 & 28; Van Vlierden (1995), p. 85, no. 56.
92. *Insular Manuscripts*, no. 65.

Porticus or *pastophorion*? Eighth-century St Martin, Utrecht, between Anglo-Saxon and Frankish traditions

by Raphaël Rijntjes

INTRODUCTION

In the summer of 1993 the chapel of the Holy Cross was partially re-excavated, some sixty years after major excavations on the Cathedral square (*Domplein*) took place. Back then, the search for the Roman history of Utrecht had been the main concern. The chapel received little attention and was considered to be a tenth- or eleventh-century addition to the episcopal complex, consisting of St Salvator's to the south and the St Martin's to the north. In 1993, however, renewed interest in the Holy Cross-chapel did arouse some publicity, especially on account of its supposed connection with Willibrord: new research and interpretation of the old excavation reports suggested that a much earlier date for the chapel was possible.[1]

In two separate articles the city archaeologist, H. L. de Groot, and I, independently came to more or less the same conclusions: the walls and foundations of the chapel of the Holy Cross were older than had been assumed, apparently pre-dating the Norman attacks on Utrecht from AD 857 onwards. Because of the earlier date, the chapel must have been one of the two early medieval churches within the old Roman *castellum*: St Martin or St Salvator.[2] During pre-war excavations, remains of a predecessor of the Romanesque St Salvator were found beneath the former crossing. According to recent research by Jos Stöver, these remains must belong to the first eighth-century church of the Salvator.[3] This left only one option: the 'newly' found church must have been St Martin's, the predecessor of the Romanesque and Gothic cathedral to the north.

These conclusions have not yet been generally accepted.[4] Furthermore, radio-carbon dating of three samples of charred wood, extracted from the mortar of the walls, indicate a date between AD 876 and 1008. Yet there are strong reasons for holding on to an early, pre-Norman date for the church. The main characteristics of the plan can be found almost all over early medieval Western Europe, especially in Spain, Northern Italy, Switzerland, Germany and England. In this article I will try to determine some aspects of the plan as it occurs in the different regions, and make some suggestions for possible new directions for current research. I present first the results of the recent excavation of parts of the Holy Cross-chapel in 1993.

THE 1993 EXCAVATIONS

Before the 1993 excavation, it was assumed that the two lower annexes were added to an already existing nave and chancel. It turned out to be different: nave, chancel and north annex were of one construction, and entirely made of re-used Roman *tufa*, bricks and tiles and concrete (Pl. IIA). However the south annex differed in fabric, masonry and foundation technique from the other parts (Pl. IIB). No concrete was used in the foundations or walls, the masonry was of much better quality and the wall was not set back but in (vertical) alignment with the foundation, whereas all the other parts showed

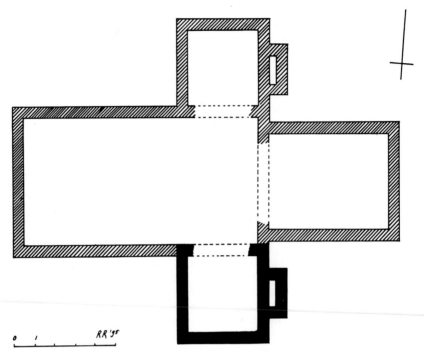

FIG. 1　Simplified plan showing the building-phases I (black) and II (hatched) (author 1995)

a clear setting back of approx. 10–15 cm. (Pl. IIc). The joint connecting the south annex to the nave, a place marked by a huge rough fragment of Roman concrete, clearly demonstrated a discontinuous foundation (Pl. IId). Moreover, it offered a comparative chronology of the two parts: because the fabric of the nave was partly laid over the foundation of the south annex — the figure shows a joint that goes from up left to down right — the south annex must be the older structure (Fig. 1).

Questions were posed by the attempt to date the two building-phases archaeologically. The stratigraphy, as it was documented during the excavations in the thirties, was complicated and the finds were not very well recorded. The interpretation of the stratigraphy and the subsequent dating of the walls of the chapel by the leading archaeologist at the time, Van Giffen, can be shown to be wrong — he misinterpreted a drawing made by his assistant. More reliable is the reconstruction of the original levels of foundations, floors and surface, published by De Groot in 1994, although many details remain unclear. An overall picture of the excavation reveals the proximity of Late-Roman levels to the floor level of the chapel (Pl. IIIa, b and c). Despite this, no precise relation between Roman and early medieval structures could be established, although the chapel was built over the Roman headquarters (the *principia*) of the fort.

Like the stratigraphy, the foundations and technique of the masonry only allow similar, general conclusions, because of both a lack of comparable buildings and the reserve necessary in analysis of walls built from reused materials. The low quality, unfinished, masonry cannot be compared with any of the known tenth- or eleventh-century churches in the region, but it resembles the remains of the oldest church found at Elst (Gelderland): a foundation of rubble (here limestone instead of tufa and brick) covered with mortar, and loosely laid courses of reused stones (Pl. IIIB). As in Utrecht, masonry was found as used, thus mostly retaining the original dimensions. The church at Elst is usually dated to the second quarter of the eighth century, not on archaeological bases but merely because of its supposed connection with the missionary activities of Werenfridus (one of Willibrord's companions) in Elst after 726.[5]

The radio-carbon analysis indicated a date between AD 876 and 1008; this date is otherwise unsupported by archaeological or other evidence. Technique, finish and stratigraphy all seem to speak for a date prior to the Norman invasions in the second half of the ninth century.

TYPOLOGY AS AN INSTRUMENT

Little so far has been said yet about the plan of the church itself, though it offers much valuable information concerning the two building-phases. The archaeological evidence suggests the incorporation of an original free-standing building into the south annex of a later structure. A second indication of this sequence is typological. The church with its symmetrically placed annexes and — as far as we know — triple altar-arrangement, must have been planned as a whole. A separate nave, chancel and northern annex is therefore unlikely, given the need for symmetry apparent in the plan, in particular in the junction of the annexes to the shoulders of the nave and the rectangular altar-niches. Uncommon as it may seem, the building-sequence as proposed above best explains the unusual features of the plan and the obvious differences in technique between the parts.

In this article I will not discuss the first phase, though in its size, form and antiquity this phase is intriguing. The second phase with its lower annexes is of even greater interest, for it brings to mind the early Anglo-Saxon churches with two porticoes, the Visigothic and Asturian churches with two sacristies, and even more the continental group known as the *fränkische Pastophorienkirchen*. These three groups will now be briefly discussed.

THE ANGLO-SAXON *PORTICUS*

Most early Anglo-Saxon churches had at least one side chamber or *porticus*, as they are called in contemporary sources. They had 'a variety of functions connected with the mass, with burial and with private prayer, though it is often impossible to specify which in any particular case'.[6] One function most frequently mentioned in the written sources is that of burial-chapel. Some patterns can be discerned according to who was buried where: in SS Peter and Paul at Canterbury, archbishops were laid in the *porticus* to the north of the nave, dedicated to St Gregory. The kings were buried in the south *porticus*, dedicated to St Martin. This division is exceptional, since in most cases only one specific elite group was buried in a church. Interestingly, a different estimation of the north and the south side can be ascertained: in general, the north *porticus* of early Anglo-Saxon churches housed only the bodies of those with 'saintly potential'. When the desired status was acquired, the remains were translated to the main axis of the church.[7]

Only a few churches had symmetrically arranged *porticus'* in the initial or later phases: Reculver, Bradwell-on-Sea and both SS Peter and Paul and St Pancras at Canterbury. At Winchester and Bishopstone a single *porticus* should be completed with a hypothetical second one. None of these had a layout similar to St Martin's at Utrecht, but the seventh-century royal foundation at Winchester comes very close, the only difference being the positioning of the two *porticus'* further to the west.

Most churches mentioned above belonged to the Kentish kingdom, the first part of England to be christianized by missionaries from Rome. Not surprisingly, many elements of Kentish architecture point to Northern Italy, Tyrol and Switzerland rather than Gaul, while the plan of Winchester in the kingdom of Wessex can only be compared with the monastery of St Germanus at Speyer. The specific backgrounds of the missionaries and clergy active in Kent and Wessex, and their personal relations across the Channel could explain the different influences on the early ecclesiastical architecture of the southern kingdoms.[8]

THE VISIGOTHIC *PREPARATORIUM*

All the few surviving Visigothic churches have symmetrically placed subsidiary rooms. Again their use is not certain, but most authors agree on some sort of liturgical function.[9] The written sources give evidence for this interpretation, although none of them allow the room mentioned in the text to be precisely located.

A seventh-century source states that the tombs of the bishops of Mérida were situated in a *cellula* close to the main altar.[10] Also close to the main altar were the *ergastula* or cells of hermits in two monasteries.[11] Liturgical texts (the *Liber Ordinum*) offer four different names for what may be the same room. A *preparatorium* acts as the place of election and ordination of three church-officials: the *sacrista*, the *custos librorum et senior scribarum* and the *archipresbyter*. It also occurs as a treasury and depository for liturgical vessels and garments; the liturgical instructions sometimes required these objects to be carried to the main altar in procession.[12] The room indicated as *sacrarium* seems to have had more or less the same functions, and is also the place of benediction of wax for the candles, whereas the *secretarium* functioned as a meeting-room for councils and other gatherings.[13] Finally the *thesaurum* was a treasury, but could house other functions since the candle-wax was sometimes blessed here.[14] The obvious overlap in functions and rituals attached to the rooms is perhaps due to the fact that all terms refer to the same chamber, in which all functions were united. Unfortunately, the texts do not offer clues for the identification of the two sacristies in the apparently rigid layout of Visigothic churches.[15]

In later periods the picture is not much clearer. During the reign of Alfonso II (791–842) of Asturia the glorious Visigothic past was revived, and the Ordo Gothicus, the Visigothic liturgy, reintroduced. All the churches built in this period or shortly afterwards have two sacristies, perhaps a result of the 'neogothic' revival promoted by the king: e.g. Santa Cristina de Lena, Santa María de Bendones, San Pedro de Nora, San Julián de Los Prados ('Santullano'). This explanation may be too simple however, since similar configurations also feature in contemporary Mozarabic architecture.[16]

THE FRANKISH *PASTOPHORION*?

The most important characteristics of St Martin's at Utrecht are the way in which the two annexes join the nave — they align with its eastern wall, thus forming *Schulterannexen* as this typical disposition is known in German, — and the protruding walls partly screening the arched openings. Both characteristics apply to a Frankish group of churches with side chambers or *Pastophorien*, after the Greek *pastophorion*. This group is dealt with in Werner Jacobsen's important thesis of 1981, which covers more than is implied by the subtitle.[17] Jacobsen also contributed to the *Nachtragsband* of the well-known corpus of Vorromanische Kirchenbauten.[18] According to Jacobsen the *Pastophorienkirchen* can be found mainly in the old Burgundian kingdom, and most of them date between AD 600 and 750, e.g. Romainmôtier, St Maurice, and Domdidier. To him, the decisive element in the similarity of the liturgy explains the similar plans: like the Visigothic and Mozarabic rite, the Gallican mass employed a ritual of Byzantine origin, namely the preparation of the Eucharist at a table or altar in a separate room, followed by the solemn procession to the main altar. Like the Byzantine churches, the Frankish group has two *pastophoria* or side chambers, one of which served as the preparation-room and often as the place where the Eucharist was kept, the *prothesis*, the other as the room where the faithful could place their offerings on a table, the *diaconicon*. According to Jacobsen, this particular arrangement disappears around AD 750, when an uniform Roman liturgy was introduced to the Frankish realm.[19]

Some remarks need to be made concerning this theory. Firstly, some sources do contain indications for the practice of a Gallican rite, but these sources are rare and the indications vague, too vague to imply the Byzantine disposition of *prothesis* and *diaconicon*. The sources mention only the procession of the Eucharist to the main altar, not the place of preparation. Besides, this could explain only one of the two annexes. More importantly, there was no such thing as 'the Gallican liturgy': uniformity in the rite was first implemented by the Carolingians; until then a great variety in practices existed.

Secondly, more recent studies concerning Byzantine liturgy and architecture have made clear that the terms *prothesis* and *diaconicon*, implying a regimented use of specific rooms in a well-defined architectural layout, cannot be applied indiscriminately to all churches with two annexes. These terms are only valid in a limited area — Syria — and a specific period — from the fifth (or perhaps mid-seventh) to the ninth century. Other periods and other areas present a more complex picture: annexes appear in different forms and sizes, and may have many different functions, such as funerary chapel, archive or treasury. Furthermore functions were frequently combined. The author of a recent article on such annexes in churches in Ravenna, where the Byzantine rite was practised, wisely chose the neutral term 'side chamber'.[20] When even Byzantine architecture does not offer a clear functional differentiation of the side chambers of the churches, the more reason there is to be very careful when applying Byzantine terms to western churches, despite obvious similarities in the plans. A simple reference to Byzantine influence is not enough. Similar plans do not necessarily imply similar liturgy, especially when the exact location of the altar is unknown. In general, liturgy very seldom offers a satisfactory explanation for specific architectural forms (or vice versa). The neutral terms annex, side chamber or even sacristy seem more appropriate than the Greek *pastophorion*.

Finally, the confinement in space and time made by Jacobsen is somewhat too strict. To the Swiss examples some northern counterparts can be added: the sixth- or seventh-century monastery of St Germanus at Speyer already mentioned; the female house founded in 700 by Adela at Pfalzel near Treves; the recently excavated Merovingian church at St Genès de Villemomble (France); the abbey of St Trudo, dated around 657, in the Belgian city that bears her name (St Truiden); also in Belgium the monastery of St Hermes at Ronse/Renaix, presumably founded by Amandus around 630; the *Christuskirche* at Hochemmerich, dating from the first quarter of the ninth century.[21]

Despite these comments, the definition of the Frankish group remains intact, and retains its validity: all these churches in my opinion belong typologically to the same group, with side-compartments placed at the east end of the nave. However the plan cannot be explained by simply assuming that analogous rituals (if any) lead to analogous architecture.

THE LOCATION OF ST MARTIN'S, UTRECHT

Although it has its idiosyncrasies (the niches at the east of the side-chambers, and the unusually large chancel), the Utrecht plan corresponds to the Frankish group. The rectangular form of the niches is unique and owes its existence to the unusual building sequence, the north annex following the early structure to the south. Such an imitation is only meaningful if an altar was placed in both the niches. This would suggest that in this phase the church must have had at least three altars, for at least one (main) altar can be assumed to have stood in the nave or chancel. The external reflection of the internal altar-arrangement is a Carolingian rather than Merovingian architectural feature. I therefore propose a date for building-phase II towards the end of the period in which the Frankish group occurs, i.e. second half of the eighth or first quarter of the ninth century.

THE FUNCTION OF THE SIDE-CHAMBERS

The evident similarity of St Martin's at Utrecht to a group of Frankish churches has previously been stressed; the plan of SS Peter and Paul at Winchester was possibly also derived from this type, via Speyer. A lack of knowledge of the rituals performed in the churches discounts liturgy as a possible key to their understanding. Written sources mention a variety of functions without distinguishing the different rooms.

However, one important characteristic remains: symmetry. Most Anglo-Saxon and Visigothic sources refer to only one altar.[22] Proximity to the main altar must be one of the most important reasons for adding the annexes to the nave, both for burials and for diverse liturgical functions. It is also the most natural explanation for the symmetry. The location close to the main altar is explicitly mentioned in many texts, especially when a place of burial is described.

Since I believe the relation to the main altar is one of the clues to the solution of our problem, I want to refer to two hypotheses put forward by German scholars.

THE BASILICA APOSTOLORUM AS A MODEL

In his major work on the royal burial churches of the Franks, Anglo-Saxons and Lombards, Karl Krüger suggested a direct link between the Basilica Apostolorum, the mausoleum of Constantine the Great, and two early medieval royal foundations: the church founded near Paris by the Merovingian king Childebert and Ethelbert's monastery just outside Canterbury.[23] There are some striking similarities: the location outside the city walls, the dedication to the apostles, the cruciform layout, and, most convincing in my opinion, the use of the church for both royal and episcopal burials in different parts of the building. Some difficulties remain however, not least among them the much disputed (cruciform or basilical) plan of Constantine's original memorial. Undisputed is the fact that in 356/67, following the arrival of relics of the apostles at Constantinople, the tomb of Constantine was transferred from the centre of the church to a mausoleum to the south; according to Krautheimer, this was done because of the excessively ostentatious position in the centre of the crossing, where Constantine was venerated as the 'Thirteenth Apostle'.[24] An annex close to the main altar was the most suitable place for an emperor (or king) to rest in, a priviliged position eagerly followed by other elite groups. Plausible as it may seem, Krüger's hypothesis is perhaps too simple. Other important structures are not included, for instance Theoderic's mausoleum at Ravenna, another imitation of Constantine's Church of the Apostles. The Basilica Apostolorum founded by Ambrose at Milan must also be derived from it. Perhaps it acted as an intermediary between 'model' and 'imitations', between east and west.

The possible notion of humility associated with the burials just outside the church is an important one; it is in perfect accordance with the second hypothesis I want to consider.

HUMILITY OR HUBRIS?

In a recent article Arnold Angenendt interprets burial just outside the church as a deliberate expression of humility.[25] He locates a theological base for the practice in the classification by St Augustine of the dead, which ranged from the *valde boni* in Heaven to the *valde mali* in Hell. In between Augustine discerned two categories: the *non valde boni* who had to remain outside Heaven, and the *non valde mali* that ended in Purgatory. In particular the *non valde boni,* or good but not saintly people (just) outside Heaven, formed an attractive category for those who had not lived a saintly life, but would like to secure a place at the threshold of Heaven. This corresponded with their place of burial: as only saints could be buried in the main axis of the church, in the proximity of the main altar, the next category chose a place just outside the church itself. Hence, according to Angenendt, the striking number of burials of both laity and clergy *ante limina, in porticu, in atrio, in sacrario* and so on.

In my opinion Angenendt overlooks one important factor: although superficially similar — all spaces indicated are outside the church — there are considerable differences between the terms which he more or less equalizes. A humble burial with only a slab near the entrance can not be compared with a carved tomb in a chapel as close as possible to the main altar; at least one should discern a degree of humility. And sometimes, the virtue of humility is so openly demonstrated that its goal must have been the opposite.

Another difficulty is a lack of clear definitions of the terms Angenendt collected: for instance a *porticus* can indicate many things, depending on the local use and situation.[26] Even more ambiguous is the term *sacrarium*: besides sacristy it can also refer to the sanctuary, thus contradicting Angenendt's theories.

CONCLUSION

Despite its shortcomings, the study of Angenendt, together with the daring but stimulating hypothesis of Krüger, opens new ways of interpreting some puzzling architectural concepts. After all, typology is only the first step in ordering data: real understanding requires a much deeper analysis. The number and position of the altars, the opening between nave and chancel, the subdivision of the nave; all this has first to be established before more can be said of the possible origins of a plan or concept. The excavation at Utrecht does not permit a reconstruction of the early-medieval interior;

the plan itself is the only source available. So far only rough indications can be given about date and origin of the plan of St Martin's at Utrecht, though the wider context can to some extent be redrawn. Hopefully more can be said in future.

REFERENCE

1. In 1994 a special issue of the Bulletin KNOB was published, dedicated chiefly to the 1993 excavation, but also containing articles on St Salvator and on the urban liturgy: *Bulletin KNOB*, XCIII nr 4/5 (1994).
2. H. L. de Groot, 'De Heilige Kruiskapel te Utrecht. Die Tatsachen bleiben, die Interpretation schwänkt', *Bulletin KNOB*, XCIII nr 4/5 (1994), 135–49; R. Rijntjes, 'De ecclesiola in het Utrechtse castellum. Bouwhistorische interpretatie van de resten van de Heilig-Kruiskapel', *Bulletin KNOB*, XCIII nr 4/5 (1994), 150–61.
3. R. J. Stöver, 'De afmetingen van de Salvator- of Oudmunsterkerk in de afbeeldingen van de Monumenta van Van Buchel en in de collectie Booth: toetsing en interpretatie aan de hand van opgravingsresultaten', *Bulletin KNOB*, XCIII nr 4/5 (1994), 169–85.
4. Two historians strongly oppose the identification of the chapel with the earliest St Martin, and favour St Salvator instead. They have proposed a somewhat complicated building sequence that — not only in my opinion — seems to overlook the archaeological facts and the earliest written sources. Their most comprehensive publication: C. J. C. Broer, M. W. J. de Bruin, *De eerste kerken in Utrecht: Sint-Thomas, Sint-Salvator, Sint-Maarten* (Utrecht 1995).
5. For the excavations at Elst: J. E. A. Th. Bogaers, *De Gallo-Romeinse tempels te Elst in de Over-Betuwe* (Den Haag 1955); the most recent publication discussing the date of the church: H. Stoepker, 'Church archaeology in the Netherlands. Problems, prospects, proposals', *Medieval Archaeology in the Netherlands. Studies presented to H. H. van Regteren Altena* (Assen/Delft 1990), 199–218.
6. E. Fernie, *The Architecture of the Anglo-Saxons* (London 1983), 42.
7. M. Biddle, 'Archaeology, architecture, and the cult of saints in Anglo-Saxon England', *The Anglo-Saxon church. Papers on history, architecture, and archaeology in honour of Dr H. M. Taylor*, ed. by L. A. S. Butler, R. K. Morris (CBA Research Report 60) (London 1986), 11.
8. Fernie (note 6) (1983), 42–46.
9. For example J. Yarza, *Arte y Arquitectura en España 500–1250*, 7th edn (Madrid 1994), 15–16.
10. R. Puertas Tricas, *Iglesias hispánicas (siglos IV al VIII). Testimonios literarios* (Madrid 1975), 62–63, 99, 238.
11. Puertas Tricas (1975), 121.
12. Puertas Tricas (1975), 134.
13. Puertas Tricas (1975), 135–36 (sacrarium), 137 (secretarium).
14. Puertas Tricas (1975), 143–44.
15. Puertas Tricas (1975), 154.
16. L. Arias, *Prerrománico Asturiano. El arte de la Monarquía Asturiana* (Gijón 1993), 48 (Santullano), 114 (Santa María de Bendones), 119 (San Pedro de Nora), 198 (Santa Cristina de Lena).
17. W. Jacobsen, *Der Klosterplan von St. Gallen und die karolingische Architektur. Entwicklung und Wandel von Form und Bedeutung im fränkischen Kirchenbau zwischen 751 und 840*, (Berlin 1992).
18. W. Jacobsen, L. Schaefer, H. R. Sennhauser, *Vorromanische Kirchenbauten. Katalog der Denkmäler bis zum Ausgang der Ottonen. Nachtragsband*, (Munich 1991); the original edition of 1966–1971 was reprinted in one volume in 1991.
19. Jacobsen (1992), 262–64.
20. J. Ch. Smith, 'Form and Function of the Side Chambers of Fifth- and Sixth-Century Churches in Ravenna', *Journal of the Society of Architectural Historians*, XLIX (1990), 181–204, with extensive bibliography on the subject, esp. in note 7.
21. For a short notice of the excavation and plan of St Genès de Villemomble, see: *Bulletin Monumental*, 152-I (1994), 107; all the other churches: *Vorromanische Kirchenbauten* (Munich 1990) and *idem*, *Nachtragsband* (Munich 1991).
22. H. M. Taylor, 'The position of the altar in early Anglo-Saxon churches', *The Antiquaries Journal*, 53 (1973), 52–58; Puertas Tricas (1975), 84.
23. K. H. Krüger, *Königsgrabkirchen der Franken, Angelsachsen und Langobarden bis zur Mitte des 8. Jahrhunderts. Ein historischer Katalog* (Munich 1971), 459–65.
24. R. Krautheimer, 'Zu Konstantins Apostelkirche in Konstantinopel', *Mullus. Festschrift Theodor Klauser* (Jahrbuch für Antike und Christentum, Erg.bnd 1, 1964), 224–29.

25. A. Angenendt, 'In porticu ecclesiae sepultus. Ein Beispiel von himmlisch-irdischer Spiegelung', Iconologia Sacra. Mythos, Bildkunst und Dichtung in der Religions- und Sozialgeschichte Alteuropas. Festschrift für Karl Hauck zum 75. Geburtstag, ed. H. Keller, N. Staubach (Arbeiten zur Frühmittelalterforschung 23) (Berlin/New York 1994), 68–80.

26. D. Parsons, Books and buildings: architectural description before and after Bede (Jarrow Lecture 1987) (Jarrow 1988), 24–27.

St Salvator's, St Martin's and Pepin the Younger[1]

by Eelco van Welie

The early history of the diocese of Utrecht is usually seen as an important aspect of the Anglo-Saxon missionary movement on the Continent, mainly through its connection with Willibrord.[2] This Anglo-Saxon missionary, in founding a missionary centre in the former *castellum Traiectum* in close connection with both the east Frankish magnates and the papacy, set an important precedent for future missionary expansion on the Northern frontiers of *Francia*. Rudolf Schieffer pointed to the close connection between Willibrord's episcopal foundation and its associated Pippinid donations as another 'zukunftsträgtige Entwicklung' first seen in Utrecht.[3]

The picture of Utrecht as an episcopal see founded by Willibrord has, however, become the subject of debate. Instead of a static idea in which *sedes episcopalis*, cathedral, and episcopal ordination all come about in one single act of foundation and form an integrated whole, it has become clear that the establishment of the diocese of Utrecht hardly was completed by the time of Willibrord's death.[4] In fact, we will see that it was a process which continued for a large part of the eighth century. Furthermore, the central position usually alloted to Willibrord as the founder of a new strategy in the Anglo-Saxon missionary movement on the Continent, has recently been criticized as well.[5]

As a consequence, attention should focus not only on Willibrord, but also on his successors. Of these, Boniface is noteworthy, not least because of his peculiar position as caretaker for Utrecht in the conflict with Cologne in 752–53. To this I shall return. In addition, the question of whether the establishment of Utrecht as *sedes episcopalis* was all but completed by the time of Willibrord's death or was not even foreseen, has its consequences for our perception of the function of the churches within the former *castellum Traiectum*; consequences which as yet have not been fully recognized. This is especially and obviously true as regards the long-running debate on the problem of identification and localization of the cathedral in eighth-century Utrecht, the so-called 'kathedraalkwestie'.[6] Yet simply denying the existence of a cathedral in the time of Willibrord far from settles the problem.

To get a clear picture of the origins and early development of Utrecht as an ecclesiastical centre, one must distinguish between the different factors usually present in the process of the foundation of a diocese. In the areas of missionary activity on the fringes and outside the former Roman Empire, bishop and diocese are more often than not separate issues, determined by different institutions, and therefore may be established in different ways and at different times.[7] The same holds true for the establishment of an episcopal centre. We must therefore evaluate the notions of *episcopus*, or even *archiepiscopus*, *sedes episcopalis*, and *ecclesia cathedralis* separately.

First, there is the episcopal title. In the case of Willibrord, it is problematic. The title of *archiepiscopus* is recorded by Bede, but might also be deduced from the passage on Willibrord's inauguration in the *liber Pontificalis*, which furthermore mentions Willibrord's appointment *'in gentum Frisonum'*.[8] Other sources however, including the famous calendar note ascribed to Willibrord himself, mention only the title of *episcopus*.[9] Either way, it was from Rome that Willibrord got his title.

Second, there is the *locus cathedrae episcopalis* (as Bede puts it): it is the place where Willibrord was to have a base from which to operate.[10] There seems to be no question in contemporary sources as to who provided it. According to Bede, Pepin II, who in 690 had just gained control over the former Roman *castellum Traiectum* on the borders of the Rhine, ensured that Willibrord began his missionary activities from there.[11] The subsequent donations by Charles Martel show clear Frankish support for Willibrord's *monasterium*.[12]

Third, there is the cathedral church. The word cathedral is derived from the late-antique *cathedra*, the symbol of the authority of the bishop; its main function can be described as housing the official pontifical liturgy.[13] However, it is not possible to determine whether Willibrord celebrated an 'official pontifical liturgy' in Utrecht.[14] In addition, there is no mention of an *ecclesia cathedralis* (or *episcopalis*) in the time of Willibrord.[15] The term 'cathedral' is, therefore, perhaps best avoided when discussing the functions of the churches in the former *castellum* in the eighth century, with which we will deal in a moment.

As the *Liber Pontificalis* does not mention a *sedes* from which Willibrord was to embark on his missionary work, it seems clear that the pope played no part in providing a *locus cathedrae episcopalis* for Willibrord. Furthermore, in contrast with Augustine's campaign in England nearly a century earlier, there is no indication of any papal prescription as to the number or the location of future episcopal sees among the *gens Frisonum*.[16] This was hardly un-Roman: the setting-up of a *domus* for Boniface and of individual *episcopia* in the area of the *Thuringi et Germaniae populo* was explicitly left to, indeed asked of, the people addressed by Pope Gregory II in 724.[17] This, however, does not mean that the functions that were associated with the title of archbishop did not at least *imply* the setting up of an ecclesiastical organization, including the appointment of bishops in newly converted areas.[18] On the other hand, Willibrord, who saw no problem in consecrating churches in other bishops' dioceses, or giving donations granted earlier to his *monasterium* in Utrecht to his own foundation in Echternach, hardly acted as would be expected of a truly 'Roman' legate. This 'unroman' (or, better, 'non-diocesan') behaviour, to which Arnold Angenendt has drawn attention, has been ascribed to the Irish and Anglo-Saxon background of Willibrord.[19] It might also mean that the Northumbrian missionary himself did not think of Utrecht as his *sedes* at all. Apart from this, political events may have frustrated any initial attempt at establishing a *sedes* in Utrecht. For Willibrord was presumably forced to leave following Pepin's death in 714, and it was not until after 719 that Charles Martel was able to secure Utrecht and the area to the north.[20] Even this did not stop Willibrord from making his donations to Echternach.[21] In addition, Angenendt has argued that it might have been Frankish fear of Frisian separatism that put a stop to any plans for a Frisian church province, and this might also have affected the continuity of the *sedes episcopatus* in Utrecht.[22] In any case, during Willibrord's lifetime, evidence for the institution or existence of a diocese with Utrecht as *sedes* seems to be lacking after 719.[23]

In conclusion, one might say that any attempt at founding a Frisian church province, implied by the papal ordination of Willibrord as archbishop *in gentem Frisonum*, was frustrated by the political events unfolding in the Frankish/Frisian border-areas, by Willibrord's own perception of the function of a bishop, and possibly by the reluctance of the Frankish authorities to accept the possibility of a Frisian 'national' church province.

How, in this context, should we see Willibrord's major church foundation in Utrecht, dedicated to Christ Salvator? Boniface, in a famous letter to the pope of 752–53, ascribed to Willibrord the rebuilding of a second, older church *de fundamento*, which the missionary dedicated to St Martin.[24] However, in strictly contemporary records, there is no indication of any clear function for, or indeed functioning of, a second church alongside St Salvator's. The first donation by Charles Martel from 723 only speaks of a *monasterium vel ..casam dei*, and in the second donation three years later, St Salvator's is named as the sole beneficiary.[25] This does not seem to be compatible with a supposed 'Anglo-Saxon' scheme of St Salvator's as the cathedral and St Martin's as a 'minster' complementing it, and in this way creating a 'Frisian Canterbury' in Utrecht, as Schieffer among others argued.[26] If Willibrord founded a second church besides St Salvator, the parallel escaped Bede. This is hardly surprising, given the fact that it was only the patron saints of the main churches in Utrecht and Canterbury (Salvator) that matched. St Martin's in Canterbury was a separate foundation, unconnected to Augustine's main churches, whereas St Peter and St Paul's performed the function of a monastery complementary to the cathedral, and housing the graves of St Augustine and his successors[27] a function which in Utrecht St Salvator's seems to have performed until the episcopate of Balderic (917–76).[28] As regards the functional structure, it is not at all clear how much Willibrord felt himself familiar with the *familia* in Canterbury; his known horizons were the monasteries of Rathmelsighi and Ripon.[29] If an episcopal parallel were to be drawn, York seems more appropriate, being the see of Willibrord's master Wilfrid.[30] A more important consideration, however, is that groups of churches were nothing special in Ireland, England or, indeed, on the Continent in the seventh and eighth centuries: one need not look at Canterbury to find examples of the association of two or more churches in monastic or episcopal contexts.[31] In conclusion, then, a supposed 'Canterbury scheme' of cathedral and associated monastic church as a model for whatever Willibrord had in mind for Utrecht, does not really provide a plausible option.

The question does not seem to be why Willibrord founded two churches in Utrecht, but rather, why he decided not to choose the existing church as the centre of his *monasterium*. Evidence for a clear-cut division between groups of ecclesiastics around Willibrord (e.g. between sexes or nationalities) is lacking, although later the community surrounding Gregory, who governed the church of Utrecht without an episcopal title between 747–752 and *c.* 775, is said to have been international, and to have included men and women.[32] Nor are there any indications of a sharp divide between clerics and laity associated with one or other of the churches. Indeed, it is St Salvator's which is mentioned consistently in our evidence: it is the recipient of the donations by Charles Martel, and later tradition attaches baptismal rights to this church, a point supported by the earliest references to the font.[33] Moreover, Liudger recorded that abbot Gregory was brought to the entrance of St Salvator's in the hour of his death (perhaps in 775). In addition, Liudger himself, according to his *vita* by Altfrid (written between 839 and 849) used to sleep during his years in the Utrecht community 'in the solar of the church of the holy Salvator, which saint Willibrord built'.[34] This last passage is particularly revealing in that it sheds some light on the perception of this church in the eyes of the ninth-century hagiographer: it was St Salvator, the church of Willibrord, with which these clerics were connected. In these two *vitae,* no mention at all is made of a second church in Utrecht. This clear focus on St Salvator's (or, better, the absence of references to St Martin's) seems to exclude any functional status for St Martin's as monastic church besides St Salvator's.

There seems, thus, to be no alternative to the conclusion that St Salvator was, simply, *the* church of Utrecht, not only in the time of Willibrord, but also in the perception of Gregory's and Liudger's hagiographers. Yet this was not the perception of all the parties involved.

For Pepin, by contrast, St Martin's was the sole recipient in two confirmations of immunity and tithe for the *episcopatum* of Utrecht of 751–53, made by the him as king;[35] the grant of tithe was renewed in 769 by Charlemagne and once again by Louis the Pious in 815.[36] Indeed, St Salvator disappears entirely from the scene and it is not until 944 that it appears as co-recipient, with St Martin's, in a donation by Otto I.[37] By then, however, St Martin's had received all donations and privileges granted to the church of Utrecht for nearly two hundred years. What had happened?

The crucial document here is the aforementioned letter which Boniface addressed to pope Stephen in 752 or 753. It concerns a conflict between Boniface, who was acting as caretaker for Utrecht, and the Bishop of Cologne (Hildegar), who claimed Utrecht (called explicitly a *sedes episcopatus* by Boniface) as subordinate to his see. The letter has been the subject of numerous speculations concerning the status of Boniface in relation to Utrecht, the status of Utrecht as an episcopal centre, Willibrord as bishop and St Salvator's as cathedral.[38] However, serious doubts have been put forward as well with respect to the reliability of the information Boniface presents to the pope. Consensus now regards Boniface's account of things as highly coloured, or indeed completely false.[39] A renewed attempt to evaluate the historicity of Boniface's argument here seems rewarding, for the source is crucial for our purpose in assigning very specific functions and meanings to both St Salvator's and St Martin's. Certainly, it is for the conflict of 752–53, and not the time of Willibrord, that this document provides crucial evidence.

The rhetoric in Boniface's letter is directed entirely at finding a counter-argument for Cologne's claim to Utrecht. This claim, which must be accepted as historical as a consequence of the existence of the letter itself, is based, Boniface says, on the alleged donation of a church in Utrecht to a former Bishop of Cologne by the Frankish king Dagobert.[40] The fact that the Anglo-Saxon does nothing to contradict this, proves perhaps not so much the historicity of the donation, as Boniface's acceptance of it as a credible and legal basis for Hildegar's claim. The argument Boniface directs against Hildegar is concerned with rather different issues.

First, Boniface states that the *castellum Traiectum* and its ruined church were donated to the diocese of Cologne on condition that the bishop would preach to and christianize the Frisians. This, says Boniface, the bishop did not do, thus invalidating Cologne's claim to Utrecht.

Second, Boniface points out that the church donated to Cologne lay in ruins, and did not amount to very much anyway: it is degradingly called an *ecclesiola*, devastated by pagan raids and neglected by the Bishops of Cologne. What validity could a claim have that is based on 'the foundations of a small church, destroyed by the pagans', which Willibrord had to rebuild completely?[41]

Third, Boniface goes to great lengths to prove that any claim that could be laid upon Utrecht by Cologne would be 'overruled' by the more recent and successful association of Willibrord and Utrecht. Here the construction of Boniface's argument requires close examination. First, Boniface recalls Willibrord's papal ordination and commission to preach to the pagan Frisians 'in the coastal areas of the western ocean' (*in littoribus oceani occidui*). He then states that Willibrord erected 'an episcopal *sedes* and a church in honor of St Salvator ... in the place and the fortress which is called Traiectum' (*sedem episcopalem et aecclesiam in honore sancti Salvatoris ... in loco et castello, quod dicitur Traiectum*). Attachment of the patrocinium of St Salvator to both *sedes* and *ecclesia* is suggested by the repetition of the whole phrase in the next sentence, which alsostates that it was there that Willibrord stayed until his old age (*ad debilem senectutem*). The reason for this tying together of Willibrord, *sedes episcopalis* and St

Salvator's becomes clear when Boniface draws his conclusion: what Cologne was trying to usurp was not just a church, it was the *sedem . . . episcopi Clementis* [i.e. Willibrord's] *a Sergio papa ordinati*. This construction has an obvious advantage: it presents Utrecht as a *sedes*, erected by Willibrord, but as a consequence of that missionary's papal commission, subjected to the pope (*subjecta Romano pontifici*). This makes for a strong argument: touch Willibrord's *sedes*, and you touch Rome. It also implied a commitment on the part of the pope, which Boniface could use very well. Giving in to Cologne would mean that Rome would loose its direct control over Utrecht. Whence Boniface concludes, a papal prescription which has Utrecht's subordination to Rome as its consequence should weigh more than the poor remains of a ruined *ecclesiola*, devastated as a result of pagan aggression and neglect on the part of Cologne. How could a pope object to such an argument?

We do not know if Boniface's argument convinced the pope, but it has certainly convinced scholars, who have drawn various conclusions from it.[42] However, given the highly biased state of affairs presented in the letter, as well as Boniface's obvious partiality, the information requires careful treatment: what is crucial for his argument seems most likely to be subjected to bias.

The building by Willibrord of a church dedicated to St Salvator can be deduced from its mention in the charter of 726;[43] as we have seen, the notion that Willibrord built this church was still vivid in the *Vita Liudgeri*. For Willibrord's rebuilding of the second church, there is less evidence from other sources. However, the existence of an older church in Utrecht seems plausible in the light of Cologne's claimed donation by Dagobert, which Boniface left untouched. The least one could say is that the church existed in some form before 752–53. The rebuilding of the church by Willibrord seems quite another matter, and its historicity is not to be taken completely for granted because of the function this alleged rebuilding played in Boniface's account of the matter: it served literally to undermine the basis for Cologne's claim by stating that it was only through the complete rebuilding by Willibrord that the older church could function at all. However, its existence before 752–53 leaves only a few possible candidates as (re)builders. Finally, Boniface appears particularly biased in his presentation of Sancti Salvatoris Willibrord's *ecclesia* and his *sedes* in Utrecht as quasi-identical. As we have seen, this is a construct designed to couple Willibrord's papal commission and his foundation of St Salvator's so as to be able to present Utrecht as a *sedes, subiecta Romano ponifici* in opposition to Cologne's affiliation with the older *ecclesiola*. The repeated use of the term *praeceptum* in the second part of the letter was considered by Wolfgang Fritze as an indication that Boniface (who had worked with Willibrord between 719 and 721) could recall from memory a papal *praeceptum* stating that Willibrord should have a fixed *sedes*.[44] Had this been the case, however, Boniface would surely had made this clear at the beginning of the text, where he related how Willibrord got his papal commission; in that particular passage, however, mention is made only of Willibrord's ordination as *episcopus*, his mission to the Frisians, and his commission to preach there. Boniface, who must have known that it was only through a Frankish mayor of the palace that Willibrord could set up his mission station in Utrecht, carefully omits this episode and makes Willibrord's missionary activity among the Frisians central, ascribing to him alone the merit of having constituted a *sedem episcopalem* in Utrecht. The direct subordination of Utrecht to the apostolic see, therefore, depends on no papal *praeceptum*, but follows from Boniface's combining of Willibrord's papal ordination, and his founding of a church in Utrecht.

The conclusion of our analysis of Boniface's argument is that, in the highly politicized context of 752–53, very distinctive meanings were attached to each of the two churches in Utrecht. St Salvator's emerges as the church of Willibrord *par excellence*, St Martin's provides as the legal basis on which Cologne's claim to Utrecht rested. Any actual function for that church within the community at Utrecht indeed its existence before the conflict with Cologne, remains without support from strictly contemporary written evidence. It is plausible, however, that it was rebuilt before 751–53.

In clear contrast with the state of affairs presented in Boniface's letter, the two aforementioned charters of Pepin the Younger name St Martin's as sole recipient. Scholars have interpreted this contrast in different ways. Based on the assumption that Utrecht presented the 'Canterbury scheme' in which St Salvator's as the cathedral was complemented by a *monasterium* dedicated to St Martin, Schieffer considered the shift to the benefit of the latter as the more or less 'evolutionist' outcome of the development of the early bishopric: the discontinuity in the episcopal succession meant that the *monasterium* of St Martin, presided over by an abbot (Gregory) would become, if not in principle, in fact, the cathedral.[45] Van Winter and Leupen interpreted the shift towards St Martin as a gesture on the part of Boniface (considered as the initiator of the transaction in both documents) towards Pepin, as the *patrocinium* of Martinus was considered as typically 'Frankish'.[46]

Both interpretations, however, are not satisfactory. Schieffer's assumption that St Martin's must be considered as the monastery alongside St Salvator's as cathedral has no other basis than the alleged and and as we have seen questionable influence of a supposed 'Anglo Saxon cathedral scheme', notably Canterbury.[47] Moreover, this interpretation is not in keeping with the picture we get from the *vitae* of Gregory and Liudger, and if the latter's account has little to impress historians, the reference to Gregory and Salvator comes from one who knew the community in Utrecht from his own experience. At least he knew what he was talking about.

On the other hand, Leupen's and Van Winter's interpretations scarcely follow the consequences of their supposition. It is one thing for Boniface to flatter the Frankish authorities with a 'Frankish' *patrocinium*, yet quite another to give up the whole idea of a 'Romverbundenen' *sedes et ecclesia sancti Salvatoris* in favour of an *episcopatum vel . . . ecclesiam sancti Martini*.[48] For that is what the donations of 751–53 amount to, if only in terms of setting the tone for future developments. There must, then, be more.

The charters of 751–53 have not survived in their original form, but doubts as to their authenticity have not been found credible.[49] The undated charter is modelled exactly after the *formula* of Marculf,[50] and reads in fact like an exercise in filling in the blanks.[51] If the document is to be scrutinized for its value in the context of Utrecht in the years 751–53, the focus should therefore be on the passages which fill out the general wording of the *formula*. The most interesting of these is the reference to a former donor, in the *formula* indicated with a simple *ille rex*. In the Utrecht charter, this reference is worked out very elaborately: *antecessores nostri vel parentes Clotharius quondam rex et Theodebertus quondam*. The indication of these kings as *antecessores . . . vel parentes* is particularly striking.[52] They could have been identical with Chlotarius II (613–29) and Theudebertus II (595–612), which would make a perfect succession with Boniface's mention of Dagobert (if it is Dagobert I (629–39) he is referring to). Blok and Eckhardt however, independently concluded that *Theodebertus* had to be emendated in *Theodericus*, which would make a succession of Chlotar IV (before 3 Feb. 718–19) and Theudericus IV (721–37), thus taking the alleged first privilege back to the time of Willibrord's activity in Utrecht.[53] Either way, the reference by the new king to his Merovingian predecessors is clearly stressed.

Pepin's *coup d'état* of 751 has been a celebrated subject of discussion, especially as to the meaning and the importance of Pepin's appeal for papal approval, and the subsequent anointing of the newly enthroned king. Both events have been seen as crucial for the success of Pepin's take-over. Recent scholarship however, regards this as less important. Yet although Rosamond McKitterick has played down the importance of Pepin's request for papal approval and his subsequent anointment as king, as only the outcome of the gradual accumulation of wealth and power under his Carolingian predecessors, and Janet Nelson has emphasized that these events only followed after the approval of the Frankish aristocracy,[54] it seems clear that Pepin's actions were motivated by a desire to secure 'some veneer of legality for his *coup d'état*'.[55] In any case, the new *rex Francorum* as the proud opening sentences of the charters read certainly appears eager to portray himself as the heir of the kings named as the original donors to St Martin's.

What could be the implications of this heightened awareness of royal patronage? It would seem somewhat strange that the new king expressed these pretentions in a document for a church in a border-area of his kingdom. For whom was this message intended? one would need to ask. Besides a charter for Worms,[56] no other royal privilege of any *episcopatum* is extant from the period of Pepin's reign as king. And it seems difficult to see Utrecht as another St. Denis, the support of which Wallace-Hadrill saw as 'decisive in swaying the loyalties of the Frankish Church from the Merovingians to the Carolingians.'[57] However, the issue of granting a privilege to an ecclesiastical foundation formerly favoured or believed to have been favoured by the Merovingian kings is the same.

It is not a matter for us here to establish whether or not there was any royal privilege for St Martin in the days of Willibrord or even before, nor is it our purpose to prove that Dagobert really gave a church to the bishop of Cologne. What matters is that in the middle of the eighth century there existed on the part of Cologne, Boniface as well as the new king of *Francia*, a clear notion that a tradition of royal patronage and indeed ownership was attached to St Martin's. It was not to St Martin as a patron of the Franks, but to this tradition that the charters refer. If, for anything, Cologne lost its credibility as patron of St Martin's in Utrecht because of its failing to meet its part of the deal (i.e. christianizing the Frisians), it ceded that credibility by implication to the Frankish king, not to the English missionary, nor to Rome.

In patronizing St Martin's instead of St Salvator's Pepin put a stop to the possibility of an episcopate that would have escaped his influence, because of its direct subordination to Rome. In doing so, he also brought the church clearly under his royal patronage. In this way, Pepin might not be doing much more than he and his Carolingian predecessors had done with so many *monasteria* which they brought under their *defensio vel mundeburdium*.[58] One might even ask whether Pepin, in patronizing an *episcopatum sancti Martini*, was perhaps deliberately ousting Hildegar, who himself must have favoured a subordinate church within his jurisdiction rather than the prospect of a diocese in his back yard. After all, Friedrich Prinz considered Hildegar as 'ein Mann, der wohl eher zum Schlage Milos und Gewilibs zu rechnen ist': the kind of bishop, then, which in the words of Rosamond McKitterick, 'constituted the principal threat to Pippin's position'.[59]

With both opponents dead (Boniface while preaching to the pagans, Hildegar while campaigning against the Saxons in 753), another episode begins. Gregory's sending of the Anglo-Saxon Alubert to York to be ordained as his *corepiscopus* is perhaps still indicative of the unease between Utrecht and its rival further up the Rhine.[60] But with the consecration of Gregory's nephew Alberic by the Bishop of Cologne after 777, the hierarchy is clearly established. Utrecht's 'Alleingang' had ended.

From what has gone before, it seems reasonable to conclude that the conflict between Boniface and Cologne heightened the notion of the various traditions attached to the two churches in the former *castellum*. St Salvator's appears as Willibrord's church, the church of his successors as leaders of the community in Utrecht. St Martin's emerges as the church to which a tradition of royal tutelage was attached, and which Pepin now firmly established as the church that was to be identified with the *episcopatum* of Utrecht, perhaps thereby in one stroke ruling out the possibility of a diocese directly dependent on Rome, as well as a church which the Bishop of Cologne could claim as his property. Schieffer's hypothesis of a strong connection between *sedes* and royal donations in the eighth century can therefore be extended to the domain of individual churches: the royal patronage, expressed in the series of donations and privileges from 751–53 onwards not only fixed a *sedes episcopatum* in Utrecht, but implied, if only in time, a cathedral status for St Martin's. The list of landed property belonging to the church of Utrecht (probably from the ninth century) simply added 'sancti Martini' to the individual properties as an indication of Utrecht's ownership.

SHORTENED TITLES USED

DOCUMENTARY SOURCES

HE *Bede's Ecclesiastical History of the English People*, eds B. Colgrave and R. A. B. Mynors, Oxford Medieval Texts (1969).

OB Utr. *Oorkondenboek van het Sticht Utrecht tot 1301 I (695–1197)*, eds S. Muller and A. C. Bouman (Utrecht 1920).

Vita Gregorii Liudgeri Vita Gregorii abbatis Traiectensis, ed. O. Holder-Egger Monumenta Germaniae Historica, Scriptores, XV/1 (1887), 63–79.

Vita Liudgeri Vita sancti Liudgeri auctore Altfrido, ed. W. Diekamp, Die Geschichtsquellen des Bisthums Münster, IV, (1881), 1–53.

Vita Sturmi Die Vita Sturmi des Eigil von Fulda: literarkritisch-historische Untersuchung und Edition, ed. P. Engelbert, Veröffentlichungen der Historischen Kommission für Hessen und Waldeck, XXIX (1968), revised and updated in Id., 'Eigil: das Leben des Abtes Sturmi', *Fuldaer Geschichtsblätter*, 56 (1980), 17–49.

Ep. 109 *Die briefe des Heiligen Bonifatius und Lullus*, ed. M. Tangl, Monumenta Germaniae Historica, Epp. Sel., 1 (1916), no. 109, 234–36.

SECONDARY WORKS

Angenendt (1973) A. Angenendt, 'Willibrord im Dienste der Karolinger', *Annalen der Historische Verein für den Niederrhein*, CLXXV (1973), 63–113.

Angenendt (1989) A. Angenendt, 'Willibrord als römischer Erzbischof', *Willibrord. Apostel der Niederlände. Gründer der Abtei Echternach. Gedenkgabe zum 1250. Todestag des angelsächsischen Missionars*, eds G. Kiesel and J. Schroeder (Luxemburg 1989), 31–41.

Blok (1962) D. P. Blok, 'Het immuniteitsdiploma van Koning Pippijn I voor de St. Maartenskerk te Utrecht', *Tijdschrift voor Geschiedenis*, LXXV(1962), 40–43.

Eckhardt (1975) K. A. Eckhardt, *Studia merovingica*, Bibliotheca rerum historicarum, II (Aalen 1975).

Kaiser (1990) R. Kaiser, 'Bistumsgründung und Kirchenorganisation im 8. Jahrhundert', *Der hl. Willibald Klosterbischof oder Bistumsgründer?*, ed. H. Dickerhof (Regensburg 1990), 29–67.

Leupen (1990) P. Leupen, 'Sint Salvator en Sint Maarten, Willibrord en Bonifatius', *Willibrord, zijn wereld en zijn werk* (as Angenendt 1990), 317–27.

McKitterick (1983) R. McKitterick, *The Frankish Kingdoms under the Carolingians 751–987* (London–New York 1983)

Schäferdiek (1994) K. Schäferdiek, 'Fragen der frühen angelsächsischen Festlandmission', *Frühmittelalterliche Studien*, XXVIII (1994), 172–95.

Schieffer (1975) R. Schieffer, 'Über bischofssitz und Fiskalgut im 8. Jahrhundert', *Historisches Jahrbuch*, XCV (1975), 18–32.

Schieffer (1976) R. Schieffer, *Die Entstehung von Domkapiteln in Deutschland*, Bonner Historische Forschungen, XVIII (1976).

Van Winter (1975) 'Utrecht am Rhein: Mittelalterlicher Rheinlauf und Entstehungs- geschichte der Stadt Utrecht', *Festschrift E. Ennen* (Bonn 1972), 138–53.

Wallace-Hadrill (1985) J. M. Wallace-Hadrill, *The Barbarian West 400–1000* 2nd edn (Oxford 1985).

Weiler (1989) A. G. Weiler, *Willibrords missie. Christendom en cultuur in de zevende en achtste eeuw* (Hilversum 1989).

Werner (1982) M. Werner, *Adelsfamilie im Umkreis der frühen Karolinger. Die Verwandtschaft Irminas von Oeren und Adelas von Pfalzel*, Vorträge und Forschungen, Sonderband, XXVIII (1982).

Wood (1994) I. Wood, *The Merovingian Kingdoms 450–751* (London–New York 1994).

REFERENCES

1. I thank Ian Wood for reading and correcting the text of this paper.
2. W. Levison, 'Willibrord and his Place in History', *Aus rheinischer und fränkischer Frühzeit. Ausgewählte Aufsätze*, ed. W. Holtzmann (Düsseldorf 1948), 320–26; Angenendt (1973), 63, cites Levison, pointing to the symbolic overtones in Levison's picture; A. Angenendt, ' "Er war der Erste. . ." Willibrords historische Stellung', *Willibrord, zijn wereld en zijn werk. Voordrachten gehouden tijdens het Willibrordcongres, Nijmegen, 28–30 september 1989*, Middeleeuwse Studies, VI (1990), 29–30 with further references; Kaiser (1990), 50 and no. 72, cites approvingly Fritze (1971), 109, who saw Utrecht as 'Ausgangspunkt einer roma-zentristischen Kirchenorganisation in den altheidnischen Ländern nördlich der Alpen'.
3. Schieffer (1975), 25–26 and 32 (citation).
4. Weiler (1989), 152; Leupen (1990), 321, takes a rather radical position in stating that there were not even plans for a new diocese.
5. Schäferdiek (1994), 186 and 195.
6. For the literature on this issue, cfr the article of L. Bosman in this volume.
7. For Utrecht, cfr Weiler (1989), 152–54.
8. *Le Liber Pontificalis. Texte, introduction et commentaire*, ed. L. Duchesne, I, 2nd edn (Paris 1955), 376. Bede also testifies to Willibrord's attachment to the Frisians rather than to Utrecht: *HE* v.11, 486. For a recent survey of sources on this matter, cfr A. Angenendt (1989). For the function of *archiepiscopus*, cfr R. Kottje, 'Erzbischof', *Lexikon des Mittelalters*, III (1986), 2192–94.
9. *The Calendar of St. Willibrord*, ed. H. W. Wilson (London 1918), fol. 39ᵛ, marginal note.
10. *HE* v.11, 486. Leupen has recently suggested that Bede's reference to *Traiectum* should be taken at its most direct: as designating the place in which the *cathedra* of the bishop was placed (unpublished paper presented at the symposium *Mission to Millennium. The Diocese of Utrecht AD 695–1000*, Utrecht 1995).
11. *HE* v.11, 486.
12. OB Utr. no. 35 (723, Jan. 1), OB Utr. no. 36 (726, June 9).
13. In the late antique *civitates*, however, the cathedral was not always clearly set apart from other churches, nor can it always be identified with a single building. In Rome, for instance, this ambiguity can be found in the complementing functions of the *Basilica Constntiniana* and the *Basilica S. Petri*, which both claimed the title of *caput et mater* but formed together with the *Basilica S. Mariae* the nucleus of the pontifical liturgical organization throughout the middle ages: S. L. de Blaauw, *Cultus et Decor. Liturgia e architettura nella Roma tardoantica e medievale* (Studi e Testi, CCCLV, 1994), 47–48.
14. For Willibrord's liturgy, cfr. Y. Hen, *Culture and Religion in Merovingian Gaul, A.D. 481–751* (Cultures, Beliefs and Traditions, Leiden 1995), 102–06.
15. Eigil's life of Sturm speaks of an 'ecclesia maior' in Utrecht in 754 (*Vita Sturmi* 15, 148–49). There, however, the term is set against an 'ecclesia minor', and is part of a particular narrative structure. There is no clear indication that the 'maior ecclesia' is seen as a cathedral.
16. Cfr I. Wood, 'The mission of Augustine of Canterbury to the English', *Speculum*, LXIX (1994), 1–17.
17. As cited by Kaiser 1990, 57–58 with nn. 109–110. Boniface's own appointment as an archbishop did not include any indication of *sedes* either, cfr Bonifatius, ep. 28 (Monumenta Germaniae Historica, Ep. Sel. I, 49–52). In fact, Boniface didn't care to settle until the (unsuccessful) campaign for an appointment to the see of Cologne in 745.

18. In favour of Roman plans for a Frisian church province: Kaiser (1990), 52, Angenendt (1989), 41 and Fritze (1971), 124. Sceptical: Leupen (1990), 321 and Weiler (1989), 155. For the concept of universality and focus on *gentes* rather than on territorial structures, cfr W. Fritze, 'Unversalis gentium confessio. Formeln, Träger und Wege universalmissionarischer Denkens im 7. Jahrhundert', *Frühmittelalterliche Studien* III (1969), 78–130, and Schäferdiek (1994), 176–80.

19. Angenendt (1973), 91–92; Angenendt (1989), 39–40.

20. Fritze (1971), 145–48, and Wood (1994), 267–71. It was probably only in 733–34 that Charles was able to push the line further, up to the Lauwers in the north-east of *Frisia*. Given these circumstances, it seems hardly plausible that Willibrord could establish bishops in subordinate dioceses, as states Kaiser 1990, 53 and no 84, with reference to the 'antistes' Bede decribes as instituted by Willibrord.

21. OB Utr. no 38 (726/27).

22. Cfr above, no 16.

23. Bede's *locus cathedrae episcopalis* refers to the period before 719, for the author clearly states that it was provided by Pepin (*HE* v.11, 486). The donations by Charles Martel mention only a *monasterium* and an *ecclesia* (Cfr above, no 10).

24. Ep. 109.

25. Cfr above, n. 10.

26. This title has been assigned to Utrecht by Schieffer (1976, 178), and, earlier, by N. B. Tenhaeff, *De oorkondenschat van den heiligen Willibrord* (Groningen 1929), 6. The 'Canterbury model' was accepted by subsequent scholars, e.g. Angenendt (1989), 39, and Werner (1982), 299 no 539, but not by E. Ewig, 'Der Martinskult im Frühmittelalter', *Spätantikes und fränkisches Gallien. Gesammelte Schriften (1952–1973)*, II, ed. H. Atsma (München 1979), no 146.

27. Cfr N. Brooks, *The Early History of the Church of Canterbury. Christ Church from 597 to 1066*, Leicester 1984, 87–92.

28. According to later medieval tradition. If one leaves out Gregory and his successor Alberik (who both may well have been buried at Susteren), the list starts with Theodardus († 790). Radbod († 917), while in exile, was buried in Deventer. Cfr Werner 1982, 284–88.

29. M. Richter, 'The Young Willibrord', *Willibrord. Apostel der Niederlände. Gründer der Abtei Echternach. Gedenkgabe zum 1250. Todestag des angelsächsischen Missionars,* eds G. Kiesel and J. Schroeder (Luxemburg 1989), 25–30.

30. Cfr R. Morris, 'Alcuin and the Alma Sophia', *The Anglo-Saxon Church. papers for H.M. Taylor*, ed. L. A. S. Butler and R. K. Morris, CBA research report, LXI (London 1986), 80–89.

31. For the Insular evidence, cfr. J. Blair, 'Anglo-Saxon minsters: a topographical review', *Pastoral Care Before the Parish*, eds J. Blair and R. Sharpe (Leicester–Londen–New York 1992), 226–66, and H. M. Taylor and J. Taylor, *Anglo-Saxon Architecture*, I, (Cambridge 1965), fol. 13, and III (Cambridge 1978), 1020. For the Continent, J. Hubert and E. Lehmann among others have drawn up extensive lists of 'cathédrales doubles' or 'Kirchenfamilien', which however depend often on projections from secondary evidence: cfr E.G. van Welie, 'Double churches — some aspects of the form and function of a phenomenon in fourth- to seventh-century church architecture', *Boreas*, XVI (1993), 165–80, with further references.

32. *Vita Gregorii* xi, p. 75 and xv, p. 79. Schieffer (1976), 179, pointed to the mention of *monachorum vel canonicorum* in a charter from 753 (OB Utr. nr 43, see below) as indicative of a division within the community at Utrecht. As these clerics are mentioned in connection with one *Casa Dei sancti Martini* only, there is no indication that they constituted two separated bodies of clerics associated with S. Salvator's and S. Martin's respectively. Anyway, we should not project this evidence back to the period of Willibrord. The charters of Charles Martell mention only one *monasterium* (OB Utr. no. 35), or one *basilica* (OB Utr. no. 36).

33. As far as can be seen at present, the earliest evidence comes from the *ordinarius* of S. Martin, to be dated *c.* 1200, (*Ordinarius S. Martini Traiectensis*, ed. P. Séjourné (Utrecht 1921), [31].

34. *Vita Liudgeri* i.18, 21: *in solario ecclesiae sancti Salvatoris, quam sanctus Willibrordus construxerat* .

35. OB Utr. no. 40 (undated, 751, Dec. 13 754, June 5) and no. 43 (753, May 23).

36. OB Utr. no. 45 (769, March 1), and no. 56 (815, March 18).

37. OB Utr. no. 106 (944, July 17).

38. e.g. recently Leupen (1990), 319–20, and Angenendt (1989), 39.

39. For a recent critique of Boniface as a forger, M. Mostert, 'Bonifatius als geschiedvervalser', *Madoc*, IX (1995), 213–21.

40. The Merovingian King Dagobert I (623–632) is most likely to have been the one Boniface had in mind, which leaves Cunibert (*c.* 626 — after 648) as most probable bishop. For a discussion of Dagobert's interest in the northern parts of *Francia*, cfr. Wood (1994), 293–303 and 317–21.

41. Ep. 109: *fundamenta cuiusdam destructae a paganis ecclesiolae.*

42. E.g. Wolfgang Fritze (see below).
43. OB Utr. OB Utr. no 36; convincing identification with St Salvator's in Utrecht by J. E. A. T. H. Bogaers, *De Gallo-Romeinse tempels te Elst in de Overbetuwe* (The Hague 1955), 189–202. For the archaeological evidence and the problems of identification and dating, cfr (with summaries in English) H. de Groot, 'De Heilige Kruiskapel te Utrecht', *Bulletin KNOB* XCIII (1994), 135–49, R. E. Th. M. Rijntjes, 'De *ecclesiola* in het Utrechtse castellum. Bouwhistorische interpretatie van de resten van de Heilig-Kruiskapel', *Bulletin KNOB* XCIII (1994), 150–61, and R. J. Stöver, 'De afmetingen van de Salvator- of Oudmunsterkerk in de afbeeldingen van de Monumenta van Van Buchel en in de collectie Booth: Toetsing en interpretatie aan de hand van opgravingsresultaten', *Bulletin KNOB* XCIII (1994), 169–85.
44. Fritze (1971), 118–19.
45. Schieffer (1976), 178.
46. Van Winter (1975) and Leupen (1990). Before these, I. H. Gosses, 'Merowingisch en Karolingisch Utrecht', *Bijdragen voor vaderlandsche geschiedenis en oudheidkunde,* 4th series, IX (1911), 209–66 first made this point.
47. Cfr above.
48. The wording is from OB Utr. no. 40; St Martin is referred to as *ipsa casa dei . . . vel . . . illo episcopoatu* in OB Utr. no. 43.
49. OB Utr. no. 40: Blok (1962); OB Utr. no. 43; *Nederlandsch Archievenblad*, XXVIII (1919–1920), 98–99. Both documents are represented in Bishop Radbod's cartulary.
50. *Monumenta Germaniae Historica, Formulae Merowingici et Karolingini aevi, Formulae Marculfi,*I, ed. K. Zeumer (Hanover 1886), no. 4, 44.
51. To this, Karl August Eckhardt has drawn attention (Eckhardt 1975, 43–49). The title of Boniface as *Traiectensis episcopus* for instance, seems a direct 'translation' of the *illius civitatis episcopus* in the Marculf *formula*, and therefore says nothing about the actual status of Boniface with regard to Utrecht. Boniface could boast his archiepiscopal title in order to legitimate his actions anyway, did so in the charter of 753, that charter not being restricted by a clear formula-template. It is not necessary, either, to suppose that Boniface actually showed charters with the privileges Pepin confirmed in the charter of 751–53 to that king, as Van Winter (1975), 70, supposes. The passage on which Van Winter based her argument is an exact copy of the text of the *formula*, and has therefore little value as a source for reconstructing the situation in Utrecht.
52. It is however not necessary to follow Eckhardt's hypothesis of a possible blood-link between Pepin and his merovingian predecessors.
53. Blok (1962), 43 and Eckhardt (1975), 51–54.
54. McKitterick (1983), 35–36; J. Nelson, 'The Lord's anointed and the people's choice: Carolingian royal ritual', *Rituals of Royalty. Power and Ceremonial in Traditional Societies,* eds. D. Cannadine and S. Price, Past and present Publications (Cambridge 1987), 142 and 180.
55. J. Fleckenstein, *Lexikon des Mittelalters*, VI (1993), 2168–70 sums up the consensus in stating 'Das Problem, das es zu lösen galt, lag in dem Mit verhältnis, das zwischen dem machtlösen könig und dem Inhaber der tatsächlichen Macht bestandt, der keinen Königsgeschlecht angehörte. . . .Es kam darauf an, die fehlende Legitimität seines (i.e. Pippin's) Geschlechts auf andere Weise zu ersetzen'.
56. *Monumenta Germaniae Historica, Dipl. Karol.*, I, ed. E. Mühlbacher (Hanover 1906), nr 20, 28–29. The core of the document is supposedly from *c.* 764, but was subsequently reworked in the 10th century.
57. Wallace-Hadrill)1985), 163.
58. McKitterick (1983); J. Semmler, 'Pippin III und die fränkischen Kloster'. *Francia*, III (1975), 88–146.
59. F. Prinz, *Klerus und Krieg im früheren Mittelalter* (Stuttgart 1971), 70 n. 118; McKitterick (1983); E. Ewig, 'Milo et eiusmodi similes', *Spätantikes und fränkisches Gallien. Gesammelte Schriften (1952–1973),* II, ed. H. Atsma (München 1979), 189–219.
60. *Vita Liudgeri* i.10, 15.

Willibrord's Cathedral: An investigation of the First Phases of the Construction of the Salvatorkerk in Utrecht[*]

by Jos Stöver

Qui (Willibrordus) per L annos predicans prefatum gentum Fresorum maxima ex parte convertit ad fidem Christi, fana et dilubra destruxit et aecclesias construxit et sedem episopalem et aecclesiam in honore sancti Salvatoris constituens in loco et castello, quid dicitur Traiectum.[1]

INTRODUCTION

During the Middle Ages, three churches stood in close proximity on the site of Utrecht's Roman fort. The northern area of the former *castellum* was, and in part still is, occupied by the Cathedral of St Martin. Only a few metres to the south stood the much smaller Chapel of the Holy Cross (demolished in 1826) and the larger church of Jesus Christ the Saviour, also known as the Oudmunster (Old Minster), a derivation from the Latin Vetus Monasterium.[2] This church, demolished in 1587 just after the Utrecht Alteration, is the subject of this article. (For clarity and ease of understanding the Dutch term 'Salvatorkerk' will be used in references to this church in the remainder of the paper.) The ecclesiastical complex of Utrecht originates from the enterprise of the Anglo-Saxon missionary Willibrord (ob. 739). In 695 Willibrord was ordained Archbishop of the Frisians. A letter to Pope Stephen II from Boniface (ob. 754), who had undertaken the administration of the Frisian area after Willibrord's death, states that Willibrord intended the Salvatorkerk to be his Cathedral.[3] It is generally accepted that Willibrord's wishes followed the tradition established by other cathedrals such as that at Canterbury, established by Papal instigation and also dedicated to the Saviour.[4] Similarly the eighth-century missionary bases at Wurzburg, Fulda, Erfurt and Eichstätt had churches dedicated to Christ which, over a period of time, developed into cathedrals.[5]

The dedication to the Saviour appears to have its origins in the Lateran Church in Rome, the first church built by Emperor Constantine. This church was built to serve as cathedral for the city of Rome and mother church to the whole of the Roman Empire; in fact the Lateran was the first cathedral ever in the Empire.[6] Both Willibrord and Boniface had strong bonds with Rome, both having been ordained Archbishop by the Pope.

Nevertheless, the Salvatorkerk at Utrecht did not become the Cathedral of the see into which the Frisian area had developed by 780. The Salvatorkerk is the only foundation in Utrecht mentioned in the few written sources for the period before 750.[7] However, according to written sources from the period around 750 and later,[8] Saint Martin was considered the patron saint of the diocese and this patronage was connected to a second church which, according to Boniface's letter, had also been built by Willibrord. The Chapel of the Holy Cross, mentioned above, can most probably be identified with Willibrord's St Martin's.[9]

At the beginning of the eleventh century the patronage of St Martin was transferred to a new church, the third within the walls of the former Roman *castellum*. This was

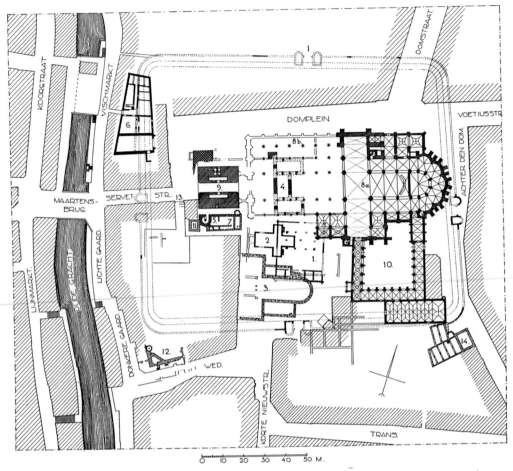

FIG. I.   Roman and medieval buildings on the Domplein at Utrecht: 1. walls, gates and
praetorium of the Roman fort; 2. Chapel of the Holy Cross; 3. Church of the Saviour;
4, 5, 7. Foundations of the Romanesque cathedral; 6. Remains of the imperial palace of Lofen;
8a. Choir and transept of the gothic cathedral; 8b. Former nave of the gothic cathedral; 9. Gothic
cathedral tower; 10. Cloisters of the cathedral with chapter; 12. Remains of the episcopal palace;
13. Gate of the bishop's area.

*Source: E. J. Haslinghuis, De Nederlandse Monumenten van Geschiedenis en Kunst, II, Iste stuk, afl. 1
(The Hague 1956) 12.*

the great cathedral of Bishop Adelbold (1010–26), which was rebuilt in the Gothic
manner about 1250 (Fig. 1). Thus, unlike the missionary churches in Canterbury,
Eichstätt and Wurzburg, the Salvatorkerk was probably not considered a cathedral in
the latter part of the eighth century and certainly not from the beginning of the eleventh
century when a new cathedral church was built. This makes the original function of the
Salvatorkerk rather obscure but it is evident that the church had some specific episcopal
privileges. Up to the episcopate of Baldric (918–75) most bishops of Utrecht were
buried in the Salvatorkerk.[10] Of more importance, and rather peculiarly, the oldest
baptismal font was located in the Salvatorkerk. From liturgical sources it is very clear

that the cathedral of St Martin did not have its own font.[11] Thus, for one of the most important of parochial rights, the Cathedral of Utrecht was completely dependent on a neighbouring church. Furthermore, an extensive system of mutual stations existed between the two churches, indicating a specific and special alliance.[12] Although, during the later Middle Ages, Old Minster was, in fact, an ordinary collegiate church, the mutual dependence, privileges and established customs show the Salvatorkerk's position as being unusual but important. So far research into the ecclesiastical complex of Utrecht has resulted in disagreement as to how the Salvatorkerk functioned.[13]

Until its demolition in 1587 the Salvatorkerk was constantly being enlarged, altered and embellished. The Reformation halted this process and, indeed, led to its demise. On 11 November 1587 the building was sold and soon afterwards torn down.[14] The building was completely razed to the ground and even most of its foundations removed.

Fortunately the Salvatorkerk did not fall into complete oblivion. The building is reasonably well documented in both pictorial and written sources and most of the accounts of its maintenance, from 1347 onwards, still exist.[15] Additionally some of the so-called *ordinarii*, in which the liturgy of the church services were set down, are also preserved.[16] A description of the interior of the Salvatorkerk was written by a canon of the Chapter, Johannes Mersman, just after the building had been demolished.[17] Sources such as these give important detail of the spatial arrangements of the building and its liturgical disposition.

Shortly after, or maybe even during demolition, some drawings and paintings were made of the ground plan and elevation of the Salvatorkerk. Two drawings in particular have proved especially valuable for the present investigation. A sketch of the ground plan and elevation is contained within a historical work by Arnout van Buchel (ob. *c.* 1640); the other, unattributed, work is in the collection of Cornelis Booth (ob. 1678), a former Mayor of Utrecht and a keen historian (Pl. IVA).[18] The drawings provide significant information about the dimensions of the Salvatorkerk: linear measurements of various parts of the ground plan of the building are given in both. Of equal importance are the archaeological excavations on the Domplein carried out in the 1930s by Van Giffen, Vollgraff and Van Hoorn.[19] Immediately beneath the pavement of the Domplein remains of the Salvatorkerk, the Chapel of The Holy Cross and of Adelbold's romanesque cathedral were found. These sources, when combined, provide an abundance of material to reconstitute the history of the building of the Salvatorkerk.[20]

ANALYSIS OF THE WESTERN PART OF THE GROUND PLAN. CONCLUSIONS CONCERNING THE DIMENSIONS AND PROPORTIONS OF THE NAVE AND WESTERN BLOCK

In an article published in 1994, an analysis of the dimensions of the Salvatorkerk was presented.[21] Data from all relevant sources were combined and verified, and the result is a fairly accurate reconstruction of the ground plan (Fig. 2). This close study allowed the formulation of theories concerning the dimensions and shape of what is presumably to be identified with the first phase of the Salvatorkerk's construction. This phase of building will be discussed in some detail in the remainder of this article.

In its final phase, the proportions of the Salvatorkerk were remarkable. The eastern part of the building consisted of a long, deep transept flanked to the east by a great choir. Beneath the choir was a large crypt consisting of three aisles no less than eight

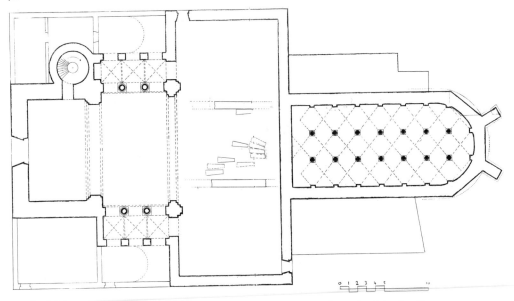

FIG. 2.   Reconstruction of the ground plan of the Salvatorkerk by Jos Stöver
Drawing: Wijnand Bloemink, Deventer

bays in length. Two annexes opened on either side of the choir, only one of which, that of the north, belong to the original plan. Transept, choir and north annex do not form part of the first period of building but are additions made to the original fabric, probably shortly after 1050. The choir is of a specific type known as a 'langchor', a type of construction used elsewhere during this period.[22]

The western part of the Salvatorkerk, as it existed prior to demolition and consisting of an arcaded nave on columns and a western block, is less well documented. Vestiges of this part of the building may lie under houses built on the Domplein at the end of the last century. The presence of these houses made archaeological investigation of this area impossible. From a liturgical point of view, the western parts of the Salvatorkerk are presumably less important than the choir, the liturgical focus of any church. Sources such as the *ordinarii* therefore offer little information about these parts of the building. However it has been possible to draw up a fairly accurate plan. The dimensions of the eastern parts of the Salvatorkerk given on the drawings were found to be surprisingly accurate when compared with measurements taken during the archaeological investigations. Given this close agreement, there is little room to doubt the accuracy of the proportions of both nave and tower given in the drawings.

The western parts of the Salvatorkerk had extraordinary proportions. The nave hardly deserved the name for it was exceptionally short. Each arcade had only three bays. Over all the length of the nave must have been approximately 10 m. Compared to its length the nave was extremely wide, more than 12 m and flanked on either side by narrow, apparently ill-proportioned aisles, each some 2.5 m wide. According to medieval building proportions, aisles should be half as wide as the nave, a ratio of 1:2. Such proportions were the norm even in Carolingian times. However the ratio of the nave and aisles in the Salvatorkerk is approximately 1:5.[23] On the western side a monumental westwork was connected to the nave, having almost the same dimensions

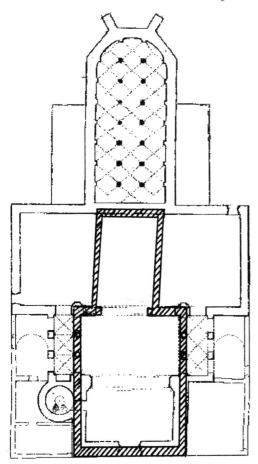

FIG. 3. The ground plan of the eighth-century hall-church incorporated in the ground plan of the later church

as the nave. On its northern side, the westwork was flanked by a stair turret; there may have been a corresponding turret on the southern side. The unconventional proportions of the plan of the Salvatorkerk, do not conform to the usual proportional systems of construction of the Middle Ages. This nonconformity can only be explained by the assumption that the western part of the church is in fact the result of the addition of units at different times to the layout of a pre-existing building. In the writer's opinion the plan of the nave and western block together comprise the plan of a sizeable hall-church, 18 m long and 12 m wide (internal measurements). This hall-church, as will be seen, was connected to a constricted, rectangular eastern annex or porticus (Fig. 3). Using the ground plans of the earlier stages of a building as the starting point of further building is common practice.[34] Many churches stand on the foundations of earlier buildings. The plan of the hall-church in Utrecht thus must have been 'split' to allow the construction of the basilical structures of nave and tower. The unconventional proportions of the aisle when compared with the nave lead to the hypothesis that these were the only parts that were actually added. The 'hall-church' stage of the Salvatorkerk in Utrecht could have been the first in its structural evolution, built in the early eighth century during the administration of Willibrord. In the region around Utrecht hall-churches frequently occur from about 700. Such buildings as Willibrord's church in Echternach or the churches of the seventh-century monastic complex at Nivelles are examples, but not the only as will be shown. The dimensions of the hall, around 18 m long and 12 m wide, result in a width–length relationship of 3 to 2, not unusual for hall-churches.[25] However, and as far as these dimensions are concerned, even in recent literature it has been assumed that eighth-century missionaries could not afford the huge expense of constructing large churches, having to make do with small, possibly thatched and often wooden structures of modest proportions.[26] The impressive Salvatorkerk in Utrecht may be hard to accept in this context, however it should not be overlooked that missionaries such as Willibrord were also important political figures. In fact Willibrord and his immediate successors played an active role in the incorporation of the Frisian territory, only recently conquered by the Franks. Indeed Willibrord was strongly supported by the Frankish mayors of the palace.[27] The aspirations of the Frankish rulers, and their missionaries, necessitated majestic architecture.

At Echternach. Willibrord built an abbey church on land he obtained from Pippin, and his wife Plectrud, in 700.[28] This church was much smaller than the Salvatorkerk but the decoration of this building must have been fairly rich and, even today, shows artistic refinement. Some of the original furnishings still exist, parts of the stone screens around Willibrord's tomb and the fine ambo.[29]

Early examples of churches of comparable size to the Salvatorkerk are also known. At Eichstätt for instance, a missionary base founded by Boniface in the first half of the eighth century, Bishop Willibald had a church built around 742. This building was dedicated to the Saviour and the Virgin, and had dimensions comparable to those of the Salvatorkerk. During excavations in the 1970s, it was discovered that the arcades of the nave of the present cathedral were built on the foundations of an early hall-church. The distance between the old walls, that is the width of the old hall-church, was about 12 m. Unfortunately the original eastern parts of the earliest structure were obliterated by the construction of a crypt in the twelfth century (Pl. IVB).[30] Not far from Utrecht, at Elst in the Betuwe region, traces of a hall-church were found beneath the present church of St Martin. This church, probably founded by Werenfried, a companion of Willibrord, was around 22 m in length and about 12 m wide (external measurements). A small, constricted, square sanctuary with traces of an altar against the eastern wall, was connected to the eastern side of this hall.[31]

A great church dedicated to the Saviour during the eighth century in Utrecht would not have been unique and can be traced back to its origins in the hall-church. This particular type of church, the hall-church, is more appropriate to the seventh century rather than the ninth, tenth or eleventh centuries. It is true that the hall-church was a type employed quite commonly until far into the thirteenth century but, even before 800, its use was beginning to be restricted to buildings of a lower status such as parish churches or chapels. Conversely, and again before 800, due to Carolingian desire to copy Roman monumental construction, more important churches were (re)built with basilical attributes, which emphasized the monumentality of these establishments in comparison with the smaller, less significant churches. The church founded by Boniface in Fulda, for instance, was meant to be a replica of St Peter's in Rome,[32] and Willibrord's church at Echternach was completely rebuilt on a much greater basilical plan after 750.[33] Even during the period of strict reform, directed by Benedict of Aniane (ob. 821), in which Carolingian architecture lost much of its monumentality, the basilical design endured.[34]

This raises an argument as to the type of church built by Willibrord at Utrecht. Documentary evidence shows that Willibrord built the Salvatorkerk and it is perhaps unlikely that the hall-church concept would have been utilized again if Willibrord's original church had been replaced after 750 by a building of a different kind. As important an episcopal foundation as the Salvatorkerk would most probably have demanded a reconstruction of the basilical type. In 850 the see of Utrecht was raided by Vikings, and the clergy forced to flee the former *castellum*, preventing any building activities. Some seventy years later Bishop Baldric returned to start recovery of his scattered diocese, protected by the patronage of the Ottonian King/Emperors. It is said that he restored the existing churches by simply patching them up.[35] Nothing is known about new building schemes during Baldric's reign although he was active in reorganizing the Church of Utrecht. He might have started the construction of a new cathedral[36] but, if he had rebuilt the Salvatorkerk, he would probably have chosen a contemporary concept for one of the most important churches in his see.

At some point the hall-church must have been (partly) demolished and the plan divided into two more or less equal parts. A basilical structure arose on the eastern side with the addition of aisles, whilst on the western half a three-tower-westwork was built. The small eastern annex remained untouched. But for the aisles, the area covered by the original hall-church was not exceeded — apparently it was not a large church that was needed but one of a different type. The new basilical structure was half the size of the former hall-church. Its plan must have had almost centralizing proportions and does not appear to have been capable of accommodating a large congregation. The church which emerged from the reconstruction is reminiscent of a private oratory or palace church. Such a function is conceivable for the Salvatorkerk as it had always been connected with the residence of the bishops and served as their funerary church.[37]

Palatine churches appear in episcopal complexes from 1000. It may be assumed that this is around the time of the alterations to the Salvatorkerk. A three-tower-westwork, apparently inspired by that of Charlemagne's palace-chapel at Aachen, was built around 1000 in the bishopric of Liège, by Bishop Notker (972–1008). This period coincides with the episcopate of Bishop Ansfried (995–1010). As Notker, Bishop Ansfried was an important representative of royal power in Lotharinga, a constantly troublesome area from the point-of-view of the German emperors. There is thus good reason to attribute the rebuilding of the Salvatorkerk at Utrecht to Bishop Ansfried.[38] In his dissertation the writer will more extensively revert to this building-stage. It is sufficient here to state that a major rebuilding of the Saviour's Church took place around 1000. The transformation from hall-church to episcopal palace-church most probably concerned the old and very patched-up church built by Willibrord.

MATERIAL INDICATIONS OF THE ORIGINAL BUILDING OF THE SALVATORKERK: THE CONSTRICTED EASTERN ANNEX

The reconstruction of the plans of the hall-church was only possible from analysis of the ground plans of the western parts of the later church. However, material evidence of a constricted eastern annex is available. During the excavations of the Domplein in the 1930s, parts of two parallel walls of great antiquity were found in the former crossing of the church. These walls were constructed of irregularly shaped blocks of tufa, probably taken from the walls of the Roman *castellum*. The distance between the walls was 7.85 m, each wall having a thickness of 0.75 to 0.8 m. The depth of construction was about 3 m above N.A.P.[39] The walls did not show any constrictions so the remnants probably consisted solely of foundations. The axis of the building to which the walls once belonged differed from the axis of the western part of the church; a small deviation in orientation was also observed.

The archaeologists who carried out the excavations of the Domplein have dated the remains to the tenth century, to the episcopate of Baldric. This date is provided by the recovery of finds of pottery, etc., found near or between the walls. According to the excavators only a few Merovingan or Carolingian traces were found, whilst so-called Pingsdorf ware was relatively abundant.[40] This presumably makes the finds all the more valuable. The accuracy of this dating, however, is not entirely reliable as the archaeologists failed to record their findings accurately; nothing, for instance, is said about the depth or layers at or in which the material was found. Such knowledge would be indispensable for the interpretation of their findings: the ground on which the Salvatorkerk once stood has been thoroughly disturbed by several building phases and countless burials in and around the church, as is clear from the discovery of several tombs. The demolition in 1587 included the removal of the foundations requiring wide, deep ditches to accomplish the task, irreparably destroying the stratigraphy.

It is believed that the oldest remnants of the Salvatorkerk can be positively dated to Willibrord's days. The base of the wall's foundation was about 3 m above N.A.P., comparable with that of the Chapel of The Holy Cross. Except for traces of later, more extended, building requiring deeper foundations below the 3 m level, only vestigial traces of Roman levels were found. Furthermore there is a striking resemblance between the material used, reused debris from the Roman fort, and the construction methods, an irregular loose bonding technique. The Chapel of The Holy Cross was re-excavated in 1993 by the archaeologist from Utrecht, H. de Groot, with Raphaël Rijntjes. Their work suggests an eighth-century date for the chapel. They both identified the small church with Willibrord's St Martin's.

Of crucial importance in dating the oldest of the walls of the Salvatorkerk was the finding of a considerable number of limestone sarcophagi cut from large, single blocks of stone, some of which had lids. Only one of the sarcophagi was retained, the remainder disappeared. They were photographed and some of the photographs show both their type and individual detail. The sarcophagus which was saved is kept at the Central Museum of Utrecht; it has its lid and is adorned with braided bands and zig zag patterns (Fig. 4).

Most of the sarcophagi were found between the remnants of the old walls, having been buried inside the structure to which the walls once belonged. All were laid in the same plane as the walls. In the middle of the eastern half of the annex a group of four were clustered as if laid before an altar. The tops of the lids were all at one level just beneath the floor level of the church. These discoveries may indicate that the sarcophagi were buried whilst the structure was still in use. The monolithic limestone sarcophagi, sometimes provided with carved detail such as braided bands, lines, St Andrew's crosses, or circles in very low relief are dated to the eighth or ninth centuries. Similar sarcophagi have been found in other places such as Xanten, Maastricht, Bonn, Metz and Echternach.[41]

In considering the position of the remains with regard to the hall (reflected in the plan of the later church), the structure to which these remains belonged can only have been a constricted annex or porticus. The considerable quantity of sarcophagi give a hint as to the function of this porticus, it must have been a burial chamber. Similar usage of an (eastern) annex is seen quite frequently elsewhere.[42] Willibrord's tomb, for instance, was initially placed behind and later mounted in front of, and partially

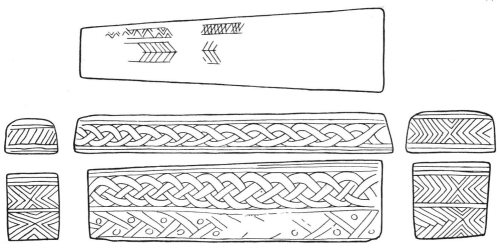

FIG. 4.   Limestone sarcophagi. Eighth or ninth century.
*Source: C. W. Vollgraff en G. Van Hoorn, Opgravingen op het Domplein te Utrecht, Wetenschappelijke
verslagen III (Haarlem 1936) 82, ill. 42. This sarcophagus is kept at the Central Museum Utrecht*

beneath, the altar in the eastern annex of his church in Echtemach.[43] At Nivelles an
irregular, square burial chamber, in which Gertrud of Nivelles (ob. 659) was interred,
was connected to a great hall. This annex was accessible from the hall and was enlarged
after Gertrud had been declared a Saint.[44] It would appear that eastern annexes were
used as burial chambers in England; from written sources it is known that, at
Monkwearmouth, important clerics were buried *in porticu*.[45] It is to be expected that
such a burial chamber would be found in the Salvatorkerk. Willibrord was, at his own
wish, buried at Echternach but Boniface, who was martyred at Dokkum, was interred,
if only temporarily, in the Salvatorkerk.[46] Following Boniface's interment nearly all of
the bishops of Utrecht, up to the time of Bishop Baldric, were buried in the
Salvatorkerk.[47] The tombs found during the excavations in the 1930s may well have
been those of the first bishops and senior clerics who governed the budding diocese in
the eighth and ninth centuries. In 1421, during the laying of foundations for a rood-
gallery in the crossing of the church, a coffin containing the bones of St Gregory
(ob. 780), an abbot who ruled the monastery at Utrecht after Boniface's martyrdom,
was found. His remains were exhumed immediately and an altar, dedicated to his
honour, was built under the northernmost bay of the rood-gallery in the vicinity of the
original place of burial.[48] Even in the seventeenth century, the Chapter of Old Minster
were still aware of the significance of this area in the crossing of their former
Salvatorkerk. The Chapter, then resident in the abbey church of St Paul, were embroiled
in a serious clash with the city of Utrecht's plan to build a road over 'the ground of the
belly of the demolished church, where many of her deceased, some of extraordinary
rank, were buried'.[49]

CONCLUSION

The dimensions presented on the drawings and plans of the Salvatorkerk are indicative
of a great hall-church. The plan of the hall-church constituted the starting point for the

construction, probably about 1000, of a basilical structure with a centralized chapter and a westwork. This structure survived until the final demolition of the building.

Based on a typological argument, the hall-church may be considered as Willibrord's church and, thus, the first stage of the building which eventually became the Salvatorkerk. The substantial dimensions of the building were not unique in this period. Churches of the type, and comparable in dimensions to the Salvatorkerk in Utrecht, were built at Eichstätt and Elst in the Betuwe region in Holland.

Connected to the eastern end of the hall-church in Utrecht was a constricted annex, traces of which were found during excavations. These traces can probably be dated to the eighth century, a dating reinforced by the monolithic limestone sarcophagi found lying within the remains of the walls. This porticus was, very probably, used as a burial chamber for the first bishops of Utrecht.

REFERENCES

*   I am greatly indebted to Ian Wallace, Bebington, England for the checking and correction of this entry.
1.   Reinhold Rau, *Briefe des Bonifatius. Willibalds Leben des Bonifatius, nebst einigen zeitgenössischen Dokumenten* (Ausgewählte Quellen zur deutschen Geschichte des Mittelalters, Freiherr vom Stein-Gedächtnisausgabe, ivb) (Darmstadt 1988), 338–43.
2.   The church was called in a charter of 1238: *ecclesia Sancti Salvatoris, quae vetus monasterium nuncupatur*, although in a charter of 1108 Oldminster was already *ecclesia Salvatoris que Vetus dicitur*. *Oorkondeboek van het Sticht Utrecht tot 1301*, S. Muller Fz. and A. G. Boumann (below abbreviated as OBU) (Utrecht 1921), I and II, nrs. CCLXXVIII and CMXXXII.
3.   Reinhold Rau (1988), 338–43.
4.   I only mention here Rudolf Schieffer, *Die Entstehung von Domkapiteln in Deutschland* (Bonner Historische Forschungen, XLIII) (Bonn 1976), 171–91.
5.   Fulda as a missionary centre did not evolve into a cathedral, but became an important Royal Abbey. The cathedral status was obtained only in this century. Short descriptions of the mentioned churches in Friedrich Oswald, Leo Schaefer and Hans Rudolf Sennhauser, *Vorromanische Kirchenbauten. Katalog der Denkmäler bis zum ausgang der Ottonen* (München 1966–71) and the socalled *Nachtragsband* under the direction of Werner Jacobsen, Leo Schaefer and Hans Rudolf Sennhauser (München 1991) (below abbreviated as Vorrom. Kirchenb.).
6.   The Lateran church, founded by Constantine after his God-given victory over his rival Maxentius, nowadays is dedicated to St John (San-Giovanni-in-Laterano). The basilica Salvatoris was called 'omnium ecclesiarum urbis et orbis mater et caput'. See Adolf Ostendorf, 'Das Salvator-Patrocinium, seine Anfänge und seine Ausbreitung im mittelalterlichen Deutschland', in: *Westfälische Zeitschift*, C (1950), 357–76.
7.   For example a charter of 726. The church was called 'basilica[m], que est constructa in honore Savatoris domini nostri Jesu Christ et beate Marie genitricis Dei, sed et beatorum apostolorum Petri et Pauli omniumque apostolorum, sanctique Johannis Baptiste vel ceterorum sanctorum . . .' OBU I, nr. XXXVI.
8.   For the first time in a charter of 753, OBU I, nr. XLIII.
9.   H. L. de Groot, De Heilige Kruiskapel te Utrecht. Die Tatsachen bleiben, die Interpretation schwänkt, in: *K.N.O.B.-Bulletin*, XCIII, 4/5 (1994), 135–49; Raphaël Rijntjes, De *ecclesiola* in het Utrechtse castellum. Bouwhistorische interpretatie van de resten van de Heilig-Kruiskapel, in: *K.N.O.B. Bulletin*, XCIII, 4/5 (1994), 150–61.
10. See in this volume the contribution of J. M. van Winter.
11. Statement by Eelco van Welie (5 October 1995).
12. On several occasions throughout the year the clergy of the two churches combined for religious observances. For example the clergy of St Martin's celebrated mass in the Salvatorkerk on St Boniface's feast day, one of the most important liturgical celebrations of Old Minster. The clergy of the Salvatorkerk are known to have visited St Martin's on Easter Day and, of course, on St Martin's Eve. See Paul Sejourné, *Ordinarius S. Martini Trajectensis* (Utrecht 1919–21) and A. A. J. van Rossum, Kerkelijke plechtigheden in de St Salvatorskerk to Utrecht, in *Archief voor de geschiedenis van het Aartsbisdom Utrecht* (below abbreviated as *AAU*), III (1876), 109–259 (See also note 16).
13. See the contributions of H. L. de Groot and of Raphaël Rijntjes in the *K.N.O.B. Bulletin* (note 9). See in that issue also the contribution of Eelco van Welie, 'Omnes canónici. Een verkenning van de Utrechtse Stads liturgie' Charlotte J. C. Broer and Martin W. J. de Bruijn, De Heilig Kruiskapel in Utrecht:

Sint-Maarten of Sint-Salvator? Latter authors have recently published a booklet on this subject C. J. C. Broer and M. W. J. de Bruijn, *De eerste kerken van Utrecht: Sint-Thomas, Sint-Salvator, Sint-Maarten* (Utrecht 1995). For a reaction on this publication see the contribution in this volume of Van Winter, note 26.

14. A survey of the events concerning the demolition of the church see G. G. Calkoen, *Aanteekeningen omtrent de voormalige burch Trecht en hare inrichting* (Utrecht w.y.), fol. 163. The tufa used in the construction of the Salvatorkerk was a much sought after material that could be used in the production of mortar.

15. A review of these accounts was made by G. G. Calkoen, *De Burch van Utrecht en hare naaste omgeving. Aanteekeningen en beschouwingen omtrent de Kapittelkerk van St. Salvator of Oude Munsterkerk na circa 1200. Deel C.* (Utrecht 1914). This work was never published but is available for inspection at the Municipal Archive of Utrecht.

16. Some of these liturgical books were published. The ordinarius of Saint-Martin's cathedral is published in: Paul Sejourné, *Ordinarius* (note 12). An elaborate manual for the sexton of Oldminster (the so called ordinarius of candles) was edited and translated by A. A. J. van Rossum, Kerkelijke Plechtigheden (note 12), 109–259. Another ordinarius was composed in the early fourteenth century for the vicarii of the Saviour's church by dean Egidius Pansier. This was published in Hugo van Rijn, *Historie ofte Beschrijving van 't Utrechtsche Bisdom, behelzende De Oudheden, Kerkelijke en Geestelijke Gebouwen, Kapellen, Kommandeurschappen, Abdijen, Koosters, Overste en Geleerde mannen, Getrokken uit de Oude Handschriften der kerken en Abdijen, etc. Deel I: Van de Oudheden en Gestichten der stad Utrecht*, 180–83: A late fourteenth-century ordinary of the Saviour's church is kept at the Royal Archive at Utrecht.

17. Johannes Mersman's 'Topographia sive interna descriptio vetustissimi et splendidissimi Templi Sancti Salvatoris Trajectensis' was published and translated into Dutch in Oudmunsterkerk te Utrecht, in: *AAU* (noot 12), I (1875), 337–85. Mersman finished his text in 1592, so after the church had been demolished.

18. Van Buchel's drawing is his 'Monumenta passim in templis ac monasteriis Trajectinae urbis'. This work is kept in the Municipal Archive of Utrecht. Booth's collection is kept at the Royal Archive at Utrecht.

19. The results of the excavations were defectively and only in part published in the so-called scientific reports: A. E. van Giffen, C. W. Vollgraff and G. van Hoorn, *Opgravingen op het Domplein te Utrecht: wetenschappelijke verslagen*, I–IV (Haarlem 1934–38). The greater part of the results of Van Giffen's excavations were not recorded in these reports, however information is available from the original drawings, sketches, notes and photos, made during the excavations. Most of this material is kept at the Archaeological and Buildinghistorical Centre at Utrecht. I would like to thank drs. Huib de Groot for his cooperation.

   A thorough survey of the excavations with regard to the Roman *castellum* and its periods can be read in L. R. P. Ozinga and T. J. Hoekstra c.a., *Het Romeinse Castellum te Utrecht. De opgravingen in 1936, 1938, 1943/44 uitgevoerd onder leiding van A. E. van Giffen, met medewerking van H. Brunsting, aangevuld met latere waarnemingen* (Utrecht 1989).

20. The results of the searches and analysis will be set down in a dissertation, in course of preparation by the author, and to be published in the near future.

21. R. J. Stöver, 'De afmetingen van de Salvator- of Oudmunsterkerk in de afbeeldingen in de Monumenta en in de Collectie Booth: toetsing en interpretatie aan de hand van opgravingsresultaten', in: *K.N.O.B. Bulletin*, XCIII, 4/5 (1994), 169–85.

22. Choirs of this type, usually indicated with the German term 'Lanchor', were built in Cologne (St Gereon, St Severin and St Andrew) and Bonn (St Cassius and Florentius). All, Oldminster in Utrecht included, were built during the second half of the eleventh century. The 'langchor' seems to be connected with the veneration of special saints. Gereon, Cassius and Florentius and Severin were martyrs and saints from the time the see of Cologne came into existence. The first three were the members of the so-called Theban Legion, a Roman army unit that converted to Christianity and were therefore slaughtered. Severinus was one of the first bishops of the see. These saints had played their part in the sacred origin of the archbishopric and the presence of their relics emphasized its respectable age. At Utrecht the same can be said of Boniface and his companions. This martyr was considered the founder of the see of Utrecht. Just like its counterparts in Cologne and Bonn, the 'langchor' of the Salvatorkerk therefore may be considered Boniface's shrine, a sort of foundation monument.

23. Chantries were added to the exterior of the aisles in the fourteenth and fifteenth centuries as were annexes to both sides of the tower. These additions will not be considered in this paper.

24. Some examples of early hall-churches that were extended into basilicas on the basis of their former shape: Bremen: Dom, stage III (858–60); Gerpinnes (Belgium), St Michael, stage II (c. 1000); Landen: St Gertrud, stage IIa (early ninth century); Tiel (Holland): St Martin, ninth-century hall-church extended with aisles around 1000; Waha (Belgium): St Martin, stage II (ninth or tenth century). Information from Vorrom. Kirchenb. (note 5).

25. For this fact, early examples can also be given: Nivelles, St-Paul's, seventh century; Büraburg, St Brigid's, eighth-century; Canterbury, St Martin's, seventh century; Kirk-Hammerton/Yorkshire, 600–800. In formation from Vorrom. Kirchenb. (note 5) and Taylor and Taylor, *Anglo-Saxon Architecture* (Cambridge 1965).

26. As Prof. Dr. C. J. A. C. Peeters has stated in a recent article on the early buildings stages of the churches at Utrecht. C. Peeters, 'Kerk- en Kloosterbouw in de missiegebieden van Willibrord', in *Willibrord, zijn wereld en zijn werk. Voordrachten gehouden tijdens het Willibrordcongres, Nijmegen, 28–30 september 1989* ed. by P. Bange and E. Weiler (Nijmegen 1990), 361–73, especially 367.

27. A. Angenendt, 'Willibrord im Dienste der Karolinger', in: *Annalen des historischen Vereins für den Niederrhein*, CLXXV (1973), 63–113.

28. Heinz Cüppers, 'Die Basilika des heiligen Willibrord zu Echternach und ihre Vorgängerbauten', in *Hémecht. Zeitschrift für Luxemburger Geschichte*, XXVII, 2/3 (1973), 346–53.

29. About the remnants of the church and its furnishings, Cüppers, Basilika (note 28), 332–46.

30. W. Sage, 'Die Ausgrabungen in den Dom von Bamberg und von Eichstätt', in *Jahresberichte der bayerischen Bodendenkma lpflege*, XVII/XVIII (1976–77), 195–206.

31. J. E. A. T. H. Bogaers, *De Gallo-Romeinse Tempels in Elst in de Overbetuwe* (Den Haag 1955), 195–206. The remains of the oldest church in Elst resemble the oldest works of the Salvatorkerk and the Chapel of the Holy Cross in Utrecht both in material and its application: a loose bonding of Roman debris (see below: section III). The first church of Elst was built on the remains of a Gallo-Roman temple.

32. Werner Jacobsen, *Der Klosterplan von St. Gallen und die karolingische Architektur. Entwickelung und Wandel von Form und Bedeutung im fränkischen Kirchenbau zwischen 751 und 840* (Berlin 1992), 193–99.

33. Cüppers, Basilika (note 28), 353–60 and Jacobsen, St Gallen (note 32), 218–22.

34. Jacobsen, St Gallen (note 32), fol. 262.

35. For an outline of tenth-century history of the diocese of Utrecht, see Rolf, *Das Bistum Utrecht und seine Bischöfe im 10. und frühen 11. Jahrhundert* (Cologne, Vienna, 1987), especially 17–19 and 30–101.

36. This is indicated by Baldric having divided the monastery at Utrecht in two Chapters, one dedicated to St Martin, the other to the Virgin (who was, according to a charter of 726, the second dedicand of the Salvatorkerk) see OBU I (note 2), nr. CVI (944). This can be seen as a thorough reorganization of the Church of Utrecht. According to later sources, some time after 950 Bishop Baldric obtained relics of several saints which he may have used for the furnishing of a new church, Johannes de Beke (ed. by H. Bruch), *Cronieken van den Stichte van Utrecht ende van Hollant* (The Hague 1982), 51. Building activities are very often accompanied by translation or elevation of relics: the construction of 'langchöre' for example always coincided with the elevation of holy bones. In Cologne relics of the Theban legion were found to furnish archbishop Anno I's (1056–75) 'Langchor' that he added to St Gereon's church. At Utrecht a 'Langchor' (mentioned above) was built in the same time by Bishop William (1054–76) in order to serve as shrine for relics of St Boniface. See also note 22.

37. The episcopal palace in the later Middle Ages was situated in front of the Western façade of the Salvatorkerk. In this façade the main portal of the church was built on the bishop's land and not on that of the church itself. See for an overview of the medieval situation: M. W. J. de Bruijn, *Husinghe ende Hofstede. Een institutioneel-geografische studie van de rechtspraak over onroerend goed in de stad Utrecht in de middeleeuwen* (Utrecht 1994), especially 111–20, 144–65 and Pl. 8 (82–83).

38. About Bishop Ansfried's episcopate: Rolf Grosse, *Das Bistum Utrecht* (note 35), 115–209.

39. N. A. P.: Normaal Amsterdams Peil; Normal level at Amsterdam. A fixed water level, the base from which all water and ground levels in Holland are measured.

40. Vollgraff and Van Hoorn, *Opgravingsverslagen* (note 19), III, 79.

41. For an excellent overview of the limestone sarcophagi found in Holland and surrounding countries see S. Lammers, 'Medieval Christian Interments in Stone: Monolithic Limestone Sarcophagi', in *Berichten van de Rijksdienst voor Oudheidkundig Bodemonderzoek*, XXXIX (1989), 377–434.

42. Peeters, Kerk- en Kloosterbouw (note 26), 370. See also Arnold Angenendt, 'In porticu ecclesiae sepultus. Ein Beispiel von himmlisch-irdischer Spiegelung', in *Iconologia Sacra. Mythos, Bildkunst und Dichtung in der Religions- und Sozialgeschichte Alteuropas. Festschrift für Karl Hauck zum 75. Geburtstag* (Berlin, New York 1994), 68–80.

43. Christian Beutler, *Die entstehung des Altaraufsarzes. studien zum Grab Willibrords in Echternach* (München 1978), 51–67 and 102–03 (notes). Willibrord's sarcophagus was surrounded by the beautiful screens mentioned above.

44. Vorrom. Kirchenb., Nachtragsband (note 5), 309–11.

45. H. M. Taylor, 'The Position of the Altar in early Anglo-Saxon Churches', in *The Antiquaries Journal*, LIII (1973), 52–58, especially note 1, 54: *Sepultus est autem Benedictus in porticu beati Petri, ad orientum altaris, ubi postmodum etiam reverentissimorum abbatum easterwini et Sigfridi sunt ossa translata.*

46. Rau, *Briefe des Bonifatius* note 1), 518–19: Corpus vero beati pontificis prosperis velis ventorumque flatibus trans fretum quod dicitur Aelmere (sed et aliorum martyrum) post dies non multos perductum est ad supradictum urbem quae dicitur Trecht ibique conditum ac sepultum, donec a Magontia religiosi et fideles in Domini fratres a Lullo episcopi successore quidem huius sancti pontificis et martyris Christi directi navigio ad perducendum beati viri cadaver ad monasterium, quod vivante construxerat et secus ripam fluminis quod dicitur Fulde situm est, advenerant.

Cumque honorabilis tam sanctae consocietatis fratres ad praedictam urbem pervenerunt, tunc quippe aliquantula eis abbiam populi erat congregata collectio, eiusdemque urbis praefecti, eis audientibus, quomadmodum a glorioso rege Pippino exivit edictum, insonuit interdictum et, ne inde praedicti pontificis corpus amoveretur, indictum est. Sed quia omnipotentis magis quam hominum convalescit fortitudo, mirabile statim ac memorabile cunctis adstantibus angelica magis quam humana. peractum cognitione, auditum est miraculum, aecclesiaeque gloccum in signum ammonitionis sancti corporis, humana non contiguente manu, commotum est, ita ut omnes repentino timoris pavore perculsi maximo tremore obstupuerunt et iusti huius reddendum esse corpus proclamaverunt. Sicque statim redditum est corpus et a praedictis sanctae recordationis fratribus cum psalmis hymnisque ablatum ac sine remigantium labore tricesima obitus sui die perductum est ad civitatem supradictam Magontiam.

47. Although Utrecht was still in the hands of the Vikings and the bishop and his clerics resided at Deventer, Bishop Odilbald (866–99) was nevertheless, at least according to later sources, buried in the Saviour's church. Of his successor Radbod (900–17) is known that he occasionally visited the tombs of his episcopal ancestors. See Beka, *Cronieken* (note 36), 48–50; Mersman, *Topographia* (note 17), 361.

48. Calkoen, *Salvatorkerk* (note 15), 31.

49. Calkoen, *Burch* (note 14), pp. 220–21. The original old-Dutch reads as follows: *de gront van de buyck haerl. Gedemolieerde kercke, daeronder veele ja de principaetste doden liggebn begraven . . .*

The large round-bottomed Medieval boats excavated in the municipality of Utrecht

by Robert Vlek

INTRODUCTION

Holland is well known as a country where water and land are always at hand. In many places there was once land where there is water now and vice versa. In some cases the shift was man-made, by land reclamation (polders) or peat production (plassen). In other cases there were natural causes like erosion and changing rivers (Fig. 1).

Ships and boats of our ancestors sank and were buried in this process for centuries only to be found accidentally. These historic (and prehistoric) ship- and boat-finds occurred many times in our history, but only a few have been recorded from the previous century onwards. Apart from recording, the next step was preserving the

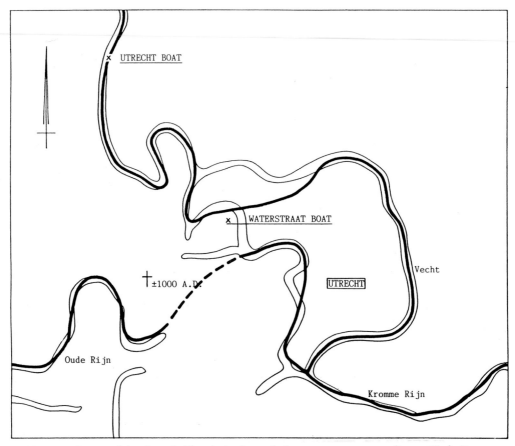

FIG. 1.   Course of the rivers in Utrecht in the period AD 1050–1122 according to H. de Groot

vessel itself. All this was successfully done for the first time in Holland in the 1930s with the 'Utrecht Boat', in analogy with the earlier Nydam boat in Schleeswig and the Viking ships in Oslo.

DISCOVERY AND EXCAVATION

The first traces of the 'Utrecht boat' were found in early December 1930 while digging a ditch by hand at the Van Hoornekade, on behalf of the new housing project in the north of the city of Utrecht.

The site was geologically surveyed and the profile showed that the wreck of a large vessel was situated in an undisturbed fluvial sand deposit of a former bed of the nearby Vecht river. This made clear that the vessel was very ancient although no absolute date could be stated at that time (Pl. Va).

It was big news at the time. Many people came to take a look and a multi-disciplinary team was formed ad hoc under the supervision of Dr W. C. Schuylenburg, the director of the local Central Museum, to deal with the excavation and preservation. Despite the economic depression Dr Schuylenburg did an excellent job of fund raising among the harbour magnates in Amsterdam and Rotterdam.

PRESERVATION

In the mean time the vessel was taken apart and shipped to the largest cellar of the Central Museum where it is still located (Pl. Vb).

According to the advice of Professor Van Griffen, the preservation would be executed in 'dry mode'. All the wood would be treated on the surface with creosote and linseed oil for some time, after which it would be left to dry more or less controlled during and after the reconstruction. This process was earlier successfully applied in Oslo with the Oseberg and Gokstad Viking ships.

The Utrecht boat proved to be more difficult to conserve in this way because the oak members were much thicker and more waterlogged due to the burial in sandy deposits.

The saturation of the wood with creosote began in the autumn of 1931. Gradually the solution was mixed with a higher percentage of linseed oil. Nevertheless about a year later the first traces of shrinkage appeared and would continue until a new stable situation was reached.

RECONSTRUCTION

The reconstruction started in the autumn of 1931 with the bending of the deformed logboat base to its original shape. All parts of the vessel were drawn to a scale of 1:10 and a model was made accordingly. In this way the original shape and feature became clear, prior to the actual rebuilding (Fig. 2).

It was decided that the missing parts of the strakes would not be replaced by new ones and this decision meant that the vessel had to be supported in one way or another to provide the necessary cohesion. For this purpose a number of steel jigs were made and attached to the floor of the cellar replacing earlier wooden support. In this steel 'harness' the vessel was left to dry.

In the autumn of 1936 the conservation and the reconstruction were finished and the largest object in the museum was finally open to the public.

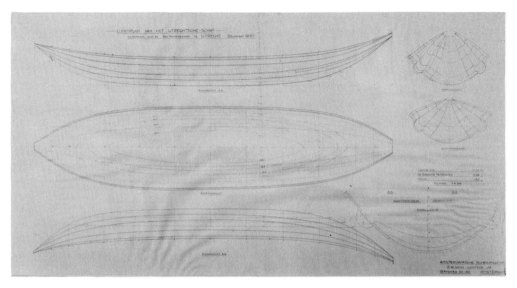

FIG. 2.   The log boats in Utrecht

INTERPRETATION

It took even longer to arrive at any official publication. This was due to the lack of funds, missing expertise in this field and finally World War II. A number of articles, however, were written in the thirties that gave rise to a number of mistakes that were copied many times over the following decades.

The most difficult subject concerned the dating of the vessel. It was generally taken for granted that the vessel was built in the second century AD and could be connected with the Roman *limes*. This date was derived from the geological reports and the unusual construction with the logboat base, compared to the size. The archaeologist, Professor Van Griffen, who was consulted at the site of the excavation, rather thought of the Carolingian period due to some pottery sherds that were found near the wreck. This date was never published however.

The second most important misinterpretation concerned the additional envisioned parts. It was suggested that the vessel was fully decked, double bottomed and had sailing capacities beyond the coastline. Even a model was made to support this view and put on display next to the ship. When the second find of a vessel of the same type was made in the Waterstraat in Utrecht in 1974, a number of things became clear.

CONSTRUCTION CHARACTERISTICS

The most characteristic part of the Utrecht type is the enormous longitudinally and transversely arched logboat base made from the trunk of a large oak. The size of the logboat base of the Utrecht boat measures 14.30 m long and 1.93 m wide, the breadth of the logboat base of the Waterstraat boat measures 1.57 m (length is not known because the stem is missing).

Due to the fact that large oaks tend to rot in the core and are mostly hollow, the logboat base of the Utrecht boat had to be enlarged with extension boards fore and aft. This seemed not to be necessary for the smaller Waterstraat boat, the core is present in the stern. To prevent splitting, a heavy plank was fastened with tree-nails over it on the inside. This plank also served to fasten the strakes.

The enormous oak trunks that were to become the logboat base were first shaped by axe and adze on the outside after which a large number of holes of a specific depth were bored and filled with tree-nails serving as thickness gauges when the inside was hollowed out. In this way an average thickness of 6 cm was assured. It is probable that the logboat bases were expanded by fire and water treatment to make them broader and give them a structural inward tension to secure the cohesion with the ribs.

Given the fact that trees are wide at the base and taper to the top, the broad part was used in both vessels for the stem. In the Utrecht Boat, the forward extension board was also larger than the one at the stem. So not only was the stem higher but the whole front section was broader than the after section. This is the correct shape for floating downstream with little steering.

Because hollowed-out tree trunks easily tend to warp and crack due to localized dehydration, a great number of ribs, made from oak branches, were inserted. Both vessels have their own unique rhythm of alternating long and short ribs. All ribs have limber holes to drain rain and bilge-water towards midships. There was a small mast step in the rib positioned in the forward part at one third of the length. This was probably used to equip a short mast for a tow-line.

The garboard strakes consisted of two halves, pegged with a great number of tree-nails in clinker fashion to the logboat base. They were split out of a straight oak trunk and adzed to the correct thickness. The halves join exactly in the middle with a flat scarf.

One of the most remarkable features of the Utrecht type are the thick half round wales running from stem to stern over the full length of the ship. They are made from the same straight tree trunk and provide the longitudinal stiffness and enough material to fasten the sheerstrakes. Apart from their structural function, the wales must have had a transverse stabilizing effect when the boats were in use with full cargo capacity.

The sheerstrakes were made in similar fashion as the garboard strakes and attached to the inside of the wales. The sheerstrakes were lined with rubbing strakes to enforce and protect the top sides. All strakes and wales ended to squared-off bow and stern knees. The round endpieces on the Utrecht boat are over-enthusiastic reconstructions in accordance with aesthetic concepts of streamlining in the thirties.

This type of construction and the craftsmanship involved meant that caulking of the seams was an absolute necessity. This was done with large quantities of a moss that was suitable to fill large cavities. The twigs of the moss were placed on top of each other to make a compact and dense string. These were hammered between the strakes and in some places moss-laths were used to keep the caulking in place. The moss-laths were fastened with iron clamps (Dutch: *sintels*) of a specific type that was used in the eleventh century.

Apart from the '*sintels*', the only iron used were nails to fasten small plants over cracks and knots on the outside of the logboat base of the Utrecht boat, but these were later additions. Every structural connection was made with numerous (willow) treenails, secured with oak wedges on a side to expand the top.

DATING

The dating of the Utrechts boats has been very complicated and the methods attempted have not given equivalent results. The 'Utrecht boat' was dated by means of stratigraphy, typology of various aspects, C14 and dendrochronology. None of the methods were decisive due to various circumstances. The 'Waterstraat boat' was dated based on pottery sherds and dendronchronology with the same results.

The most probable date for the 'Utrecht boat' is the first half of the eleventh century. The 'Waterstraat boat' could be somewhat younger, probably from the second half of the twelfth century. So the full size Utrecht type was probably a feature of the period AD 1000 to AD 1200.

These dates also rule out any direct relations with the depicted seagoing ships on Carolingian coins from Dorestad and the ship drawings of the famous 'Utrecht Psalter'. Though the predecessors of the Utrecht type will have been around in that period and geographical location in the form of extended dug-out canoes of various sizes.

CONSIDERATIONS ABOUT THE 'UTRECHT TYPE'

Given the above description of the 'Utrecht type' based on the two vessels that are recorded, we can proceed with the interpretation of the type e.g.: to what tradition can the Utrecht type be connected? Why are they found around Utrecht? Who built them and who used them and for what purpose?

In nautical archaeological literature it is stated that the Utrecht type could be the predecessor of the illustrious hulk, the voluminous bulk freighter of the late Medieval period. The hulk is known from illustrations and historical sources but no definitely determined wreck has been found so far. The hulk was a seagoing vessel for the Baltic and North Sea and had a 'tubby' shape with round planking on stem and stern for maximum loading capacity. This is absolutely not the case with the Utrecht type.

Stem and stern were raised above the water-line and cargo could only be placed in the middle. No structural detail can be connected to further development of seagoing vessels of the hulk type.

Instead of looking forward in development, it probably suits better to look backwards to evaluate the Utrecht type in its context. The Utrecht type formed the ultimate development of the ubiquitous logboat, known to exist since prehistory, starting with the logboat from Pesse which is dated in the sixth or seventh millennium BC. So the Utrecht boat rather marks the end of a development in local rivercraft production with minimal means. It constitutes a traditional product, that makes optimal use of the materials at hand, as the variation in details shows.

Its distribution is regional as far as we now know, but though the two finds were made in Utrecht these vessels are probably made somewhere in Germany. The German dendrochronological sequences provide the best fit to the curves of the samples taken. So the vessels probably both ended up in Utrecht in the eleventh century floating downstream on the river system with an unknown cargo.

At that time Utrecht was a major staple and trading place in north-west Europe with trade links to England. The boats of the Utrecht type could have played some part in Utrecht's eastern branch of trading, but other types of ships must have taken part in the western trade link across the sea.

POSTSCRIPT

A few years ago a monument to this boat was erected, constituting the only memorial to an archaeological shipwreck in the Netherlands.

BIBLIOGRAPHY

R. Vlek, *The Mediaeval Utrecht boat*, BAR International series 382, National Maritime Museum Greenwich, No. 11 (Oxford 1987).

R. Vlek, Van zolderschuit tot kelderschip, *Flevobericht*, nr 280 (Lelystad 1987), 39–43.

D. P. Snoep, *Het Utrechtse schip* (Utrecht 1980) (Brochure Centraal Museum).

T. J. Hoekstra, *Schepen met geld* (Utrecht 1976).

T. J. Hoekstra, Note on the ancient ship found in Utrecht, *International Journal of Nautical Archaeology* 4.1 (1975), 390–92.

J. P. W. Philipsen, The Utrecht Ship, *Mariners Mirror 51* (1965), 35–46.

E. P. von der Porten, The Utrecht boat, *Mariners Mirror 49* (1963), 50–51.

P. H. van der Wijk, Beschouwingen over het Utrechtse schip, *Jaarboek Oud Utrecht* (1933), 28–47.

A. Köster, De Utrechtse scheepsvondst, *Maandblad Oud Utrecht 7*, nr 5 (1932), 36–37.

P. H. van der Wijk, Een merkwaardige Sinterklaasverrassing, *Maandblad Oud Utrecht 5*, nr 12 (1930), 89–93.

The invention of a notion: on the historiography of the churches of Bishop Bernold and the cross of churches in Utrecht

by Lex Bosman

Developments in science in the twentieth century seem to grow at an ever faster pace. Changes and developments in the history of architecture on the other hand often take decades instead of months, but can look very impressive in retrospect. Ideas about building dates, related types of architecture and their origins, or the reasons why particular buildings came into existence, are often only adopted after scholarly battles have been fought. The next generation of scholars most often studies the results, not the genesis of these thoughts. The risk of such a process may of course, be, that newly accepted elements in architectural history are more or less taken for granted, instead of being tested over and over again.

Although most students of the history of Dutch medieval architecture are well aware of the fact that many of our romanesque churches reveal more of their nineteenth-century appearances than of their medieval origins, few of us fully realize how art history, and therefore architectural history, is largely formed by the nineteenth century. We still owe it to that century that we have a system of classification of the material we work with, however obsolete this sequence of styles within regions or countries has become. In the case of the romanesque chapter churches in Utrecht, and those in Deventer and Emmerich (now Germany, but once part of the diocese of Utrecht), the indebtedness to the pioneers of Dutch architectural history is of considerable interest. We will focus our attention on those buildings which form part of the cross of churches in this city, and on those which are referred to in modern literature as the churches of Bishop Bernold (1027–54). Both groups largely, but not completely, overlap.

In a description, published in 1758 as part of a series of descriptions of the provinces of the Netherlands, the church of St Peter's in Utrecht is mentioned as the first of the chapter churches in this town, second only to the cathedral (Fig. 1). Bishop Bernold is mentioned as its patron, but no details about the architecture are given. The same goes for the second chapter church in the sequence, that of St John's.[1] So only the common patron of these two churches, Bishop Bernold, was known to the anonymous author, but similarities in the architecture of the buildings were still beyond the horizon of eighteenth-century knowledge and, indeed, interest. Not surprisingly so, since understanding of what is commonly called romanesque architecture in general, was very limited in Europe at that time. Furthermore it should be mentioned, that the series of which the volume cited is a part, was intended to publish what was known about the history of the provinces of the Dutch Republic and its cities, with strong emphasis on its institutions.

Almost a century later, we find different statements about the churches in Utrecht. The first one to study the history of medieval architecture in the Netherlands, as irrespective of existing prejudice or tradition as possible in the decades before and after the middle of the nineteenth century, was F. N. M. Eyck van Zuylichem. In several publications he described ground-plans, characteristics and details of medieval churches in the Netherlands and gave the first classification of Dutch medieval architecture. For

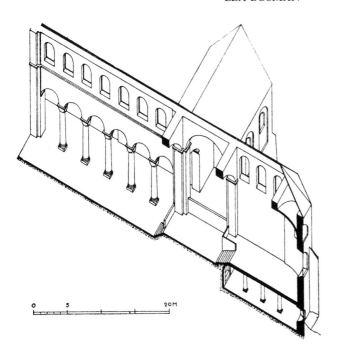

Fig. 1.   Utrecht, St Peter's.
Reconstruction of the eleventh-
century building (Ter Kuile 1959)

more than a century his observations were cited in scholarly literature. The differences
between Roman and Romanesque architecture for instance, in his time a rather tricky
problem, was made considerably clearer by Eyck van Zuylichem.[2] In 1849 this pioneer
of architectural history published a lengthy article, although entitled *Short survey*, on
medieval churches in the Netherlands, in which the basis of the group of Bernold-
churches can be found. Similarities between the churches of St Peter and St John in
Utrecht are keenly observed: ground-plan, the clerestory walls, the windows. Of the
church of St Lebuin in Deventer Eyck had noticed, that its choir and crypt bear strong
resemblances to St Peter's. The same ground-plan of a crypt was found by Eyck in St
Martin's at Emmerich (Fig. 2). Because of differences in the forms of the columns and
capitals in the Emmerich crypt, he suggested a somewhat later date for this building
than for the churches in Utrecht and Deventer: Emmerich could date from the late
eleventh or early twelfth century.[3] Noteworthy here is the method Eyck van Zuylichem
used: the ground-plan of St Martin's showed its connection with Utrecht, while the
presumed later building date was suggested by details, the columns and capitals. The
crypts of St Peter's in Utrecht and of St Lebuin's at Deventer do indeed look more alike,
not so much in their ground-plans — which stem from the same root as the ground-
plan of Emmerich — but in the form of the columns, where shafts are used with spiral
decoration. For a pioneer these observations were not at all a bad start.

  Interestingly, Eyck tried to assign another building to Bishop Bernold, the church of
St Plechelm at Oldenzaal. Here it was the simplicity of the exterior that made Eyck van
Zuylichem suggest a building date during the episcopate of Bernold. Nevertheless, he
was felt compelled to admit that this church of St Plechelm's showed more features of
what he called 'foreign' churches, than of the churches built by bishop Bernold in

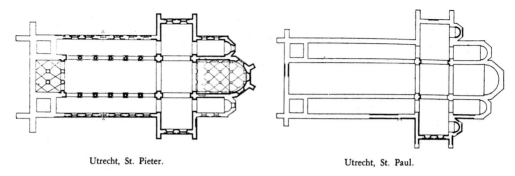

Utrecht, St. Pieter.   Utrecht, St. Paul.

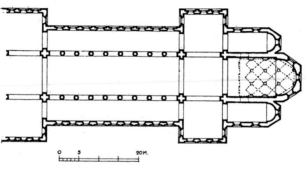

Deventer, St. Lebuinus.

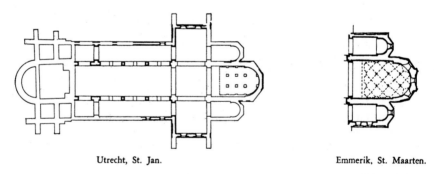

Utrecht, St. Jan.   Emmerik, St. Maarten.

FIG. 2. Reconstruction (1959) of ground-plans of the churches of Bishop Bernold (Ter Kuile 1959)

Utrecht.[4] A trace of nationalistic feelings about the architecture can be read in this
remark, no exception of course in the nineteenth century.

In a book published in 1858, Eyck van Zuylichem took up most of his thoughts on
Dutch medieval architecture, and tried to classify the material into chronological
periods. Here attention is focused on Romanesque architecture, which was divided into

three main periods. The first group contains churches dating before the eleventh century. Of this group only one still existed, the octagonal chapel at Nijmegen, which 'undoubtedly' dated from the time of Charlemagne, a date later rejected.[5] A second group was centred around the activity of Bishop Bernold in the first half of the eleventh century. The style of this architecture was dominated by plain arches, according to Eyck. St Peter's at Utrecht is cited as the best example of the architectural style of this period. Again, Oldenzaal is incorporated into the Bernold-group, while the crypt at Emmerich was dated half a century later than the other churches built by Bernold. Using style as a tool by which to classify material, Eyck van Zuylichem attributed to Bishop Bernold the predecessor of the existing church of St Michael's, Zwolle, relying on the archaic, simple style of the tympanum with Abraham, reused in the eastern part of this church. There were indeed connections between the famous bishop and this church, but its eleventh-century appearance is as unknown to us as it was to Eyck.[6] Finally the third group of buildings was described by Eyck van Zuylichem as featuring a transitional style, dating mainly from the twelfth century into the thirteenth.

To summarize, it is fair to say, that Eyck van Zuylichem published the first attempts to classify medieval Dutch architecture according to its style, resulting in a few main categories, with which he followed examples given in other countries. Architectural details were used to define the date of building, but written sources were consulted as well. An attempt was also made to define a certain geographical group of Dutch medieval churches as opposed to foreign architecture, as becomes clear in the description of Oldenzaal. Again, Eyck van Zuylichem followed foreign authors, in that important period in the nineteenth century, when the classification of architecture was the main concern of architectural historians.[7] Eyck formulated the group of Bernold-churches focusing on the two churches in the city of Utrecht, St Peter's and St John's, with which St Lebuin's at Deventer was closely and St Martin's at Emmerich more loosely connected. St Plechelm's at Oldenzaal was attributed to Bernold as well, although the architecture of this church showed far less the characteristics of the other four.

The main body of this group would remain intact to this day. I will just observe some of the changes in the definition of the group of Bernold-churches. To observe what Dutch architectural research has discovered from the days of Eyck van Zuylichem until well into the twentieth century, it is interesting to read Vermeulen's ambitious survey on the history of Dutch architecture, published in three parts and six volumes between 1928 and 1941. Oldenzaal had already been removed from the group of churches built by Bernold; it had become clear that this building dated from the twelfth rather than from the eleventh century. No longer its austere exterior, but the ground-plan and architectural details were the elements of later research.[8] Emmerich did not receive much attention in Vermeulen's book, and while nowhere in his treatise is it denied that St Martin's belonged to the Bernold-churches, no argument in favour of this idea is given either. However, a third church of Bernold in Utrecht was granted some attention, the church of the former abbey of St Paul's. Towards the end of the sixteenth century this complex was demolished and merely a part of a transept wall remains to be admired. St Lebuin's at Deventer continued to be firmly attached to the Bernold-churches in Utrecht. The arguments are scattered throughout the book: thus the ground-plans of the crypts are discussed in a section on crypts, the columns and capitals in a section on ornamentation.[9] In this way many kinds of architectural elements are examined by Vermeulen together with their supposed origins, before a geographic classification is given. Only in this last section is mention made of the patron, bishop Bernold of Utrecht. Of course this is a result of the arrangement of the book, an arrangement quite common at the time of publication. The need for classifying data still obscured other issues, later to be found essential.

Still, even after the preliminary arrangement of the material within the framework of the sequence of styles quite a few problems remained to be solved. Since the choir of the church of St John in Utrecht was rebuilt in the first half of the sixteenth century, relatively little was known about the original appearance of that part of the building. The plan of St Paul's remained entirely to be investigated, while at the radically rebuilt churches of St Lebuin at Deventer and of St Martin at Emmerich medieval and later alterations still obscured much of their original layout. Meanwhile, the patron himself was rather shadowy as a person: where did he come from? What positions had Bernold held before he was made a bishop? Was the place or region where he was educated of importance for a better understanding of the architecture of his churches? Some of these questions were tackled in the decades after the publication of Vermeulen's study.

Ozinga summarized in 1949 what was known then about Bernold's churches. He followed the established idea of a group of churches built by this bishop sharing some common characteristics, like the crypts of St Peter's, St Lebuin's and St Martin's or the exteriors of St Peter's and St John's.[10] Important new material was found during the course of archaeological investigations in St John's and at the site of the former church of St Paul in 1948 and 1949. The ground-plan of the eleventh-century choir of St John's was revealed, which proved the great resemblance of this church to St Peter's. The plan was the same, with small differences in dimension. A reconstruction of the ground-plan of St Paul's could be drawn after archaeological examination. Both similarities and differences with the other two churches of Bernold in Utrecht came to light: the choir not only had two smaller chapels at either side, but in addition to that there were two small apsidioles, to be entered from the transept as well. A few years later more details were revealed about St Peter's, after which the results were published by Temminck Groll.[11]

In 1949 an attempt was also made to describe Bishop Bernold's background, in an article by Lieftinck.[12] He proposed a theory about Bernold, as supposedly originating from Germany and, perhaps recruited from the circle around the German King Conrad II. Real proof was lacking however. Despite the hypothetical character of these thoughts, they were used as guide-lines for research in the field of architectural history. Since the rows of columns between nave and aisles were considered as one of the main characteristics of Bernold's architecture — although still existing in only one of his five churches — the supposed background in southern Germany and the idea of a column basilica were brought together.[13] The churches with rows of columns at the Reichenau and in Einsiedeln were thus seen as possible models for Bernold's churches. This idea could not really be squared with the ground-plan of the choirs: the choir flanked by smaller chapels, each ending in an apsidiole, was not found in south Germany, but is usually labelled 'Cluniac'. Observations of this nature were published in 1959 by Ter Kuile.[14] Although some of his thoughts no longer hold, his article remains valuable because of his attempt to consider Bernold's churches in an international context, in a more thorough way than did Vermeulen.

Some of Bishop Bernold's churches were made the subject of monographs. Research done during the much needed restoration of St John's in the seventies resulted in new facts. The most important of these was, that it could now be proved that the nave and aisles of this church were originally also divided by two rows of columns, later altered into piers on rectangular bases. Some of these piers still hid the eleventh-century circular column within. This of course made the case for the definition of the Bernold-church as a column basilica much stronger. Van Wezel published an accurate article on the building history of this church.[15] After a thorough restoration of St Peter's in Utrecht, Temminck Groll published an article with detailed information about the building history of this church.[16] St Martin's at Emmerich also received more attention; during an extensive campaign to restore this mutilated church, the architect carefully examined the eleventh-century structure and later published his results.[17] Already early this century the restoration of St Lebuin's at Deventer led to a publication with a reconstruction of the eleventh-century building. Later, it was Ter Kuile who published a new reconstruction, which was replaced only recently in a new study by a group of scholars.[18]

In 1988 the study of the churches of Bishop Bernold, of the older cathedral and of Bernold himself was given new impetus as a result of a joint effort between historians and architectural historians, at a congress concerned with these themes. In her paper the historian Van Winter firmly attacked Lieftinck's till then uncontested theory about Bernold's background. She argued instead in favour of an older tradition, in which Bernold appears as chaplain in the Dutch town of Oosterbeek, before being called to the high position of bishop. As with Lieftinck's, her hypothesis lacks conclusive evidence: neither can really be proven. However, it seems of importance to me that research has stopped focusing attention on the south of Germany, in search of models for the type of Bernold's column basilica. Parallel with Van Winter's observations on Bernold's origins, Mekking broke away from the old path to southern Germany and tried to locate the models for specific architectural elements elsewhere: Limburg a. d. Haardt and Ravenna.[19] In his opinion it was not just Bishop Bernold who decided on the concept of the churches in Utrecht, Deventer and Emmerich, but the involvement of Emperor Henry III seems to have been significant. While the group of Bernold-churches itself remained firmly established for decades, a new theory was launched only recently, adding a sixth church to the five. The convincing and carefully composed reconstruction of the original structure of the church of St Walburga at Zutphen shows a striking resemblance to the main characteristics of the five other churches: a basilica based on a Latin cross, side chapels flanking the main choir and giving access to the crypt, the specific ending of the apses, half-round on the interior and polygonal at the exterior.[20] If only Eyck van Zuylichem, so eager to find traces of Bernold's building activity, could have known this addition to the group!

With these contributions the most recent phase of scholarly work is reached, but the other important question now deserves some remarks. Let us shift our attention then to the cross of churches in the city of Utrecht. Three of the Bernold-churches already mentioned belong to this cross: to the north of the cathedral St John's was built, to the east St Peter's — where Bishop Bernold was buried — and to the south St Paul's. A few decades after Bernold's death in 1054, in the last quarter of the eleventh and the first half of the twelfth century, St Mary's arose to the west.[21] In Dutch and in international literature this specific arrangement of four churches around the cathedral, in the form of a cross, is mentioned quite often and is evidently well known, in the Netherlands as well as abroad. In 1962 for instance the German art historian Günter Bandmann mentioned the Utrecht cross of churches as one example among a few others of a lay-out with specific symbolism, in an article dealing with the meaningful placing of altars in medieval churches. Ten years later the same author discussed the meaning of pre-Gothic architecture as representations of the Heavenly City and referred to the cruciform arrangement of churches in order to reproduce the same meaning.[22] For Bandmann, one of the pioneers of the iconography of architecture, not only was the symbolical meaning of the cross important, but the arrangement of well-chosen patron saints around the cathedral, establishing an ideal of the Heavenly City on earth was essential as well.

Utrecht also appears, together with the German cities of Hildesheim, Paderborn and Fulda, as an example of a cross of churches in the respectable *Lexikon der christlichen Ikonographie* in the section about the cross as a symbolic form in architecture.[23]

In these references the Utrecht cross of churches was merely mentioned as an example, but its concept was not elaborated upon. The symbolic meaning of the Utrecht cross of churches, as well as of some other examples, was recognized by Peeters in 1966, but his article dealt with the oldest episcopal churches in Utrecht, so the paragraph on the cruciform layout of the eleventh-century chapter churches isn't much more than a footnote.[24] The idea of the unusual situation of the cross of churches in Utrecht has cropped up in writings on varied aspects of the history of medieval architecture, although no literary tradition about this concept can be traced. The anonymous eighteenth-century author mentioned at the outset of this essay, wasn't aware of architectural details of Bernold's churches, let alone the cross of churches. Nor did the nineteenth-century architectural historian Eyck van Zuylichem make any mention of it. Aimed at classifying the architecture in periods and regions, the position of the Bernold-churches in Utrecht amidst their built surroundings, or their specific position in relation to each other, were matters not yet dealt with in general, in writings on architectural history in his time.

Being well-acquainted in our time with the concept we can easily recognize the cross of churches on a city-map of Utrecht. But one could assume that quite some time ago someone, for some reason gazing at a map of Utrecht, suddenly realized that the sites of the four churches around the cathedral were well-chosen, rather than that these churches were haphazardly scattered around the eleventh-century city. I believe this person can be identified as S. Muller, a famous and very productive archivist and historian in Utrecht in the last quarter of the nineteenth and the first quarter of the twentieth century. Muller wrote numerous books and articles on different aspects of the history of Utrecht, so he was familiar with historical outlines and details as well. Probably inspired by literature on the cross of churches in German Paderborn and on the rudimentary layout in Münster, Muller mentioned the cross of churches in his own city, initiated by Bishop Bernold, in a footnote to an article on the church of St Saviour in Utrecht, which was demolished in the late sixteenth century.[25] He tried to provide a reconstruction both of the history and of the building of St Saviour, and followed its history up to Bernold's episcopate. As a side effect of his reading, to compare the historical situation of Utrecht with that of other cities, Muller was launched on a track which led to his 'discovery' of the cross of churches. The idea was repeated in the introduction to his book of 1911 on old houses in Utrecht. As parallels once more he named Paderborn and Münster, but he did not have much more to say about this concept.[26] The place of Muller's remarks on the specific topographic situation in Utrecht is not as peculiar as it may seem. Interested as he was in differences between old houses in several parts of the city, he must have noticed that these differences could partly have been caused by the fact that some of the houses were built in former immunities of the chapters. Also in more recent literature the effects of the plots in the immunities, on the type of houses are generally recognized.[27]

It would take a few decades however before Muller's crucial thought of the cross of churches was taken up again, although we can assume that the idea itself has become widespread. While Vermeulen merely mentioned the cruciform arrangement of the churches around the cathedral, in 1939 the Utrecht cross of churches was taken as a starting-point for a comparison of the early topographic development of Paderborn and Utrecht.[28] Rather than study the symbolic implications of the cruciform arrangement of the four churches around the cathedral and those of the dedications, the author described the early development of Utrecht as a bishop's city. A few more parallels were mentioned by Haslinghuis: Fulda, Corvey, Werden and Bamberg, as well as Münster and Paderborn.[29]

Though not discussing Utrecht in detail, it was probably Bandmann who brought this example into the context of architectural symbolism in general and the symbolic meaning of the intended arrangement of altars in churches and of church buildings themselves.[30] Bandmann had already published his book and several articles dealing with crucial aspects of the iconography of medieval architecture, while other authors contributed their parts to this interesting field of study.[31] In his still important book on medieval architecture as a bearer of meaning Bandmann did not refer to the concept of the cross of churches, although some paragraphs come close to doing so. Wolfgang Braunfels, in his book on medieval cities in Tuscany, discussed the possibilities of city walls as symbols and of the recreation of the models both of Rome and of the Heavenly City in medieval towns and cities.[32] Possibly such notions encouraged Bandmann to interpret the crosses of churches in a similar way as he had done with single buildings.

With the publication of Herzog's study on the Ottonian city the matter was approached from a different angle. Not limiting himself to either the topography, or to several branches of history, or even to art history, Herzog tried to use and incorporate as many possible keys to a better understanding of the genesis and development of medieval cities. A ring of churches allowed a looser arrangement of churches, of monasteries and chapters around the cathedral, and Herzog mentioned quite a number of examples. As a specific form of the ring of churches Herzog, described the cross of churches and called Utrecht the most regular example of this concept.[33] So now the Utrecht cross of churches could be recognized as bearer of meaning, and its importance for the creation and development of the city from the eleventh century onward had become more obvious. Still, it was only in 1988 — at the congress mentioned above — that finally the full content of meanings was studied in a variety of ways. Aart Mekking searched for answers to relatively simple though highly important questions: when was it decided to create the cross of churches in Utrecht? What would have been the occasion that triggered this building activity? Who could be seen as patron: only the well-known Bishop Bernold or others as well? Why was the form of a cross decided on? What did it mean to the patrons?[34]

No easy answers were at hand, but comparison with the similar layout in Paderborn and Bamberg helped Mekking to formulate his interpretation. Only in these three cities of Bamberg, Paderborn and Utrecht was the cross of churches planned, though not always completed, while in other places an existing situation was converted into a cruciform arrangement. The death of the Emperor Conrad II in 1039 in Utrecht caused his son and successor Henry III to honour and commemorate him with the building of the cross of churches to shield Conrad II's heart, buried in the cathedral, against evil forces. Bishop Bernold's role in this enterprise was less crucial in Mekking's point of view than had hitherto been assumed. The seemingly obvious reference to Rome in the choice of patron saints — Peter, Paul, John and Mary — was denied by Mekking, a matter that could well be discussed again. I don't believe it to be necessary that, as Mekking stated, St Peter's, should show a distinct feature of the famous Constantinian basilica of St Peter's in Rome, other than the rows of columns.[35] The example of Utrecht, as well as others, as a cross of churches richly laden with symbolical meaning recently appeared again in another context, that of the layout of Liège in the last decades of the tenth and the first decade of the eleventh century, interpreted as an architectural copy not only of Jerusalem, but bearing associations to Rome and Aachen as well.[36]

The development of the study of the churches of Bishop Bernold and of the cross of churches in Utrecht mirror the changes in art history in general since the early nineteenth century. Following the model of such famous architectural historians as Arcise de Caumont, Eyck van Zuylichem described the framework for Dutch medieval architecture. The sequence of styles, the supposed regional features, led among much more to the formulation of the group of Bernold-churches, to which later St Paul's in Utrecht and St Martin's at Emmerich were added, and possibly even St Walburga's at Zutphen. Half a century after Eyck it was Muller who, studying other historical questions, recognized the cross of churches. But in a period when classifying the material was still prominent in Dutch architectural history, the comparison of forms and tracing forms to their alleged origins left alone other important questions. It was only in the last thirty or so years that new impulses were given to this field of study by bringing the cross of churches as well as the individual buildings Bishop Bernold commissioned into the iconography of architecture. No longer is the careful study of forms a goal in itself, but a necessary step in the process to gain answers to other questions, dealing with the meaning of architecture and the intentions of the patrons. Seen from this point of view the examples described above reflect the development of Dutch architectural history in an interesting manner. Learning what the aims and limits of the research of our older predecessors were, can be an inspiration in deepening our understanding of medieval architecture.

SHORTENED TITLES USED

Bandmann (1951) Günter Bandmann, *Mittelalterliche Architektur als Bedeutungsträger* (Berlin 1951).

Bouwen en duiden (1994) *Bouwen en duiden. Studies over architectuur en iconologie*, ed. E. den Hartog a.o. (Alphen a.d. Rijn 1994).

Bulletin KNOB Bulletin van de Koninklijke Nederlandse Oudheidkundige Bond.

Eyck van Zuylichem (1849) F. N. Eyck van Zuylichem, 'Kort overzigt van den bouwtrant der middeleeuwse kerken in Nederland', *Berigten van het Historisch Gezelschap te Utrecht*, Vol. 2, 1st part (1849), 67–146.

Fillitz & Pippal (1985) eds, Hermann Fillitz & Martina Pippal *Akten des XXV. Internationalen Kongresses für Kunstgeschichte Wien. Vol. 3: Sektion 3 Probleme und Methoden der Klassifizierung*, Vienna/Cologne/Graz 1985.

Herzog (1964) Erich Herzog, *Die ottonische Stadt. Die Anfänge der mittelalterlichen Stadtbaukunst in Deutschland* (Berlin 1964).

Mekking (1988) Aart J. J. Mekking, 'Een kruis van kerken rond Koenraads hart', *Utrecht kruispunt* (1988), 21–53.

Mekking (1992) Aart J. J. Mekking, ed., *De Grote of Lebuïnuskerk te Deventer* (Clavis Kunsthistorische Monografieën 11) (Utrecht/Zutphen 1992).

Ter Kuile (1959) E. H. ter Kuile, 'De kerken van bisschop Bernold', *Bulletin KNOB* 58 (1959), 145–64.

Utrecht kruispunt (1988) *Utrecht kruispunt van de middeleeuwse kerk. Voordrachten gehouden tijdens het congres ter gelegenheid van tien jaar Mediëvistiek Faculteit der Letteren Rijksuniversiteit te Utrecht 25 tot en met 27 augustus 1988* (Clavis Kunsthistorische Monografieën 7) (Zutphen 1988).

Vermeulen (1928) F. A. J. Vermeulen, *Handboek tot de geschiedenis der Nederlandsche bouwkunst*, Vol. 1 ('s-Gravenhage 1928).

REFERENCES

1. *Tegenwoordige Staat der Vereenigde Nederlande, elfde deel, behelzende eene beschryving van de provincie van Utrecht* (Amsterdam 1758), 371–72.

2. See for instance: Raphaël Rijntjes, 'De heidense kapel te Utrecht', *Bouwen en duiden* (1994), 207–18.

3. Eyck van Zuylichem (1849), 83–85, 87, 91–92.

4. Eyck van Zuylichem (1849), 85–86.

5. F. N. M. Eyck van Zuylichem, *Les eglises romanes du Royaume des Pays-Bas* (Utrecht 1859), 6. Nowadays this small building is commonly dated to the eleventh century, cf. J. J. F. W. van Agt, 'De Sint-Nicolaaskapel op het Valkhof', *Het Valkhof te Nijmegen* (Nijmegen 1980), 53–58; Matthias Untermann, *Der Zentralbau im Mittelalter* (Darmstadt 1989), 131–32.

6. The date of the tympanum is still somewhat controversial. For a discussion of the iconography see: Elizabeth den Hartog, 'Kinderen van God, kroost van Abraham. De iconografie van het Abraham-tympaan te Zwolle', *Bouwen en duiden* (1994), 147–61.

7. Cf. Willibald Sauerländer, 'From Stilus to Style: Reflections on the Fate of a Notion', *Art History* 6 (1983), 253–70; Peter Lasko, 'The Concept of Regionalism in French Romanesque', Fillitz & Pippal (1985), 17–25; Willibald Sauerländer, 'Die Geographie der Stile', Fillitz & Pippal (1985), 27–35.

8. Vermeulen (1928), 336.

9. Vermeulen (1928), 189, 198, 307–08, 315–17.

10. M. D. Ozinga, *De romaanse kerkelijke bouwkunst* (Amsterdam 1949), 84–88.

11. C. L. Temminck Groll, 'De vroeg-romaanse kerken van Utrecht', *Bulletin KNOB* 58 (1959), 35–50.

12. G. I. Lieftinck, 'De herkomst van bisschop Bernold van Utrecht (1027–1054)', *Jaarboekje Oud-Utrecht* 1949, 23–40.

13. Vermeulen (1928), 181, already pointed to southern Germany.

14. Ter Kuile (1959), 145–46; Vermeulen (1928), 189. For the churches on the Reichenau cf. Alfons Zettler, *Die frühen Klosterbauten der Reichenau* (Sigmaringen 1988), esp. 263–85; Wolfgang Erdmann, *Die Reichenau im Bodensee. Geschichte und Kunst* (Königstein 1993).

15. G. W. C. van Wezel, 'De bouwgeschiedenis van de St.-Janskerk te Utrecht tot 1700', *Restauratie vijf hervormde kerken in de binnenstad van Utrecht*, Jaarverslag 6 (1979–1980–1981), 105–58.

16. C. L. Temminck Groll, 'De St.-Pieterskerk te Utrecht', *Bulletin KNOB* 81 (1982), 75–118.

17. Helmut Flintrop, *Die St. Martinikirche zu Emmerich. Ein Vorposten des Hochstiftes Utrecht* (Clavis Kunsthistorische Monografieën 10) (Utrecht/Zutphen 1992).

18. F. A. Hoefer, *De Sint-Lebuïnuskerk te Deventer naar onderzoekingen van W. te Riele Gzn.* (Haarlem [1902]); Ter Kuile (1959). For the modern reconstruction of the building history see: J. W. Bloemink, 'De bouwgeschiedenis van de kerk tot ca. 1450', Mekking (1992), 29–49; A. J. J. Mekking, 'Herkomst en betekenis van het concept en de hoofdvormen van de elfde-eeuwse kerk', Mekking (1992), 50–70.

19. J. M. van Winter, 'Bisschop Bernold, afkomst en persoonlijkheid', *Utrecht kruispunt* (1988), 9–20; A. J. J. Mekking, 'De zogenoemde Bernold-kerken in het Sticht Utrecht. Herkomst en betekenis van hun architectuur', *Utrecht tussen kerk en Staat*, ed. R. E. V. Stuip & C. Vellekoop (Hilversum 1991), 103–51; Aart J. J. Mekking, 'Die ottonische Tradition in der Architektur des ehemaligen Herzogtums Lothringens im 11. Jahrhundert', *Productions et Échanges artistiques en Lotharingie médiévale* (Actes des 7es Journées Lotharingiennes) ed. Jean Schroeder (Luxemburg 1994), 65–80.

20. Aad Bastemeijer, 'De zesde kerk van bisschop Bernold van Utrecht. Oorsprong en betekenis van de St.-Walburgskerk te Zutphen', *Madoc. Tijdschrift over de middeleeuwen* 9 (1995), 8–20.

21. H. M. Haverkate and C. J. van der Peet, *Een kerk van papier. De geschiedenis van de voormalige Mariakerk te Utrecht* (Clavis Kunsthistorische Monografieën 2) (Utrecht/Zutphen 1985). St Mary's was finally demolished in the first half of the nineteenth century.

22. Günter Bandmann, 'Früh- und Hochmittelalterliche Altaranordnung als Darstellung', *Das erste Jahrtausend. Kultur und Kunst im werdenden Abendland an Rhein und Ruhr*, ed. Victor H. Elbern, Textvol. 1 (Düsseldorf 1962), 283–84; Günter Bandmann, 'Die vorgotische Kirche als Himmelsstadt', *Frühmittelalterliche Studien*, 6 (1972), 78–79.

23. See 'Kreuz', *Lexikon der christlichen Ikonographie*, Vol. 2, ed. Engelbert Kirschbaum (Rome etc. 1970), 588.

24. C. J. A. C. Peeters, 'De oudste bisschopskerken van Utrecht', *Feestbundel F. van der Meer* (Amsterdam/Brussels 1966), 75.

25. S. Muller, 'De St. Salvatorskerk te Utrecht. Een merovingische kathedraal', *Archief voor de geschiedenis van het aartsbisdom Utrecht* 25 (1898), 59 note 2. For Paderborn and Münster see: Herzog (1964), 102–15, 242–43.

26. S. Muller Fz., *Oude huizen te Utrecht* (Utrecht 1911), 8.

27. See Marceline J. Dolfin, E. M. Kylstra & Jean Penders, *Utrecht. De huizen binnen de singels* (De Nederlandse Monumenten van Geschiedenis en Kunst, Geïllustreerde Beschrijving. De provincie Utrecht. De gemeente Utrecht, Deel IIIA) ('s-Gravenhage 1989), Vol. 2, 6–8, 37–54.

28. Vermeulen (1928), 306; Daan Jansen, 'Utrecht en Paderborn. Bisschopssteden in hun vroegste ontwikkeling', *Jaarboekje Oud-Utrecht* 1939, 59–72.

29. E. J. Haslinghuis, *De Nederlandse Monumenten van Geschiedenis en Kunst. Geïllustreerde Beschrijving.* Deel II De provincie Utrecht, Eerste stuk: De gemeente Utrecht ('s-Gravenhage 1956), 16. For Fulda and Bamberg, see: Herzog (1964), 171–81, 250–51.

30. See note 18.

31. Bandmann (1951). For some notes on the historiography of iconology/iconography of medieval architecture, cf.: A. F. W. Bosman, *De Onze Lieve Vrouwekerk te Maastricht. Bouwgeschiedenis en historische betekenis van de oostpartij* (Clavis Kunsthistorische monografieën 9) (Utrecht/Zutphen 1990), 10–17; Lex Bosman, 'Speaking in stone. On the meaning of architecture in the Middle Ages', *Argumentation* 7 (1993), 15–17, 25–26; Lex Bosman, 'De Sensus Allegoricus van middeleeuwse gebouwen, of: architectuur-iconologie in historisch perspectief', *Bouwen en duiden* (1994), 1–14.

32. Bandmann (1951), 84 ff., 146–59; Wolfgang Braunfels, *Mittelalterliche Stadtbaukunst in der Toskana* (Berlin 1953), 45–50, 131–39.

33. Herzog (1964), 241–51, esp. 246–47.

34. Mekking (1988).

35. Mekking (1988), 40. Cf. Helmut Maurer, 'Kirchengründung und Romgedanke am Beispiel des ottonischen Bishofssitzes Konstanz', *Bischofs- und Kathedralstädte des Mittelalters und der frühen Neuzeit*, ed. Franz Petri (Cologne/Vienna 1976), 47–59.

36. E. den Hartog, *Romanesque Architecture and Sculpture in the Meuse Valley* (Leeuwarden/Mechelen 1992), 33–55.

A Cross of Churches Around Conrad's Heart:
An analysis of the function and symbolism of the Cross of Churches in Utrecht, and those of Bamberg and Paderborn*

by Aart J. J. Mekking

THE FOUNDATION OF THE CROSS OF CHURCHES IN UTRECHT: THE HISTORICAL SETTING OF THE FOUNDATION AND ITS PATRONS

'In the year 1039 after the incarnation of Our Lord', emperor (1027–39) Conrad (II), seeing that nearly everything in his kingdom was going according to his wishes, was celebrating holy Whitsun (June 3) in Utrecht, a city in Friesland, in the confidence that his son — now that his kingship had become reality — might hope for the emperorship. As he strode to the table while celebrating the most holy festival in great splendour with his son and the empress, the crown on his head, he appeared in some pain which he nonetheless endured. When the following day the illness, which would prove fatal, struck violently and the bishops present in Utrecht gathered around his deathbed at his request, he had the body and blood of the Lord and the Sacred Cross with the relics of the saints brought to him. All in tears he raised himself up and received the last sacraments and the absolution of his sins through a pure and sincere confession and a fervent prayer that he carried out with the greatest possible humility. He thereupon bid farewell to the empress and to his son king Henry after having admonished him with all his heart. Then he died on (Whit) Monday, the fourth of June in the seventh indiction. The emperor's remains were interred in Utrecht and the king enriched the burial place with gifts and inalienable goods.'[1]

King from 1039 and emperor between 1046 and 1056, Henry III seems to have had a very strong bond with his father Conrad.[2] Perhaps for this reason he remained so well disposed towards Utrecht, the city in which his beloved father's remains were interred (Pl. VIA). No other king or emperor of the Holy Roman Empire visited as often the episcopal see to attend the solemn celebration of the great feasts there.[3] Henry's generosity towards the church of Utrecht is accounted for by a document of 21 May 1040: 'We have entrusted the entrails of our father to Martinus as a precious deposit, so that we are now in his debt'. This is followed with a list of the rich gifts bestowed upon the church of Bishop Bernold (1027–54).[4]

The entrails were regarded as the most important parts of the body. The source of all life was believed to be contained in the entrails. The heart, the most important of all entrails, was thought to be the seat of the soul and of the mind, which joined the soul to the body.[5] This may explain Henry's devotion to, and patronage of his father's final resting place; it was Henry's wish that his own heart and entrails be buried in his favourite place, at Goslar, his 'patria' and 'lar domesticus'.[6] The annals of Pöhlde describing Henry's death say that he on 5 October 1056, from his deathbed in Bodtfeld,

---

* Translated from Dutch by K. Ronnau-Bzadbeer

ordered that his remains be transferred to the imperial family's funerary oratory at Speyers.[7]

Just as the entrails of his father were deposited in a tomb before the high altar of the Utrecht Cathedral,[8] so Henry's heart and entrails were interred in front of the high altar of the monastery of Simon and Judas in Goslar,[9] which he himself founded. According to the annals of Pöhlde, Henry instructed that his heart be buried there, 'because his heart had always been there', but his heart also went out to the place where the heart of his emperor and father was interred.

The affection of Henry III for his father Conrad II of which the sources speak was, in my opinion, the impetus for the foundation of the cross of churches in Utrecht. It was not built around the oldest cathedral, the venerable Salvator, upon which the new churches depended.[10] Nor did the cathedral precinct lie in the centre of the cross. Rather it was the Cathedral of St Martin where the most important physical remains of the first Salic emperor lay which lay at the heart of the cross of churches. This configuration expresses Henry's design: to establish a cross of churches around Conrad's heart, just as his father's predecessor Henry II had himself buried at the centre of a cross of churches he founded for the purpose at Bamberg.

That the foundation of a cross of churches at Utrecht was carried out at the initiative of Henry III may be apparent from the consecration of altars to the king's chosen patron saints, Simon and Judas (Pl. VIB). One of the altars is preserved in the eleventh century cathedral, the other in the Pieterskerk. The latter is particularly significant as the Pieterskerk may have been the first in the sequence of churches to be built.

According to one tradition, the Pieterskerk in Utrecht was consecrated on 1 May 1048. This tradition (one of the very few that have a bearing on the time of construction of the eleventh-century church in Utrecht), fits well with the widelyaccepted belief that the cross of churches in Utrecht was founded shortly after 1039. The intervening period of seven or eight years must have been more than enough to build at least one church.[12]

Two passages from medieval texts suggest that Bishop Bernold himself was active in the establishment of a cross of churches in the 'capital' of his bishopric. The following statement, which must be dated to 1050 and which refers to the construction of the Paulusabdij (Paul's Abbey), appears in the earliest of two texts: '(. . .) I, the unworthy person of Bernold, bishop of the see of Utrecht, have had built a monastery in the southern part (meridiana plaga) of this same city'.[13] One could infer from the choice of words used to describe the location of the Paulusabdij, that the author's conception of the layout of the city is informed by its arrangement around the four cardinal points of the compass; churches built on these points had the effect of notionally dividing medieval cities into quarters.

The second passage, from the Ordinals of the Cathedral which is dated to 1200, deals with the first vespers of the evening before the feast of the Invention of the Cross (3 May). On this evening the canons of all the chapters joined in solemn procession to the cathedral in order to celebrate liturgical offices before the great reliquary-cross there.[14]

It appears to me that a connection may exist between this custom and the choice of the first of May (1048) for the consecration of the Pieterskerk. The intention may have been to move from the newly consecrated church to the Cathedral for vespers on the evening of 2 May to return to the Pieterskerk for the rites of the feast of the Invention of the Cross on 3 May.[15] The procession on the evening of 2 May, which continued in later centuries, was without doubt intended to express the close relationship between the collegiate churches and the cathedral in elaborate and public liturgy.

The most significant aspect of all this is, however, that both the procession and the consecration of the Pieterskerk were held on the most important feast of the cross in the western church's calendar, the Invention of the Cross. However, the choice of this feast for the consecration of the Pieterskerk is not accidental.[16] The ceremonies scheduled for the first three days of May 1048 mark not only the consecration of the Pieterskerk, but announce the official installation of the cross of churches in Utrecht.

The only 'hard' evidence for the existence of the cross of churches in Utrecht is provided by the four eleventh-century churches themselves. The Pieterskerk in the east, the Mariakerk in the west, the Janskerk in the north and the church of Paulus in the south stand at the four cardinal points around the cathedral, the axis of the cruciform configuration of churches.[17]

When Bishop Conrad (1076–99) added the Mariakerk, and so completing the arrangement, he fulfilled the plan initiated under Bishop Bernold.[18] Even the consecration of the new church to the mother of Christ, Mary, was based on a criteria established by Bernold. Mary had been one of the patron saints of the old cathedral church of Salvator which, as we have already seen, provided the dedications of the three other churches which formed the 'cross'.

That Bishop Bernold presided over the foundation of the other three churches has long been accepted, and for good reason. That king Henry III has also to be considered as the chief patron can, in my opinion, be supported not only from the evidence outlined above, but also on the basis of the wider implications of the choice of such a plan and the forms of the individual churches.[19]

CROSSES OF CHURCHES

Only two other instances of programmes for the creation of crosses of churches are known from the Holy Roman Empire — at Bamberg and Paderborn. The imperial implications of these projects were resonant at Utrecht, and certainly provided the motive for the building of a cross of churches there. At Bamberg and Paderborn, as at Utrecht, the cathedral stood at the centre of a cross spanning the city, each of the four arms of which were marked by collegiate churches or cloisters.[21] In all three cases the construction of the cross of churches was begun in the first half of the eleventh century. In Bamberg and Paderborn the king of the Holy Roman Empire was active in the foundation and construction of the new churches.[22] This may also be the case in Utrecht. The three cities enjoyed similar status in the first half of the eleventh century: they are all episcopal seats with which the king had both personal concerns and a political interest in their position and livelihood.

With the exception of the complexes at Bamberg, Paderborn and Utrecht, all the other crosses of churches in the eleventh century Holy Roman Empire of a scale larger than that of a cathedral immunity or a monastic complex,[23] came into being through the restructuring and transformation of pre-existing churches.

Perhaps the earliest example of this kind is the so-called 'Kirchenkranz', which is interpreted as a reference to the Heavenly Jerusalem. It is assumed that the 'wreaths' of churches which lay around the cathedrals of Cologne and Strasbourg were transformed but not expressly built, to form crosses.

Similarly triangles of churches were arranged in symbolic reference to the Holy Trinity. Such a configuration of churches within the monastic enclosure at Fulda was modified to form a cross during the eleventh century.[25]

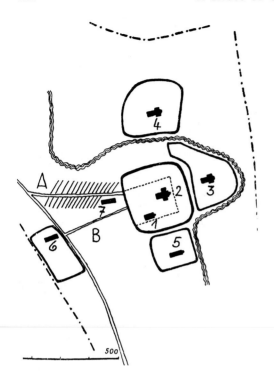

FIG. 1.   Utrecht, diagrammatic plan showing
the Cross of Churches: 1. St Salvator or Old
Minster; 2. Cathedral of St Maarten;
3. Pieterskerk; 4. Janskerk; 5. Pauluskerk;
6. Mariakerk; B. 'Via Triumphalis' or
'procession route of the Emperor' (from
E. Herzog, *Die ottonische Stadt* (Berlin 1964),
p. 150)

At Hildesheim a sequence of churches built around the cathedral in no apparent order was later fitted into a cross formation.[26]

THE CROSS AS IDEOGRAM

Just like the arrangement of churches at the vertexes of a hypothetical triangle, the position of churches at the extremities and the intersection of a hypothetical cruciform has to be interpreted as an ideogram. That is to say that the architectural patron expressly wanted to refer to one or more specific concepts with one or other configuration. The ideogram of the cruciform is much richer in referential meanings than that of the triangle which I must assume referred exclusively to the Holy Trinity and the related theological connotations.[27]

The cross of churches refers not only to specific elements of the Christian religious tradition but also to cosmology and politico-historical ideals and events. While the above-mentioned references to Christian theology are historically best characterized by the concept 'clerical-allegorical', the designation 'politico-allegorical' does most justice to the specifically medieval references to cosmology and politico-historical nature.[28]

In the medieval world the cruciform figuration is naturally associated with the cross of Christ. The monks and canons who inhabited the ecclesiastical institutions of the cross of churches in Paderborn were known as 'servants of the crucified'.[29]

The sign of the cross was first and foremost the standard of the triumphant Saviour who with it had conquered death and its cause, sin. Alongside this soteriological interpretation, the apotropeic power of the cross must not be overlooked.

In this case the sign of the cross is regarded as a defence against the powers of evil, particularly against those forces which threaten the salvation of the human soul. This talismanic magic effect of the Christian cross has its origins in pre-Christian cultures and may be derived from symbols of salvation found in prehistoric art. Closely related to the apotropeic power of the cross is its use in the consecration of a specific area. The ancient custom of creating a 'templum', an angle piece of heaven on earth, by using a cruciform was assumed by Christianity and prominently deployed in the laying out of churches, monastic complexes and other foundations which are earthly reflections of the heavenly Jerusalem.

As the most essential characteristic of the structure of the Heavenly City, the cross refers to the eschatology, the end of time when Christ will appear in heaven with the trophy of the cross and when the Heavenly Jerusalem will descend to earth to receive the righteous as the fellow citizens of God and his Saints. The written tradition surrounding the cross of Paderborn contains references to the eschatological significance of the arrangement of the churches.

Utrecht

In the first paragraph of this study, I tried to show that the occasion of the foundation of the cross of churches in Utrecht was the interment of the entrails of emperor Conrad III in the cathedral there. The cross of Bamberg was established along with its bishopric, and that of Paderborn is associated with the 'Renovatio' of the see there. Despite the different circumstances, the foundation of each of the three crosses enjoyed the harmonious co-operation of emperor and bishop and are perhaps best viewed against the political contexts in which they took place. Each project is associated with the élite patronage of the imperial court, be it on a central level as at Bamberg, or a regional level as at Paderborn and Utrecht.

THE CROSS OF CHURCHES: AN IMAGE OF THE CHURCH

At both Paderborn and Utrecht, one church in each sequence was appointed 'ecclesia mater'. At Paderborn the cathedral functioned as such; in Utrecht the rôle was assumed by the former episcopal church which was known by the name of 'Oldminster'. There is, however, one essential difference: at Paderborn, the main invocation was transferred from the cathedral to both the named churches; at Utrecht, however, each of the four churches were dedicated to one of the secondary patrons of the Oldminster (Pl. III).[33]

While at Paderborn the main patron of the newly-founded churches is the same though the church buildings themselves were quite different from each other, at Utrecht the opposite can be observed. As far as can be judged by their architecture, the churches dedicated to St Peter, St Paul and St John the Baptist had rather similar forms. The fact that the Mariakerk is an exception to this is undoubtedly a consequence of the fact that it was built some decades later, under the authority of a different emperor and bishop.

It is not only striking that the three churches built following the episcopal funerary — church dedicated to Peter display the same principal forms. It is equally remarkable

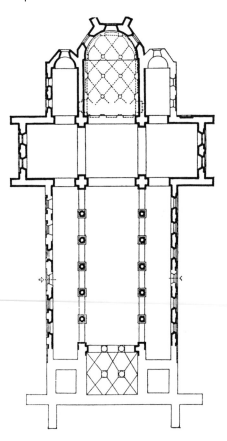

FIG. 2.   Utrecht, ground-plan of the Pieterskerk.
(From E. H. Ter Kuile, 'Kerken van bisschop
Bernold', *Bulletin Koninklijke Nederlandse
Oudheidkundige Bond* (1959), 145–264

that the Pieterskerk itself did not contain a single architectural reference to the St Peter's
in Rome in spite of its dedication (Fig. 2).

As Richard Krautheimer has already established, an outward resemblance between
two churches in the Middle Ages is no basis on which to identify the older church with
the newer one. For that purpose, a uniformity in dedication was apparently sufficient.[34]
Thus the Pieterskerk in Utrecht, in spite of the absence of architectural references to the
first St Peter's, Rome, par excellence, was regarded as the local version of the first
church in Christendom.

This is clear from an event which took place about thirty years after the dedication
of the church. In 1076, Bishop Willem — contrary to custom — celebrated the solemn
Easter mass not in the cathedral but in the Pieterskerk; this in spite of, or precisely
because of the fact that emperor Henry IV was present at the ceremony. The emperor
had heard the news of his excommunication by the pope some days before. Perhaps for
this reason he had Bishop Willem stage the solemn Easter rites in the church built as the
local representative of the papal basilica. Thus Henry and his leading cleric were able
visibly to appropriate the favour enjoyed by the bishops of Rome, the descendants and
heirs of St Peter; in this context Henry appears as Christ's appointed vicar on earth.
The same concept is apparent in a charter detailing the emperor's sponsorship of the

Pieterskerk, issued a short time later. In it Peter is called amongst other things 'defender of the kingdom and empire'.[35]

Another reason why the Pieterskerk in Utrecht may have been regarded as an image of the funerary oratory of the first bishop of Rome is the fact that the new church dedicated to Saint Peter became the episcopal funerary church. Thus each bishop is referentially associated with the successors of the Apostles. The church is then itself an embodiment of the universal ecclesiastical authority.

The position of the Pieterskerk at the eastern extremity of the cruciform may have underlined the role of the church as an expression of ecclesiastical authority. It corresponds with that of the eastern presbytery of the church building itself, which, in this period, was considered the architectural symbol of the priesthood.

Similarly the west end of the church, particularly of the 'Kaiserdome', was seen as a prominent architectural allegory of emperorship.[36] It is therefore perhaps no coincidence that — albeit more than forty years after the foundation of the other three churches — the emperor's church was built at the western extremity of the cross. That this was part of the original plan is clear from the dedication of the church and the form of its west end. The church was dedicated to the Virgin Mary. This dedication was often chosen for royal chapels and altars during the Middle Ages in both the Eastern and Western Empire. In the Holy Roman Empire, the association of the Virgin Mary with royal sanctuaries doubtless owes much to the fact of the dedication to Mary of Charlemagne's palace chapel at Aachen (Pl. Va).

Thus the church of St Mary at Utrecht was the coronation church of the emperor. From the coronation church the sovereign of the Holy Roman Empire, newly-clad in the vestments and regalia of imperial office, would process to the principal church to attend and participate in the solemn celebration of liturgy.[38] (Pl. VIb)

The fact that the Mariakerk in Utrecht, unlike the three other churches of the cross, was not built during the episcopate of Bernold makes clear that the concern for the construction of this church rested from the beginning not solely with the bishop, but with the king. The cause of the long delay in the completion of the scheme may lie in this consideration. The church may have had a low priority in the eyes of the sovereign or — and this possibility must certainly be considered seriously — it may be that royal plans for the Mariakerk were so ambitious that it may be that their execution ran up against great financial difficulties. The plans may have included not just a single church, but an entire complex of ecclesiastical, residential and service buildings, in short, a royal palace, as Labouchère has suggested.[39]

The fact that Henry IV king from 1056 and emperor between 1084 and 1105 finally became serious about the construction of the Mariakerk between 1085 and 1090 will have been a consequence not only of the political and strategic value that Utrecht had for him in this period, but is perhaps also to be especially good relationship he enjoyed with Conrad, bishop of Utrecht (1076–99), Conrad, to whom he entrusted the responsibility for the upbringing of his son and successor Henry V.[40]

A number of royal investment and coronation churches were built on the confines of a (pre)urban settlement. Such is the case with the Mariakerk. Sometimes a very straight and frequently wide thoroughfare linked the palace-chapel with the western entrance of the principle local church, usually a cathedral. At Utrecht, a broad and completely straight road which corresponds with the (noticeably long) western arm of the cross linked the Mariakerk with the gatehouse of the atrium of the Cathedral of Adelbold.[41]

There can be no doubt that this road — which more or less corresponds with the line of the present Servetstraat, Maartensbrug and Zadelstraat — was the most important route to the cathedral complex even before the planning of the cross of churches. It determined the line of the western arm of the cross of churches. The far western end of this road, the (junction) with the very old Springweg, was the logical place to erect the coronation church needed for ceremonial occasions.[42]

The analogy with the arrangement, parts and functions a church building, which lies at the basis of the concept of the cross of churches in Utrecht, emerges not only from the connection of the 'sacerdotium' of the church which formed the eastern arm to the 'regnum' at the end of the western arm. It is equally apparent from the strong mutual resemblance of the three churches completed by Bernold. An expression of the unity of the earthly church is presented by a number of similary-planned churches.

This symbolism may be associated with the ecclesiastical policy of the royal patron, Henry III. Henry's great achievement was to integrate church and state. This he achieved with the assistance of a number of reformist popes with whom he entered into new co-operation.[43]

The cross of churches in Utrecht expresses this newly wrought unity of the *ecclesia*, the worldly kingdom of God governed harmoniously by emperor and pope. Hence the reference to the church, and the '*regnum*' and '*sacerdotium*'. From its early Christian origin the church in its form articulates the concept of *ecclesia*.

The architectural arrangement of the churches may reveal the political motivation which lay behind the creation of a cross of churches in Utrecht. The churches have 'Ravennate', choirs, and 'Ravennate' niches (blind arcading) In the exterior walls of the naves. The façades have twin towers. The architectural vocabulary is derived from traditions of imperial church building (Fig. 2 and Pl. VIIA). These elements referred to the reformist emperorship.

The Ravennate elements seem to be taken in particular from the imperial abbey of Saint'Apollinare in Classe and refer to the reform of the monastic community there by Otto III, king from 983 and emperor from 997 to 1002, and Romuald (*c.* 950–1027), son of the duke of Ravenna.

Perhaps more important is the fact that, even before its reform by Henry III in 1046, the ecclesiastical architecture of the popeless alternative to Rome — as beloved Ravenna was regarded by the Ottonians and early Salians — could in no way be associated with the corrupt papacy which had been usurped by the Roman nobility. This same consideration undoubtedly accounts for the fact that the Pieterskerk in Utrecht makes no reference to Saint Peter's in Rome.

Two principle motives underlie the reception of elements of the architecture of Sant'Apollinare in Classe by the churches of Utrecht. Firstly, the process may be attributed to the first Salians, anxious to define themselves as descendants of the Ottonians. There was the greatest need for legitimation on the part of the new dynasty with respect to its founder, Conrad II. The tomb for his entrails in Utrecht was also surrounded by highly visible references to the Ottonian church in Classe.

Secondly, the sensational penance to which emperor Otto III submitted himself in this church during the spring of 1001 will have considerably increased the utility of its architecture in Henry's eyes. Henry, the uncompromising opponent of simony, knew all too well that his father Conrad was guilty of this 'heresy'. He thus sought to furnish his father's tomb with a highly-visible and referential symbol of faith, to reproduce in enduring, monumental form the great remorse shown by Conrad at his death and described by Wipo. Where Otto III performed his penance, Henry expressed his father's prayer for salvation in architecture.[45]

ACKNOWLEDGEMENTS

This article is a much shortened, updated summary of 'Een Kruis van kerken rond Koenraads hart. Een bijdrage tot de kennis van de functie en de symbolische betekenis van het Utrechtse Kerkenkruis alsmede van die te Bamberg en te Paderborn' by the same author. This article appeared in 1988 in the collection 'Utrecht Kruispunt van de middeleeuwse kerk. Voordrachten gehouden tijdens het congres ter gelegenheid van tien jaar Medievisitek Faculteit der Letteren Rijksuniversiteit te Utrecht 25 tot en met 27 augustus 1988' (Clavis Kunsthistorische Monografieen, VII, Zutphen, 1988).

SHORTENED TITLES USED

Balzer (1982)   M. Balzer, 'Zeugnisse fur das Selbstverständnis Bischof Meinwerks von Paderborn', *Tradition als Historische Kraft* (Berlin 1982).
Deutscher Aberglauben—*Handwörterbuch des deutschen Aberglaubens*, vols. 1–10, ed. H. Bachtold-Staubli and E. Hoffman-Krayer (reprint) Berlin 1987.
Bandmann (1962)   G. Bandmann, 'Mittelalterliche Altaranordnung als Darstellung', *Das Erste Jahrtausent-Kultur und Kunst im werdenden Abendland an Rhein und Ruhr*, ed. V. Elbern (Düsseldorf 1962), vol. 1, 371–411.
Binding (1986)   G. Binding, *Städtebau und Heilsordnung* (Düsseldorf 1986).
Haverkate en Van der Peet 1985   M. Haverkate en C.-J. van der Peet, *Een kerk van papier. De Geschiedenis van de voormalige Mariakerk te Utrecht*, (Clavis Kleine Kunsthistorische Monografieen vol. 2), (Zutphen, 1985).
Herzog (1964)   E. Herzog, *Die Ottonische Stadt* (Berlin 1964).
Jahrbücher   *Jahrbücher des deutschen Reichs unter Heinrich III*, ed. E. Steindorff (Jahrbucher der deutschen Geschichte vol. 1), Leipzig.
Kirschbaum (1970–76)   *Lexikon der christlichen Ikonographie*, ed. E. Kirschbaum (Rom, Freiburg 1970–76).
Ter Kuile (1959)   E. H. ter Kuile, 'De kerken van bisschop Bernold', *Bulletin van de Koninklandsche Oudheidkundige Bond*, Series 12 (1959), 145–64.
Kunstdenkmale Goslar (1979)   *Die Kunstdenkmale der Stadt Goslar*, ed. K. Wolff, A. von Werth, U. Hölscher (Kunstdenkmälerinventare Niedersachsens. Neudruck des gesammten Werkes 1889), Bd. 23, Osnabruck 1979.
Linssen (1981)   C. A. A. Linssen, 'Lotharingen 880–1106' *Algemene Geschiedenis der Nederlanden. Deel I. Middeleeuwen*, ed. D. P. Blok and A. Verhulst (Haarlem 1981), 305–53.
Mekking (1988)   A. J. J. Mekking, 'Een Kruis van Kerken rond Koemraads hart. Een bijdrage tot de kennis van de functie en de symbolische betekenis van het Utrechtse Kerkenkruis alsmedevan die to Bamberg en te Paderborn', *Utrecht Kruispunt van de middeleeuwse kerk. Voordrachten gehouden tijdens het congres ter gelegenheid van tien jaar Medievisitek Faculteit der Letteren Rijksuniversiteit te Utrecht 25 tot en met 27 augustus 1988* (Clavis Kunsthistorische Monografieen vol. VII) (Zutphen 1988), 21–53.
Mekking (1991)   A. J. J. Mekking, 'De zogenoemde Bernold-kerken in het Sticht Utrecht', *Utrecht tussen Kerk en Staat*, ed. R. Stuip and C. Vellekoop (Hilversum 1991).
Mekking (1993)   A. J. J. Mekking, 'Die ottonische Tradition in der Architektur des ehemaligen Herzogtums Lothringen im 11. Jahrhundert'. *Productions et échanges artistiques en Lotharingie médiévale* Actes des 7es Journées Lotharingiennes, ed. J. Schroeder (Luxembourg 1993).
OBU I   *Oorkondenboek van het Sticht Utrecht*, ed. S. Muller and A. C. Bouman, vol. 1 (Utrecht 1920).
Peeters (1964)   C. J. A. C. Peeters, 'De oudste bischopskerken van Utrecht', *Opstellen aangeboden aan Prof. dr. F. G. L. van der Meer* (Amsterdam, Brussel 1964).
Post (1957)   R. R. Post, *Kerkgeschiedenis van Nederland in de Middeleeuwen* (Utrecht, Antwerpen 1957).
Séjourné (1919)   P. Séjourné, *Ordinarius S Martini Trajectensis* (Utrecht 1919–21).
Vogt (1957)   H. J. Vogt, *Konrad II im Vergleich zu Heinrich II und Heinrich III. Ein Beitrag zur Kirchenpolitischen wie religiösgeistlichen Haltung der drei Kaiser* (Frankfurt a.M. 1957).

REFERENCES

1.   Wipo, *Das Leben Kaiser Konrad II*, Uebersetzt von W. Pflüger, ed. W. Wattenbach (fourth edition) (Leipzig *c.* 1892) (Die Geschichtschreiber der deutschen Vorzeit. Zweite Gesamtausgabe Band 41),

caput 39, p. 81; *Wiponis Proverbia Tetralogus Heinrici regis vita Chuonradi II. Imperatoris*, ed. G. H. Pertz (Hannover 1854) (Monumenta Germaniae Historica Scriptores XI), 243ᵛ, caput 39, 'de obitu imperatoris', 274; rerum germanicarum in usum scholarum separatim editi) (Hannover/Leipzig 1915), caput 39 (58–59).

2.   Von Giesebrecht, *Geschichte der deutschen Kaiserzeit* (Leipzig 1885), vol. 2, 340.

3.   R. R. Post. 1957, vol. 1, 73; E. Muller, *Das Itinerar Kaiser Heinrich III (1039 bis 1056)* (Berlin 1901), (Historische Studien, Heft XXVI), 15, 27, 31, 56; Jahrbücher 1874, Whit Sunday 1039: 45, 49; 21 May 1040: 86; 13 February and Easter 1041?: 101–02; Easter 1046: 294.

4.   'quasi pro pignore paterna sepelivimus viscera, ut beatus Martinus nobis quasi debitori nostra requirat servitia', see: OBU I, nr. 192, 179–80; Jahrbücher 1874, 49 and 86.

5.   Not only was an esteemed Roman author such as Pliny convinced of this, but also a highly developed Medieval nun like Hildegard von Bingen. Bargheer, 'Eingeweide', *Deutscher Aberglauben*, vol. 2, kk. 703–04; Bargheer, 'Herz', *Deutscher Aberglauben*, vol. 3, kk. 1794–1813 i.h.b.k. 1797.

6.   Hendrik III celebrated Christmas in the palace in Goslar and had it restructured fifteen times. See Kunstdenkmale Goslar, 1979, p. 14.

7.   'quia corde semper fuerit Goslariae', see: *Annales Pallidenses*, ed. G. H. Pertz 1895 (MGH SS. XVI), Hannover 1895, 48–98, i.h.b. 69. De Poehlder Annalen were written between *c.* 1182 and 1390; (Jahrbücher 1881), vol. 2, p. 356. Bargheer, 'Herz', *Deutscher Aberglauben*, vol. 3, k. 1799.

8.   When on 23 May 1125, after a solemn Festkronung on the occasion of the high feast of Whit Sunday, king (1106)/emperor (1111–25) Henry V died in Utrecht, his entrails were buried in the Cathedral, in the same tomb in which the entrails of Conrad II were laid to rest, the so-called Sepulchrum Imperatorum in medio choro. See: H. C. Hazewinkel, 'De Keizergraven in den Dom', *Jaarboek Oud-Utrecht* 1929, 31; OBU I, nr. 318 (p. 291); (Séjourné, 1919), 200, note 1.

9.   Kunstdenkmale Goslar 1979, 46, 65.

10. A. van den Hoven van Genderen, *Het Kapittel-Generaal en de Staten in het Nedersticht in de vijftiende eeuw* (Stichtse Historische Reeks XIII, Zutphen 1987), 140. Peeters (1964), 85; OBU I, XXXVI 26. With the exception of the Pieterskerk, there is no indication that the ordinations of the churches that form the cross in Utrecht were extended to refer to the Roman Basilicae consecrated to the same saints. See: Haverkate and Van der Peet (1985), 19.

11. D. Von Winterfeld, *Der Dom in Bamberg* (Berlin 1979), 1, 24. For the altar of Simon and Judas in the cathedral see: Séjourné 1919, sub 28 oktober. The altar of Simon and Judas in the Pieterskerk was located 'a latere sinistra chori', in the northern side choir, see: G. G. Calkoen, *Beschrijving der St. Pieterskerk te Utrecht (1903–1906)* (ms. Gemeentelijke Archiefdienst Utrecht), 64. Also compare the altar of Simon and Judas in the Sint-Servaaskerk in Maastricht the foundation of which most probably goes back to Henry III (consecration of 1039), see: '*Bijdragen tot de Bouwgeschiedenis van de Sint Servaaskerk te Maastricht, deel II, Het Schip*', ed. A. J. J. Mekking (Publications de la Societé Historique et Archeologique dans le Limbourg, Tome, CXVI–CXVII, 1980–81).

12. Mekking (1991), 123; Mekking (1994).

13. '(. . .) ego Bernoldus indignus Traiectensis sedis episcopus in meridiana plaga eiusdem urbis construi feci monasterium (. . .)', see: *Oorkondenboek van Holland en Zeeland tot 1299, deel I*, ed. A. C. F. Koch, ('s-Gravenhage 1970), LXXXI, 151. J. M. van Winter, 'Bisschop Bernold, afkomst en persoonlijkheid', *Utrecht Kruispunt van de middeleeuwse kerk. Voordrachten gehouden tijdens het congres ter gelegenheid van tien jaar Medievistiek Faculteit der Letteren Rijksuniversiteit te Utrecht 25 tot en met 27 augustus 1988*' (Clavis Kunsthistorische Monografieen VII) (Zutphen 1988), 13–20, 17.

14. Séjourné (1919), 73 and 120.

15. A. Verheul, 'Kerkwijding', *Liturgisch Woordenboek*, ed. L. Brinkhoff e.a. (Roermond, 1965–68), II, kk. 1322–28.

16. For the reference of the cruciform arrangement of churches to the cross of Christ, see: '*Liber Luciani de laude Cestrie*', ed. M. V. Taylor (Lancashire and Cheshire Record Society Publications LXIV), (London 1912), 45 and 53; G. Binding, 'Städtebau und Heilsordnung', (Düsseldorf, 1986), 36ᵛ, and note 32. The cross of Christ was seen early on as the basis of the ground plan of the cruciform church. See: E. Dinkler and E. Dinkler-von Schubert, 'Kreuz', in: Kirschbaum 1970–76, II, k. 588; Fr. Mobius and H. Sciurie, '*Symbolwerte mittelalterlicher Kunst*', (Leipzig 1984), 86–87; W. Braunfels, *Abendländische Klosterbaukunst*, (Köln 1969), 279–80; R. Krautheimer, 'Introduction to "An Iconography" of Mediaeval Architecture', *Journal of the Warburg and Courtauld Institutes*, V (1942), 11. The arrangement of five stones in the shape of a cross was given as the basis for the image of the cross of Christ. Examples: at the foundation of his cathedral by Thietmar von Merseburg 'posuit lapides in modum Sancti crucis [see: *Thietmari Merseburgensis episcopi chronicon*, ed. W. Trillmich (Ausgewählte Quellen zur deutschen Geschichte des Mittelalters. Freiherr Von Stein-Gedächtnisausgabe) (Darmstadt 1974) liber VII, caput 13,

p. 366] and at the foundation of the new cathedral by bishop Poor of Salisbury [see: N. Pevsner, *The buildings of England. BE 26. Wiltshire* (Harmondsworth 1963), 350].

17. Jansen, 'Utrecht en Paderborn. Bisschopssteden in hun vroegste ontwikkeling', *Jaarboek Oud-Utrecht* (1939), 59–72; Ter Kuile (1959); Bandmann (1962), 383ᵛ; Peeters (1964).

18. Haverkate and Van der Peet (1985).

19. Ter Kuile 1959; G. I. Lieftinck, 'De herkomst van bisschop Bernold van Utrecht', *Jaarboek Oud-Utrecht* 1949, 23–40. Mekking 1991, 123; Mekking 1994.

20. When crosses of churches are mentioned in the literature, the question is seldom posed whether they were meant as such and almost never whether different types can be distinguished. So there were crosses of churches founded with and without a centre. These crosses could be made up of collegiate churches, cloisters or parish churches. From the examples mentioned, it is often not clear whether they were indeed built as crosses of churches or are the result of a later expansion. Sometimes it appears that a coincidental cruciform configuration of churches was labelled as such subsequently. It involves the following places: Liège [see J. J. Morper, *Die Mitte Deutschlands. Zur Reichssymbolik der Tattermannsäule* (Bamberg 1957), 13] Corvey, Werden and Münster I. W. [see: E. J. Haslinghuis, *De Provincie Utrecht, eerste stuk, de Gemeente Utrecht* (De Nederlandse Monumenten van Geschiedenis en Kunst II) (Den Haag 1956), 16]; Straatsburg and Aachen [see: E. Herzog, *Die Ottonische Stadt* (Berlin 1964), 244–45 and ill. 50 and M. Schmitt, *Die Städtebauliche Entwicklung Aachens im Mittelalter unter Berücksichtigung der gestaltbildenden Faktoren* (Aachen 1972) 70, 71]; Minden and Trier [see: Balzer 1982, 274]; Saint Albans [see: J. E. A. L. Struick, *Utrecht door de eeuwen heen* (Utrecht/Antwerpen 1968) 36 note 2]; Chester [see Herzog 1964, 251 and 255]. Then there are also a number of places, inside and outside the Holy Roman Empire, where the cathedral is flanked by two churches or encircled by three, of which it is unclear due to lack of written sources whether this disposition was supposed to develop into a cross of churches. The fact that this last possibility must not be ruled out is taught by the example of Paderborn, where only two of the four planned churches came into being, while it is in any case certain that these churches were supposed to have been a part of a cross of churches.

21. The most important written source on the cross of churches in Bamberg goes as follows: locus Babenbergensis ecclesiis et patrociniis sanctorum in modum crucis undique munitus', in 'Adelberti vita Henrici II', Liber I, caput 6 (*c.* 1150), O. Lehmann-Brockhaus, *Schriftquellen zur Kunstgeschichte des elften und des zwolften Jagrhunderts* (Berlin 1938), IC; see also Mekking (1988), p. 27 and — for the individual churches in Bamberg — Mekking (1988), note 24. Further details about the churches which form the cross of churches in Paderborn can be found in Herzog (1964), 102–15 and 251; Mekking (1988), 36–40.

22. Herzog (1964), 250; H. Bannasch, *Das Bistum Paderborn unter den Bischöfen Rethar und Meinwerk* (Studien und Quellen zur Westfälischen Geschichte XII) (Paderborn 1972), 159 vv.; Balzer (1982), 267ᵛ.

23. The most elementary adaptation of the cruciform as the basis for a form of ecclesiastical architecture is certainly the concept of the cruciform church (see note 16). Furthermore, the cruciform is encountered as a scheme for the arrangement of the sanctuaries within the specific areas of an episcopal immunity or a monastic complex, for example: Milan, Glanfeuil, Schaffhausen [Bandmann (1962), 384].

24. According to Günther Binding, this was the case with the so-called 'Kirchenkranz' [see: Herzog 1964, 243–44] of Cologne in which a cross of churches would be distinguished through the construction of the church of Salvator and Maria in Deutz around the year 1000. The fact that the consecration (in the year 1003?) Took place on the feast of the Invention of the Cross (3 May) will certainly have been no coincidence; compare the consecration of the Pieterskerk in Utrecht on 1 May 1048 which is also associated with the feast of the Invention of the Cross for this. See also: Binding 1986, 13–15, 21–22, 24 and 32.

25. According to the 'Vita Bardonis Maior', Abbot (1018–39) Richardus had the trio of ecclesiastical foundations around the abbey in Fulda expanded to a cross of churches by having a cloister with a church (consecrated 1023) erected in the west on the Neuenberg. See: Bandmann (1962), 84 and note 65; Herzog (1964), 250–51; Binding (1986), 34. In contrast to that which Herzog claims on p. 251, the churches in Fulda are decidedly not at the extreme ends of the axes of a 'crux decussata' with the abbey as centre (Bandmann (1962), illustration on p. 384), but here it has to do with an adaptation to the situation of the landscape in which it was strived — just as in Hersfeld — to situate the churches as far as possible on the crests of prominent hills. In imitation of the triangle of churches in Fulda, a similar configuration was brought into being in Hersfeld. Around the abbey a Benedictine deanery rose on both the Petersberg (1002–05) and on the Johannesberg (1012–24) which, together with the already existing parish church on the Frauenberg, had to form the sign of the Trinity. The resemblance to Fulda extends to the patrocinia. See: Herzog (1964), 249. This late and persistent preference for the Trinity symbolism was perhaps characteristic of the Benedictine order. See: E. Hempel, *Geschichte der deutschen Baukunst* (München

1956), p. 57; P. von Naredi-Rainer, *Architektur und Harmonie* (Kölm 1982), 47ᵛ, and 143; A. Reinle, *Zeichensprache der Architektur* (Zürich/München 1976), 143.

26. In 1010 the first stone for the monastic church of Saint Michael was laid by Bishop Bernward to the north of the cathedral. See: H. Beseler and H. Roggenkamp, *Die Michaeliskirche in Hildesheim* (Berlin 1954), 169). His successor Godehard founded three more collegiate churches around the cathedral: that of Maria to the east, that of Mauritius to the west and that of Bartholomeus to the north-east. Together with the church of Saint Michael they formed the cross of churches of Hildesheim. See: E. Lehmann, 'Bemerkungen zu den baulichen Anfängen der deutschen Stadt im frühen Mittelalter, *Settimane di studio del centro italiano di studi sull'Alto Medioevo VI. La citta nell'Alto Medioevo 10 a 16 aprile 1958* (Spoleto 1959), 581.

27. Bandmann (1962), 385.

28. Mekking (1968), 61–85.

29. Possibly the fact that these clergymen were denoted as such in the chapter of the Vita (caput 218, p. 131) in which the question of the foundation of the cross of churches is also brought up has to be regarded as an indication that the latter aroused a direct and strong association with the cross of Christ. See also note 16 and note 21.

30. 'Als Bannung in ein Heilszeichen das aus der Welt aussondert, in besonderer Beziehung zu den himmlischen Mächten bringt und damit Schutz gewährt': Bandmann (1962), 385. See furthermore: G. Bandmann, *Mittelalterliche Architektur als Bedeutungsträger* (Berlin 1951), 146ᵛ.; F. Mobius, 'Ueber und unter dem Bogen. Zur Ausdruckhsbedeutung zweier Formzönen', Festschrift Johannes Jahn zum XXII November MCMLVII, Leipzig 1957k, 75ᵛ.; W. Braunfels, *Die Kunst im Heiligen Römischen Reich* (Munchen 1980), II, 164 and 314; W. Muller, *Die Heilige Stadt (Stuttgart 1961), Hoofstuk A.3; Kirschbaum 1970, 1976*, II, kk. 562–90, i.h.b. kk. 587–88; Straberger-Schusser, 'Kreuz', Deutscher Aberglauben (1987), v, kk. 478–84. Paderborn: see Mekking (1988), 38.

31. Mekking (1988), 30–40.

32. I agree with the view of P. Kehr that Hendrik III strenghthened the position and standing of the bishop of Utrecht in order to put up a dam against the all too power hungry regional lords like Gottfried-met-de-Baard, the duke of Lotharingen; Dirk IV, earl of Holland; Herman, earl of Henegouwen and Boudewijn V, earl of Flanders. See: P. Kehr, 'Vier Kapitel aus der Geschichte Kaiser Heinrichs III.', *Abhandlungen der Preussischen Akademie der Wissenschaften. Jrg 1930 Philosophisch-Historische Klasse* (Berlin 1931), 22, 24 and 25. See furthermore: I. H. Gosses and R. R. Post, *Handboek tot de staatkundige geschiedenis der Nederlanden. I. De Middeleeuwen* ('s-Gravenhage 1974), 65–67. Linssen (1981), 340ᵛ.

33. B. Van den Hoven van Genderen, *Het Kapittel-Generaal en de Staten in het Nederstich in de vijftiende eeuw* (Stichtse Historische Reeks XIII) (Zutphen 1987), 140; Peeters (1964), 85; OBU I, XXXVI, 26. There is no single indication for the supposition that, with the exception of the Pieterskerk, one consciously wanted to refer to the Roman Balisicae which are consecrated to the same saints with the name-giving of the churches that form the cross in Utrecht. See: Haverkate and Van der Peet (1985), 19.

34. Krautheimer (1942), 18.

35. Saint Peter's in Rome as the most important papal basilica: S. De Blaauw, *Cultus et Decor. Liturgie en architectuur in laatantiek en middeleeuws Rome. Basilica Salvatoris Sanctae Mariae Sancti Petri* (Delft 1987), 259. With respect to the Easter service in Utrecht in 1076 see: Post 1957, 98–99. '. . . regni vel imperii defensorem . . .', see OBU I, nr. 236, 214. See also Mekking 1988, note 100.

36. Mekking (1986), sub vocibus: Regnum en Sacerdotium.

37. G. Bandmann, 'Die Vorbilder der Aachener Pfalzkapelle', *Karl der Grosse. Lebenswerk und Nachleben. Karolingische Kunst*, ed. W. Braunfels (Düsseldorf 1965), 437–39 and 458–62; A. Reinle, *Zeichensprache der Architektur* (Zürich/München 1976), 145–46; Mekking (1986), 301–03.

38. In Goslar and Halberstadt, the churches which were used as coronation churches were also consecrated to Mary. See W. Noack, 'Stadtbaukunst und geistlich-weltliche Repräsentation im XI. Jahrhundert', *Festschrift Kurt Bauch. Kunstgeschichtliche Beiträge* (München 1957), 29–49.

39. Th. Haakma Wagenaar, 'Enige hypothesen van Dr. G. C. Labouchère over het middeleeuwse Utrecht', *Jaarboek Oud-Utrecht* (1972), 13–33.

40. Linssen (1981), 349; Haverkate and Van Der Peet 1985, 15. i.h.b. p. 21; Post 1957, 1, 97–100.

41. T. J. Hoekstra, 'De dom van Adelbold II, bisschop van Utrecht (1010–1026)', *Utrecht Kruispunt van de Middeleeuwse kerk* (Clavis kunsthistorische monografieen vol. VII) (Zutphen 1988), 104; Th. Haakma Wagenaar, *Memorandum Domtoren* (typoscript) (Utrecht 1975), 'Architectuur en Bouwgeschiedenis', 7, 'Tekeningen en foto's, ill. 2.

42. Zadelstraat is the oldest known paved street of Utrecht (recorded as 'Via Lapidea' in 1196), see: 'Archeologische Kroniek 1978/79/80', ed. T. J. Hoekstra, *Maandblad Oud-Utrecht* III (1981), Nr. 23 (p. 65), and 'Archeologische en Bouwhistorische Kroniek 1984', ed. T. J. Hoekstra and A. F. E. Kipp, *Maandblad Oud-Utrecht*, IV (1985), Nr. 72 (p. 186).

43. Vogt (1957), 72–75; A. Hauck, *Kirchengeschichte Deutschlands*, Berlin/Leipzig 1954, vol. 3, 665 and 673;
     U. Duchrow, *Christenheit und Weltverantwortung* (Stuttgart 1970), 344; A. Dempf, *Sacrum Imperium*
     (München 1962), 170.
44. J. Sauer, *Symbolik des Kirchengebäudes und seiner Ausstattung in der Auffassung des Mittelalters*,
     Freiburg i.Br. 1924, 99–100.
45. Vogt (1957), 72–73 and 126–37; K. J. Benz, 'Kaiser Konrad II. (1024–39) als kirchlicher Herrscher', *Archiv
     fur Liturgiewissenschaft*, XX/XXI (1978/1979), 80; Mekking (1991), 118–33 and 138–42; Mekking (1994),
     73–76.

The Utrecht Parishes and their Churches

by Karel Emmens

THE DOM-PARISH

From at least the eighth century a settlement of merchants flourished next to the cathedral-complex, on the west side of the former Roman castellum. This settlement, called Stathe (staithe), was situated in the surroundings of the Steenweg on the south bank of the (former) bed of the Rhine. Its importance grew from the late tenth century onwards, as it took over a small part of European trade previously handled by Dorestad, and driven by the needs of the bishops and clergy who demanded a supply of goods and the availability of craftsmen.[1] During the tenth and eleventh centuries two new settlements of merchants developed nearby. One was situated north of Stathe on the south bank of the river Vecht (Waterstraat-area) and the other south of Stathe on the east bank of the Rhine (Tolsteeg-area).[2]

The burghers living in these three areas formed the nucleus of the Utrecht parish. This so-called Dom-parish was very large for it stretched for several miles beyond these settlements: in the north to Maarssen and to the east up to and including the village of De Bilt. Both the burghers and the inhabitants of these rural areas worshipped in the Dom, the cathedral church of Sint-Maarten (St Martin).[3] Baptism, however, probably took place in the chapter church of St Saviour.[4]

THE BUURKERK, THE FIRST PARISH CHURCH

During the eleventh century three new chapter churches and one abbey were founded in Utrecht.[5] The growing number of ecclesiastical structures, and the increased number of clergy coupled with the growth of the civilian population, seems to have led the burghers to demand a more independent position. In 1122 finally their wishes were met with the granting of city rights.[6]

One of the first signs of this emancipation may be seen in the erection of a separate parish church in the oldest and most important settlement, in Stathe. Perhaps this was a sign of civic consciousness, although the Dom chapter may at the same time have felt a need to alleviate their increasing burden of liturgical obligations without the disturbing presence of the citizens.

This new parish church was dedicated to Our Lady and was called Maria Minor to distinguish it from Maria Maior, the nearby chapter church.[7] It is referred to as the church of the burghers, the buurt (neighbours) and therefore has retained the name of Buurkerk until the present day.[8] The Buurkerk-parish had the same boundaries as the earlier Dom-parish, which it succeeded.[9]

Without written evidence for the Buurkerk in this early period the precise date of its foundation is unknown. It is assumed to have been built sometime between the late tenth and the late eleventh century. Two hypotheses are in favour of an early establishment. In 1007 the merchants set Stathe on fire when they saw armed Vikings approaching Utrecht. The Vikings left without causing any further damage and the burghers may have taken the opportunity to erect a new church in the centre of their settlement while it was being rebuilt.[10] The other argument concerns the orientation of the building which is similar to that of St Salvator and the chapel of the Holy Cross at

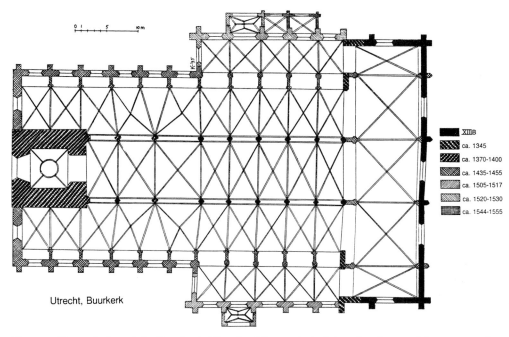

FIG. 1.   Ground-plan of the Buurkerk, Utrecht. The symbols define the phases of the construction of this church. (K. Emmens (1995), based on ground-plans of Van Traa and Haakma Wagenaar.)

Utrecht, while the Dom and the chapter churches are slightly differently orientated. By following this (probably) older scheme, the Buurkerk may appear to precede the foundation of the chapter churches.[11] On the other hand the Dom-parish appears in eleventh-century documents, so the Buurkerk may have been established as late as the end of the eleventh century.[12]

Very little is known of the first phase of the Buurkerk. Only the foundations of the tower have been researched, so apart from indications regarding its orientation, the appearance of this romanesque building cannot be reconstructed.[13] The tower, constructed of tufa, stood in the third bay east of the present tower (Fig. 1).[14] It may belong to the late tenth century but might be as late as the twelfth century.

THE DIVISION OF THE BUURKERK-PARISH

During the twelfth and thirteenth centuries the growth of the population and its wealth continued. At the same time, during the episcopacy of Bishop Godebald (1114–27), the Gregorian Reform of the Utrecht diocese resulted in increased pastoral care.[15] In addition the residents of the settlements in the north and in the south may have felt the need to express their wealth in parish churches of their own. These factors probably led to the division of the large Buurkerk-parish into four smaller ones. Beside the Buurkerk the Jacobikerk (St James's church), the Klaaskerk (St Nicholas's) and the Geertekerk (dedicated to St Gertrude of Nivelles) were established.

Again, no documents exist that tell us about this division. It is generally assumed that the three new parishes were founded at the same time, so the earliest written evidence for the existence of one of these churches provides a *terminus ante quem* for them all. The Jacobikerk appears in a document of 1173, and in 1204 the Klaaskerk is referred to as a parish church. Some years before 1259 the Geertekerk was rebuilt within the city walls.[16] This division must have been accomplished not later than 1173.

Of the four new parishes, that of the Buurkerk is still the largest within the city walls. The chapters immunities all lay within this parish, as did most of the huge so-called city castles, the houses of the richest Utrecht merchants.[17] The parish of St James's served the northern quarters at both sides of the Oude Gracht (Waterstraat-Breedstraat), the Klaaskerk, the poor south-eastern part (Twijnstraat-Agnietenstraat) and the Geertekerk, the very small, south-western, quarter of the city. At the Smeebrug the parishes of the Buurkerk, Klaaskerk and Geetekerk met. South of the bridge the Oude Gracht divided the parishes of the Geertekerk and Klaaskerk. This part of the Oude Gracht is most likely to have been excavated around 1120 and the fact that the parish-boundary follows this canal indicates that the division must have taken place between 1120 and 1170.[18]

All four of these parish churches were subordinated to the chapter of the Dom.[19] In Utrecht the other chapters did not receive the right to establish parish churches of their own, in a situation rather different to that of Maastricht and Cologne, for instance, where parish churches were erected alongside the chapter churches.[20] Without this tie to other Utrecht chapters and with the Buurkerk already very near to the Dom, the new Utrecht parish churches were founded in those areas where they were most needed, at the two other settlements. In the north (Waterstraat-area) the Jacobikerk was built and in the south (Tolsteeg-area) the Klaaskerk. Originally the Geertekerk was erected outside the city walls, though its exact location is unknown.

THE KLAASKERK A PARISH CHURCH AS WELL

The structure of the Klaaskerk contains the oldest surviving remains of any of the four parish churches (Fig. 2, Pl. VIIIA). Between 1100 and 1130 a choir with two side-chapels, transepts and the westwork were built. Traces indicate that the original plan was for a vaulted cruciform basilica with an arcade and clerestory. In 1130, however, the plan was modified and an aisle-gallery introduced. As a result, the nave was higher than the older parts of the church.[22]

This change of plan tells us more about the unknown primary status of this church. An aisle-gallery and vaults with band-shaped ribs had been used at the Utrecht chapter church of Maria Maior, which was remodelled in this form some years earlier on the instructions of Emperor Henry V.[23] The church's dedication is instructive, many parish churches in the Netherlands are dedicated to St Nicholas, the patron saint of sailors and merchants, and protector against flooding. This devotion to St Nicholas was established during the twelfth century.[24] But before then St Nicholas was probably an imperial saint of the Holy Roman Empire: St Nicholas was the patron of the Concordat of Worms in which Henry V had played a very important role. Henry died in Utrecht in 1125, his burial in the Dom reveals the close connections between Utrecht and the imperial House. So it is possible that the Klaaskerk was originally either a chapter church or part of an imperial monastery.[25]

In 1204 this church appears to have served the parish in the south-eastern part of Utrecht and a large rural area outside the city walls.[26] It was probably in order to fit this new function that the building was internally modified. A new polygonal apse crowned the raised transepts and choir. The nave was extensively altered and modified.

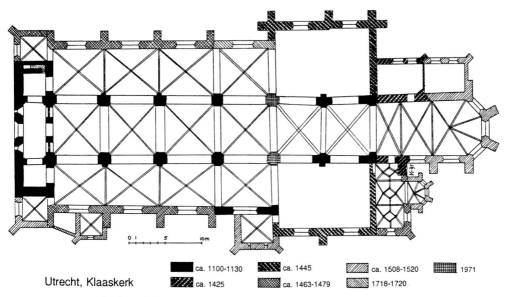

FIG. 2.   Ground-plan of the Klaaskerk, Utrecht, with its phases of construction. (K. Emmens
(1995), based on ground-plans of Van Traa and Haakma Wagenaar.)

The bays of the side-aisles were enlarged by removing the piers in the middle of each
bay and the two connecting arches were transformed into one large round arch. The
aisle-gallery was therefore lost.[27] In this way all the now disfunctional parts of the
building were removed, creating a spacious interior with a number of altars for the
church's large congregations. Especially the diamond-shaped windows in the transepts
indicate that the restructuring may be dated to around 1200.[28]

THE THIRTEENTH CENTURY: THE BUURKERK AND JACOBIKERK

Although we know nothing of the form of the Buurkerk or the Jacobikerk in their
earliest phases, we can conclude from the Klaaskerk that the basilical plan was
commonly in use and may even have been the norm for a parish church in the late
twelfth century.[29] If the present structures follow earlier arrangements, it is not unlikely
that the Buurkerk and the Jacobikerk were laid out as basilicas in their earliest phases.
These churches were erected in the second half of the thirteenth century, at the same
time that the Dom was enlarged and the present ambulatory added.[30]

   The Buurkerk was the largest of the three churches. It had a cross-basilica added to
the east of the old tower. The arcade was supported by cylindrical piers flanked by four
columns (Pl. VIIIc). Whether there was a triforium or an aisle-gallery between the
arcade and the clerestory is unknown. Even the form of the clerestory is unclear as the
walls were later extensively re-modelled. The vaulting over the long transepts was
lower, probably to around the same height as the vaults in the later demolished choir.[31]

   The form of the nave piers is rather unusual. Similar piers were used in the
ambulatory of the Dom. Around the same time, during the second half of the thirteenth
century, similar capitals supported the vaulting (now destroyed) of St Lebuinus at
Deventer. In the case of the Dom, these forms appear to be derived from French

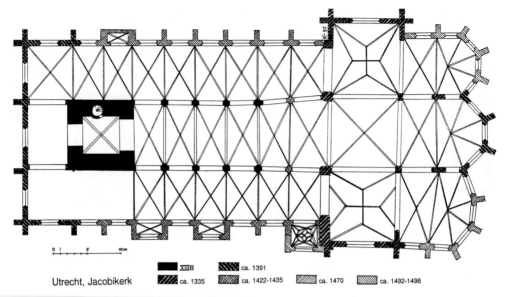

■ XIIIB		ca. 1391	
ca. 1335		ca. 1422-1435	ca. 1470	ca. 1492-1498

Utrecht, Jacobikerk

FIG. 3.   Ground-plan of the Jacobikerk, Utrecht, with its phases of construction. (K. Emmens (1995), based on ground-plans of Van Traa and Haakma Wagenaar.)

cathedrals mediated through the Dom of Cologne.[32] This source is less likely in the case of the Buurkerk. Did the burghers of Stathe try to impress their neighbours and seek to accentuate the supremacy of the Buurkerk among the other parish churches with forms derived from French cathedral architecture?[33] Or were the same masons who built the Dom employed to build the Buurkerk? It should be pointed out that these forms are found in the thirteenth century in churches of the mendicant orders as well.[35] The mendicants established priories in Utrecht from 1250.[36] Until then a combination of late-Romanesque and Gothic conditioned the appearance of churches, as may be seen in the nave of the Walburgskerk in Zutphen (c. 1240).[37]

The construction of this phase is usually assumed to have started shortly after the fires of 1279 or even that of 1253.[38] Recent studies show that destruction by fire or any other accident is usually followed by restoration of a building's former shape.[39] The building of this part of the Buurkerk belongs to the second half of the thirteenth century; without further evidence it cannot be more precisely dated.[40]

The pre-eminence of the Buurkerk among the other Utrecht parish churches is clear as the city council had its own chapel there. In this chapel the council worshipped and city resolutions were proclaimed. Practically every guild in the city had an altar in the church. The church-tower functioned as a watch-tower, and next to the parish bell hang two city bells.[41]

In the same period (c. 1290) the Jacobikerk was rebuilt as a smaller and more simple cross-basilica (Fig. 3, Pl. VIIIB). Its piers are oblong with columns on two sides. The capitals in the side-aisles are still present (to their original height); the vaulting of the nave was raised later.[42] Special attention should be given to the tower, the first Gothic tower at Utrecht, built around 1250 or at the same time as the basilica itself (c. 1290).[43] Its original height was more or less equivalent to that of the older twin towers of the Dom, the chapter churches, the monasteries and probably that of Buurkerk.[44] Around

1350 the tower of the Jacobikerk reached its present height.[45] During those years it was the highest and most impressive tower in Utrecht; the tower of the Dom was begun in 1321 and completed in 1382.[46]

From this period onwards many cities erected new churches which follow those of Utrecht in their design: among others the Sint-Joriskerk at Amersfoort (St George, c. 1300) and St Nicholas at Amsterdam (Oude Kerk, c. 1300).[47] Utrecht was in this period the most important city in the Northern Netherlands[48] and by taking over the concept of the cross-basilica the burghers of those cities may have sought to advertise their autonomy as the Utrecht burghers did earlier.[49]

THE FOURTEENTH CENTURY

The position of Utrecht in inter-regional trade diminished and the economy was increasingly oriented towards local markets.[50] Due to the expansion of the city outside the northern walls during the late thirteenth and fourteenth centuries, the parish of St James' grew.[51] In this new district (the Bemuurde Weerd) the potters lived and worked, using the clay-sediment of the Vecht.[52] Next to the crossing and transepts of the Jacobikerk new larger and higher transepts were built, combined with a new choir flanked by two smaller chapels. The choir was provisionally finished and consecrated in 1334.[53]

A very curious restructuring took place in the last decades of the century. Onto the west side of the tower a nave of one bay with smaller side-aisles was added. In this so-called achterkerk (the part of the church behind the tower) consecrated in 1391, the font was placed creating a pseudo-baptistry, with its own altars.[54] Between 1334 and 1391 the roof of the nave was raised together with the extant vaulting to match the new crossing and transepts. The apse of the choir was probably completed at the same time. Despite these changes the church remained a basilica with two transepts.[55]

Several churches seem to be in competition with each other in this period. Did the parishioners of St James try to overrule the supremacy of the Buurkerk? Some years after the new transepts of the Jacobikerk were built in 1344 the transepts of the Buurkerk were enlarged by moving the western walls one bay westwards into the nave.[56]

Around 1370, some twenty years after the completion of the tower of the Jacobikerk and twelve years before the completion of the famous Dom-tower, the parishioners of the Buurkerk built a new tower and choir. The first stage was completed in 1380 and the choir around 1390. By building the new tower several metres west of the old one (demolished in 1388) the nave was lengthened by three bays; this was completed in 1404.[57] Thus the church was considerably enlarged and in borrowing the octagonal form of the Dom-tower the parishioners may be seeking to renew the Buurkerk's status as the city's principal parish church. However the octagonal second parish stage of the tower was never built.[58]

HALL-CHURCHES IN UTRECHT

In the beginning of the fifteenth century, from 1421 to 1433, the side-aisles of the Jacobikerk were widened, the clerestory dismantled and a pseudo-basilica created. The old crossing and transepts were added to the nave. The Dom's master mason, Willem van Boelre, was involved in this project.[59] With this transformation the concept of the cross-basilica appears to have lost its supremacy in Utrecht and this phase of the Jacobikerk may represent an intermediate step towards a new scheme.

The concept of a hall-church was introduced in Utrecht in the third decade of the fifteenth century in the Buurkerk. Outside Utrecht the concept was already employed as early as *c.* 1300 in the Bovenkerk at Kampen.[60] Kampen was the most important and richest city in the Northern Netherlands during the fourteenth century, and it is perhaps for this reason that the idea was reproduced in other cities.[61] St Michael at Zwolle and the Sint-Joriskerk at Amersfoort were (partially) transformed into hall-churches in the second half of the century, as was the Oude Kerk at Amsterdam some decades earlier.[62] The Utrecht parish churches are later, probably because the city lost its dominant role during the thirteenth century.[63] From as early as *c.* 1350 a new development was underway, again starting with the Bovenkerk at Kampen. A huge cathedral-like basilical choir with ambulatory and radiating chapels was erected.[64] This was the starting point for the erection of numbers of similar churches in the Netherlands up till *c.* 1450.[65]

The Utrecht parish churches did not participate in this development, as perhaps the burghers wanted to distinguish their churches from the cross-basilicas of the clergy.[66] The hall church could contain larger congregations and multiple altars, and on account of the great height of their walls the hall church formed a conspicious element of the city-scape.[67] It is striking that this concept was being introduced at a time when a former master mason of the Dom fabric, Willem van Boelre, was involved — we have met him above, working on the Jacobikerk too.[68]

The side-aisles of the Buurkerk were adjusted in accordance with the new concept (Fig. 1, Pl. VIIIc). Although buttresses appear on the outside of the aisles they are used in the interior as well, flanking very small barrel-vaulted chapels. The same arrangement can be found in the transepts. In the first instance it was intended to replace the old arcade, for, as the outer walls clearly show, the number and scale of the bays of the side-aisles do not correspond with those of the nave. Yet the piers were maintained and only the upper walls of the nave were extensively transformed. When in 1454 the transepts along with the nave and aisles were vaulted by Bernt van Covelens from Zwolle, the building was completed. All three aisles were spanned by one enormous saddle roof. The ridge of this giant roof was nearly as high as the tower gallery.[69] In the first decades of the sixteenth century the church was completed when the last side-aisles and side-choirs were finished.[70]

Following the impressive transformation of the Buurkerk, the Jacobikerk was also transformed in this period. This was a fairly simple task for the side-aisles only needed to be made higher to match the nave. In 1461 this transformation had begun and was probably completed around 1465 or 1470. The so-called achterkerk to the west of the tower was reshaped and now matched the nave on the east side of the tower. When the southern side-chapel was transformed into a side-choir in the 1490s the Jacobikerk was completed.[71]

Finally, the Klaaskerk remained unchanged until around 1445 when four large chapels were added to the east side of the eleventh-century transepts, two on either side of the nave. This gave the building something of the appearance of a hall-church. But in the 1460s the entire building was transformed into a true hall-church and the vaulting was replaced. Jacob van der Borch, a master of the Dom, was involved in the transformation of the Klaaskerk as well as the Buurkerk. The present apse was added *c.* 1500 to complete the church.[72]

The Utrecht hall-churches all have stone vaults. In Holland and Zeeland barrel vaulted waggon ceilings dominate the hall-churches, as for instance in the Grote Kerk of Edam. Exceptional are the Grote Kerk at 's-Gravenhage (The Hague) and in part the

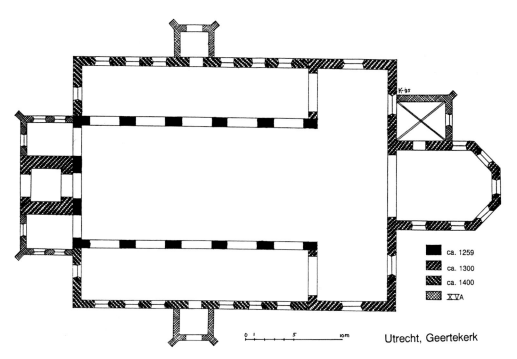

FIG. 4.   Ground-plan of the Geertekerk, Utrecht, with an indication of its phases of construction.
(K. Emmens (1995), based on a ground-plan of Van Traa.)

Oude Kerk at Amsterdam, where the size of the bays equals that of the transepts. East
of Utrecht the hall-churches all have stone vaulting, for instance the churches in
Amerfoort and Zwolle. The Utrecht churches fit into this east-Netherlandish tradition[73]
and maybe Bernt van Covelens — who had vaulted St Michaels at Zwolle as well — is
not merely to be attributed with the vaulting at the Buurkerk.

THE GEERTEKERK

The simplest of the four parish churches is the Geertekerk. Its history is still rather
obscure. The church of 1259, a large oblong building of reused tufa, was first
transformed into a cruciform church and then, in the fifteenth century, into a hall
church with a barrel vaulted waggon ceiling (Fig. 4).[74] Despite these changes it never
achieved the grandeur of the other three Utrecht parish churches, so the parish of the
Geertekerk is presumably to be regarded as the poorest of the parishes.

    With the Alteration in 1580 all the churches in Utrecht passed into the control of
protestants and the parishes dissolved.[75]

REFERENCES

  1. Kai van Vliet, 'Middeleeuws Utrecht, een markt in ontwikkeling', *Markten in Utrecht van de vroege
    middeleeuwen tot nu*, Jan Brugman, Hans Buiter & Kai van Vliet (Utrecht 1995), 9–17. Marceline J.

Dolfin, E. M. Kylstra and J. Penders, *Utrecht, de huizen binnen de singels: beschrijving* ('s-Gravenhage 1989), 8–9.

2. Dolfin (1989), 11, 14.
3. Dolfin (1989), 9, 11–12.
4. As Eelco van Welie has suggested. The presence of a font in both the Dom and St Salvator and their positions in the Utrecht urban liturgy is described by the following authors. C. L. Temminck Groll, *De romaanse kerken van Utrecht* (Utrecht 1988), 10, 15. E. J. Haslinghuis and C. J. A. C. Peeters, *De Dom van Utrecht* ('s-Gravenhage 1965), 147, 161. Eelco van Welie, 'Omnes canonici. Een verkenning van de Utrechtse stadsliturgie', *Bulletin K.N.O.B. 93* (1994), 186–92.
5. The chapter churches of St Peter's, St John's and St Mary's and the abbey of St Paul's. Dolfin (1989), 6–8. Temminck Groll (1988), 17–36.
6. Dolfin (1989), 9–10. A similar development took place at Cologne, the seat of the archbishop to whom the bishop of Utrecht was subordinated, that received its privileges of a city in 1114. (Werner Schäfke, *Kölns romanische Kirchen, Architektur — Ausstattung — Geschichte* (Cologne 1984), 15.)
7. Th. Haakma Wagenaar, *De bouwgeschiedenis van de Buurkerk te Utrecht* (Utrecht 1936), 78–79. Temminck Groll (1988), 29–36.
8. Flip Delemarre, Ada van Deijk and Pieter van Traa, *Middeleeuwse kerken in Utrecht* (Utrecht 1988), 40.
9. Dolfin (1989), 9, 11.
10. Van Vliet (1995), 17. Haakma Wagenaar (1936), 80.
11. Haakma Wagenaar (1936), 85–95, 102–08. Th. Haakma Wagenaar, 'De bouwgeschiedenis van de Buurkerk', *Restauratie vijf Hervormde kerken in de binnenstad van Utrecht*, jaarverslag 1982/1983/1984 (Utrecht 1985), 149, 152.
12. Dolfin (1989), 9, 11.
13. Might this church have had any resemblance with the parish churches at Cologne? If so, it probably was a romanesque cross-basilica with galleries (Schäfke (1984), 184).
14. Haakma Wagenaar (1936), 89–95, 102–08, figs 33, 36. Haakma Wagenaar (1985), 146–50, 152.
15. Dolfin (1989), 11, 13.
16. Dolfin (1989), 11, 13.
17. Dolfin (1988), 13. A. F. E. Kipp, 'Große mittelalterliche steinerne Wohnhäuser in Utrecht', *Hausbau in den Niederlanden*, G. Ulrich Grossmann ed. (Marburg 1990), 258–59.
18. Dolfin (1989), 7, 11, 13. Tarquinius J. Hoekstra, 'Utrecht, Entstehung und räumliche Entwicklung bis etwa 1700, ein Überblick', *Hausbau in den Niederlanden*, ed. G. Ulrich Grossman (Marburg 1990), 211.
19. Delemarre (1998), 10.
20. Schäfke (1984), 68. The parish church of St Peter's was established in the tenth or eleventh century being the only example left in Cologne of this disposition. The parish church of the chapter of St Gereon at Cologne, St Christoph, was first mentioned in 1172 (Schäfke (1984), 122).
21. Hoekstra (1988), 211. Dolfin (1989), 7.
22. Th. Haakma Wagenaar, 'Verslag bouwhistorische begeleiding restauratie binnenstadskerken: Nicolaï-kerk', *Restauratie vijf Hervormde kerken in de binnenstad van Utrecht*, jaarverslag 2 1971/1972, Utrecht s.a.; 38, 40–54. Haakma Wagenaar (1977/1978), 67–83. Both Maria Maior and the Klaaskerk were vaulted according to this system: on one square bay of the nave corresponded with two square bays of the side-aisles. So the side-aisles had twice as many bays as the nave itself.
23. H. M. Haverkate and C. J. van der Peet, *Een kerk van papier. De geschiedenis van de voormalige Mariakerk te Utrecht* (Utrecht/Zutphen 1985), 32–38. Only one vault of this type remains in the Klaaskerk, being the only example left in Utrecht because Maria Maior has been demolished.
24. H. J. Kok, *Proeve van een onderzoek van de patrocinia in het middeleeuwse bisdom Utrecht* (Assen 1958), 14, 23, 151–52.
25. As is suggested by A. J. J. Mekking in his lecture about the iconology of architecture at a workshop at the University of Leiden on 23 March 1995. He kindly gave me a written copy of his talk (not published) which I quote in this article: A. J. J. Mekking, *Essay t.b.v. 'Verbeelding van sociale posities'* (Onderzoekschool Mediëvistiek/Onderzoeklijn 2, Workshop Leiden 23 maart 1995), 1–4. The octagonal chapel of St Nicholas at the imperial palace of Nijmegen, the Valkhof, was built during the reign of the Emperor Henry III (1039–56) as a commemoration of his victory over a revolt of Lotharingian nobles, who had destroyed the Valkhof-palace. (Mekking 1995, 2–3). Based on different arguments Haakma Wagenaar came to the same conclusion (Haakma Wagenaar (1971/1972), 52).
26. Dolfin (1989), 13.
27. Th. Haakma Wagenaar, 'Verslag bouwhistorische begeleiding restauratie binnenstadskerken: Nicolaï-kerk', *Restauratie vijf Hervormde kerken in de binnenstad van Utrecht*, jaarverslag 2 1971/1972, Utrecht s.a.; 38, 40–54. Haakma Wagenaar (1978), 67–83.

28. Haakma Wagenaar (1971/1972), 51. These diamond-shaped windows appear also in the transepts and choir of the chapter church of St Peter (Temminck Groll (1988), 21).

29. The romanesque parish churches of Cologne for instance, which have all but one been destroyed, were basilicas as well (Schäfke (1984), 184).

30. Haslinghuis (1965), 171–73, 336–37, Fig. 24.

31. Haakma Wagenaar (1936), 78–125. Haakma Wagenaar (1985), 151–57. In his reconstruction he assumes that there was neither a triforium nor an aisle-gallery.

32. E. H. ter Kuile, 'De architectuur', Duizend jaar bouwen in Nederland, I: Middeleeuwen, S. J. Fockema Andreae, E. H. ter Kuile and R. C. Hekker (Amsterdam 1948, 197. Haslinguis (1965), 227 (note 1), 336–37. Delemarre (1988), 33.

33. Until now I have discovered only two other parish churches with similar elements that appear to be derived from French cathedrals, both in Germany. The one is the Liebfrauenkirche in Trier (started 1227) and the Elizabethkirche in Marburg (started 1235). (L. Helten, Steit um Leibfrauen. Eine mittelalterliche Grundrißzeichnung und ihre Bedeutung für die Liebfrauenkirche zu Trier (Trier 1992), 16–46).

34. Despite the proximity of both churches there were very few contacts between the fabrics of the Dom and the Buurkerk. Sometimes they made use of the same masters and artists, or took over some material from one another (W. H. Vroom, De financiering van de kathedraalbouw in de middeleeuwen (Maarssen 1981), 351–52; R. Meischke, De gotische bouwtraditie (Amersfoort 1988), 85).

35. The Dominican (c. 1300) and Franciscan (fourteenth century) churches at Maastricht for instance show these elements as well. In both churches the triforium is only indicated by tracery. The Franciscan church has cylindrical piers flanked by four columns, like the fourteenth-century churches of Meerssen and Sittard (Ter Kuile (1948), 197–99, 255).

36. Temminck Groll (1988), 42–43.

37. Ter Kuile (1948), 205–06. The only Utrecht example of this combination of romanesque and gothic we know of is the tower of the House of the Regular Canons. They used this complex, built earlier that same century, since 1290 (Temminick Groll (1988), 41–42, 47).

38. Haakma Wagenaar (1936), 78–126. Haakma Wagenaar (1985), 151–58. Frans Kipp, 'Water en vuur', Het vuur beschouwd, ed. H. L. de Groot (Utrecht 1990), 78–80.

39. Meischke (1988), 8. K. Emmens, 'Van toren tot toren. Vier eeuwen bouwen aan de Sint-Joriskerk te Amersfoort', Flehite 22 (Amersfoort 1992), 27–28.

40. In my doctoral thesis I will try to establish the sources of these forms, what caused their application and who were involved in their use.

41. Vroom (1981), 345.

42. Th. Haakma Wagenaar, 'Geschiedenis van de bouw en de restauratie van de Jacobikerk', Restauratie vijf Hervormde kerken in de binnenstad van Utrecht, jaarverslag 1975/1976 (Utrecht s.a.), 44–47. Ter Kuile (1948), 213–14. The sketch Kipp made of the Utrecht conflagrations shows that the Jacobikerk was only struck in 1279, where the Buurkerk was struck both that year and in 1253 (Kipp (1990), 78).

43. Haakma Wagenaar (1975/1976), 44–47. The shape of two capitals attached to the eastern corners of the tower indicate the middle of the thirteenth century.

44. Temminck Groll (1988), 10–43.

45. Haakma Wagenaar (1975/1976), 48–51.

46. Haslinghuis (1965), 413, 459.

47. Emmens (1992), 27. A. van Rooijen, De Oude Kerk in Amsterdam in vogelvlucht (Amsterdam 1985), 15–16.

48. Van Vliet (1995), 26.

49. Many cities in the Netherlands received their privileges in this century, for instance Amersfoort in 1259 (granted by the bishop of Utrecht), Delft in 1246 and Dordrecht in 1220 (both by the count of Holland) to name just three examples (C. A. van Kalveen, 'De Sint Joriskerk in het middeleeuwse Amersfoort', De Amersfoortse kerken (Amersfoort 1984), 12; Kunstreisboek: Zuid-Holland (Amsterdam/Zeist 1985), 61, 85).

50. Van Vliet (1995), 28–30.

51. Dolfin (1989), 18.

52. Huib de Groot & Cees van Rooijen, 'Door het vuur en voor het vuur', Het vuur beschouwd, ed. by H. L. de Groot (Utrecht 1990), 12–16.

53. Haakma Wagenaar (1975/1976), 47–49.

54. Haakma Wagenaar (1975/1976), 51–53.

55. Haakma Wagenaar (1975/1976), 51.

56. Haakma Wagenaar (1936), 126, 130, 133–37. Haakma Wagenaar (1985), 157.

57. Haakma Wagenaar (1936), 126–33, 136–48. Haakma Wagenaar (1985), 156–58.

58. Haakma Wagenaar (1936), 153–65. Haakma Wagenaar (1985), 158.
59. Haakma Wagenaar (1975/1976), 53–54. Meischke (1988), 86.
60. E. H. ter Kuile, 'De bouwgeschiedenis van de St. Nicolaaskerk te Kampen naar de gegevens van de restauratie', *Bulletin K.N.O.B.*, nr. 71 (1972), 72–86. L. Helten, *Kathedralen für Bürger* (Utrecht/Amsterdam 1994), 80–82, Figs. 98, 99.
61. Van Vliet (1995), 26. Helten (1994), 11.
62. Meischke dates the hall-choirs of Zwolle and Amersfoort resp. before 1406 and 1442 (Meischke (1988), 9). Emmens (1992), 28. K. Emmens, 'De koorpatij van de Amersfoortse Sint-Joriskerk', *Nieuwsbrief Stichting Bouwhistorie Nederland*, nr. 9 ('s-Hertogenbosch 1994), 4–17. In this article I date the hall-choir of this church between 1370 and 1390. H. Janse, *Houten kappen in Nederland 1000–1940* (Delft 1989), 35. He dates the construction of the hall-nave of the Oude Kerk between *c.* 1325 and 1350.
63. Van Vliet (1995), 26–29.
64. Helten (1994), 17–60.
65. Meischke (1988), 9–11. Helten (1994), 11.
66. Or is it due to the fact that the Dom fabric had no relations whatsoever with those of the parishes, contrary to the position in other cities? Maybe the city council did not see any necessity to expand one of the four parish churches into a prestigious building (Meischke (1988), 85). In fact, four parish churches in Utrecht was too many and the Buurkerk was now not one of the more important parish churches in the diocese (Vroom (1981), 351).
67. Ter Kuile (1948), 290–91.
68. Ter Kuile (1948), 291–92, 311. Meischke (1988), 85–88.
69. Haakma Wagenaar (1936), 168–247. Haakma Wagenaar (1986), 158–69. This giant roof was struck by the storm of 1674. Since then three separate roofs cover the aisles of the nave (Haakma Wagenaar (1985), 181.
70. Haakma Wagenaar (1985), 168–77. Haakma Wagenaar (1936), 248–306. The three choirs were demolished in 1586, only six years after the Reformation and replaced by houses (Haakma Wagenaar (1985), 177–81).
71. Haakma Wagenaar (1976), 55–59.
72. Haakma Wagenaar (1978), 83–85. Meischke (1988), 88–89.
73. Ter Kuile (1948), 291–95, 314–15. Meischke (1988), 9–11. There is no explanation yet concerning this diversity of forms. The only difference of importance between the church of Edam and for instance Amersfoort is the material of the vaulting (resp. wood and stone), the bays remain oblong. The bays of the church at The Hague are square and only very few piers divide the space.
74. Delamarre (1988), 46–47. It is a puzzle why both the nave and the tower are romanesque in their appearance whereas, at the same time, two other parish churches were erected nearby in the new fashion gothic.
75. Dolfin (1989), 28. Delemarre (1988), 8. Vroom (1981), 352.

The Mariakerk at Utrecht, Speyer, and Italy

By Peter Kidson

Without a doubt, by far the most interesting of the medieval churches in Utrecht is the one that is no longer there — the Mariakerk. The last vestiges were removed 150 years ago in 1843. But like the Cheshire Cat, it had been in process of vanishing slowly over the previous 200 years; and were it not for one of the most remarkable exercises in architectural recording of the seventeenth century, our knowledge of it would be confined to a handful of brief, repetitive, and certainly not very informative, notices in documentary sources from the Middle Ages and the centuries that followed.

We owe the record to the anxieties of the ecclesiastical authorities who were in charge of the church in the 1630s. At that time the Mariakerk was used in a discreet but clandestine fashion by the small catholic community of Utrecht, which was tolerated, but only barely so, by the predominantly Calvinist majority of the citizens. The situation was always volatile, frequently ominous. The church had already been threatened with demolition in 1581; and 55 years later the dean and chapter, fearful for its survival, but immensely proud of it both as a building and as an institution, decided in a mood of antiquarian piety, somewhat reminiscent of our own times, that a visual memorandum ought to be made before it was too late. For this purpose they secured the services of the Haarlem artist, Pieter Saenredam, who specialized in drawing and painting buildings. Saenredam came to Utrecht in the summer of 1636, and spent, so we are told, twenty weeks there,[1] in the course of which time he made eleven drawings of the interior of the Mariakerk and three of the exterior. On his return to Haarlem, seven of the interiors were immediately worked up into paintings; the rest followed at a more leisurely pace. It is these drawings and paintings that now represent the building for us. Saenredam was clearly an archaeologist manqué. Neither drawings nor paintings were romanticized, and they were accompanied by diagrams and measurements that have every appearance of being mathematically accurate. What they reveal is a church that fully justified the concern of the clergy, for it was a work of conspicuous originality, a totally unexpected maverick among the churches of Romanesque date in the city and the surrounding region. Moreover, if the chronology that can be extracted from the documents really applied to the monument that Saenredam painted, the Mariakerk was a building of European significance, which ought to be ranked with the handful of buildings that betokened a major epoch in medieval architectural history. However, the chronology has never been firmly established, and the purpose of the present essay is to re-examine the whole question in the light of evidence not previously taken into account. The importance of the subject is my only excuse for trespassing on a well-cultivated piece of art-historical territory to which I have no prescriptive right of access.

The extant manuscript sources date from the middle of the fourteenth century,[2] but these were compiled from earlier chronicles and obit rolls, which contained a basic list of dates and events to be commemorated, that are not really open to doubt. The one event which caught the attention of the early chroniclers was not the foundation of the church so much as the murder of its founder. This was noticed by Sigebert of Gembloux who put it in 1098; otherwise the briefest of the local references occurs in the *Annales Egmundenses*, which state under the year 1099 that Bishop Conrad was struck down while celebrating mass '*in proprio domo*', and was buried in the *ecclesia sanctae Mariae* which he himself had built at great expense.[3] The entry is in the first part of the chronicle, which up to the early twelfth century, was little more than excerpts from obit rolls. One other death that the annalist thought fit to mention was that of Emperor Henry IV in 1107 [sic], though there is nothing to indicate that this had any significance for the Mariakerk.

The Mariakerk had its own annals,[4] which simply recorded the killing of Bishop Conrad in 1099; but this was subsequently augmented by the scribe with the information that he was stabbed by a 'plebian'. The martyrologium adds that he was 'the founder of our church', and credits him with the establishment of the 'fratrum prebendam', i.e. the distribution of the endowments among the canons. Under 1106 the death of Henry IV was again listed without further comment. But the martyrologium reveals the reason for his inclusion. There the emperor was referred to as 'our benefactor, who ordered the church to be consecrated and confirmed our possessions'.

Another fourteenth-century source was a list of bishops of Utrecht, of whom the last to be named by the original compiler was Johannes de Arkel (1342–64).[5] This adds two further details to the medieval tradition about the origin of the Mariakerk. One is that Conrad built the church up against the walls of Utrecht in a manner reminiscent of a church at Milan which Conrad himself had destroyed. The other is that the murder was committed in the bishop's own hall by a certain Frisian who managed to escape when the deed was done.

As given in the list of bishops the story of the Milanese church is pure fantasy. Needless to say there is no evidence that a Lotharingian bishop was involved in the destruction of any Milanese church at the time when the Mariakerk was founded; and how such a curious fiction came to be fabricated is itself a substantial problem. One might easily conclude that by the middle of the fourteenth-century legends were forming around the Mariakerk. An alternative explanation, however, might be that a substantially true account has been rendered incomprehensible by abbreviation and corruption. Of this, more in due course.

The identification of the 'plebian' of the martyrologium as a Frisian is also not beyond the need of further elucidation, though it is not in itself historically incredible. A much fuller version is given in the chronicle of Johannes de Beka,[6] where it reads like the precis of one of Chaucer's tales. Here the plebian has become a certain Frisian by name Pleberus. The crafty bishop is said to have cheated him of the exorbitant payment he demanded for solving the problem of how to lay the foundations of the church; and in revenge the Frisian plotted the bishop's murder. De Beka does not mention the Milanese church, from which it may be inferred that he was not familiar with the list of bishops or its source. But the fact that he turned *plebeo* into the Frisian *Pleberus* suggests that he had access to other texts, if only to misread and embellish them.

For the fullest account of all, however, it is necessary to turn to one of Saenredam's interiors (Pl. IX). Apparently there were some not very distinguished latin hexameters displayed on the crossing piers, purporting to describe the origins of the church.[7] Given Saenredam's meticulous attention to detail, it may be assumed that these were faithfully reproduced in the painting. The translation reads as follows:

> Should any wish to know when and why
> This ancient church was built, these verses will instruct you.
> When Henry IV swayed sceptre over the Roman Empire
> And had subdued all Italy with his victorious troops,
> Milan alone dared close to him its rebellious gates.
> Capturing it at last, at first the victor took his spoils,

Then destroyed the town, in flames which did not spare
Even the white marble temple of the Holy Virgin Mary.
This saddened him. His soul afire with pious love
He resolved to have another built
Wherever else on earth he could.
At that point Conrad, bishop of Utrecht,
His former teacher and fervent comrade in arms,
Rendered the emperor a service by founding,
On an elevation in this place,
A high-towered church, built to last through the ages.
In this he was helped by presents and a large donation
From the emperor. So you see it,
Standing on its firm columns,
The vault covering in perpetuity the lofty site.
The venerable bishop took it upon himself
To serve as primate of the church, instituting prebends
And canons to sing an everlasting song to you, O Virgin Mary.
After the passage of three times six years
From the church's beginnings, the fatal hour arrived
When the holy bishop was killed through infamous murder,
For this reason: when the foundations for the walls
Were being laid, the masons ran into a bottomless
And squelchy mire. Work came to a halt.
None of the experts could deal with the problem.
They could not believe that their highly paid staff,
With unlimited funds, was unequal to the task.
When all hope was given up, a boorish Frisian
Guaranteed that he would fill the pit. But when
They heard his quite immodest fee, they balked,
He quit, and work was stopped once more.
The man having a son he loved, the bishop called the lad
And offered him a bribe. With his mother's help,
He got his father drunk, wheedled the technique out of him and,
Behind his father's back, told it to the priest.
At once the work, after long delay, was recommenced,
And all were overjoyed to know the secret trick.
The Frisian, though, enraged at being so deceived,
Was driven to despair. Beside himself,
He killed the bishop with a sharp knife
As he descended the stairs after celebrating Mass.
His death is commemorated in April by the inhabitants of Tivoli
      (Sic! — the latin is Tiburti).
In the year 1099.

    The text of these verses does not appear in the preparatory drawing in the Utrecht Municipal Archives, no doubt because the drawing was less than one third of the size of the finished picture. A pedestal and canopy on the left-hand pier, which had once been occupied by a statue, were also omitted in the drawing. To make room for the text on the left-hand pier, the picture was extended further to the left than the drawing. From all of this it can be inferred that the dean and chapter insisted that a legible account of what they took to be the origins of the church should be preserved for posterity in the painted version.

At first sight this narrative seems like nothing but an expanded version of the cryptic remarks in the list of bishops, making it even more of a farrago of nonsense. The tale of the Frisian's revenge was evidently based on Beka, or Beka's source. But by adding the detail that the murder took place eighteen years after the foundation, it deprives the story of whatever credibility Beka's version of it may have had. Either the problem of the foundation was insoluble for most of the eighteen years, or the Frisian nursed his grievance for a similar length of time. Neither seems likely, and more plausible explanations can be proposed. It was said that Bishop Conrad was murdered because he was a schismatic;[8] but it could just as well have been an episode in the on-going feud between the bishops of Utrecht and the counts of Holland, which from time to time erupted into active warfare.[9] Either of these would imply that the motive for the murder was political. It is hard to believe that a mere artisan, whose identity must have been known, could have got clean away, and eluded retribution for several years, if he was acting entirely on his own. In the end the crime was punished. In 1110, when the daughter of Henry I of England was on her way to become the Empress Matilda, the wife of Henry V, the happy pair, having met at Liège, moved on to Utrecht, where they celebrated Easter and were formally betrothed. In the course of the festivities the Emperor Henry found time to order the execution of an unnamed man who was alleged to have plotted the death of Bishop Conrad.[10] No doubt a great deal about the affair will never be known, but one thing is certain: the case of a Frisian artisan would never have been referred to the Emperor. If imperial authority was needed for his execution, the plotter was a man of some social distinction. The actual assassin may have been a Frisian, and he may have been engaged in the building of the Mariakerk, but much more was involved than a personal quarrel between him and the bishop, and much of the story may be apocryphal.

The really important new item in the Saenredam text, was the prominent part assigned to the Emperor Henry IV. There was no precedent for this among the extant medieval sources apart from his designation in the martyrologium as 'our benefactor'. On the other hand, the reference to the Milanese church in the list of bishops can almost certainly be taken to imply that something akin to the Saenredam text was in circulation by the middle of the fourteenth century, for when the two are put side by side, it is clear that one is simply an abbreviated quotation from the other. With this in mind it is worth taking a closer look at the question of the Milanese church.

As history, the Saenredam text is, for all the extra detail, no great improvement on the list of bishops, but marginally it does make better sense to attribute the destruction of an Italian church to the emperor than to the bishop. At no time in his turbulent reign did Henry IV sack Milan or destroy a Milanese church. He was in Milan on precisely one recorded occasion, 14 April 1081, and then only briefly en route for Pavia and Rome.[11] There was, however, one north Italian city which was besieged and captured by Henry IV. This was Mantua. In 1090 he mounted an expedition to Italy with the express intention of dispossessing the Countess Matilda, the staunchest ally of his arch-enemy the Pope, of the vast estates between the Apennines and the Po, which she had inherited at the age of nine in 1055. The siege lasted from June 1090 to April 1091. Whether it ended with a sack is not recorded, but it is just possible that a church of the Virgin was destroyed on that occasion, for there is no such dedication among the older churches of the city. Bishop Conrad of Utrecht was with him on this campaign,[12] and was present when Mantua fell. Thus it transpires that a verifiable historical event was turned into a romantic fable by the corruption of the single word *Mantova* into *Mediolanum*.

The Saenredam text concludes with another bit of mystification by introducing the *Tiburti*, i.e. the inhabitants of Tivoli. But here again a simple emendation is all that is needed to bring sense out of nonsense, for the correct word was obviously *Traiecti*, i.e. the citizens of Utrecht. How these misunderstandings came to infect the transmission is in itself an interesting question; but the fact remains that far from being the sheer make-believe that it is often taken to be, the Saenredam text needs remarkably little editorial attention to turn it into a potentially useful historical document.

There is abundant evidence that the Henry IV connection was a source of pride and accepted without question at the Mariakerk in the late Middle Ages. A fifteenth-century cushion cover has survived in which he is depicted standing on one side of the Virgin with Bishop Conrad on the other, in a manner that clearly assigns to them equal status as founders. There was also a statue of the emperor on the roof of the choir, almost certainly medieval in date, which the chapter had restored in 1632.[13] By then it was no doubt expedient for the catholics of Utrecht to draw attention to this particular imperial founder, for his life-long hostility to the Roman papacy would *ipso facto* make him something of a hero in the eyes of the Calvinist reformers; and it was perhaps with this in mind that, in 1641, the chapter paid out quite a large sum for a portrait of the emperor, whom they explicitly named as 'our founder'.[14]

What is curious about the whole business is not so much that the early sources were decidedly reticent on the subject of Henry IV, but that signs of real interest cannot be inferred until the story of the Milanese church began to circulate, i.e. not much before the middle of the fourteenth century, by which time would-be historians were distinctly hazy about what actually happened. It is hardly surprising that in the twelfth century ecclesiastical chroniclers should have been at pains to play down the connection between the Mariakerk and Henry IV, for papal anathemas had left him with a reputation little short of anti-Christ. But what caused the pendulum to swing the other way, 250 years later, is harder to discern. It is perhaps conceivable that the fortuitous operations of the laws of inheritance had something to do with the revival of half-forgotten memories of former imperial associations. When Count William IV died, in 1345, the County of Holland passed to his sister Margaret, who happened to be the wife of the German emperor of the day: Louis of Bavaria. If it was the social rank of founders and benefactors that gave prestige to churches, the canons of the Mariakerk may well have decided that the cachet of having an imperial founder more than outweighed any stigma attached to his name. But in that case the only thing that mattered was Henry's title.

Put like that, the value of the Saenredam text, even when amended, as a reliable source about the origins of the Mariakerk, remains open to question. Nevertheless, it considerably augments the other documentary material, and if there had been no pictorial evidence, the building history of the church might be summarized in something like the following terms.

Alone among the sources, the Saenredam text gives the date of the foundation. It was eighteen years before the bishop's murder, in *c.* 1081. The documents are unanimous that Conrad was the founder, and there is nothing to suggest that Henry IV's participation began until after the 'sack' of Mantua in 1091. But if the bishop acted on his own initiative in 1081, it is unlikely that he looked far beyond Utrecht itself for ideas about the sort of church that he intended to build. In 1043 one of his predecessors, Bishop Bernoldus (*c.* 1027–54), had founded the Pieterskerk; and like Conrad in 1099, he was buried in his own church when he died.[15] The Pieterskerk lay to the east of the cathedral, and the Janskerk to the north was also ascribed to Bernoldus. As the

Mariakerk lay due west of the cathedral, it has been inferred that Bernoldus planned to build a cross of churches with the cathedral at the centre, to be named after the four great basilicas of Rome, and that Conrad's church was part of the implementation of this scheme. If so, there is a strong probability that it would have been conceived as a basilica of the kind that can still be seen in the Pieterskerk or the Janskerk.

The annals of Egmond state that 'the great expense' of the church was incurred by the bishop alone. The martyrologium called Henry 'our benefactor', but then specified that he 'authorised the dedication of altars and confirmed our possessions' which, rather carefully perhaps, stops well short of presenting him as co-founder. The author of the annals of St Mary's thought it important to add as an afterthought to entries reporting the murder of the bishop and the coronation of Henry V at Aachen, that the altar of the Virgin, which was later removed to the west end, had been consecrated by Conrad as the high altar — as though this proved that the church was indeed Conrad's. And though the omission of any mention of Henry IV in the reference to the Milanese church in the fourteenth-century list of bishops is confusing, it does at least preserve intact the article of faith that Conrad alone had been the founder of the Mariakerk.

That might be described as the early house tradition. But a quite different picture could be constructed from sources outside Utrecht. This starts from what modern historians would probably think to be the most important thing about Conrad, namely that for twenty-three years, between 1076 and 1099 — the period when the power struggle between the pope and the emperor for control of the German church was at its height, he never once wavered in his support for the emperor. His origins are unknown, but he was said to have come from Swabia, and all the early steps in his career were taken in German churches such as Hildesheim and Goslar.[16] He owed his elevation in 1076 entirely to the emperor and his loyalty was as valuable to the imperial cause as it was rare among German ecclesiastics. The backing which he gave to Henry's attempt to depose Gregory VII, and his support for the anti-pope, Clement III, had the inevitable consequence of making him *persona non grata* at Rome, where technically he was in a state of schism. In 1087 he was put in charge of the education of Henry's son, the future Henry V, and in this capacity he must have spent much time at court. It is inconceivable that he was not familiar with the emperor's own architectural project at Speyer. Conrad was at Speyer with Henry IV in 1090, and was his companion in Italy for the first part of the campaign which culminated in the siege of Mantua. His murder in 1099 deprived Henry of one of his few personal friends, and the loss was all the more grievous in the unhappy circumstances of the last years of his reign. It would have been entirely appropriate if he had adopted the Mariakerk as a gesture of gratitude for his dead friend, whether or not he was suffering pangs of remorse for deeds of violence done at Mantua.

It is obvious that the Saenredam text is the only document in the case that does anything like justice to the close relationship between the emperor and the bishop. It is also quite explicit that it was 'this church', i.e. the church in which the verses were displayed, that received the benefit of Henry's generosity, and that there was only one church in which the emperor and the bishop were involved. It should therefore follow that the house tradition and the Saenredam text were referring to the same building. But were they, and if not, which of the two was mendacious?

This is where the visual record enters the argument. Saenredam's pictures should, indeed in the last resort they must, dovetail with the documentary evidence to sustain a single, historically coherent interpretation of the chronology of the building. But it is precisely here that the complications begin, for architectural historians have been virtually unanimous that the church depicted by Saenredam could not have been built in the time of Bishop Conrad or Henry IV. The consensus of recent opinion is that it belonged to the second quarter of the twelfth century.[17] A previous generation even brought it forward into the second half of the twelfth century. The fact that the documents might lead to a different conclusion was regrettable, but, as a distinguished art historian once said 'if style tells me one thing and documents another, I will always trust my sense of style'; and the Mariakerk is a case in point. To escape from the impasse, architectural historians have postulated two Mariakerks: the first of which was founded in 1081 by Bishop Conrad; while the second was a complete rebuilding from some date in the twelfth century. The former, having satisfied the documents, then conveniently disappeared without trace; the latter was still standing in the seventeenth century. It so happens that the annals of St Mary's record under the year 1131 the occurrence of a fire in which a large part of the city of Utrecht was said to have been burnt; and the Mariakerk was one of several notable casualties singled out for specific mention.[18] At first sight this is just what appears to be needed to justify the theory of the second church; but from that point of view it is almost certainly a snare and delusion. Chronicles abound with remarks of that sort, and unless there is a follow-up, they do not always have to be taken at their face value. In the next fire to afflict the city, which happened in 1148, both the Pieterskerk and the Janskerk were said to have been burnt,[19] but it is doubtful whether many architectural historians would be prepared to redate either of them on the strength of this evidence. The year after the fire of 1131, a reconsecration service was performed by the Archbishop of Cologne and four bishops.[20] As it was not thought necessary to specify the church which received these ministrations, the obvious inference is that it was the annalist's own church, i.e. the Mariakerk. If so, the fire damage can only have been very superficial. Certainly two or three years later the church was in full commission when Floris of Swarte sought sanctuary there for three months before he was murdered (1134–35).[21] It has been claimed that the removal of Conrad's high altar to the west end is evidence that rebuilding was in progress. A date of c. 1138 has been proposed for this change of location,[22] though why a rearrangement of the altars could not have been the reason for the re-consecration service performed by the Archbishop of Cologne in 1132 is not clear.

If there was a rebuilding in the twelfth century, the clues in the annals are curiously muted and oblique. No one reading them would instantly leap to the conclusion that there was a second church, unless they were under pressure to find one. The idea was perhaps permissible as long as the narrative in the Hamburg painting could be treated as a romantic invention; but once it is recognized that there was a substratum of sound history behind the embroideries, the theory of the second church becomes an expedient of last resort. Before going to such lengths it is worth asking whether the stylistic arguments are so watertight as to exclude any other possibility. Not much more can be done about the documents, but art-historical inferences are always open to revision, and in this case they are positively crying out for re-examination.

The reluctance of architectural historians to subscribe to the view that the Mariakerk of the documents and the church painted by Saenredam were one and the same, stems from the current orthodoxy about the evolution of Romanesque architecture in the lower Rhine–Meuse area. This has come to be organized around a single critical event, namely the inception or reception of what the Germans call the 'gebundenes system' (gebonden stelsel in Dutch,[3] système Lombardo Rhenan in French). Before this arrived most of the great churches of north-west Europe still fell into the category of the unvaulted basilica, which had descended with very little change from prototypes which belonged to the early Christian period. These were essentially aggregates of large blocks of interior space shaped by walls or arcades, i.e. the nave, aisles and transepts of the familiar church plan. The *gebundenes system* may be described as the articulation of these primary spaces by the device of inserting into them smaller cells framed by wall-shafts, arches, and in theory if not always in practice, some species of cross vault. The great questions for architectural historians are when did this new type of church make its appearance in north-western Europe, and where did it originate?

The one thing about which there is no doubt, is that the Mariakerk in Saenredam's pictures was a church of this kind. It was, however, by no means a typical example. The original east end was extensively Gothicized in the fourteenth century, and for some reason Saenredam paid very little attention to the choir. But even in the parts on which he concentrated, i.e. the nave and transepts, there were three unusual features. Of thirty-three churches cited by Kubach and Verbeek as instances of the *gebundenes system* in the region,[23] all but three were two-storeyed, and only two had proper galleries above their side aisles. Both were in Utrecht. One was the Mariakerk, and the other, the Nicolaaskerk, was patently modelled on the Mariakerk.

A second peculiarity was the presence of a dwarf transept in the middle of the nave. Here again the sample in Kubach and Verbeek included no more than three instances. The second was at Kerkrade (Rolduc), near Maastricht;[24] while the third was once a feature of the Onze Lieve Vrouwekerk at Maastricht. These nave transepts were clearly related to one another, and as they were an intrusive element, the question of which came first is likely to be settled only on the basis of contact with sources outside the area.

The third rarity was the ribbed vaults of the nave and transepts. Here it was very much a question of date, for ribs became common among the later instances of the *gebundenes system*. More than anything else it was the presence of ribs which persuaded Gall that the Mariakerk belonged to the second half of the twelfth century. Firm dates were hard to find, but there was one documented date which seemed to provide a plausible peg on which the whole chronology of ribs in the Rhineland could be hung. This was 1159, when there was a fire at Speyer which provided a convenient *terminus post quem* for the ribs in the transepts there.[25] As the nave of Speyer had groined vaults and the choir was barrel-vaulted, the sense of evolution was difficult to resist. During the inter-war years and for long afterwards, it was axiomatic that ribbed vaults were later than groined vaults. It was also widely accepted that ribbed vaults originated in France, from where, by a process akin to osmosis, they gradually percolated into the surrounding areas, though not to any great extent before the second half of the twelfth century. Speyer appeared to confirm this theory to perfection, and it became the pivot around which undated or controversial ribs, like those of Worms, Murbach or Utrecht could be grouped.

In recent years, this edifice has begun to crumble. Dendrochronology produced dates between 1132–36 for the timberwork at Worms, which made a date in the 1160s for the vaults untenable.[26] Then, in the aftermath of the restoration of Speyer (1958–71), it emerged that the ribs of the transepts could not have been inserted into a structure that was not already standing.[27] Accordingly, they ceased to have any connection with the fire of 1159. If the ribs were integrated into the upper stages of the transept, they had to be part of the remodelling of Speyer that was set in motion by Henry IV; though it could still be argued that they belonged to the latest phase of that operation. This permitted a cautious revision of the chronology. Rather reluctantly, one feels, Kubach settled for a date in the 1130s,[28] and it was in the wake of Speyer that the hypothetical second version of the Mariakerk at Utrecht came to be located in the same decade.

These reappraisals have been made almost entirely on the basis of archaeological evidence. As steps in the right direction they are welcome, but an historian might think that they do not go nearly far enough. To an extent that makes it unique among European cathedrals, Speyer was deeply embroiled in the momentous events of the years when it was being updated for Henry IV, and the building cannot be properly understood without reference to them. When the purpose that inspired the work is taken into account, it becomes very hard indeed to resist the conclusion that the ribs were an essential part of Henry's project, and almost impossible to see how they could have been added to the design at any time after Henry's death in 1106. To justify these claims a digression is required into certain aspects of the emperor's quarrel with the Roman papacy.

In its first incarnation Speyer was started by Conrad II in 1030, continued by Henry III, and completed in 1061 during the minority of Henry IV. In 1030 Conrad's intention was to make Speyer his own burial church, and in this respect it was not fundamentally different from Otto the Great's Magdeburg or Henry II's Bamberg. Although the building cannot have been far advanced when he died in 1039 Conrad was in fact buried there. It was Henry III who broke with precedent. Instead of adopting or founding a church of his own for the purpose, he too elected to be buried at Speyer; and it was this decision that launched Speyer on its career as the mausoleum of the Salian dynasty. Henry IV took the idea one stage further. The inspiration of the vast campaign of works which commenced shortly after 1081 was nothing less than the wish to convert the cathedral into a vast imperial mortuary chapel, or collection of such chapels. The physical evidence of this intention is the presence of six specially prepared tomb chambers let into the thickness of the walls — two in the choir, one on each side of the high altar, and two in each of the end walls of the transept. It may be conjectured that the two choir niches were designated for Conrad and Henry III, and that the transepts were reserved for Henry IV, his son, and the royal ladies, though as the whole scheme was aborted before it was implemented, it is pointless to speculate about the details.

So far as I am aware, it has never previously been suggested that the recesses were intended for tombs; but no other satisfactory function has ever been found for them, and the circumstantial case is a strong one. The transepts were the principal beneficiaries of Henry IV's attention.[29] In Speyer I they were little more than bare boxes of masonry, devoid of both altars and articulation. The immense envelope of cladding that in stage II allowed the niches to be inserted in the end walls, also made provision on the east side for shallow apses. In other words, niches and altars arrived together. The transformation of the transepts into veritable chapels was further enhanced by the cross of arches overhead. Whatever the structural advantages of ribbed vaults, in medieval eyes they would almost certainly convey the sense of a ciborium over a consecrated space of especial holiness, or at least express an aspiration to be understood in that way. The ribs may have been an afterthought in so far as they were not foreseen in 1081, but they added an extra note of solemnity which distinguished the transepts from the nave, and which would have been meaningless unless they were introduced while it was still the purpose of the transepts to house the imperial tombs.

Externally, it was planned that the windows of the transepts should receive elaborate frames of carved ornament, and if all of them had been embellished in this way no one would have been in any doubt that the transepts were the most important part of the church. But the programme was abandoned rather precipitously in mid-window.[30] This is perhaps the most important clue of all, for the abrupt departure of the sculptors signified not just the death of Henry IV in 1106, but the premature collapse of all his burial plans.

Henry died at Liège. His wish to be buried at Speyer was not at first respected; but by order of the papal legate, the body was taken to Speyer, where it lay for five years in an unconsecrated chapel, which Godfrey of Viterbo identified as the Afrakapelle.[31] This was because he died in a state of excommunication. When in the end the Church gave way, the place of burial was not in the transept but at the east end of the nave. None of the niches was ever occupied by a tomb; and whatever soul masses were celebrated on behalf of the defunct Salians took place at the nave altar, or in the *chorus regum* which was subsequently set up over the royal tombs as a kind of collegiate chantry.

There is nothing in the documents to indicate that the withholding of burial rites was used by the Church as a bargaining ploy to confound Henry's grand design for the exaltation of the Salians. But given the architectural evidence that there was such a scheme, and the historical evidence that it came to nothing, it is reasonable to suppose that the matter was raised in the course of negotiations between Henry V and Paschal II at Rome in 1110, when the papal ban was finally lifted.

It would be a mistake to underestimate the seriousness of the tomb issue. For both sides what was at stake was a matter of principle, indeed nothing less than the issue at the heart of the quarrel between pope and emperor. Henry IV was heir to an exceedingly lofty notion of his status as a consecrated ruler, by virtue of which he considered himself entitled to exercise far-reaching powers over the affairs of the Church. His father, Henry III, consistently invoked the sacral kingship as the foundation of his authority without compunction or challenge. If necessary, precedents could be cited among his predecessors extending back through Ottonians and Carolingians to Byzantine emperors and Constantine himself. Then, in the middle of the eleventh century this whole tradition was suddenly thrown into question by a radically different conception of the right order of power in the world, emanating from Rome, and based on the fundamental distinction between secular and sacerdotal. From this point of view kings and emperors were no more than laymen, and however great their temporal privileges, these did not, or should not, allow them to cross the lines of demarcation which separated the spheres of the laity and the spiritual hierarchy. These extended to where and how laymen should be buried in church.

What Henry IV appeared to be doing at Speyer was expropriating strictly ecclesiastical symbols, like the *croisée d'ogives*, to proclaim that consecrated kings deserved the sort of veneration normally reserved for saints or relics. The gesture was all the more provocative for being made at the moment when the conflict between Henry and Gregory VII reached its climax, shortly after they had solemnly deposed one another in 1080, and when Henry was about to set out for Rome in order to be crowned emperor by his anti-pope. The Church party could not fail to construe the plan as a flagrant act of calculated defiance; it could not afford to turn a blind eye, and in the prevailing mood of intransigence had no option but to veto it. It was still a sticking point in 1110. By then, however, Henry V was no longer fighting for the sacral kingship as this had been understood by his father or grandfather. He had shifted his ground, and when at last he was in a position to wring concessions from the pope, it probably cost him little to give way on the question of where the late emperor should be buried.

It follows from this interpretation that to all intents and purposes the ribs of Speyer were already in position when Henry IV died in 1106. Unless they had passed the point of no return, they would have been jettisoned once the prime mover was no longer there. If the argument is sound, the case for postulating a second Mariakerk in the 1130s evaporates, and with it go the archaeological reasons for disregarding the account of the origin of the church (suitably corrected) given in the Saenredam text. There was only one Mariakerk. Bishop Conrad was the founder in the sense of setting up the chapter in 1081, but in all probability the church itself was not designed until the late 1090s. Given Henry IV's friendship with Bishop Conrad, and his recorded interest in the foundation, it makes good sense to suppose that the man who was responsible for the vaults at Utrecht, was seconded from Speyer when he had completed the task of putting ribs over the transepts there. The question then arises whether it was the same man who gave the Mariakerk the galleries and nave transepts which, together with the ribs, set it apart from the main body of *gebundenes system* churches in the lower Rhine–Meuse area. If so, there is a very strong likelihood that the man was Italian.

The Mariakerk has often been called an Italian church in the north, but how it got there is a question that has usually been side-stepped, as though it were a trap for the unwary, and answers have tended to be very cautious. This is another consequence of the reluctance to take the Saenredam text seriously, for the story of the Italian church seems to offer the rudiments of an explanation. If Bishop Conrad was present when Mantua was captured in 1091, and the Mariakerk became an expiatory offering for a church destroyed on that occasion, it seems rather perverse not to connect these circumstances with the Italianate appearance of the building. At least the hypothesis ought to be explored further. The problems do not entirely vanish, but they are not perhaps as intractable as sometimes supposed.

It may be accepted for the sake of argument that the Mariakerk was not the replica of a destroyed Mantuan church, which, unless it were brand new, would probably have been a simple basilica. The Italian churches that resembled the Mariakerk were not to be found in the lands of the Countess Matilda, but further west in Lombardy. There were some in Milan, but the places par excellence were Pavia and Novara. Oddly enough, the Romanesque cathedrals of both these cities, which are known to have had nave transepts, have disappeared: Pavia in the sixteenth century, Novara as lately as 1863. The evidence for the double cathedral of Pavia is meagre; but there are drawings of Novara which show it to have possessed all three of the features which made the Mariakerk exceptional: galleries, including one across the west front, combined with an internal porch, which was very rare; dwarf nave transepts, and ribbed vaults. The ribs rested on corbels, and in the nineteenth century it was inferred that they were additions,[32] but the grouping of the clerestory windows of the nave implied that vaults were always intended. It is dangerous to compare two no longer extant buildings on the basis of drawings alone, but ostensibly the cathedral of Novara and the Mariakerk were too close for them not to be related. Is it possible that Novara was the model for Utrecht?

The trouble with almost all the relevant Lombard buildings is that none of them is firmly dated. On stylistic grounds Novara has usually been put well into the twelfth century. Kingsley Porter offered a date *c.* 1125,[33] which suited the theory of a second Mariakerk well enough. The date could be disputed, but it is perhaps more to the point that Novara cannot have been the first church of its kind. It was too provincial, and too close to both Milan and Pavia to escape the influence of the architectural styles that were fashionable in those cities. Pavia in particular, as capital of Lombardy, was still able, at the turn of the century, to compete vigorously with its ancient rival in the matter of great churches, and it was probably there, rather than at Novara or Milan, that Henry IV recruited the expert who constructed the vaults of Speyer for him. Henry seems to have avoided Milan, but he was in Pavia on several occasions: in April 1081 on his way to Rome, when he presumably took the opportunity to have himself crowned king of Lombardy; again a year later; and he was there for several weeks at the end of 1092 when the Mantuan campaign was over.[34]

As far as the vaults are concerned the argument is circumstantial. There is no general agreement that large-scale ribbed vaults were to be seen anywhere in Lombardy when Henry IV was there; although the reaction which set in after the failure of Kingsley Porter's crusade to instate Italy as the true home of ribbed vaulting almost certainly went too far in the opposite direction. The crucial thing about the Speyer ribs is that they were the work of someone who was familiar with Roman vaults. That is to say there is no proper keystone. Instead one arch was built before the other, and appears to pass through the crown of the second arch, which takes the form of two arcs abutting it. This was how the brick ribs embedded in the concrete of the Baths of Diocletian were built; and it may be surmised that part of the attraction for Henry IV lay in the knowledge that the *croisée d'ogives* was Roman as well as ecclesiological — a perfect symbol for a holy Roman emperor. Though it does not follow as a matter of course that the Speyer man was Italian, the bulk of the classical evidence was to be found in Italy, and the intuition which led Kingsley Porter to the view that the first moves in adapting what was in effect a Roman practice, for use in Romanesque churches, were made in Italy rather than in France, was essentially sound. One by one, his putative list of eleventh-century examples was whittled away; but so far as I am aware one case still remains outstanding: S Nazaro Maggiore in Milan. This church was one of the casualties of the religious riots which wrought havoc in the city in 1075, and its restoration was the work of Archbishop Anselm III, who was buried there when he died in 1093. The diagonal ribs over the *nef-unique* of S Nazaro Maggiore have a span of over 20 m; which though not quite on the scale of those at Speyer (*c.* 25 m), at least proves that the necessary technology and experience were available in Italy.

With the sculpture we are on firmer ground. The idea of framing windows with broad bands of carved ornament was nowhere common, and apart from Speyer the most conspicuous instances are to be found in the choir of S Abbondio at Como, for which there was a papal consecration in 1096. One of the Como window patterns was copied, more or less move for move, in the window of a chapel in the south transept of Quedlinburg, so there were sculptors with access to the Como pattern book active in Germany at about the right time. The men who carved the Speyer windows almost certainly knew S Abbondio, but an even closer parallel can be found in the pulpit of the church on the Isola di S Giulio in the lake of Orta just north of Novara. Here the similarities extend beyond motifs and formal arrangement to the way the shapes were actually cut; and it can be inferred with confidence that the Orta sculptor worked at Speyer.

If the sculptors of Speyer came from Italy in the 1090s it becomes very difficult to postulate a different date or provenance for the author of the vaults. Speyer was a remodelling job, and references to Italy were confined to details; but given a free hand to design a complete church for his northern patrons, such a man would almost certainly come up with something out of the Pavian constellation — especially if his brief encouraged him to do so, which is precisely what, according to the Saenredam text, happened at Utrecht. All in all that seemingly fanciful document turns out to have drifted no great distance from the verifiable facts of history, and the time has come for it to be rehabilitated among the primary sources of the Mariakerk.

The conclusion that the ribbed vaults of Speyer and Utrecht belonged to the end of the eleventh century rather than a generation later is the limited objective of the present paper. It would make them almost exactly contemporary with the ribs of the choir of Durham, and open fresh vistas of speculation about the relation between Anglo-Norman architecture and the *gebundenes system*. In a more general sense it would provide prima facie grounds for reopening Kingsley Porter's argument that ribbed vaulting began in Italy; and it would do nothing but good if it helped to clarify the distinction between Romanesque and Gothic ribs. But these are all matters to be explored elsewhere.

ACKNOWLEDGEMENT

This is an amended version of the lecture delivered at the BAA conference at Utrecht in July 1993. I wish to record my particular thanks to Koos Wynia-Gils, to whom I am indebted for information about Dutch sources.

REFERENCES

1. G. Schwartz and M. Jan Bok, *Pieter Saenredam, the Painter and His Time* (London 1990), 131.
2. S. Muller, Fzn., 'Drie Utrechtsche Kroniekjes vóór Beka's Tijd', *Bijdragen en Mededeelingen* (Utrecht 1888), 465–508.
3. 'Annales Egmundenses' in *Fontes Egmundenses*, ed. O. Oppermann, *Werken uitgegeven door het Historisch Genootshap*, 3rd ser, 61 (1933), 134.
4. S. Muller, op. cit., fol. 465.
5. Ibid., fol. 482.
6. *Chronographia Johannis de Beke*, ed. H. Bruch ('s Gravenhage 1973), 94–95.
7. The picture is in the Kunsthalle, Hamburg. See G. Schwartz and M. Jan Bok, op. cit., catalogue no. 158. Latin text, 283–84, English translation, 141–44.
8. G. Meyer von Knonau, *Jahrbücher des Deutschen Reiches unter Heinrich IV und Heinrich V* (Leipzig 1890–1909), v, 68–69.
9. S. Muller, op. cit., fol. 497.
10. *Annales Patherbrunnenses*, ed. P. Scheffer-Borchorst (Innsbruck 1870), 122.
11. E. Kilian, *Itinerar Kaiser Heinrichs IV*, (1886).
12. G. Meyer von Knonau, op. cit., v, 335.
13. G. Schwartz and M. Jan Bok, op. cit., 147.
14. Loc. cit.
15. S. Muller, op. cit, 491.
16. *Series Episcoporum Ecclesiae Catholicae Occidentalis. Ser V, vol 1, Archiepiscopatus Coloniensis* (Stuttgart 1982), 193–94.
17. H. E. Kubach and A. Verbeek, *Romanische Baukunst an Rhein und Maas*, 4 (Berlin 1989), 230.
18. S. Muller, op. cit., 476.
19. Ibid., 479–80.
20. Ibid., 477.
21. Loc. cit.
22. H. E. Kubach and A. Verbeek, op. cit., 230.
23. Ibid., figs 187–88.
24. Ibid., 247.
25. R. Kautzsch, 'Der Dom zu Speyer', *Städel Jahrbuch*, I (1923), 75–108.
26. H. E. Kubach and A. Verbeek, op. cit., 232, n. 26A.
27. D. Von Winterfeld, 'Die Rippengewolbe des Doms zu Speyer', *Jahrbuch des Vereins für Christliche Kunst in München*, XVII (1988), 101–12.

28. H. E. Kubach and A. Verbeek, op. cit., 232.
29. H. E. Kubach and W. Haas, ed., *Der Dom zu Speyer. Die Kunstdenkmäler von Rheinland-Pfalz* (Berlin 1972), textband 673–77, 722–44, tafelband 9, 19.
30. Ibid., bildband pl. 760.
31. *Godfrey of Viterbo, Monumenta Germaniae Historica*, Script XXII, 253.
32. A. Kingsley Porter, *Lombard Architecture* (New Haven 1915–17), 108–15.
33. Ibid., 115.
34. E. Kilian, op. cit., 89, 118, 147.

…Foderunt manus meas et pedes meos
On the iconography of the twelfth-century reliefs in the Pieterskerk in Utrecht

by Elizabeth den Hartog

INTRODUCTION

In 1965 four more or less square reliefs (c. 81 × 82 cm) decorated with scenes from the New Testament were discovered in the Pieterskerk in Utrecht (Pl. XA and XB). The inscriptions framing the panels suggest that these originally formed two pairs. The right-hand side panel of the first pair shows a ruler seated on a faldstool and a sword-bearer. The ruler is pointing at the Crucifixion represented on the left panel. Apart from the crucified Christ, Stephaton and Longinus and personifications of the sun and the moon, this scene includes a kneeling figure hammering a nail into Christ's feet. Unfortunately the inscription is rather damaged. It reads 'MIRA DE. . . R SUB PRE.IDE .RESES CUNCTOR(UM) CUNCTOSQ(UE) SIBI MORIENDO REFORMAT' and refers 'to the Ruler of all who dies under the ruler and in dying reforms us all'. The second pair of panels shows an angel seated on the empty tomb of Christ receiving the three Marys. The inscription running round these two scenes reads 'HIC NARRAT . . . QUEM DEFUNCTUM MULIERUM MENS DEVOTA PUTAT. FELIX QUI CREDIT UTRUMQ(UE)', 'this (angel) is telling that He, who the women in their piety held to have died, is alive. Blessed is he who believes this as well as the other'.

There is some evidence that the panels originally flanked the stairs leading up to the choir and so they were reset here, with the Crucifixion and the seated ruler to the left and the angel and the three Marys to the right of the stairs.[1] If the sculpture does indeed derive from this location, it follows that there are no panels missing. On the evidence of the stone and above all the style of the work, the panels are attributed to an atelier working in Maastricht and surroundings from about 1140 onwards.[2] They are likely to date from shortly after 1148, when a fire swept over Utrecht and during which the Pieterskerk was damaged.

THE ICONOGRAPHY OF THE PIETERSKERK PANELS

The Crucifixion panel shows Christ being nailed on to the cross, a subject not often represented in western art, nor indeed in Byzantine art. The earliest example in the West is a ninth-century wall painting in the crypt of St Maximin in Trier.[3] All further examples — and they are few and far between — are from the twelfth century or later.[4] Apparently, the nailing scene originated in Byzantine psalter-illumination, the oldest example appearing in the ninth-century Chludov psalter as an illustration to Psalm 22(21), 17 '. . . me foderunt manus meas et pedes meos.'[5] It shows four figures driving nails into Christ's hands and feet with the cross slanting at an angle.[6] This image is rather more realistic than the Utrecht one, where the cross is already erect.

The headgear worn by the Utrecht soldiers is also interesting. The sword-bearer and two of Christ's tormentors are wearing conical caps, Longinus a sort of helmet. This is not the normal headgear of Roman soldiers. More often than not Stephaton and Longinus are shown bare-headed and only occasionally is one or are both of them wearing a Phrygian cap. Being unusual, such caps probably had a specific meaning. According to Schreckenberg,[7] already long before the fourth Lateran council of 1215 during which the wearing of a specific form of headgear became obligatory for Jews, both the Phrygian and conical cap — and their many variations — were used in western art to denote certain figures as Jews, or at any rate as coming from the east, as strangers. It is therefore likely that the Utrecht soldiers represent Jews, thus implying that the Jews should be denounced as the murderers of Christ.[8]

Even more remarkable is the inclusion of the seated ruler pointing at the Crucifixion. The only parallel for this is an eleventh-century ivory from Cologne (now in a private collection in Freiburg), which for this reason has been considered as the direct model of the Utrecht reliefs.[9] Most scholars identify the Utrecht ruler as Pilate on the evidence of the inscription 'SUB PRE.IDE'. This is however a very general phrase that could have been derived from something like the Credo and may serve merely to specify the time of Christ's Crucifixion. It does not necessarily refer to the seated ruler on the panel. In my opinion it is very unlikely that the ruler is indeed Pilate. Why would Pilate be shown almost as a mirror-image of the angel, as if he were the foremost witness to the Crucifixion, a role not borne out by the Gospel narratives, an image unique in western art? With only four reliefs to fill there should have been compelling reasons for including Pilate in this way and to my mind these do not exist. So if he isn't Pilate, who is he?

Firstly, the ruler is shown with all the attributes of high station; he is dressed in finery, carrying a rod, seated on a faldstool with his feet resting on a footstool and accompanied by a sword-bearer. Thus he forms a strong contrast with Christ, the heavenly Lord, whose only regal attributes are the suppedaneum under his feet and the rather smart loincloth, that has a beaded hem similar to that of the ruler's tunic.[10] Another contrast is formed by the ruler's sceptre and that of the angel; the former is a bare stick, the latter terminates in a trefoil. The contrast seems deliberate and probably signifies that the rule of the heavenly king is eternal while earthly rule is finite. Even a contrast between Ecclesia (the Tree of Life) and Synagoga (the Arbor mala, or 'bad tree', that carries no fruit) may have been intended,[11] as on the evidence of his clothing, the seated ruler too is probably Jewish. His cap, consisting of a band decorated with a chevron pattern and a lobed top, resembles the headgear of the destroyed Old Testament prophets and patriarchs of the west façade portals of St Denis near Paris (1137–40), as depicted on Montfaucon's engravings of 1729. Moreover, the Utrecht ruler is shown wearing a cloak fastened under his chin by a disc-shaped fibula, while on the so-called 'Eedsrelief' in the church of Our Lady in Maastricht — a work by the same atelier as the Pieterskerk panels — a similar ruler is portrayed wearing a cloak with the more usual shoulder fastening. This suggests that the attire of the Utrecht ruler may have some significance. Steger has in fact argued that the centrally-fastened cloak appears from the ninth century onwards in representations of King David and gained popularity by the eleventh century. From the twelfth century onwards it even became part of the regal attire. The origins of this way of wearing the cloak are unclear, but it may well derive from representations of Old Testament high priests and prophets, who are shown wearing similar attire already from the sixth century onwards.[12] According to Steger this type of cloak was intended to identify David as both rex and sacerdos, a priest-king.

DAVID, PROPHET AND KING

Could the Utrecht ruler represent King David? David after all was the author of Psalm 22(21), that contains the passage '. . . et foderunt manus meas et pedes meos'. The first lines of this psalm were quoted by Christ when he died on the cross. If the seated ruler can be identified as David, this would not only explain the appearance of the otherwise rare nailing scene as an illustration of one of David's main prophecies, it would also account for the inclusion of Stephaton and Longinus rather than Mary and John. Their presence reflects psalm 69(68); 'they gave me also gall for my meat; and in my thirst they gave me vinegar to drink'. Moreover, the juxtaposition with Christ makes perfect sense if the ruler is indeed David. Was it not King David who had prophesied the coming of the Messiah, His death on the cross as well as the Resurrection? Also, according to Christian doctrine Christ was descended from the house of David, for had not God promised David that a son of his seed would rule in eternity. In addition, David was often seen as a type of Christ.[13] David would thus be pointing at the Crucifixion to show that both his prophecies and God's promise to him had been fulfilled in Christ, that Christ is indeed the Messiah, the Saviour of mankind. The juxtaposition of David and Christ could also have a typological significance. They could be placed next to each other as the Old and the New Jerusalem, the Old and the New covenant, as the Old and the New Testament, the one foretold by the other.

The appearance of David in representations of the Crucifixion is not unique in contemporary Meuse-valley art. A particularly interesting example (Pl. XIA) occurs in the evangeliary of Averbode (c. 1150–60).[14] Above the arms of the cross, where one would expect to find personifications of the sun and the moon, there are two busts of figures holding scrolls. The inscriptions identify these figures as Isaiah and King David. David's scroll reads '. . . foderunt manus meas et pedes meos.' In the Floreffe Bible, the illustrations of which are very similar to those in the evangeliary of Averbode, David is represented in much the same way, although the inscription on his banderole differs (Pl. XIB). Interestingly, in this case David is actually pointing at the Crucifixion.[15] There are also several Byzantine images showing David in connection with the crucified Christ. As with the nailing scene most of these representations are to be found in the marginal psalters (Pl. XIC). The earliest examples occur in the Chludov psalter, where David is repeatedly depicted standing and looking at a medallion or icon containing the bust of Christ. In some instances he is even standing next to the Cross that bears a medallion with the image of Christ (fols 4 and 86).[16] Even more explicit is the three-tiered illustration on fol. 172^v (illustrating Psalm 131:6, 7, 11), with David predicting the Messiah and the Crucifixion and David pointing at Christ in Majesty.[17] The Byzantine psalters also contain pictures of David witnessing the Resurrection.[18] Again the earliest examples appear in the Chludov psalter, where David is shown peering into the empty tomb of Christ, with the soldiers sleeping in the foreground (fol. 6) and as witnessing the visit of the Marys to the tomb (fol. 44). In Pantokrator 61, a manuscript at the monastery of Mount Athos, Christ is twice shown leaving the Holy Sepulchre with David looking on (fols 24^v and 26^v). A similar scene also appears in the so-called Bristol psalter.[19]

ADVERSUS JUDAEOS

David's pointing gesture emphasizes that Christ truly is the Messiah, a point on which Jews and Christians strongly disagreed. The Jews also denied the Resurrection. The inscription on the Resurrection panels, 'Blessed is he who believes this as well as the other' seems to indicate that the controversy between Jews and Christians may have had some bearing on the iconography of the reliefs and that their purpose was similar to that of the many polemical treatises dealing with this controversy from the third century onwards.[20] As Jews were often not schooled in Latin and had no access to these 'adversus Judaeos' texts, they were obviously not written in order to convert Jews to christianity. Likewise, Jews would not have been able to see the decoration inside churches. Both texts and images served to strengthen the faith of laity and clergy alike on the main points of Christian dogma.

Further, the panels not only demonstrate the fulfilment of the Messianic prophecy, they also depict Jews as tormentors of Christ. What can the reason for this strong anti-Jewish bias be? Why would the artist (or more likely his patron) have felt compelled to use imagery of this kind round about the middle of the twelfth century? As there is no evidence for a Jewish community at this time in Utrecht or in the Meuse Valley, it is unlikely that Jews posed a serious problem here.[21] In this context it is interesting to look again at the Byzantine marginal psalters, where the same problem occurs. Although the imagery in these psalters was in the first place directed against the iconoclasts, the opponents most often depicted or addressed are not iconoclasts but Jews.[22] However, as Corrigan has pointed out:

contemporary Jews alone did not present enough of a threat to elicit the systematic condemnation found in the psalters. More important to the Byzantines would have been the cleansing of their church of all heresy after the divisive period of Iconoclasm, and the defence of Christianity against its newest and most powerful opponent, Islam. Arguing the Christian position through the condemnation of the Jews made perfect sense: Over the centuries the process of Christian self-definition had always involved differentiating Christianity from Judaism, and the Christians often condemned their enemies by comparing them to the Jews. And in the ninth century it seemed to Orthodox Christians that the Iconoclasts and the Muslims had derived many of their arguments against Christianity from the Jews. Although most of the polemical images in the psalters are directed against the Jews, and some against Iconoclasts, it is likely that ninth-century readers would have seen these images as a refutation of the beliefs of all their opponents.[23]

Significantly, ninth-century Byzantine writers sometimes referred to Muslims as 'new Jews'.[24]

Unlike the Jews, the Muslims accepted that Christ was the Messiah foretold in the Old Testament and was a messenger of God, but they denied His divinity, i.e. that he could be the Son of God, thus also rejecting the Holy Trinity. Another point of disagreement between Muslims and Christians concerned the reality of Christ's Death and Resurrection. In Muslim opinion it was merely Christ's likeness that had been crucified. Corrigan[25] pointed out that illustrations of Psalm 22(21) in the Chludov and Pantokrator psalters, both including the nailing scene, should be seen as an affirmation of the reality of Christ's Passion and Crucifixion, and therefore as a rebuttal of the claims of the Muslims. This point was also elaborated on in several anti-Muslim tracts of the ninth century. The Muslims argued that if Christ was crucified against his will, he was weak and could not be God. If he had died of his own free will, then the Jews should not be condemned, for they were simply doing the will of Christ. The Christians responded that, despite the fact that Christ died of his own free will, the Jews were still to be condemned for their evil intentions. According to Corrigan, the Christian defence of the reality of Christ's Death on the cross therefore depended in part on the portrayal of the Jews as evil-natured and motivated by hatred of Christ.

HISTORICAL BACKGROUND

In Utrecht historical conditions similar to those in ninth-century Byzantium may well have underlain the iconography of the panels, for if they were indeed made shortly after the 1148 fire this places them exactly in the period of the Second Crusade. In 1147 Louis VII of France and Conrad III of Germany set off to the Holy Land to free Jerusalem from the infidel and returned from this disastrous expedition in 1149. Clergymen, like the provost of St Servatius in Maastricht, accompanied their kings on this mission. Clearly, the Muslim world would have attracted considerable attention on the homefront at this time but, as Kedar[26] has shown, knowledge about Islam was slight. The Muslim religion was considered to be a mixture of pagan, Jewish and Christian elements. As a result Jews and Muslims were often held to be collaborators, the Jews supplying the Muslims with arguments against Christian doctrine.[27] It is thus not difficult to understand how the Jews came to be scapegoats. In the Rhineland ideas like these led to mass murder and other excesses. In France Peter of Cluny preached that Jews were worse than Saracens and wondered what use it was to fight enemies of the faith in countries far away, when Jews could go on living in the midst of the Christian community. It needed the preaching genius of Bernard of Clairvaux, who argued that their continued and miserable existence should be taken as living proof of the 'veritas christiana', to prevent a massacre.[28]

However, feelings towards the Jews were rather ambivalent at this time. On the one hand anti-Jewish feelings prevailed, on the other the Crusades stimulated a renewed interest in the Old Testament and its great heroes.[29] The Holy War against the infidel was compared to the great battles described in the Old Testament; Christian leaders were repeatedly parallelled with Judas Maccabeus, Moses or Joshua. This renewed interest in the Old Testament even generated regard for the Hebrew Bible, as scholars became increasingly aware that the Vulgate translation was not correct on all points. Putting aside the idea that the Jews had manipulated certain passages of the Bible to suit their own purposes, new translations were made and the Vulgate text improved.[30] These ambivalent sentiments concerning Jewry and Old Testament are also manifest on the Utrecht panels. On the one hand the Jews are depicted as evil-doers, on the other there is the positive figure of King David.

There was also hope that the Jews and pagans would convert at the end of time, an idea dealt with in many twelfth-century texts.[31] According to Bernard of Clairvaux, in a letter written in 1146, Jews were not to be annihilated as their survival was necessary to fulfill Paul's prophecy in Rom. 11, 25–26 concerning their conversion at the end of time.[32] These same hopes of eschatological conversion were held with regard to the Muslims from about the middle of the twelfth century.[33] In October 1147 leaders of the French army participating in the Second Crusade declared in Constantinople that their aim was 'to visit the Holy Sepulchre and, by the command of the Supreme Pontiff, wipe out our sins with the blood or conversion of the pagans.'[34] Gerhoch of Reichersberg uttered the hope that the expedition to Jerusalem might succeed and the hitherto unconverted nations attain salvation.[35] And Helmold of Bosau, writing about the Second Crusade in the 1160s, asserts that Bernard of Clairvaux had exhorted the faithful 'to set out for Jerusalem in order to repress and bring under Christian laws the barbarous nations of the Orient, saying that the time draws near in which the fullness of nations ought to enter, and thus all Israel will be saved.'[36]

Interesting in this context is the Utrecht sword-bearer, who is wearing a conical cap, which indicates that he is either a Jew or an oriental. He is also holding his beard, a gesture pertaining to the taking of an oath. What oath could this be? The illustration of Psalm 18(17) in the Golden Psalter of St Gallen depicts David enthroned under a large arch. In front of the arch there are two groups of people. Those on his right are dead; those on his left are standing, displaying their swords. David is here shown at the height of his power, almost as if directing the Last Judgement. It is the Good and the Bad that are being separated here. According to Eggenberger the good soldiers are taking an oath, illustrating verse 45 of the psalm, 'populus quem non cognovit, servivit mihi', that was often considered to have eschatological significance.[37] It is possible that the Utrecht sword-bearer has a similar meaning. That the reliefs have some eschatological significance seems confirmed by the figure of the crucified Christ, whose feet rest on a suppedaneum standing directly on the ground; i.e. Christ is not suspended from the cross and the suppedaneum has no supportive function whatsoever. It therefore seems significant that Mount Sion was sometimes referred to as a footrest.[38] If Christ is indeed standing on Sion, what is represented here may well refer to the fulfilment of Isaiah's (2, 2–3) eschatological prophecy. What is more, the conversion of the pagans and Jews at the end of times was also prophesied by David in Psalm 22(21), 28–31.

CONCLUSION

To conclude, in my opinion the unusual figure of the seated ruler pointing at the Crucifixion should be identified as King David, who foretold Christ's Passion and Resurrection and who was regarded as a type of Christ. If this is so the appearance of the nailing scene makes perfect sense. It serves to illustrate one of David's most important prophecies, '. . . foderunt manus meas et pedes meos'. The prominent appearance of an Old Testament king round about the middle of the twelfth century is not surprising, for at this time — no doubt as a consequence of the Crusades — the Old Testament and its heroes were held in high regard. Similarly, the anti-Jewish bias that is manifest in the reliefs seems to fit in well with ideas concerning the Jewry and other unbelievers prevalent at the time of the Second Crusade.

   If the seated ruler is indeed David, it follows that the present sequence of the panels is wrong for David should be pointing at the Resurrection as well as at the Crucifixion, since he predicted both. The sequence should read, from right to left, first the seated ruler, then the Crucifixion followed by the three Marys and the angel. In terms of composition this arrangement is certainly more pleasing. The Crucifixion scene, which is at present more or less tucked away in a corner, would become more conspicuous and the two pointing figures would actually open (prophecy) and close (fulfilment) the sequence.[39]

REFERENCES

1. C. L. Temminck Groll, 'De St.-Pieterskerk te Utrecht', *Bulletin van de Koninklijke Nederlandse Oudheidkundige Bond* 81 (1982), 106–07 and Pls 41 and 42.

2. J. J. M. Timmers, *De Kunst van het Maasland I*, Assen 1971, 272–74; R. B. Green, 'The Mosan reliefs from the Pieterskerk, Utrecht: Iconography and Sources', in *Album amicorum J.G. van Gelder*, The Hague 1973, 135–39; B. Brenk, 'Die Werkstätten der Maastrichter Bauplastik des 12. Jahrhunderts', *Wallraf-Richartz Jahrbuch* 38, 1976, 46–64; E. den Hartog, *Romanesque Architecture and Sculpture in the Meuse Valley*, Leeuwarden/Mechelen 1992, 122–33; A. van Deijk, *Romaans Nederland*, Amsterdam 1994, 187–89.

3. M. Exner, *Die Fresken der Krypta von St. Maximin in Trier*, Trier 1989, 107–22.

4. Other examples include

— Mantua, Biblioteca Communale, Ms 340/C.III, a psalter from Polirone, *c.* 1125.
— the so-called Latin Hamilton psalter (Tuscan, *c.* 1150, Staatl. Museen Preuss. Kulturbesitz, Kupfer-stichkabinett Berlin, Ms 78 A 5)
— London, BL. Harley 2895
— Paris, Louvre (coll. Le Roy): a reliquary casket
— a reliquary casket from the Servatiuschurch in Siegburg
— a wall painting in Råsted in Denmark (*c.* 1200)
— a baptismal font in Löderup (Skåne, Sweden)
— a baptismal font from Dortmund-Aplerbeck (Städtisches Museum, Dortmund)
— Biblioteca Apostolica Vaticana, Ms Ross.181, fol. 17[v] from the Peterskirche in Erfurt (1202?). In the thirteenth century the nailing scene makes a far more regular appearance and even depictions of the virtues nailing Christ onto the Cross exist (H. Kraft, *Die Bildallegorie der Kreuzigung Christi durch die Tugenden*, Frankfurt 1976).

5. Moscow, Museum of History, nr. 129 II, fol. 20[r].
6. A similar, but late eleventh-century example occurs in the Barberini psalter (Rome, Bibl.Vat. Barb.gr.372, fol. 33[v] (37[v])). The London Theodor psalter (BL, Add. 19 352, fol. 23[r]), dating from 1066, shows an upright cross and four hands at work driving in the nails. In Bibl.vat. gr.1927, fol. 34[r]. the nailing scene also includes Stephaton and Longinus.
7. H. Schreckenberg, *Die christlichen Adversus-Judaeos-Texte (11.-13.Jh.). Mit einer Ikonographie des Judenthemas bis zum 4. Laterankonzil*, Frankfurt am Main 1988, 629–35.
8. Schreckenberg (1988), 587.
9. Brenk, 50–53. The identity of this ruler is unclear. Brenk identifies him as Pilate, A. von Euw as Herod, cf. 'Elfenbeinarbeiten des 9. bis 12. Jahrhunderts', *Rhein und Maas. Kunst und Kultur 800–1400*, Exhibition catalogue, (Cologne 1972), 381.
10. E. Grubbe, 'Majestas und Crucifix. Zum Motiv des Suppedaneums', *Zeitschrift für Kunstgeschichte* 20, 1957, 268–87, has shown that the suppedaneum was a royal attribute, denoting Christ's majesty.
11. Hildegard of Bingen wrote 'das Alte Testament ist wie der Winter, der alles grün in sich verhüllt: Das Neue Testament hingegen ist wie der Gräser und Blumen hervorbringende Sommer' (PL 197, 1021, (Schreckenberg 1988), 227).
12. H. Steger, *David, Rex et Propheta. König David als vorbildliche Verkörperung des Herrschers und Dichters im Mittelalter, nach Bilddarstellungen des achten bis zwölften Jahrhunderts* (Nürnberg 1961), 30–34.
13. Migne PL 219, 244; E. A. Gosselin, *The King's Progress to Jerusalem: Some Interpretations of David during the Reformation Period and their Patristic and medieval Background* (Malibu 1976); Steger, 1–2.
14. Liège, Universitary Library Cod. 363c, fol. 87[r]; J. Hoyoux and M. Delcourt, *L'Evangeliaire d'Averbode, manuscrit conservé a la Bibliothèque generale de l'Université de Liège* (Liège 1979), 42–45.
15. London, BL, Add. Ms 17738, fol. 187; Other relevant examples are to be found in:

— Brussels, Bibl. Royale Ms 10527
— an evangelistary in the Trier Dombibliothek (Ms 142) of about 1190 (Helmarshausen?).
— related to this manuscript is a single leaf from a sacramentary showing the Crucifixion (Westfälischen Landesmuseum, Münster, Inv.nr. BM 1745)
— a typological window in the cathedral of Châlons-sur-Marne of Meuse-valley provenance.
— the ninth-century Drogo sacramentary (Paris, Bibliothèque Nationale, fol. 43[v]). The figure of a seated old man pointing at the crucified Christ and holding the terrestial globe, that signifies world rulership, may also represent David; F. Unterkircher, *Zur Ikonographie und Liturgie des Drogo-Sakramentars*, Graz 1977, 17–19.

16. Other examples are to be found in the eleventh-century Theodore psalter (fol. 3[v]), illustrating Psalm 4:7; in Vatican, Barb.gr. 372, fol. 5[v] (Psalm 4:7) and fol. 115[r], illustrating Psalm 85:19 (86:19).
17. S. Der Nersessian, *L'illustration des psautiers grecs du Moyen Age II. Londres, Add. 19.352*, Bibliothèque des Cahiers Archéologiques (ed. A. Grabar/J. Hubert) (Paris 1970).
18. S. Dufrenne, *L'illustration des psautiers grecs du moyen age I* (Paris 1966).
19. London, BL, Add. 40 73, fol. 21[v].
20. H. Schreckenberg, *Die christlichen Adversus-Judaeos-Texte und ihr literarisches und historisches Umfeld (1.-11.Jh.)*, Frankfurt-am-Main/Bern 1982; Schreckenberg 1988. In the Low Countries too, treatises of this kind enjoyed considerable popularity, cf. W. Bunte, *Juden und Judentum in der mittelniederländischen Literatur (1100–1600)* (Frankfurt-am-Main 1989), 67.

21. J. Zwarts, 'De oudste geschiedenis der Joden te Utrecht', *Jaarboekje van Oud-Utrecht* 1929, 99–113; Bunte, 71–72; D.E. Timmer, *The religious significance of Judaism for twelfth-century monastic exegesis: a study in the thought of Rupert of Deutz, c.1070–1129* (Indiana 1983), 51–53.

22. K. Corrigan, *Visual Polemics in the Ninth-Century Byzantine Psalters* (Cambridge 1992).

23. Corrigan, 5–6.

24. Corrigan, 94.

25. Corrigan, 81–82.

26. B. Z. Kedar, *Crusade and Mission. European Approaches toward the Muslims* (Princeton 1984).

27. Schreckenberg 1982, 526, 540, 546.

28. B. Blumenkranz, 'Die Entwicklung im Westen zwischen 200 und 1200', in *Kirche und Synagoge. Handbuch zur Geschichte von Christen und Juden I*, ed. E. Klett Stuttgart 1968, 84–135; reprinted in B. Blumenkranz, *Juifs et Chrétiens. Patristique et Moyen Age* (London 1977), nr. 23.

29. A. Waas, 'Volk Gottes und Militia Christi — Juden und Kreuzfahrer', in , *Judentum im Mittelalter. Beiträge zum christlich-jüdischen Gespräch,* ed. P. Wilpert (Miscellanea mediaevalia. Veröffentlichungen des Thomas-Instituts an der Universität Köln, nr. 4) (Berlin 1966), 410–34.

30. Schreckenberg (1988), 53 and 109.

31. Schreckenberg (1988), 111, 114–16, 188, 195, 36, 196 and 226–27.

32. Schreckenberg (1988), 170–71.

33. Kedar, 66–67.

34. *De profectione Ludovici VII in Orientem*, ed. and trans. V. G. Berry (New York 1948), 70–71; Kedar, 66.

35. P. Classen, *Gerhoch von Reichersberg: eine Biographie* (Wiesbaden 1960), 132, note 19.

36. *Helmoldi Cronica Slavorum*, ed. B. Schmeidler (1937), in MGH Scr. rer. Germ. 32, 114–15. According to Kedar (67) such an exhortation by Bernard does not survive in any of his extant writings.

37. Fol. 39, C. Eggenberger, *Psalterium Aureum Sancti Galli. Mittelalterliche Psalterillustrationen im Kloster St. Gallen*, Sigmaringen 1987, fol. 61.

38. H. Schmidt, *Der heilige Fels in Jerusalem. Eine archäologische und religionsgeschichtliche Studie* (Tübingen 1933), 78–102.

39. A parallel for such an arrangement is provided by the already-mentioned Cologne ivory in Freiburg.

Missionaries, masters and manuscripts: a survey of the oldest books and their patrons in the diocese of Utrecht (until *c.* 1200)

by W. C. M. Wüstefeld

INTRODUCTION

A major problem in tracing the first development of written and educational culture in the Netherlands is the lack of evidence — a problem comparable to the situation in Gaul 200 years earlier.[1] By the eighth century the main centres of book production on the continent are found in the great monasteries in the north and north-east of France and in a number of monasteries in Germany. It was in the monasteries that teachers, scholars and missionaries were trained and that the books they needed were written and copied. The number of centres making books rapidly increased in the ninth century: several scriptoria were active in the production of the Bible, liturgical books, canon law, patristic and school texts. Not only were copies made of existing works, but also original texts were drafted, among them native works, such as saints' lives, homilies and verses. Many monasteries enjoyed aristocratic patronage. In the general development of the Carolingian empire and the institution of its power, manuscripts and literacy became important instruments in the conversion of Europe's remaining pagan tribes.

Since his arrival in our region in 690, Willibrord is thought to have founded several churches both in the city of Utrecht itself and in Vlaardingen, Oegstgeest, Velsen, Heiloo and Petten. He also founded or supported the foundation of several monasteries, for instance at Utrecht (a Benedictine community, *c.* 695), Echternach (698), Aldeneyck (*c.* 700–10) and St Pietersberg, later Odiliënberg (*c.* 700) and Susteren (714). Willibrord is thought to have set up a school in Utrecht for the training of missionaries, though the date of this establishment is unknown. For daily liturgical practice and for education — books were indispensable tools. The success of Willibrord's work is much disputed and it may be that the medieval diocese of Utrecht came into being only two hundred years later, when following the Viking attacks, Bishop Balderick of Cleves settled in Utrecht and assumed control of the diocese's administrative organization (920).[2] Be that as it may, the first developments in the Low Countries started much later than in Gaul. This paper will attempt to identify the earliest books and other texts which may have been brought to Utrecht since Willibrord's time (seventh century) and describes the oldest surviving manuscripts produced in the region (until *c.* 1200).

FROM WILLIBRORD TO LIUDGER (690–809)

Although Alcuin does not refer specifically to any books in his *vita* of Willibrord,[3] it seems likely that the missionary brought books (a bible and some liturgical works) with him from overseas. We may assume that Willibrord — who visited Rome twice shortly after his arrival on the continent in order to obtain the sanction of Pope Sergius and to acquire relics for use in churches — also brought books from the south. Though

Utrecht became his episcopal see and though he is known as the 'apostle to the Frisians', Willibrord spent most of his time south of the rivers Rhine and Meuse, at Echternach. There is evidence for the existence of an active scriptorium at Echternach from as early as *c.* 704. Among Willibrord's original companions or 'disciples' at Echternach were at least two Anglo-Saxon copyists, namely Virgilius and Laurentius. The hands of both scribes reveal certain insular characteristics. Some products of Willibrord's scriptorium at Echternach survive, among them the famous Maaseik Gospels (Maaseik, St Catherine's Church, MS s.n., *c.* 704–20) presented by the archbishop of the Frisians to the convent at Aldeneyck, on the occasion of the consecration of the abbess Harlindis. Willibrord himself is attributed with a pious annotation added to a calendar (now Paris, Bibliothèque Nationale, MS Lat. 10837).[4] Although these manuscripts provide precious indications of scribal activity on the border of the diocese of Utrecht, unfortunately, no comparable manuscripts are known from Utrecht which can be associated with the first bishop or his companions.

Willibrord's missionary work was continued by several other men, among whom the best known are Winfred, called Boniface (680–754), Lebuin († 773) and Liudger († 809). Boniface received his education in the monastery of Exeter and at Nursling where he studied theology and the classics. He was widely known and regarded as a scholar and teacher and he remained committed to books and learning throughout his life. A considerable correspondence with English friends dating from his time in *Germania* (more than thirty years) has been preserved. Boniface made frequent requests for books to be sent out to him.[5] He himself was the author of a grammar and a manual of versification, but none of these were written in the Low Countries. In 716 Boniface made his first visit to Frisia, but after 722 he seems to have concentrated most of his attention to the conversion of the Saxons for which mission he became known as apostle of Germany.[6] Only shortly after 750 he returned to Frisia where he together with his companions was martyred near Dokkum († 5 June 754). On his misisonary journeys Boniface is said to have gone equipped with chests filled with books and relics. One volume believed to have been used by Boniface to shield himself from the sword blows of his Frisian assassins, may have been preserved as a relic at Fulda.[7] The author of an early life of the saint, the Anglo-Saxon priest Willibald, gathered material from the missionaries surviving disciples. The book was completed within a dozen years after Boniface's death.[78] According to a later *vita*, Willibald drafted his text on wax tablets and submitted it for approval of the archbishops of Mainz and Würzberg, before a copy was made on to vellum.

Boniface is said to have had a companion, a young man of Frankish origin named Gregory († 776). It is recorded that when the missionary first met Gregory, he asked him to read from the Psalms, which the youth did though without understanding. Years later, Gregory was to become the most distinguished teacher of the school of Utrecht. In 723, he travelled with Boniface on his second journey to Rome, from which they returned to Thuringia laden with books.[9] After Willibrord's death *c.* 739, Gregory is thought to have taken up residence in Utrecht where he became head of two priest's houses. Boniface appointed him bishop shortly before 753, but, although he ruled the diocese and the monastery with its school in the episcopal city, he was never consecrated. Under his leadership the Utrecht school flourished, as will be discussed in more detail below. Two students of the school continued Boniface's missionary work. Lebuin worked in the eastern part of the Netherlands († 773) and became known as the founder of the first church at Deventer. His name is associated with the well-known Franco-Saxon Gospels now in the Utrecht Museum Catharijneconvent (see below).

Gregory's other student, Liudger (*c.* 742–809), finally accomplished the task begun by Willibrord and Boniface. The son of a Frisian nobleman, Liudger studied in Utrecht and in York, where he was a student of the brilliant Alcuin. At York he had access to the monastery's famous library.[10] Upon returning to the continent he lived in Rome and at Monte Cassino, before Charlemagne (768–814) appointed him leader of missionary work among the East Frisians and Saxons. In 799, six years before he became Bishop of Münster, Liudger founded the abbey of Werden on the Ruhr, just outside Saxon territory and presided over the conversion of the North German lowlands south of the Elba. His *vita* records that he brought books with him to Utrecht; he may have gathered these manuscripts from England as well as from Italy. Liudger is known to have written the *vita* of his longtime teacher Gregory, and he is also thought to have stimulated others to write: thus, at Werden, the Frisian poet Bernlef may have composed the Heliand, a heroic poem based on the life of Christ.[11]

Just as Liudger wrote his master's *vita*, his own life was also described by a contemporary, namely Altfried († 849) who was his successor at Werden. This text was followed shortly afterwards by two other, more legendary versions, dating from the ninth century. Although hagiographic texts were assembled in codices since the eighth and ninth century, hardly any information relating to the lives of the early saints — with the exception of information offered by Bede or Alcuin — survives in contemporary or near contemporary manuscripts. The earliest surviving examples date to the eleventh century, though many are later.[12.]

When the so-called Lebuin codex came north remains a mystery (ABM h1, Fig.1). As the manuscript, a Gospelbook, was made in northeastern France around 825–50, this denies the possibility that it was brought or used by Lebuin himself († 773). The book is decorated in Franco-Saxon style and contains four ornamental *incipit* pages at each of the Gospels. The opening words of the four Gospels are written in large elaborately decorated initials and followed by decorative script. These pages show elaborate plant and zoomorphic motifs which exhibit distinctive insular characteristics. The manuscript bears tantalizing traces of usage, including Anglo-Saxon notes and glosses in high German, some of which may be German names. These names may suggest that the book was used as an early oathbook, a practice which continued into the first half of the sixteenth century. However, the Gospels would have been used principally during the most important liturgical feasts, when the codex was carried in procession and displayed on the high altar. The rich binding bears elements from several centuries and appears to have been restored a number of times throughout the ages. The filigree silver cross and medallions belong to the centre of the Rhine-Meuse region and date from the eleventh century. From their style and technique the small ivory reliefs of the four evangelists are datable to between 1150–75, and may be attributed to a Cologne workshop. A fine late antique head of Bacchus (first to third century, possibly originally from Asia Minor), is set prominently at the middle of the silver cross — (as if it were a depiction of Christ). Arranged around the arms of the cross are a pair of imitation cameos (sixth–seventh century).[13] It could be that the present cover dates to the second half of the twelfth century and incorporates earlier material alongside contemporary ivories.

The codex, together with two other precious manuscripts (see below), was found in the attic of the Broerenkerk in Deventer in 1860. The three must have been together at least since 1566 when they are mentioned in the Deventer church inventory, 'drie olde boeken myt sylver beslagen ende gesteente up eyne zydt'. It has been suggested that the books were once part of the Utrecht cathedral treasury. However, the Lebuin codex, may have been brought to Deventer already in the ninth century by Utrecht ecclesiastics seeking refuge from the Vikings. The bishops of Utrecht resided at Deventer from c. 880 until 920.[14]

THE UTRECHT SCHOOL: MASTERS AND MANUSCRIPTS

Education can hardly be imagined without (at least some) books. The episcopal schools of the seventh century were modest establishments. Evidence about the schools in the Carolingian era is sparse and ambiguous, and generally consists of mere references to schools rather than precise information about them. In the *Admonitio Generalis* of 789, the wishes of Charlemagne are clear: 'let schools be established in which boys may learn to read. Correct carefully the Psalms, grammar, calendar and so in each diocese, because often some desire to pray to God properly but they pray badly because of their incorrect books' (chapter 72). Every bishop was to set up schools for the education of priests and in which learned men were to teach according to 'Roman tradition'.[15]

Precisely when the Utrecht school was established is unknown. It is assumed that Willibrord set about the education of priests and missionaries soon after his arrival. However the earliest recorded events are found in Liudger's description of the life of Gregory. Under Gregory's direction, the school and its library — presumably located within the enclosure of the Benedictine abbey of St Salvator — attracted not only the sons of the local nobility, but also students of Anglo-Saxon, Frankish, Frisian, Bavarian and Swabian origin.[16] The extent to which these claims may be accepted must of course be referred to the context in which they appear, a posthumous *vita* strongly flavoured by its author's intention to flatter his master's achievement

Because Willibrord, Boniface and Liudger came from or studied in England, it may be presumed that the curriculum at the Utrecht school bore strong Anglo-Saxon influence. However, as Utrecht was part of the Frankish kingdom Charlemagne's educational policies had to be observed. Utrecht stood on the peripherery of the Carolingian empire, and its position was not comparable to that of York, or Aachen, Echternach or Fulda. Liudger insisted on returning to York to continue his studies under Alcuin the most famous teacher of his time and this may be an indication that what he found in England was not available in Utrecht. Yet, the presence of such a learned teacher as Liudger in Utrecht may provide an indication of the high level of education on offer there. Although no precise information on the Utrecht school curriculum has been preserved, the curriculum followed by other schools is fairly well attested. The traditional education consists of the seven *artes liberales* with special emphasis on grammar. The primary reading matter in any school was the Latin psalter: St Benedict's rule stipulated that the entire psalter should be sung through every week.[17] For Latin, the grammars of Donatus and Priscian were chosen. Education was geared to understanding and paraphrasing the Bible and certain didactic treatises. The reading and copying of saints' lives presumably formed an important part of Carolingian education. It is most likely that Alcuin's didactic works were available in Utrecht, perhaps brought by Liudger from York. According to Liudger, Gregory returned from Rome with *plura volumina sanctarum scripturarum*, and he is known to have had copies of Augustine's *Enchiridion* and the *Regula Benedicti*.[18]

The presence of texts by classical authors in the region is attested by a manuscript owned by a bishop, who may also have been a teacher at the Utrecht school. A late eighth-century inscription in an Italian manuscript of Titus Livy's *Ab urbe condita L. XLI–XLV* (Vienna, ONB, cod. 15, first half of the fifth century) mentions the name

Theutbert. Theutbert, Thiatbrad or Theodrad was teacher under Bishop Alberic (775–84), Gregory's cousin and successor.[19] In his turn Theutbert also became bishop (784–90). This Italian manuscript was not the only text to travel far. Books came on loan to be copied in monasteries and were not always returned as requested. At Fulda, Hrabanus Maurus (776–856) complained that the scribes of Utrecht had not returned the copy of a commentary on St Matthew's Gospel which he had lent them.[20] If a codex from Fulda was copied at Utrecht in the ninth century how would it have looked, what would its codicological characteristics have been and, what is more, would we recognize it today as having been drafted by a scribe at Utrecht?

Hrabanus Maurus sent his commentary on the Gospel of Matthew, together with other books to Frederic (c. 820–35), the eighth Bishop of Utrecht and also a former student of the Utrecht school. Frederic requested his friend Hrabanus Maurus to write a commentary on the book of Joshua, which the author later dedicated to him. The same scholar composed a Latin lyric for the bishop, perhaps on the occasion of his consecration. It may be reasonable to assume that all these texts were at Utrecht in the early ninth century. Frederic himself is thought to have been a scholar and author. He is tentatively identified with the *presbyter Ultrajectensis*, the otherwise anonymous author of a life of Boniface.[21]

DEVELOPMENT DISRUPTED

While information concerning ecclesiastical literary culture in this period is sparse, almost nothing is known of books in secular circles in the early Middle Ages. When he stayed at his *villas* near Nijmegen and Meersen, on the borders of the diocese of Utrecht, Charlemagne and some of his court companions will undoubtedly have brought books with them. The fate of the emperor's famous library at Aachen remains obscure[22] but his codices may not have all been lost as his successor, Louis the Pious continued to maintain a library at Aachen. One of the court librarians, Gerward, later lived at Gannita, a manor just north of Nijmegen where he kept a collection of books. His library is the only one known in our region at this time and included several manuscripts with Anglo-Saxon associations and perhaps even the famous Palatine Vergil. He amassed a number of other valuable codices. Upon his death these were taken from Gannita and passed into the possession of the monastery of Lorsch, to which Gerward bequeathed a total of 27 volumes.[23] However, any connection between these books and the intellectual and liturgical life of the diocese of Utrecht is speculation and further discussion of this collection is beyond the scope of this paper.

Sometime around 850 the Viking invasions probably ended educational and scribal activity in Utrecht. In 857 the Vikings sacked the city and its churches and drove Bishop Hunger (854–63) away. Fleeing the see, the bishops of Utrecht first settled at St Peter's abbey at Berg on the Ruhr (later Odiliënberg). Hunger's successor Adelbold (866–99) transferred the bishops' residence to Deventer (c. 880–82), and after him, Radbod (900–17) remained in the east. This by no means deprived him of learning. Radbod enjoyed the education of the cathedral school in Cologne and the courtschool of Charles the Bald. He is known to have written a *Libellus de miraculis S. Martini*, poems and *sequentiae*, perhaps a *cantus nocturnalis* in the honour of St Willibrord and a *sequentia* on Lebuin.[24] However, Radbod remained in exile throughout his life († 917) and it was his successor, Balderick of Cleves (918–76) who was the first bishop to return to Utrecht (after 920). A new era began. Balderick started the reconstruction of the city and its churches, and presumably renewed the school's activities. Ten years later he received Bruno, son of emperor Henry I (1919–36), as a student at the Utrecht cathedral school. Young Bruno spent more than ten years at Utrecht (from his fourth until his fifteenth year); later he became Archbishop of Cologne and is widely known as a scholar. Contacts between Utrecht and Cologne became increasingly frequent, also on an intellectual level: the names of both Bishop Balderick and later Bishop Adelbold (1010–c. 1025/26) are listed among others entitled to access and borrow books from the Cologne cathedral library.[25]

A MONASTERY'S MANUSCRIPTS: THE BOOKS OF EGMOND ABBEY (c. 975–1200)

Following the Viking incursions into the Low Countries, two important political powers developed in the region: the bishops of Utrecht in the centre and the counts of Holland in the west. By the tenth century the rulers of the Holy Roman Empire restored much of the power previously exercised by the Carolingians. As part of this process, the German emperors granted certain rights in return for feudal loyalty and support. The Utrecht bishops, who had political control over a large part of the diocese willingly complied with the emperors. Further away on the outskirts of the Holy Roman Empire, the counts of Holland enjoyed relative autonomy. Although the Court of Holland is not known to have possessed a library of any importance before the fourteenth century, the first layman known to have donated a book to a monastery in the diocese of Utrecht is Count Thierry II of Holland. His patronage of St Adalbert Abbey in Egmond has left us the oldest surviving drawings depicting Dutch people and buildings. Two miniatures, presumably made in Ghent and added (c. 975) to a Gospel book made in Reims (c. 850–75), depict Count Thierry II († 988) and his wife Hildegard († 990) presenting the codex on the occasion of the dedication of the abbey church (Fig. 2). The manuscript, at that time bound in a gold cover enriched with precious stones, represents one of the oldest church treasures still extant.[26]

St Adalbert's Abbey at Egmond in Kennemerland was founded by Thierry II, count of Holland, around 950, close to where his father Thierry I, had built a convent (before 922).[27] Throughout the ages the abbey developed into a rich and influential intellectual centre and housed one of the most important libraries in the country. From its foundation liturgical books and books for use during community prayer must have been present. The monastic library may have been established with a grant from Archbishop Egbert of Trier (c. 977–94), son of Thierry II, who gave the abbey twenty-four texts in seventeen codices. As a boy, Egbert is thought to have received his education from Bruno, Archbishop of Cologne, himself a former student of Utrecht.[28] His gift to Egmond consisted mainly of liturgical books, scripture, patristic writings, hagiography, and treatises on grammar, arithmetic and music. One of these manuscripts, a copy of Martianus Capella, *De nuptiis Philologiae et Mercurii*, is preserved in Leiden University Library (MS BPL 87).[29]

Like the first patrons of Egmond's library — the Count of Holland and his son the Archbishop — other early patrons such as the abbots were of noble birth also. A twelfth-century booklist (surviving in a sixteenth century copy), records the abbots and other donors contributing many new acquisitions. Abbot Stephen (1057–†1105; 1071–76 exiled in Ghent) eagerly supported the *artes liberales* and acquired many books for the monastery, several of which he had copied especially, *scribi fecit vel procuravit*. The booklist mentions fifty-one books added by Stephen, altogether containing about eighty texts. Copying may have been carried out by scribes at Egmond. During the abbacy of Stephen, the library also received a donation of thirteen volumes by Magister Baldewinus, possibly a schoolteacher and Flemish friend of the abbot.[30] Four of the books presented by Baldwin are still extant. One of his donations is a Priscian (no. 75 on the old booklist) written in 838 by Irishmen in France, annotated by John the Scot and containing some poetry from the Carolingian court at Soissons.[31] The other three are M. Lucanus, *Pharsalia libri decem* (eleventh cent.; Leiden, UL, Cod. 4°, Burm. Q 1); Sedulius, *Carmen paschale* (Glasgow, Hunter library, no. 57); and Sallustius, *De conjuratione* (together with other texts, Brussels, RL, MS 10057–62). J. P. Gumbert has discovered palaeographic similarities with other books dating from the last decennia of the eleventh century and presumably written in Egmond during the last period of Stephen's abbacy (1076–1105). These similarities are found in manuscripts of works by Cicero (Leiden, UL, Lips. 30), Gellius (once bound with the Cicero MS, now Brussels, RL, MS IV 625, frg. 60), Willeram (Leiden, UL, MS BPL 130) Caesar (Oxford, Holkh. Misc. 34), and Einhart (London, BL, MS Cott. Tib. C.xi).[32]

During the abbacy of Adalardus (1105–20) ten volumes are known to have been copied, mostly liturgical books, selected partly by the abbot, partly by the *custos*. Among others he *scribi fecit . . . musicam Guidonis*, a musical treatise by Guido di Arezzo (*c.* 995–1050). Abbot Ascelinus (*c.* 1122–30) otherwise known as a weak administrator, added some very precious books, which make up seventeen entries on the list, but comprising about twenty-five separate volumes. His successor Walter of Ghent (1130–61) reconstructed the sacristy into a library and added at least sixty-five volumes (*scribi fecit vel acquisivit*).[33] During Walter's abbacy a psalter (no. 123) was written for *frater* Inghelbertus, and another *frater* Symon may have been the copyist of the *Historia de profectione Iherosolimitana* (no. 137), a text of twelve books in one volume and of Augustine's *De civitate Dei*. Under Walter several monks donated manuscripts when they entered the monastery: priest Symon gave eleven books (including five classical authors); magister Joseph offered the book of Genesis and five books of the New Testament; and priest Deddo of Rijswijc presented a further five volumes. Some of these survive, such as a copy of Palladius, *De agricultura* and a copy of the philosophical treatise by Guillaume de Conchis; both showing traces of regular use (Leiden, UL, MS BPL 102). By the end of the twelfth century Egmond Abbey possessed some 200 codices. Today around fifty medieval manuscripts from the Egmond library have been identified, many in Leiden University Library. Although several publications have been devoted to Egmond manuscripts, the publication of Gumbert's new study of this important library and his new edition of the old booklist is eagerly awaited.

MONKS AND TEXTS: LATIN AND VERNACULAR

Throughout the eleventh century Egmond Abbey on the periphery of the Christian world in the *extremus margo mundi* remained a small foundation with never more than thirty-five monks. The monastery status is based on its early hagiographic and historiographic production. The oldest narrative source about Egmond, the *Vita Sancti Adalberti confessoris* (on the founder of Egmond Abbey, supposedly a companion of Willibrord) is in fact not an Egmond product. Although the *Vita* was inspired by Egbert of Trier it was written *c.* 985 in the German abbey Mettlach by two monks, one of whom is identified as Ruopert.[34] Around 1060 the *Vita et Passio Sancti Ieronis* — Jeroen, martyr of Noordwijk near Egmond — was composed; the life is now considered the earliest surviving hagiographic text written by a monk at Egmond. Sixty years later, *c.* 1120, the *Annales Egmundenses* (covering the period 877 until 1111) were begun. The annual entries include information on events in Holland and Utrecht and contain miracle stories, strange happenings, anecdotes and astrological annotations. The *Annales Egmundenses* survive in a composite codex now in the British Library in London (MS Cotton Tib. C.xi). They are the earliest Dutch Annals and represent the beginnings of Dutch historiography.[35] Another early historiographic work from Egmond is the so-called Rijmkroniekje, a rhyming chronicle, dating *c.* 1125–30 and describing the lives of the counts of Holland from Thierry I († *c.* 941–42) until Floris II († 1121). Around 1130–40 the *Miracula Nova Sancti Adalberti* was written in the Abbey, recording, among other things, miraculous healings inspired by St Adalbert, patron of the monastery.[36]

Important as it is for the historiographical tradition of Holland, Egmond's production cannot be compared to that of Fulda, Fleury or St Denis. Although the library and the rich archives of the monastery attracted authors and scholars, one should bear in mind that Egmond's importance is measured not on a European but on a regional level. The library's contents have further significance in the context of vernacular tradition. Whereas missionaries and clerics were representatives of a written culture, the songs and texts of the indigenous culture were transmitted mainly orally. What may have been written down in vernacular before the eleventh century is hardly known. The baptismal vow and pagan practices mentioned above (p. 146, nt. 6) may witness local practice of the eighth century though this survives in a German record. The oldest book extant in old-Dutch or *Diets* dates to around 1100 and is the work of an anonymous Benedictine monk in Egmond Abbey who transposed abbot Willeram of Ebersberg's commentary (*c.* 1060) on the Song of Songs, a text with parts in Latin verse and parts in German prose. The manuscript of this translated version bears the registration mark of Egmond (Leiden, UL, MS BPL 130) and also appears in the old booklist (no. 56).[37]

Some fifty years after the work of the anonymous monk, the first poet known to have composed in 'old-Dutch' was Hendrik van Veldeke. He lived and worked in courtly circles in the Meuse region (today's Belgian Limbourg) during the last quarter of the twelfth century. He has left a considerable number of works, such as a rhymed translation of the Aeneïd (1174), a legend of St Servaes (1170–80) and about thirty love songs written in the vernacular.[38]

UTRECHT: BISHOPS AND BOOKS (*c.* 920–1200)

Following the return of the bishops to Utrecht (*c.* 920), the city developed once again into a regional centre of political power and cultural activity. Its recovery was based primarily on the patronage of the bishops, many of whom came from or were acquainted with the entourage of the imperial court. Balderick (918–76) was the confident of emperor Henry I († 936) and friend and tutor of two of his sons, Otto I (936–72) and Bruno (953–65). Ansfrid (995–1010) was appointed by Otto III (983–1002). This bishop set about rebuilding St Salvator and St Martin, and he is also known as the founder of the Benedictine abbey at Hohorst, near Amersfoort (near Utrecht). Adelbold (1010–26) was counsellor of Henry II (1002–24) who, in 1023, attended the consecration of the reconstructed St Martin's, now Utrecht cathedral. The origins of Bishop Bernold (1027–54) are unknown, but his appointment supposedly was secured by Conrad II (1024–39). A good and trustful administrator, Bernold received several gifts from Conrad's son and successor Henry III (1039–56). He owes most of his fame to his building programmes, the results of which still determine the appearance of the city today. He turned Utrecht into a typical Ottonian episcopal see, surrounding the old cathedral with collegiate churches and an abbey. He not only relocated the Benedictine abbey of Hohorst to Utrecht (later known as St Paul's Abbey), he also founded the churches of St Peter and St John. Close relations between the bishops and the emperors continued at least until the reign of Frederick Barbarossa († 1190).

Not surprisingly a number of books in Utrecht are connected to bishops mentioned above, but the provenance of several others remains unresolved. A Sacramentary (Berlin, Staatsbibliothek zu Berlin-Preussischer Kulturbesitz, theol. lat. qu. 2) of the end of the tenth century has a claim to be the earliest known surviving book to have been written (perhaps partly) in the Utrecht diocese.[39] A Gospel-book of the eleventh century (Darmstadt, Hessisische Landes- und Hochschulbibliothek, ms. 1954) may also have been written here, as is suggested by a full complement of Utrecht saints.[40] Whereas provenance and use of these books are obscure, more is known of the so-called codices of Ansfrid and Bernold, once part of the Utrecht cathedral treasury and now exhibited in Museum Catharijneconvent (Utrecht, ABM h2 and ABM h3).

The so-called Ansfrid codex is a finely decorated manuscript from St Gall (c. 950–1000) presented by Bishop Ansfrid to St Martin's, the Utrecht cathedral church. The book is an *Evangelistarium* containing the lectures of the Gospels in the order of the liturgical year. The opening words of the texts of each important feast in the church calendar (Christmas, Easter, Pentecost etc.) are rendered in large decorated initials in gold in the style of St Gall. The binding is the result of a restoration of c. 1500 comprising several older elements. The silver plate and fittings on the cover date from c. 1000 and belong to the original binding. The plaque shows an image of Bishop Ansfrid (995–1010) surrounded by an inscription, *Ornatu lapidum rutilans auroque politum praesulis Ansfridi Martino munus obivi*, 'decorated with sparkling gems and shining gold, am I [*the book*] a present of bishop Ansfrid to Martin [the Utrecht church of St Martin]'. The front of the original binding embellished with gold and gems is now lost. The present cover is decorated with a cross in silver filigree (thirteenth century) with octagonal centre piece and splaying arms. The decoration consists of engraved alsengems (sixth-seventh century) and decorated medallions of enamelled silver (fourteenth and fifteenth century). For the front cover an older thirteenth century binding may have been re-used applying stones, medallions and a filigree cross to wooden boards sheathed with gilt silver. Though the filigree cross reveals a different technique, the composition of the book cover is very similar to the binding of the Bernold codex (Utrecht, MC, ABM h2 and ABM h3, Figs 3 and 4), and may have been informed by it.[41]

Utrecht cathedral is known to have possessed at least seven codices in precious bindings. The context of these codices is attested by the plaque of Bishop Ansfrid and by copies of two charters (included in the Ansfrid codex) relating donations of emperors Otto I and Henry III to Bishops Balderick (944) and Bernold (1040). The manuscript also contains an inscription (c. 1100) recording donations by Bishop Bernold to the Utrecht cathedral (f. 1r).

A psalter presumably owned by Ansfrid's contemporary Wolbodo has been identified in the past as an early Utrecht manuscript but is now connected to Trier, possibly made c. 1000 for Utrecht use (Brussels, RL, MS 9188–9189). Perhaps originating from Flanders, Wolbodo is known to have been provost and scholaster (leader of the cathedral school) of the Utrecht cathedral chapter c. 1000 and later became bishop of Liège (1018–21). Because the litany in the codex enumerates saints specially venerated in Utrecht it has been suggested that the book was made for use in Utrecht. However, this interpretation is not definitive as saints particular to Trier are also listed. Furthermore palaeographical evidence also points to Trier as place of origin. However, the possibility that the codex was made for Utrecht use is not only enhanced by the list of Utrecht saints, but also by the glosses of the psalm texts. These contemporary marginal glosses suggest that the book was not made for liturgical purposes, but for study, meditation, education or for the preparation of sermons. Together with the manuscript's date (*c.* 1000) this observation may be used to associate the book with the scholaster of Utrecht.[42]

Bishop Bernold (1027–54) known as administrator, active builder and maecenas of several churches, is frequently mentioned in relation to treasures donated to Utrecht churches. Two books presented by him survive. He is mentioned as the donor of a *Martinellus* to St Peter's in a short note in that book (Leiden, UL, MS Vossianus Lat. Q. 74, f. 71r). The codex contains texts about St Martin (including his *Vita* and the *Dialogi* by Sulpicius Severus), the patron saint of Utrecht cathedral. The partitions in *lectiones* indicate liturgical use. Lieftinck supposed the manuscript to have been an Augsburg product, but Gumbert found no distinctive German palaeographical characteristics and suggested that the book may have been written in Utrecht, *c.* 1000–50, indicating a comparison with Leiden, UL, MS Lipsius 30, an Egmond manuscript from the end of the eleventh century (see p. 151, Cicero).[43] It is a very beautifully written but simply decorated codex. The leaves show many traces of sustained use: considerable wear and tear, dirty spots resulting from frequent handling and stains of burning wax candles. Bernold gave the manuscript to St Peter's, a church founded and built during his office. Interestingly, two other *Martinelli* survive, both made in Utrecht and once belonging to St Martin's cathedral chapter. The oldest is dated *c.* 1000–50 (fols 1–75), and contains additions made *c.* 1100–1200 (fols 76–109) and later (Utrecht, UL, MS 122). The second was written *c.* 1175–1200 (Utrecht, UL, MS 124).[44] G. I. Lieftinck noted a striking textual conformity among the manuscripts suggesting a direct relationship between all three Utrecht *Martinelli*. However, he also indicated that Bernold's manuscript presented to St Peter's cannot have been the model for the other two copies as they contain titles not found in the oldest text, which was left unfinished. One may therefore conclude that another, complete and presumably older copy must have been present in Utrecht at this time.

Although it contains no inscription relating to its ownership or donation the so-called Bernold codex, an eleventh-century *Evangelistarium*, has been associated with the Utrecht bishop. The manuscript certainly is not a Utrecht product. Both its script and illumination are datable to *c.* 1040–50 and can be attributed to the *scriptorium* of the South-German monastery of Reichenau. While there is no solid basis for this assumption, Bernold may have brought the book north from one of his German trips before presenting it to Utrecht cathedral.[45] The manuscript was written by four scribes and contains fourteen miniatures which reveal the hands of three different artists. Eight miniatures, including those of the Evangelists Mark (Fig. 5) and John, are flanked by a decorated page. Nine illustrations represent scenes from the Life of Christ, and furthermore there are miniatures of the Parable of the Unjust Tenants, the Death and Assumption of the Virgin and the Last Judgement. These miniatures show a strong relationship with the illustrations in the Gospels of Otto III (Munich, BS, Clm 4453), not only in style but in iconography. With its 230 decorated initials the manuscript is the richest extant codex known to have been in use in Utrecht at this period.

The cover of the Bernold codex (Fig. 4) is enriched with gilded silver plate, which postdates the manuscript itself, presumably dating from the beginning of the thirteenth century, as is indicated by the form of the filigree cross, the enamelled medallions and two tondi (rosettes) set in the middle of the border. The four symbols of the evangelists were added to the front cover during a restoration in the fifteenth century. The three small alsengems date from the sixth or seventh century; two other somewhat larger alsengems are lost. At the centre of the arms of the cross there is a black/bluish and grey coloured onyx, and at the end of the arms a late antique female head, a piece of dark red glass and a brown striped agate. The similarity in the composition of the bindings of both the codices of Ansfrid and Bernold suggests an early association for the two books.

UTRECHT: MANUSCRIPTS OF MONASTERIES AND CHAPTERS

During the tenth century, Oldminster or St Salvator, Willibrord's first monastic foundation in Utrecht, failed to recover its earlier position, finally losing its role as cathedral church to St Martin's. After Bernold brought Ansfrid's monastery at Hohorst within the city of Utrecht, as St Paul's this abbey became the most important and one of the richest monasteries of the town. It accommodated a limited number of monks — fifteen to twenty at most. Although the abbey is known to have had many possessions throughout the Northern Netherlands, very little is known of St Paul's as its buildings and archives were attacked and destroyed during the Iconoclasm of 1580. Thirty-four manuscripts (mostly from the fifteenth century) and sixty incunabula are all that is left of the monastery's medieval library.[46] Four surviving twelfth-century manuscripts positively identified with the *ex libris* of St Paul's provide a useful body of evidence which by comparison may help to identify other manuscripts dispersed during the sixteenth century. *Gregorius Magnus, Moralia in Job, L. I–IX and XXIII–XXXV*, in four volumes, may be the oldest of the four and is thought to have been written at the end of the eleventh or the beginning of the twelfth century (Utrecht, UL, MS 86). Several different scribes contributed to the copying of the texts which are decorated with simple ornamented initials. The best of these are found in the fourth volume. A manuscript of Albericus, *Historia Hierosolimitanae expeditiones* (Rome, BAV, MS Reg. Lat. 509) is the only codex known to have been written in the abbey as is suggested by its inscription dated 1158: *Liber sancti Pauli apostoli in traiecto scriptus anno Dominice incarnationis millesimo contesimo L. octavo*. The manuscript contains eleven finely decorated initials with interlace and stylized foliate ornaments.[47] Some initials contain intricate interlace decoration ending in a dragon's head (P, fol. 124ᵛ). Together with those in the *Moralia* of Gregory the Great already mentioned, these may be the earliest examples of dragons in Utrecht manuscript painting. Much later, in the course of the fifteenth century, dragons in different forms became the most characteristic element in Utrecht pen-flourish initials.

Two other manuscripts which once belonged to St Paul's can also be dated to the twelfth century: a fragment of the New Testament, *Epistolae Pauli* (c. 1130, with the *ex libris* of the library of Egmond Abbey, Utrecht, UL, MS 34)[48] and a fair copy of *Florus Diaconus', Defloratio epistolae ad Romanos et ad Corinthios I* (c. 1125–75, Utrecht, UL, MS 202). The latter two both contain letters of St Paul, to whom the monastery was dedicated. MS 34 has four, rather crudely decorated initials, while MS 202 is a beautifully written manuscript with two fine initials decorated with interlace and zoomorphic elements including a hare and a crane. So far, neither the script or the style of decoration of MSS thought to have been produced in Utrecht have been studied. Such research may determine whether the twelfth-century script and initials in the

Vatican manuscript (MS Reg. Lat. 509), in the *Defloratio* (MS 202), as well as in the cathedral's *Martinellus* (MS 124) represent characteristics of an early 'Utrecht' style.

In the city of Utrecht there were four chapters connected to the churches. These were the chapters of St John, St Mary, St Martin and St Peter, all presumably with a college of between fifteen and forty canons each. Responsible for the liturgical practice of the churches, the canons established within enclosed chapter immunities, a chapterhouse and private dwellings. Our knowledge of the early medieval libraries or the books owned by the canons is very limited before the fifteenth century.

One of the richest and most powerful chapters was dedicated to St Mary. The church was built between 1081–99 under Bishop Conrad of Schwaben (1076–99) and was commissioned by Emperor Henry IV. He presided at the consecration of choir and transept in 1099. On this occasion the emperor may have been the donor — a hypothetical suggestion — of what is now the chapter's oldest surviving book, an *Evangelistarium*, which was used as the canons' oathbook (Utrecht, MC, BMH h9, Fig. 6). Both its decoration and contents reveal the manuscript to be of German origin. The script is a small but regular Carolingian minuscule datable to the first half of the eleventh century (*c.* 1000–50). Its decoration — close to that of manuscripts of Minden and Verden — consists of ten large and numerous smaller initials in gold and silver with orange-red. Three of the four original *incipit* pages are lost and the surviving one is badly damaged: the leaf itself has suffered extensive damage resulting from the properties of the rich pigment, which contains silver alloyed with copper or iron.[50] In the *Proprium sanctorum* saints typically associated with Utrecht such as Willibrord, Boniface and others are absent. Prayers to Marian and Florian, two saints whose cults were popular in the bishopric of Bremen (and whose feast was celebrated there on 3 November) confirm the book's German origin. The small format and script indicate that the codex was not intended to be used for reading aloud during mass. However, as the chapter's oathbook it must have been an important and much cherished manuscript. Unfortunately there is no indication when it assumed this role. The chapter's oath formulas are inserted at the beginning and end of the book and were written by its notary Jan Gosewijnsz van Ameronghen *c.* 1520–39. The binding, presumably replacing an older, worn out cover, dates from the same period. As old fly-leaves were replaced at the same time the all possible evidence relating to the early history of the book was lost simultaneously.

Another important book associated with the chapter has survived, namely St Mary's chapterbook (The Hague, MB/MW, MS 10B17), a manuscript dated *c.* 1138. The codex contains Usuardus' Martyrology (containing many English saints), rules of Canons, excerpts from Pope Hadrian's *Decretales* of 786, rules of St Augustine and the annals and notations on the chapter's history.[51] The *Annales S. Mariae Ultraiectensis* on the opening folios of the book describe the years 539–1138, with later additions covering the period up to 1303. A note explains that the text was written in memory of Otto III, dean and priest of St Mary's church († 1130), *Anno dominicae incarnationis millesimo centesimo xxx. Obiit Otto decanus IIIus ecclesie et sacerdos pro cuius memoria scriptus est et oblatus liber iste.*

Of a later date but also belonging to St Mary's and presumably both written in the house itself are a beautiful *Collectarius* (Utrecht, UL, MS 424, *c.* 1125–50) and an *Antiphonarium* followed by a treatise on music (Utrecht, UL, MS 406, after 1130 with later additions)[52] The *Collectarius* contains six decorated canon tables and large initials. The antiphonary and musicological treatise both have several initials and show extensive signs of sustained use. The first and largest initial, an A (f. 5v) is also decorated with dragons. The antiphonary, a liturgical book containing texts recited during church office, is a typical Utrecht codex. The texts contain *inter alia* the office of the feast of St Willibrord. The date of the celebration of the dedication of the church and the consecration of its western altar, identify the book as having belonged to the chapter of St Mary's. St Mary's became one of the richest chapters in the diocese and many of its books survive. The chapter possessed at least thirteen antiphonaries, six of which are preserved. This twelfth-century songbook is the oldest and most important. It contains musical notation (especially the neumes for the tones do, fa and sibémol) which forms are typical for Utrecht.[53] These books offer good material for study. Although Utrecht manuscripts firmly adhered to the style of the German empire, the small number of twelfth-century products, deserve greater attention.

DEVELOPMENT CONTINUED

While some of the books made for the bishops, the richest monasteries and churches and the most powerful chapters of the diocese survive, no examples of the books which belonged to the parish churches are preserved, neither in Utrecht nor in other towns in the diocese. The oldest parish church in the city of Utrecht was the Buurkerk, already founded in the tenth century. Here the important events in the city calendar were celebrated, but none of its books are known to have survived before the fifteenth century.

Even less is known of book production in the environs of Utrecht and the surrounding region at the same period. The last book to be described here shows that even if a codex is known to have been used in the north of the diocese Utrecht, in Groningen, either in Bedum or Hellum or both, its provenance remains unknown. A *Missale Trajectense* (?) with prayers to a local saint, namely Walfrid, an early martyr slain by the Vikings near Bedum, may have been produced locally or was imported from Utrecht, Groningen or elsewhere (*c.* 1150–1200, Utrecht, MC, BMH h7).[54] The book cannot be attributed to a particular centre on the basis of its textual or codicological characteristics. This is still more unfortunate as the texts for Easter contain one of the earliest known Easter plays (fol. 45^v, Fig. 7), a short text with neumes indicating the parts to be sung together with an indication of the division of roles between the players.

Far from the imperial court and great intellectual centres book production in our region developed slowly from the eighth century until the twelfth century. Due to limited economic development and political instability, cultural and intellectual progress was modest and conservative, or rather provincial. Although the thirteenth and fourteenth centuries witnessed many new developments, information still remains scanty. For a long time only Utrecht and Holland enjoyed the status of regional centres of power and culture and their ecclesiastics and courts were the principal patrons. Above all the city of Utrecht extended its power as the political and cultural centre of the region above the Meuse and Rhine until the early sixteenth century when Amsterdam took over. In the fifteenth century the diocese of Utrecht was home to some of the finest Dutch manuscript painters. Because the expensive handmade book is primarily a product of personal assignment and commission, books needed patrons. Throughout the Middle Ages patronage in the region came largely from the élite classes, bishops, clerics and noblemen. Only during the fifteenth century, as a result of economic, social and religious change, did book production become more widely diffused over our region, with centres in several cities and numerous monasteries. Already by the end of the fifteenth century the 'Golden Age' of manuscript production was drawing to an end, as costly hand-written books began to be replaced by the earliest printed books. It was also the period when the Low Countries, between the British Isles and the German Empire, were absorbed by the ascendant political powers of the south, by the Burgundian dukes and their Habsbourg successors. But these are other chapters.

LIST OF ABBREVIATIONS

BAV	Bibliotheca Apostolica Vaticana
BL	British Library
BS	Bayerische Staatsbibliothek
MB/MM	Museum of the Book/Meermanno-Westreenianum
MC	Museum Catharijneconvent
ONB	Osterreichische Nationalbibliothek
RL	Royal Library
UL	University Library

BIBLIOGRAPHY

Angenendt (1990)   A. Angenendt, *Das Frühmittelalter. Die Abendländische Christenheit von 400 bis 900* (Stuttgart/Berlin/Köln 1990).

Beekman (1950)   A. Beekman (ed.) *Tien eeuwen Egmond. Ontstaan, bloei en ondergang van de regale abdij van Egmond* (Heemstede 1950).

Bischoff (1974)   B. Bischoff, *Lorsch im Spiegel seiner Handschriften* (München 1974).

CMD–NL 1 1964   G. I. Lieftinck, *Manuscrits datés conservés dans les Pays Bas* (Amsterdam 1964), 2 vols.

Carasso-Kok (1981)   M. Carasso-Kok, *Repertorium van verhalende historische bronnen uit de middeleeuwen. Heiligenlevens, annalen, kronieken en andere in Nederland geschreven verhalende bronnen* ('s-Gravenhage 1981).

Dinzelbacher (1984)   P. Dinzelbacher, 'Die Bedeutung des Buches im Zeitalter des hl. Liudger', Sierksma (1984), 45–61.

Dirks (1983)   Liesbeth Dirks (*et al.*), *Dom en onderwijs. Onderwijs aan de Utrechtse kathedral c. 700– c. 1350* (Utrechtse Historische Cahiers, 4, 1983).

Gumbert (1996)   J. P. Gumbert, 'Egberts geschenken aan Egmond.' G. N. M. Vis ed., *Egmondse Studiën 3* (Hilversum, 1996, forthcoming).

Gumbert (1993)   J. P. Gumbert, 'Wanneer werkte C? Over een Egmonds annalist en het Auctuarium van Affligem', Vis and Gumbert (1993), 183–91.

Gumbert (1990)   J. P. Gumbert, *The Dutch and their books in the manuscript age. The Panizzi Lectures 1989* (London, 1990).

Gumbert (1990)–2   J. P. Gumbert, 'Een en ander over het handschrift van de Egmondse Annalen' Vis, Mostert and Margry (1990), 55–69.

Handschriften (1984)   *Handschriften en oude drukken van de Utrechtse Universiteits-bibliotheek* (Utrecht 1984).

Horst (1989)   Koert van der Horst, *Illuminated and decorated medieval manuscripts in the University Library, Utrecht* Maarssen/'s-Gravenhage 1989).

Lampen (1950)   W. Lampen, 'De boekenlijst der oude abdij van Egmond', Beekman (1950), 75–95.

McKitterick (1989)   R. McKitterick, *The Carolingians and the written word* (Cambridge 1989).

McKitterick (1992[4])   R. McKitterick, *Frankish Kingdoms under the Carolingians 751–987* (London/New York, 1992[4]).

Mostert (1990)   M. Mostert, 'Het geschreven woord bij de Friezen in de zevende en achtste eeuw', *Willibrord, zijn wereld en zijn werk. Voordrachten gehouden tijdens het Willibrordcongres Nijmegen, 28–30 September 1989.* Eds P. Bange and A. G. Weiler (Nijmegen 1990), 256–81.

Post (1957)   R. R. Post, *Kerkgeschiedenis van Nederland in de Middeleeuwen.*
                                            (Utrecht/Antwerpen 1957), vol. 1.

Ronig (1993)   *Egbert Erzbischol von Trier 977–993,* Gedenhschrift den Diözese
                                            Trier zum 1000 Geburtstag. Ed. F. Ronig (Trier 1993), 2 vols.

Schenkeveld-van der Dussen (1993)   M. A. Schenkeveld-van der Dussen (ed.), *Nederlandse literatuur, een*
                                            geschiedenis (Groningen 1993).

Sierksma (1984)   Kl. Siersma (ed.), *Liudger 742–809. De confrontatie tussen heidendom*
                                            en christendom in de Lage Landen (Muiderberg 1984) (Stichting
                                            'Comité Muiderberg', no. 19).

Vis and Gumbert (1993)   G. N. M. Vis and J. P. Gumbert (eds), *Egmond tussen kerk en wereld*
                                            (Hilversum 1993) (Egmondse Studiën 2).

Vis (1993)   G. N. M. Vis, 'De *Historia* en de *Miracula Nova Sancti Adalberti,*'
                                            Vis & Gumbert (1993), 67–137.

Vis, Mostert & Margry (1990)   G. N. M. Vis, M. Mostert and P. J. Margry (eds), *Heiligenlevens,*
                                            Annalen en Kronieken. Geschiedschrijving in middeleeuws Egmond
                                            (Hilversum 1990) (Egmondse Studiën 1).

Vlierden (1995)   M. van Vlierden, *Willibrord en het begin van Nederland* (Utrecht
                                            1995).

Webster and Backhouse (1991)   L. Webster and J. Backhouse, *The Making of England. Anglo-Saxon*
                                            Art and Culture AD 600–900 (London, British Museum 1991).

Wüstefeld (1993)   W. C. M. Wüstefeld, *Middeleeuwse boeken van het Catharijnecon-*
                                            vent (Utrecht/Zwolle, 1993).

REFERENCES

1. See R. McKitterick, *Frankish Kingdoms under the Carolingians 751–987* (London/New York, 1992[4]),
    142; an overview for our region is: M. Mostert, 'Het geschreven woord bij de Friezen in de zevende en
    achtste eeuw', *Willibrord, zijn wereld en zijn werk. Voordrachten gehouden tijdens het Willibrordcongress*
    Nijmegen, 28–30 September 1989, ed. P. Bange and A. G. Weiler (Nijmegen 1990), 256–81 (uses of script
    in Roman inscriptions, on coins, engraved runes, letters on vellum). I kindly thank Professor Dr J. P.
    Gumbert (University of Leiden) and Drs M. van Vlierden (Museum Catharijneconvent) for their
    corrections of this paper.

2. During the Middle Ages the diocese of Utrecht encompassed the lands above the Meuse and Rhine rivers,
    excluding Nijmegen. For a concise discussion of a definition of the Low Countries, the Netherlands and
    Northern Netherlands, see, J. P. Gumbert, *The Dutch and their books in the manuscript age. The Panizzi*
    Lectures 1989 (London 1990), 3. This is a concise but very good study of North-Netherlandish medieval
    manuscripts.

3. See *Vita sancti Willibrordi,* H. J. Reichsman, *Willibrord Apostel der Friesen, Seine Vita nach Alkuin und*
    Thiofrid Lateinisch-Deutsch (Sigmaringendorf 1989) (translation after ed. B. Krusch and W. Levison.
    Vita: Passiones vitaeque sanctorum aevi merovingici cum supplemento et appendice, MGH SS rer.
    Merov., VII, 81–141).

4. Especially Gospel books can be attributed to the Echternach scriptorium, such as the Augsburg, Trier,
    Freiburg (fragment) and Maaseik Gospels, see N. Netzer, *Cultural Interplay in the eighth century. The*
    Trier Gospels and the making of a scriptorium at Echternach (Cambridge 1994), 128 ff; for the Willibrord
    calendar see L. Webster and J. Backhouse, *The Making of England. Anglo-Saxon Art and Culture AD*
    600–900 (London, British Museum 1991), 159–60, cat. no. 123.

5. Several books with his annotations survive, e.g. in Oxford, Bodleian Library, MS Douce 140; his texts are
    preserved in Fulda and Leningrad. See Webster and Backhouse (1991), 160. Boniface and later Liudger
    both procured books from England. See *Briefe des Bonifatius. Willibalds Leben des Bonifatius. Nebst*
    einigen zeitgenössischen Dokumenten, ed. R. Rau (Darmstadt 1968), see for instance 63, letter 15. From
    the Anglo-Saxon monastery Thanet Boniface ordered the Letters of Petrus in gold (Rau, fol. 114). See for
    more on Boniface and books, P. Dinzelbacher, 'Die Bedeutung des Buches im Zeitalter des hl. Liudger',
    ed. Kl. Sierksma, *Liudger 742–809. De confrontatie tussen heidendom en christendom in de Lage Landen*
    (Muiderberg 1984) (Stichting 'Comité Muiderberg', 19), 50.

6. The oldest texts related to Christianization in our regions are found in the *Indiculus superstitionum et*
    paganiarum, a *capitulare* issued either by Karloman or Pipin the Short. The oldest surviving manuscript
    (Rome, BAV, Cod. Pal. lat. 577: Mainz or Fulda, after 762), contains a baptismal vow as well as a list of
    pagan practices in vernacular (fol. 6[v]–7[r], possibly from our regions or from Saxony). This manuscript is a
    copy written in a continental Anglo-Saxon minuscule; the list of pagan practices probably was adapted

from a Northumbrian Latin original (perhaps from York) and most likely comes from a missionary centre, for which both Utrecht and Fulda have been suggested (*c.* 750). See *Corpus van middelnederlandse teksten, Reeks I: Literaire handschriften, Deel I, Fragmenten*, ed. M. Gysseling ('s-Gravenhage 1980), 19–21, 22–26; *Bibliotheca Palatina* (Heidelberg 1986), 126; M. van Vlierden, *Willibrord en het begin van Nederland* (Utrecht 1995), no. 68 (with lit.).

7.   Fulda, Landesbibliothek, MS Bonif. II, the so-called Ragyndrudis codex, containing several theological treatises. The murder is depicted in a Fulda Sacramentary of *c.* 975 (Göttingen, Universitätsbibliothek, MS 231, fol. 87^r).

8.   Post (1957), 35–36: *c.* 800 a Utrecht author went to Dokkum to find information. See also Rau (1984), no. 125.

9.   Post (1957), 34.

10. His vita records how Liudger as soon as he could walk and speak, gathered pieces of skin and bark to make 'books': *Qui statim ut ambulare et loqui erat, coepit colligere pelliculas et cortices arborum . . . consuit sibi de illis collectionibus quasi libellos . . .* Dinzelbacher (1984), 45.

11. Altfried, *Vita Liudgeri*, ed. Diekamp (1881), cap. 11 and 12. From Italy he may have brought the famous *codex argenteus* (Uppsala, University Library), which is known to have been in the abbey of Werden (perhaps since its foundation, *c.* 799) and an Italian Diatesseron. See Cor van Bree, *Lotgevallen van de codex argenteus. De wisselende waarde van een handschrift* (Amsterdam 1995), 17. For the Heliand, see R. Drögereit: *Werden und der Heliand* (Essen 1950) (Beiträge zur Geschichte von Stadt und Stift Essen. 26). However, see Angenendt (1990), 438–40.

12. See for instance M. Carasso-Kok, *Repertorium van verhalende historische bronnen uit de middeleeuwen. Heiligenlevens, annalen, kronieken en andere in Nederland geschreven verhalende bronnen* ('s-Gravenhage 1981).

13. G. A. S. Snijder, 'Antique and Mediaeval Gems on bookcovers at Utrecht', *Art Bulletin XIV* (1932), 5–52.

14. However, the book may also have arrived at Deventer much later. For instance, as a present of Bishop Bernold on the occasion of the consecration of St Lebuin's which he reconstructed in the early eleventh century. Another possibility is that the book was brought into safety from Utrecht together with the codices of Ansfrid and Bernold shortly before the Reformation. W. C. M. Wüstefeld, *Middeleeuwse boeken van het Catharijneconvent* (Utrecht/Zwolle 1993), 25 (with lit. refs.).

15. McKitterick (1992^4), 145–47.

16. Liudger, *Vita Gregorii, c.* ii; *MGH, Script.,* xv, 75 sq.; see also Siersma (1984). On the Utrecht school: Liesbeth Dirks (*et al.*), *Dom en onderwijs. Onderwijs aan de Utrechtse kathedral c. 700–c. 1350* (Utrechtse Historische Cahiers, 4, 1983).

17. McKitterick (1992^4), 148.

18. Cf. Liudger in his *vita*, MGH SS CV 78; Dinzelbacher (1984), 48; Dirks (1983), 7, 11.

19. '[I]st[e co]dex [est Th]uitberti e(piscop)i dedorostat' (fol. 193^v, Dorestad nearby Utrecht). With marginal notes in Anglo-Saxon minuscule; see E. Irblich, *Karl der Grosse und die Wissenschaft* (Wenen 1993), no. 14; B. Bischoff, *Lorsch im Spiegel seiner Handschriften* (München 1974), 55–57, 64–65; see also Mostert (1990), 261.

20. Hrabanus Maurus, PL, 108, 1000, see P. Riché, *Daily life in the world of Charlemagne* (Philadelphia, 1992^3), 211.

21. He must have found in the library: Martianus Capella, *De nuptiis . . .* , grammatical books by Priscian, Donatus, Varro and Cassiodorus; poems of Virgil, Horace, Lucanus and Prudence; rethorica by Bede and Alcuin, a Latin translation of Aristoteles' *Organum* and Boethius' translation of Greek arithmetics, Sallust, Livy, Bede, Euseby of Caesarea, the Bible, St Augustine *Enchiridion*, Gregory the Great *Liber pastoralis*, Isidore of Sevilla *De officiis ecclesiasticis*. J. W. C. Van Campen, 'De bischoppen van Utrecht' (*Jaarboekje 'Oud Utrecht'* 1953) 31; on Frederic, 32.

22. See R. McKitterick, *The Carolingians and the written word* (Cambridge 1989), 160; Mostert (1990), 256. Officially the fate was sealed in his last will: his books were to be sold at a reasonable price, *iusto pretio . . .* to anyone wishing to buy them and the money gained should be given to the poor. Whether these provisions were carried out, is uncertain but it is assumed that not all books were dispersed this way after his death.

23. See Bischoff (1974), fol. 55. Gerward held the office of *palatii bibliothecarius* sometime before 828. Several of Gerward's books were acquired from the court library of Louis the Pious and some even may have belonged to the court library at the time of Charlemagne. McKitterick (1992^4) 203; McKitterick (1989), 251.

24. Preserved in Utrecht, UL, MS 406 (see p. 156). Dirks (1983), 18.

25. See the cathedral library of Cologne, Wolfgang Schmitz, 'Die mittelalterliche Bibliotheksgeschichte Kölns', *Ornamenta Ecclesiae. Kunst und Künstler der Romanik in Köln* (Köln 1985), 2, 142–43.

26. The Hague, RL, MS 76F1, *c.* 850–75, fols 213^r–214^v. The old precious binding was lost *c.* 1571–74. See: *A Hundred highlights from the Koninklijke Bibliotheek* (Zwolle 1994), no. 1 and P. C. Boeren, *Catalogus van de liturgische handschriften van de Koninklijke Bibliotheek* ('s-Gravenhage 1988), 99–109.

27. The year of foundation is disputed, others suggest *c.* 980. See Gumbert (1990), 80, n. 7 (with lit.).

28. See J. P. Gumbert, 'Egberts geschenken aan Egmond.' ed. G. N. M. Vis, *Egmondse Studiën 3* (Hilversum, 1996, forthcoming).

29. See the previous note. Gumbert's forthcoming paper (1996) also presents a new edition of the booklist. *De nuptiis . . .* is no. 17 on the old booklist, see: W. Lampen, 'De boekenlijst der oude abdij van Egmond', ed. A. Beekman, *Tien eeuwen Egmond. Ontstaan, bloei en ondergang van de regale abdij van Egmond* (Heemstede 1950), 77; see also J. Hof, *De abdij van Egmond van de aanvang tot 1573* ('s-Gravenhage/ Haarlem 1973), 269 (Hollandse Studiën 5) and G. N. M. Vis, 'Historiografie in middeleeuws Edmond', ed. G. N. M. Vis, M. Mostert and P. J. Margry, *Heiligenlevens, Annalen en Kronieken. Geschiedschrijving in middeleeuws Egmond* (Hilversum 1990), 11. Egbert also presented a Psalter with glosses in Dutch (no. 7), although lost, still a most valuable witness of an early text in vernacular (see p. 152, nt. 37).

30. J. P. Gumbert, 'Een en ander over het handscrift van de Egmondse Annalen.' Vis, Mostert & Margry (1990), 55–69; Gumbert (1990); J. P. Gumbert, 'Wanneer werkte C? Over een Egmonds annalist en het Auctuarium van Affligem.' ed. G. N. M. Vis and J. P. Gumbert, *Egmond tussen kerk en wereld.* (Hilversum 1993), 183–91; Lampen (1950), 75–95; G. I. Lieftinck, 'Het oudste schrift uit de abdij van Egmond', Beekman (1950), 110–17. I kindly thank J. P. Gumbert for correcting my text on the abbey's books and for making available his new study.

31. Leiden, UL, MS BPL 67, CMD-NL 1, no. 168 (one named Dubthach and two others); See Gumbert (1990), 8.

32. Gumbert (1993), 183–91.

33. One of the best known works he may have acquired (no. 164) was perhaps the illustrated copy of Aurelius Prudentius Clemens, *Carmina* (a.o. *Psychomachia*), made in Northern France, perhaps in Reims in the middle of the ninth century (Leiden, UL, MS Burm. Qu 3).

34. See list Vis (1990), 21. Carasso-Kok (1981), no. 1.

35. The codex also contains the Chronicle of Regino of Prüm, Notker's life of Charlemagne, the *Annales Xantenses*, and some minor hagiographic texts, such as the *Vitae* of two nuns at Oostbroek and a narrative recording the death of Thomas Becket, written by an Egmond monk. See Gumbert (1990)–2, 54–69 and Gumbert (1993), 183–91. According to Gumbert hand C -who wrote the *Annales Egmundenses c.* 1120– also copied the *Viso Baronti*, a poem in the Glasgow Sedulius manuscript (Hunter 57), and the *Passio Christinae* (Leiden, UL, MS BPL 102).

36. Gumbert (1990), 8, Fig. 3; Vis (1993), 67–137.

37. See for Egbert's gift of a Psalter with glosses in Dutch (*c.* 980), nt. 29. However, the first poetic lines in Dutch — perhaps from a lovesong — survive in a manuscript from the Benedictine monastery of Rochester in Kent, presumably scribbled down as *probatio pennae* at the end of a manuscript containing texts in old-English (*c.* 1100–25): *quid expectamus nunc abent volucres nidos inceptos nisi ego et tu hebban olla vogala nestas hagunnan hinase hic enda thu wat unbidan we nu*, perhaps translated as 'all birds started nesting, except you and me, what do we wait now?'. Unusual for a monastic environment, the verses may represent earlier memories of the author, see F. van Oostrom, 'Omstreeks 1100: Twee monniken voeren in het Oudnederlands de pen over de liefde. De volkstaal komt op schrift.' *Nederlandse literatuur, een geschiedenis*, ed. M. A. Schenkeveld-van der Dussen (Groningen 1993), 1–6.

38. F. Willaert, 'Hendrik van Veldeke wordt de werktekst van zijn eigen 'Eneas' roman ontstolen — De Franse Hofliteratuur via het Maasland in het Duitse Rijk', Schenkeveld-van der Dussen (1993), 6–11. Dini Hogenelst & Frits van Oostrom, *Handgeschreven wereld. Nederlandse Literatuur en cultuur in de middeleeuwen* (Amsterdam 1995), 9. 20 fragments of a manuscript (*c.* 1200) from the Meuse region survive, all other witnesses are younger.

39. See *Glanz Alter Buchkunst, Mittelalterliche Handschiften der Staatsbibliothek Preussische Kulturbesitz Berlin* (Wiesbaden 1988), no. 16 (Utrecht). *Berward von Hildesheim und das Zeitalter der Ottonen, Katalog der Ausstellung* (Hildesheim 1993), V-9 (262–65, Lower Lorraine or Saxony). The miniature (f. 1r, *Te igitur*; presumably influenced by Fulda manuscript painting) is inserted and the script on the verso is by a hand slightly later than that of the book (and so are fols 50^r–52^v). The miniature depicts the benediction by the hand of God of a chalice with host on paten held by a holy priest (with nimbus). See also Vlierden (1995), no. 102.

40. L. Eizenhöfer and H. Knaus, *Die Liturgischen Handschriften . . .* (Darmstadt 1968), no. 26. Gumbert (1990), Fig. 1. Both await study!

41. See A. S. Korteweg. *De Bernulphuscodex in het Rijksmuseum Het Catharijneconvent te Utrecht en verwante handschriften.* Amsterdam 1979 and A. S. Korteweg. 'Der Bernulpuscodex in Utrecht und eine

Gruppe verwandter spätreichenauer Handschriften' *Aachener Kunstblätter* 53 (1985) 68–70 and J. M. A. van Cauteren. 'De liturgische koordispositie van de romaanse Dom te Utrecht' *Utrecht kruispunt van de middeleeuwse kerk. Voordrachten gehouden . . . Rijksuniversiteit te Utrecht 25–27 augustus 1988.* Zutphen 1988. (Clavis kunsthistorische monografieën 7), 63–84, esp. 77. Wüstefeld (1993), no. 5 (with lit.).

42. See also *Egbert Erzbischof von Trier 977–993, Gedenkschrift der Diözese Trier zum 1000. Todestag.* Ed. F. J. Ronig, Trier 1993, Band 1, nr. 26 (lit. ref.); Band 2, 153–62. In the twelfth century *vita* of Wolbodo, the monk Reiner of Liège mentions how Wolbodo himself copied a psalter and collect-prayers and presented the book to the abbey of St Lawrence in that town. Vlierden (1995), no. 109. However, J. P. Gumbert remarks that the codex does not have the appearance of a studybook (in a letter d.d. 21-12-1995).

43. G. I. Lieftinck, *Bisschop Bernold (1027–1054) en zijn geschenken aan de Utrechtse kerken, openings-college . . . 19 maart 1948*, Groningen-Batavia, 1948. More elaborate in G. I. Lieftinck, 'Der herkomst van bisschop Bernold van Utrecht (1027–54)', *Jaarboekje van Oud-Utrecht* (1949), 23–40. J. P. Gumbert, 'Die Bernold-Handschrift in Leiden: von Augsburg nach Utrecht', ed. M. Borgolte (et al.), *Litterae medii aevi, Festschrift für Johanna Authenrieth* (Sigmaringen 1988), 161–63; Gumbert (1990), 6, nt. 9.

44. Koert van der Horst, *Illuminated and decorated medieval manuscripts in the University Library, Utrecht* (Maarssen/'s-Gravenhage 1989), no. 2 and no. 7.

45. Utrecht, Museum Catharijneconvent, ABM h3; Wüstefeld (1993), no. 6. Only in the nineteenth century the book was first called 'Bernold codex'.

46. Handschriften en oude drukken van de Utrechtse Universiteitsbibliotheek (Utrecht 1984), 81.

47. In the seventeenth century the book belonged to Queen Christina who bequeathed her collection to the Vatican. A. W. Byvanck. *La miniature dans les Pays Bas septentrionaux* (Paris 1937), pl. III, Fig. 4; Horst (1989), nos 1, 4, 5.

48. The registration mark was recently identified by a student of Professor Gumbert (unpublished thesis). How and when it left Egmond and came to St Paul's remains unknown.

49. Earlier the two *Martinella* of St Peter's and the Cathedral Chapter were discussed. One of the most important functions of the Utrecht Chapters was to elect a new bishop.

50. Wüstefeld (1993), no. 7.

51. P. C. Boeren, *Catalogus van de handschriften van het Rijksmuseum Meermanno-Westreenianum* ('s-Gravenhage 1979), 44–47. CMD-NL-1, no. 119, pl. 69–72.

52. Horst (1989), no. 3 and no. 6. Handschriften (1984), no. 57.

53. G. Gerritsen-Geywitz, 'Kaarsvet en kerkwijding', *Rapiarijs: een afscheidsbundel voor Hans van Dijk*, eds S. Buitink, A. M. J. van Buuren and I. Spijker (Utrecht 1987), 45–47; Y. de Loos, Duitse en Nederlandse muzieknotaties in de 12de de 13de eeuw (diss., Utrecht, 1996). Gumbert (1990), 82, nt. 15 notes some other manuscripts as well: Brussels, RL, MS 9537–48 and Durham, Cathedral MS A.IV.34.

54. Wüstefeld (1993), no. 8.

Romanesque and Gothic stone fonts in the diocese of Utrecht

by M. Schönlank-van der Wal

I

If the position of Utrecht between two other areas, Britain and the Continent is considered as being central, then this implies a special position for Utrecht, either as an area linked artistically to one or the other (or to both areas), or as one that differs essentially from the others.

My contribution concerns medieval stone fonts and I want to show that, as far as stone fonts are concerned, Utrecht was not an intermediate area but had its own particular identity. The term 'Utrecht' here refers to the area of the medieval diocese of which the borders were not fixed, but which throughout the period 1150–1550 covered a major part of the deltas of the rivers Meuse and Rhine.

II

All the medieval stone fonts without exception, had to be imported, into the diocese because in the whole area of the present-day Netherlands, there was no material that was suitable for the manufacture of stone fonts.[1] As the import of fonts could have taken place from the many quarries in present-day Germany, Belgium, France and even England, it would make sense to presume that, in the area of the diocese of Utrecht, one would find a wide variety of fonts, if only for the reason that this area was surrounded by so many places where fonts were produced.[2] However, this assumption proves to be incorrect, because the variety of fonts in the diocese is even less than in other areas such as Denmark, western Germany, Belgium, northern France and England.

My study showed that until the beginning of the Renaissance, the whole diocese of Utrecht (as indeed almost the entire area of the present-day Netherlands) obtained every one of its fonts from two groups of quarries, namely those of Bentheim and Namur. It is even true that, though the Netherlands imported building stone from the quarry at Tournai, fonts were not acquired from there, even though Tournai fonts were exported as far as England.[3]

One can safely assume that the feasibility of transport, together with a certain degree of tradition, influenced the purchasing behaviour of the Dutch parishes, and thus of the parishes of the Utrecht diocese. Naturally, my findings as to the numbers of supplying quarries can only be derived from the medieval stone fonts existing today, either as a whole or as fragments. They number one hundred and forty in the present-day Netherlands of which seventy-seven are in the former Utrecht diocese. This total may increase a little, when new fonts are discovered. The number may seem too small to allow us to draw conclusions, but there is no reason to assume that the 'Beeldenstorm' and the 'normal' replacement of old fonts by more modern ones have had any selective effect and have spared only fonts of the two named quarries exclusively. Apart from the fact that only two quarries acted as suppliers, it is remarkable that each of them had its own separate market-area. The map (Fig. 1) shows the original locations of the fonts

○   sandstone fonts from Bentheim
●   limestone fonts from Namur
≈   rivers
—   border of the present-day Netherlands
///// border of the diocese of Utrecht in 1550

FIG. I.   Map of the original locations of the fonts

and fragments still present today, dividing them into fonts from the ateliers at Namur and Bentheim.

Though the fonts were imported as finished products (not as rough blocks of stone to be worked), certainly at the beginning of the Middle Ages this trade still posed considerable transport problems which were mostly solved by the use of ship and raft along the rivers, lakes and sea. The map shows that the rivers Overijsselse Vecht and IJssel, as well as the former Zuiderzee (now IJsselmeer), were especially important for the supply of fonts from Bentheim. Some of the fonts from Bentheim were brought to their destinations via the river Ems and the North Sea.[4] For the distribution of fonts from Namur the Meuse and the Rhine with its tributaries, for instance the Hollandse

Vecht and Hollandse Ijssel, were especially important. In that part of the diocese of
Utrecht which could be served by both supply routes and from both quarries, both
types of fonts are represented in almost equal numbers. It is remarkable that the fonts
from Namur within the area of the diocese seem to be later than those from Bentheim,
for all Namur fonts have early Gothic and later characteristics, while most Bentheim
fonts in the diocese are Romanesque in form and decoration.[5]

The question why, after the fourteenth century, the supply from the workshops at
Bentheim almost came to a halt, while the supply from Namur to the diocese went on
until the Alteration (1578), needs more investigation.

It is known that the production of fonts in the workshops at Bentheim was past its
zenith at the end of the fourteenth century. As for the diocese itself, the areas supplied
by the Bentheim quarries were hit by natural disasters and wars, with the direct and
indirect consequence of depopulation.[6] Thus the demand for fonts there came to an end
and this could explain why the Bentheim trade was not replaced by deliveries from
Namur.

III

These general considerations are followed by some more detailed remarks about the
fonts, after which, with the support of the sketches 2A and 2B, an effort will be made to
show a chronological development of the Bentheim and Namur groups respectively.

It is true of both groups that their shapes show whether they were made in the
Romanesque or Gothic periods, for in the Gothic period all fonts were octagonal in the
Utrecht diocese. (However this does not exclude the possibility that the same styles did
not prevail at precisely the same time in both places. See note 5.) For the group shown
in Fig. 2A, the change lies between the shapes 2A-d and 2A-e; for the group outlined in
2B it lies between the shapes 2B-c and 2B-d.

The fonts from Bentheim are without exception made from one piece of grainy light-
yellow to light-grey sandstone, whereas the fonts from Namur are all made from more
than one piece of hard, light-grey limestone. Apart from that, both groups can clearly
be distinguished by their design. Although, therefore, each group of fonts can be seen
as having its own type, this does not mean no variations exist within these categories.
On the contrary, no two fonts, not even when they originate from the same workshop,
are exactly the same. My research showed that the differences in appearance were not
determined by differences in the way that baptism was administered.[7] Up to the end of
the Gothic period the differences were neither determined by the artistic preferences of
the buyers, nor by the current art-forms in their areas, nor even by instructions from
the Church.

The Church limited itself to the instruction that a baptismal font had to be made of
stone and that the water it contained should be covered.[8] The great variety was almost
solely determined by the workshops themselves. In a 'seller's market' the quarries
determined the rich variety of the shapes, in spite of the fact that certain periods can be
regarded as 'periods of mass-production for the market'. The richness of form seems to
result from the ideas and preferences of the masons in the quarry workshops. By
moving around during their training as master stone-cutters, they could implement a
variety of forms in the existing tradition of their workshops.[9] Initially the designs of
monk masons often from far afield or from overseas, set the standard.[10]

FIG. 2A.   Models of fonts from Bentheim

FIG. 2B.   Models of fonts from Namur

FONTS FROM BENTHEIM

The Bentheim fonts are always made of a single piece of stone. Externally the earliest models look like stone tubs on which neither base, nor shaft or basin can be distinguished (see Fig. 2A-a). While all fonts have an average height of 90 cm the actual basin for the water has a maximum depth of 40 cm. The shape of this type of baptismal font is only externally a reminder of those wooden tubs, one can see in some illustrations in fourteenth-century manuscripts and in Gothic church windows.[11] Here the persons to be baptized are always seen sitting or standing in the tubs, which at times are made out of stone. In none of the 160 Dutch fonts that I have studied, however, could an adult person have sat. It is also a fact that the manuscript illuminations mentioned above always depict events six or more centuries prior to their production and are therefore beyond all means of verification by the artist. An example to illustrate this is the miniature in *Spieghel Historiael* by Jacob van Maerlant, dated 1323–53, showing the baptism of King Clovis and his followers in the year AD 511, but set in

Gothic (!) stone bowls on octagonal shafts. In order to contain five grown-up men they must have been made of enormous monoliths. The relationship with reality of such an image is no more than that of a saint holding a church in his hand, or a picture of eleven thousand virgins under the cloak of Ursula.[12] Whether the wooden tubs did provide enough space for complete submersion, or only a partial one, is not certain; in any case the stone fonts with a tub-like shape — such as can be found in Vledder and Ermelo — did not.

The central section of the font gradually diminished into a shaft with a base below and a bowl above such as the one in the church at Ommen (see Fig. 2A-b). Here on each of the four sides of the base, the decorative motif of a spiral in relief has been carved. Other motifs such as geometrical ones and the rope band as in Figs 2A-a, 2Ab and 2A-d, were widespread in Europe and used so often and with such a wide variety of meanings in early times that they continued to be used on Christian objects without any problem. The twisted cords, as seen on most Romanesque fonts from Bentheim, could be a reminder of the hoops of rope which held together the staves of wooden barrels and later seen on wooden tub-fonts. The arcade decoration appeared in early Christian times associated with baptisteria and later on various religious objects and in church interiors around the end of the eleventh century. After that it also appeared on stone fonts, replacing earlier pure geometrical decorations.[13] As a motif the arcade has been held to represent the Heavenly City of Jerusalem and that fact alone could explain the abundant application of this motif in various religious objects and buildings. But the suggestion has also been made that an arcade is a suitable frame for the Fountain of Life, from which the Rivers of Paradise run: Euphrates, Tigris, Geon and Physon.[14] Applied on a font, the font itself becomes the 'Fountain of Life',[15] and as such an arcade is the perfect decoration for a baptismal font.

Fig. 2A-c and Pl. XVA show us a representative of a small series of fonts made from sandstone — carved from a single piece and showing short colonnettes. They are to be found in Apeldoorn, Almen and Wesepe.[16] It is noteworthy that the rope motif and the division into friezes with which all other Romanesque Bentheim fonts are decorated, are completely absent. However, some pagan motifs were used: the capitals on the colonnettes among others show a head of Janus, a cat-like head and a ram's head. Heads of Janus were used by the Romans as a motif for the theme of separation in time and space: for gates, borders, Old and New Year, present and past. Baptism too was seen as a passing or separation, a rite of passage, a birth to a new life and also as a resurrection after death.[17] A picture of a ram was frequently used as a sign of Spring and often occurs in drawings of the Zodiac; here too it is a symbol of new life. Cat-like or devils' heads are symbols of the worldly evil that is excluded by baptism. The baptized person can no longer be its prey. A type of sandstone font widespread round Bentheim, shown in Fig. 2A-d and Pl. XVB, is represented by the font in the church at Rijssen. Some similar specimens are almost identical to each other. These fonts were made at the peak of font-production at Bentheim.

The technique used for carving in relief shows that better tools were available than before. Whereas for the first three types only the common pointed and the broad chisels were used, after that flatter, sharper and, above all, better-hardened chisels, allowed faster and surer work. Apart from the recurring rope motif separating the friezes, now one sees floral motifs like branches and so-called palmettes. Both are motifs appropriate for baptism. Vine branches are representative of the text 'I am the vine, ye are the branches' (John XV, 5), meaning Christ and his followers. Apart from that the vine motif was very common on religious subjects generally. On the lowest friezes noose-shaped, cord-like, and big-leaf shape decoration often occur (for instance in Groenlo and Toornwerd). These are roughly reproduced palm-leaves, the above-mentioned palmettes. It has been suggested that these leaves represent vegetation in Paradise, beheld by the baptized when 'he emerges from the water-grave'.[18]

The bowl of this type of font seems to be placed on a flat disc, below which are four sculpted figures. In the case of Rijssen there are four lions, crawling against the shaft, looking over their shoulders and grinning. In Christian iconography lions had either a positive meaning (the lion of Judah) or a negative one (see I ep. Petr.5:8, where the devil is described as 'a roaring lion' who 'walketh about, seeking whom he may devour'). A typological depiction of Christ as Conqueror of the Evil is often given by the image of Daniel in the Lion's den, surrounded by four prowling lions.[19] Because they prowl around the font with its sacred water, the four lions below the Bentheim fonts have a negative connotation; they symbolize the evil in the world and they make a final attempt to trap the person to be baptized, for the Sacrament of the Baptism will bring him or her out of their reach. To add to the complication, the bowl may also be supported by four human figures. One can see them squatting down below the fonts of Groenlo, Vries and Weerselo for example. Although many suggestions have been made it is not known what they symbolize. They could represent the Four Rivers of Paradise, the four Evangelists, the four Winds (of Heaven) or the entire world. Taking into account the long cowls they are wearing, it has also been suggested that they are four monks.

After the Romanesque period the shapes became, for a time, less exuberant. All fonts had now become octagonal. The number eight is also symbolic: the Resurrection of Christ is to be seen as the eighth day of the Creation. The sketches 2A-e (Markelo), 2A-f (Ontswedde, diocese of Munster) and 2A-g (Almelo) give an impression of the shapes the fonts in the Gothic period could take. In drawing 2A-h the voluptuous leaf-shapes and the masks against the shaft show the influence of the Renaissance. In the church at Den Burg on the isle of Texel, and in the Biblical Museum at Amsterdam, one can find some fonts of this model.

NAMUR FONTS

The fonts from the workshops of the quarries of Namur possibly entered the diocese of Utrecht slightly later than the sandstone fonts. All Namur fonts are made of a limestone called 'bleu calcaire de Meuse' and consist of at least three separate parts: base, shaft and bowl (the oldest, the Romanesque fonts, consist of seven parts; here four corner colonnettes were mounted separately). These Romanesque shapes (shown in the sketches 2B-a, 2B-b and 2B-c) do not occur in the diocese of Utrecht; they can only be found south of the limits of the diocese. Within the diocese we find only Namur octagonal fonts. The essential characteristic of all Namur fonts — including the earliest, roughly from the first half of the twelfth century — consists of four strongly salient heads at the rim of the bowl. They always appear on the bowl above the corners of the base and they nearly always end with their tops level with the rim of the bowl. The few fonts which do not have these heads date from the sixteenth century.

One of the two oldest limestone fonts in the Utrecht diocese is now to be found at Hoogwoud (from the first half of the fourteenth century, see Fig. 2B-d). We see an octagonal bowl with four panels vertically curved between the heads which are spaced equally around the bowl. Within the long period in which the heads were used as a motif — approximately four centuries — both the design and the theme developed strongly. This change of theme is clearly visible in the physiognomy, the styling of the hair and the head-dress. More than with the supporting figures in the sandstone fonts, there is reason here to admit a range of interpretations. The earliest (Romanesque) heads are cylindrical and almost identical on each font. Grave faces have been crudely applied to them. An interpretation of a sacred theme, such as the four Gospels, the Four Rivers of paradise or the four Patriarchs is acceptable, but no interpretation is certain.

When fonts became octagonal, in early Gothic times, there appear completely different elements in the heads and the strictly sacred theme is abandoned. We notice different facial expressions and more variations of dress. The four heads of the font at Hoogwoud, for instance, differ strongly from each other and there is no doubt that they represent four real people. Their hair-styles and their clothes are different and their facial expressions also clearly depict a wide range of human types. We even see mentally-disturbed people who grin, and people with facial deformities. In Medieval illustrations, laughing and strange facial expressions were considered to indicate foolishness (see Pl. XVc). There is reason therefore to accept the view that the four heads here would together represent 'the whole of humanity'. We see this on the fonts of Hoogwoud, Houten and Noordwijk-Binnen. On other fonts however, heads with devilish looks and pointed ears appear; sometimes we even see the head of a monkey instead of a human head. (In Christian iconography the monkey stands for: insecurity and vanity; but worst of all: the monkey — according to his description in the *Physiologus* — by aping his tricky Hunter (the Devil), smears loam on his eyes and thereby can be caught easily.[20] These themes of evil and sin were used as a warning, replacing the themes of the former sacred heads. The measurements of the heads change over a period in time. The earliest cylindrical heads were at least 30 cm high; later they become smaller. Exceptionally small are the heads on many Namur fonts shipped mainly to the Rhineland. That influence is widespread; the fonts from Wageningen (currently at Nijmegen) and at Doorn are examples of those types (see Fig. 2B-e).

With the passing of time, the rim of the bowl, and also the base and shaft, were ornamented with more profiled edges. Just as in architecture the need was felt for richer ornament, the developing dexterity of the masons and advances in the technique of stone-cutting made this possible. By means of setting points with the pointed chisel and the application of polishing methods, it was possible to create tonal differences in the colour of the hard limestone (See Figs 2B-f and 2B-g).[21] At roughly the same time the basin became less deep and smaller in diameter, whereas the outside diameter stayed the same, and, as a consequence, the heads had to cant over. Not anymore in a vertical position they could no longer face directly outwards but had to look down (see again Fig. 2B-g). Examples of such fonts are found among others at Epe and at Kuinre (currently in a church at Bolsward). The changes did not all occur at the same time, Fig. 2B-f, for instance, shows a font with profiled edges, but still with a traditional deep bowl (of about half the total height). Here the heads look straight ahead (see Fig. 6, the font of the Pauluskerk at Baarn and also the fonts at Groessen, Amersfoort and Noordeloos).

IV

In the second half of the fifteenth century the market altered. No longer was it the prerogative of the master mason alone to decide on the appearance of the font; the wishes of the buyer had to be taken into account more and more. In other words, the seller's market changed to a buyer's market. How else can the presence of four women's heads on the rim of the font of Kuinre (end of fifteenth century) be explained? From some other places as well we have inherited fonts of a particular design; these were donated to the church by rich parishioners. (These examples are all to be found in Friesland, namely at Genum, Wier and Tjalhuizum.) They were made of sandstone or hard limestone. Presumably they were not carved in quarry workshops, but on the spot. The Namur workshops modernized in the sixteenth century; the bowl came to stand on a slender shaft and, in the end, the heads at the rim were abandoned altogether (see Fig. 2B-h). Such types are to be found at Sijbekarspel, Castricum (dating from 1519), Bunschoten, Geldermalsen, Papendrecht and 'sGravenpolder (dating from 1547). In some cases these fonts have the year of their manufacture incised on them.

Changes of taste and modernization influenced the appearance of stone baptismal fonts. The rigid design of the last group could not prevent them from being practically banned by the official proclamation of the Alteration in 1578. These fonts huge and made of stone had Catholic associations, which was reason enough for their exclusion.

Even before the official Alteration the fonts had suffered during the iconoclastic period, as the Utrecht diocese was one of the hardest hit. Either they were completely smashed, or a different use was found. At one time the base was used outside the church for the verger to stand on while making announcements to the parishioners; many bowls ended up as drinking troughs for cattle or as water-basins in workshops. Some shafts even went up and down in church-towers as counter-weights for the bells. In the best case it was turned upside-down and used as a support under the newly-installed pulpit. Several fonts were buried and only recently re-appeared. In recent years an effort has been made to bring the old stone fonts back into the churches.

ACKNOWLEDGEMENT

I am grateful to P. Drake M.A. of Ipswich for advice and comments upon the draft of this contribution.

SHORTENED TITLES USED

Davies (1962)   Gordon J. Davies, *The Architectural Setting of Baptism* (London 1962).

Hall (1975)   James Hall, *Dictionary of Subjects and Symbols in Art* (London/Fakenham/Reading, John Murray (Publ.) Ltd., 1975).

Luiks (1975)   A. G. Luiks, *Baptisterium: de bediening van de doop in de oud-christelijke kerk* (Kampen 1975).

Schönlank-van der Wal (1994)   M. Schönlank-van der Wal, *Middeleeuwse stenen doopvonten in Nederland* (Amsterdam, Vrije Universiteit M.A. thesis 1994).

REFERENCES

1. M. Schönlank-van der Wal (1994), 1–75.
2. Quarries in the immediate neighbourhood were, among others, to be found at Tournai, Ecaussinnes, near Brussels, Nivelstein, in the Eifel, Baumberg, at the river Weser: see A. Slinger, H. Janse, G. Berends, *Natuursteen in Monumenten* (Zeit/Baarn 1980), 39.
3. H. Janse and D. J. de Vries, *Werk en Merk van de Steenhouwer* (Zwolle, Waanders 1991), 20–23.

4. Parishes along the coast of Friesland and Groningen and on the Dutch Wadden islands received their fonts via the North Sea.

5. There may be several reasons for these differences: for a long time Bentheim continued to make Romanesque fonts to fulfil the demand from Utrecht, while at the same time making Gothic fonts for other clients. Or the fonts from Namur in Utrecht only seem to be more recent, because Namur started producing a Gothic form of fonts about fifty years before Bentheim did. But there can also be (or at the same time) less likely causes, for instance unreliable supply via the rivers Rhine and Meuse, caused by the constant quarrels between Utrecht and Kleve, Gelre and Brabant.

6. J. H. Popping, *Schetsen uit Friesland, in het bijzonder de Geschiedenis betreffende Ooststellingwerf, Weststellingwerf, Schoterland, Opsterland en omstreken*, Wolvega 1892. J. J. van Moolenbroek, 'Caesarius van Heisterbach op reis in Friesland en Groningen, De Dialogus Miraculorum (1219–23) als historische bron', *Tijdschrift voor geschiedenis*, 98 (1985), 513–39.

7. The literature distinguishes four methods of baptism:

submersio	:	full submersion in baptismal water,
immersio	:	pouring baptismal water over a person who is standing or kneeling in a deep tub,
afusio	:	sprinkling with baptismal water over the head of a child held above a font, or over an adult standing next to the font,
. . . . .	:	submerging the head of an adult standing next to the font into the baptismal water in the font by the priest.

(See F. Bond, *Fonts and Font covers* (London/New York/Toronto, 1908, 30, aho 1985, 5–17); Davies (1962), 52, 64, R. Ligtenberg, "Romaansche doopvonten in Nederland", *Bulletin van den Nederlandschen Oudheidkundigen Bond*, serie, VIII (1915), 157; Schönlank-van der Wal (1994), 13–21; H. A. J. Wegman, *Riten en mythen. Liturgie in de geschiedenis van het Christendom*, Kampen, Uitg.mij. J. H. Kok (1991), 114, 148–51, 219–24).

8. Davies (1962), 70–71. Numerous Church Councils emphasized the necessity for stone fonts to have lids.

9. Schölank-van der Wal (1994), 42–43. H. Hagels, 'das Steinhauergewerbe in der Grafschaft Bentheim', *Jahrbuch 1979. Heimatverein der Grafschaft Bentheim* (1970), 88.

10. L. Tollenaere, *La scuplture sur pierre de l'ancien diocèse de Liège à l'époque romane* (Gembloux 1957), 172.

11. Scenes of baptism on different fonts: the copper font in Saint Barthélemy in Liège, c. 1115; the bronze baptismal font in the Cathedral in Hildesheim, c. 1220; fonts depicted on the windows of the Sainte Chapelle, Paris; 'the Baptism of Augustine' in *the Book of Prayers* of St Elizabeth of Thüringen; 'the Baptism of Constantine the Great' in the *Picture-Bible* of the Monastery Saint Bertin, fol. 157^r.

12. Hall (1975), 317.

13. Davies (1962), 68.

14. F. Nordström, *Medieval Baptismal Fonts; an Iconographical Study* (Umeâ, Umeâ University 1984), 11–13. Luiks (1975), 16, 74.

15. This theme is widely used in religious objects; e.g. Barbarossa's huge candelabrum in the Dom of Aachen.

16. Schönlank-van der Wal (1994), 45–46, 61.

17. Hall (1975), 167.

18. Luiks (1975), 162.

19. E.g. The Blassus-grave, Cemetery-church at Borsel-Youni, Tunisia: Daniel surrounded by four lions. The number four is also symbolical: it points to the Holy Centre: Christ, Who will conquer Evil.

20. The *Physiologus* is a popular-theological second-century AD treatise on the Christian virtues, by using fables. It appeared in the Middle Ages in several shortened and translated forms: the 'Bestiaria' e.g. *De Natura Rerum*, by Albertus Magnus.

21. G. A. Overeem and H. N. Karsemeyer, 'De ontwikkelingen van de bewerkingstechnieken van natuursteen in relatie met de bouwstijlen', *Restaurantie Vademecum*, RV blad steenhouwerswerk 01 (1987).

Architectural Links between Scotland and the Low Countries in the Later Middle Ages[1]

by Richard Fawcett

Scotland had active contacts with the areas that are now Holland and Belgium throughout the greater part of the middle ages. Flemings had been among those invited to Scotland by David I (1124–53) as part of his attempt to introduce feudalism to the kingdom, for example,[2] and as early as the 1180s the Cistercian abbey of Melrose — perhaps Scotland's greatest sheep farmer — was selling its wool in Flanders under the special protection of the Counts of Flanders.[3] But the closest commercial and cultural contacts were those that developed after the outbreak of Scotland's Wars of Independence with England in 1296. In fact, the architectural evidence leaves little doubt that Lowland Scotland's strongest architectural links up to that time, from the early twelfth century to the end of the thirteenth century, were with England. Already during the reigns of Edgar (1097–1107) and Alexander I (1107–24) it seems certain that masons were being introduced from England to design and build new churches, and it was under David I that such importations of English craftsmen increased most dramatically. Although the post-Reformation writer of *The Rites of Durham* was to claim that David I had brought workmen from both France and Flanders to work at Holyrood Abbey[4] it would be hard to find anything in the architecture itself which supported this idea.

From soon after David's accession in 1124 it is clear from what we can still see at the abbeys of Dunfermline, Jedburgh and Kelso, amongst other buildings, that he was drawing masons from several parts of England to design and construct the many new buildings required as part of his far-reaching campaign to modernize the Scottish church. Having lived in England since before 1100, where he was provided with extensive estates by means of a suitable marriage at a time when it seemed unlikely he would be expected to succeed to the Scottish throne, David had been well-placed to acquire a knowledge of the range of architectural ideas he would eventually wish to introduce to Scotland, as well as of the variety of forms of religious life that they might house.[5] Once established, this cross-Border exchange of ideas had continued throughout the twelfth and thirteenth centuries.

However, following the outbreak of warfare between Scotland and England in 1296, a state of only periodically broken enmity was to continue for much of the later middle ages. Of particular consequence was the contraction of architectural opportunities within Scotland for the greater part of the fourteenth century — at the very time that England was passing through an especially creative phase — which meant that artistic contact between the two countries was greatly reduced, and the likelihood of it ever being re-established was also diminished.

When architectural activity began to expand once more in Scotland from the later fourteenth century onwards, although we see some limited renewal of contact with England, as most notably in the first phase of the large-scale rebuilding of Melrose Abbey after its destruction by Richard II in 1385, in general Scottish patrons and masons began to follow a diverging path from that of England. At this period we see approaches to design gradually emerging in which new ideas from a wide variety of sources are grafted on to an established stock of solutions, resulting in a synthesis which is not quite like anything to be seen elsewhere. In achieving this synthesis the new ideas were often so extensively adapted to Scottish tastes that it can be extremely difficult to assess where the ideas would have originated, and we are dealing with a field in which there are few certainties. But it is generally accepted — and I believe rightly so — that the Low Countries must have been one important source of these ideas because of the even closer contacts that developed with that area after the breach with England. (I should state here that references to the Netherlands and the Low Countries in this paper will embrace both the modern Netherlands and Belgium.)

The links between Scotland and the Low Countries came to embrace commerce, intellectual activities and the arts and, although it probably could not be claimed that they were as important to the Low Countries as they were to Scotland, their significance to the former should certainly not be under-estimated. We see this particularly with trade.[6] Scotland's most enduring relationships were to be with Flanders, and especially with Bruges, with which the first surviving staple agreement was signed in 1359. Nevertheless, relations were occasionally soured, one problem being the curbing of piracy, while pressures applied by England on the Flemish cities could also lead to difficulties. But it is clear that, despite such difficulties, whenever a breach developed in Scottish relations with one area, other parts of the Low Countries were eager to step into that breach. In 1347, for example, all Scottish goods in Flanders were seized, but an alternative staple was quickly established at Middelburg in Zeeland. Similarly, in 1467 a Scottish Act of Parliament prohibited trade with Flemish ports, but this was reversed two years later after envoys had been sent from there to Scotland. Almost a century later, rival bids were being made by Veere, Middleburg and Antwerp for the Scottish staple in the 1530s, '40s and '50s, showing that trade with Scotland was still valued.

One of the most concrete pieces of surviving evidence for this trade is the houses on the quay at Veere which are said to have been the residences of Scottish merchants, and we also know that there was a Scottish quarter in Bruges from as early as the 1290s. Particularly significant documentation for the range of the more specialized aspects of trade survives in the trading ledger of Andrew Halyburton, Conservator of Scottish Privileges in the Netherlands between 1492 and 1503, who was mainly resident at Middelburg. His ledger itemizes a thriving trade in everything from spices, precious metals, silks and books to tombstones and building materials.[7] Apart from this, we know of the purchase of many furnishings and vestments for Scottish churches, of which the finest survivor is the altarpiece bought in the 1470s for Trinity Collegiate Church in Edinburgh from Hugo van der Goes.[8] That church had been a foundation of Mary, the queen of James II, who was herself a daughter of the duke of the Netherlands province of Guelders. One well-documented illustration of the potential problems of this trade is the purchase of stalls for the choir at Melrose Abbey. They were ordered from the leading Bruges carpenter, Cornelius de Aeltre, though by 1441 — several years after the order had been placed — they still had not materialized.[9] However, following a law suit he agreed to travel to Scotland to install them, indicating that it may not have been uncommon for craftsmen to travel from the Low Countries to Scotland. One further point worth noting here is that in the Scottish royal works of the 1530s there were masons with the names 'Flemyng' and 'Flemisman', and it was one Peter Flemisman who carved images for the chapel at Falkland Palace for James V — possibly those still surviving in the buttress tabernacles of its south flank.[10] This would seem to confirm that craftsmen from the Low Countries were no strangers to Scotland.

Allowing for such close and regular contacts it is perhaps only to be expected that architectural ideas would be borrowed from the Low Countries at a time when fresh inspiration was being actively sought in Scotland, and when many potential patrons were spending so much of their time in the area. The two best placed groups of these patrons were probably the merchants and the prelates of the church, and it is in many of the buildings raised for those two groups — the great burgh churches, and the cathedral and monastic churches in particular — that there is often the strongest case for suspecting borrowings from the Low Countries. The merchants, of course, frequently visited when transporting their goods, while several of the prelates had received part of their university training at the university of Louvain,[11] and later either visited the area on embassies or passed through en-route to the papal court.

From all of this it is evident that there was ample scope for architectural ideas originating in the Low Countries to be taken up in Scotland though, as already hinted, the transformation of those ideas at the hands of Scottish craftsmen makes positive identification of sources hazardous. It must also be remembered that many buildings which may have provided inspiration for Scottish patrons and masons have been lost. In view of the particularly close contacts with Bruges, for example, it is almost certain that a number of that city's churches would have been sources of inspiration, though the destruction or replacement of many of them has removed much of the evidence. Consequently, since we can hardly hope to identify specific sources for ideas taken up in Scotland, we can only point to buildings displaying similar traits to those found in Scottish examples as an indication that it is likely to have been from the Low Countries that inspiration was drawn.

As a starting point, one possible instance of borrowing from Netherlands prototypes could be the use of cylindrical arcade piers in a number of major Scottish churches, a usage that immediately marks them as different from the major churches of England. Among the earliest buildings to have these piers were the nave of Aberdeen Cathedral, started before 1380, the nave of Dunkeld Cathedral, started in 1406, and the south transept of St Andrews Cathedral, which was repaired after the collapse of the adjacent gable in 1409 and of which a fragment of the southern respond survives.[12] The round arches that are used at the gallery stage of Dunkeld have suggested to some writers that the cylindrical piers there represent a form of Romanesque revival. However, since the pier bases at both Dunkeld and St Andrews are of a pronouncedly late Gothic type (those at Aberdeen are of much simpler profile as a result of the use of granite there), it seems that the arcades at those churches can only be comprehensible within the context of the revival of cylindrical piers seen in many western European countries other than England.[13]

In most countries of Europe, however, the proportions of the piers tended to be more attenuated than in the surviving Scottish examples (though the St Andrews arcade piers must have been considerably more slender than those at Dunkeld and Aberdeen). Beyond this, the mouldings of the arches in the continental examples tend to be more prismatic in profile than in Scotland, and there is a frequent preference for inter-penetration of pier and arch, as illustrated by the French example at Caudebec-en-Caux, started in 1426. My own belief is that the closest parallels for the Scottish examples are to be found in the Low Countries. The late Gothic use of cylindrical piers there probably began in the duchy of Brabant — an area that seems at that time to have been more architecturally advanced than Flanders — with the rebuilding of St Rombout's Church at Mechelen in 1342.[14] It must be conceded that the piers in that church are still very lofty by comparison with the Scottish examples, but less so than in many other countries, and the flat arch soffits and clear separation between the pier and arch are closer in spirit to what we find in Scotland. Relative proportions not dissimilar from those in Scotland are to be seen in a number of churches of the coastal provinces, as in the late fourteenth-century choir of St Bavo at Haarlem, or in later examples such as St Willibrord at Hulst, where rebuilding was started in about 1462.[15]

Such comparisons by themselves are insufficient to prove the case that the Low Countries had provided the stimulus for the Scottish revival of cylindrical piers, but when we look at Aberdeen Cathedral more closely there is important supplementary evidence in support of this possibility. There, presumably at an early stage of the rebuilding of the cathedral nave by Bishop Alexander Kininmund II (1355–80), and at the east end of the nave arcades already referred to, freestone crossing piers were constructed of a kind that is unique in Scotland, with four large half-cylinders attached to a massive cylindrical core. (Pl. XVIA) This was, I believe, a type of pier that was seldom found outside the Netherlands, where it was related to the even more common type in that area which simply had four massive conjoined half-cylinders.[16] Predecessors of the Aberdeen type may have been used as early as the thirteenth century at Brussels St Gudule, and were still being used at Notre Dame du Sablon in the same city in the early fifteenth century, while later variants are to be found in the crossing piers of St Catherine's Convent in Utrecht, which belongs to work started in 1486. The likelihood of Netherlands links in this case is strengthened by the fact that Aberdeen was a port enjoying active links with the Low Countries, and was listed by Bruges in 1350 as one of the four great trading burghs of Scotland. It is perhaps also worth mentioning that Bishop John Rait, the predecessor of the bishop who started to rebuild the nave, may himself have been a canon of one of the churches of Bruges.[17] Beyond this, there might be links between one of the capital types of the Aberdeen crossing piers and a type favoured in the Meuse valley, in the way that crocket-like foliage is pushed up to just below the abacus, leaving the rest of the bell relatively bare, though I make this last point with rather less conviction.

Another of the Scottish burghs which derived much of its wealth from trade with the Low Countries was Perth and, like Aberdeen, Bruges listed it as one of the four great burghs of Scotland. Much that we now see in the nave of St John's Parish Church in Perth results from heavy-handed restorations of the 1820s and 1920s, but an engraving of 1806 in *Memorabilia of Perth* shows what appears to be the decayed relic of an abandoned scheme for rebuilding the nave as a hall church with vast aisle windows, highly enriched buttresses and wall-head parapets, and a two-storeyed porch rising the full height of the aisles.[18] (Pl. XVIB) The rebuilding of which this was evidently a part must have been a highly prestigious operation because we know that in 1496 a master mason called Walter Merlioun was working here,[19] and he was a craftsman with involvement in several building operations on behalf of King James IV, including the royal residences at Holyrood and Stirling. True hall churches — as opposed to churches simply without a clerestory — were uncommon in Scotland, though the eastern parts of Edinburgh St Giles had been built as such in the later fourteenth century.[20] The relatively high degree of architectural enrichment seen at Perth was also unusual. Considering the rarity of this type of design, it therefore seems possible that the stimulus had come from outside Scotland, and I believe it is worth speculating if the germ of the idea could have originated with one of a number of Netherlands hall churches in which ambitious double-storeyed porches play an equally prominent role as at Perth. St Joris at Amersfoot, for example, was being remodelled around the same time that Perth's nave was under construction, while the elaborate porch we see at St Michael at Zwolle was probably being added to the hall church there around the early sixteenth century.

Could there also be an element of Netherlands inspiration behind the laterally-gabled chantry chapels around the perimeter of a number of burgh churches in Scotland? Several examples are recorded at Edinburgh St Giles, while one survives of a number known to have been built at Stirling Holy Rude; a similar effect must also have been created in the outer nave aisles at Elgin Cathedral as rebuilt after the fire of 1390. The saw-tooth silhouette seen in these buildings was similar to that found at several Netherlands churches, where gabled chapels had been added in greater or lesser profusion, as at Haarlem St Bavo. The same effect is also seen in the aisle flanks of a number of churches, as at the Dominican church in the Hague, where each bay of the south nave aisle was individually gabled.

On the basis of such comparisons, and in the absence of more convincing parallels, it is at least an arguable proposition that some individual motifs to be seen in the city churches of the Low Countries were a significant source of inspiration for the burgh churches of Scotland. This is perhaps to be seen even more convincingly in the design of the west front of the parish church of St Mary at Haddington. Complete rebuilding of the church was started after an agreement in 1462 with St Andrews Cathedral Priory,[21] the body to which the parish was appropriated, though the west front was probably only completed towards the end of the operation. It is relatively unusual in a Scottish burgh parish church for so much emphasis to be placed on a towerless west front as at Haddington. Indeed, the only other major surviving burgh church which did not have a western tower, and might therefore have offered scope for a show front, was Edinburgh St Giles, though there no attempt seems to have been made to create a distinct façade before the nineteenth century. At Haddington, by contrast, an impressive frontispiece was created by marking the divisions with heavy buttresses, while the gable is set back behind an openwork parapet. Within this matrix the main emphasis is on a large six-light window subdivided by massive sub-arches, immediately above a wide doorway with a central trumeau. (Pl. XVIIA)

Since there are no surviving Scottish precedents for so self-confident a piece of design we must look elsewhere for sources, and I believe that the closest parallels — albeit on a larger scale — are to be found in the Low Countries. Such a basic formula for façade design had become common there from the fourteenth century onwards. Examples from the later part of the century may be seen in the transepts of Our Lady's Church at Dordrecht, (Pl. XVIIB) while an example perhaps more likely to have been known to Scottish traders was the west front of the Dominican church in Bruges, which is now destroyed but which we partly know from Marcus Gheeraert's map of 1562[22] and from eighteenth-century engravings. Beyond the overall formula for the design in the relationship of wall to set-back gable, and of the window and doorway both to each other and to the surrounding wall, the case for an element of Netherlands inspiration is strengthened by a number of details. The massively strong — and, in the case of Haddington, slightly disproportionate — emphasis on the sub-arches in the window, for example, is something for which the most convincing parallels are to be found in large numbers in the Low Countries. This may also be true of the design of the round-arched west doorway,[23] in which the paired openings within a larger semi-circular arch may be compared with examples at St Lebuinus' Church in Deventer and St Salvator's Cathedral in Bruges, as well as at the Bruges Dominican Church.[24]

In further support of the possibility of Netherlands debts for the façade design at Haddington it will be useful to consider here the west tower of St Mary's Church at Dundee, another major trading burgh. Rebuilding there had begun with the choir, following an agreement of 1442–43 with the appropriating body, Lindores Abbey.[25]

The tower was probably the last major part to be finished, and may have been nearing completion in 1495, when a bell was donated. This strikingly ambitious tower is of a unique design in Scotland, being of telescoped design, with the wall faces of the top two storeys set back within those of the lower stage, and with a walkway at the intake. (Pl. XVIIc) In this it shows marked similarities with a major group of towers in the Netherlands, of which both the earliest and the largest was probably that at the cathedral of Utrecht, where the main part was built between 1321 and 1382.[26] (Pl. XVIIb) However, there are many later examples of such towers in the Low Countries which are closer to Dundee in scale, including those at Amerongen and Culemborg, while Gheeraerts' map suggests there may also have been at least one example in Bruges at the old church of St Walburgha. Naturally, only certain aspects of the prototypes were copied, and while the Netherlands examples were usually eventually capped by an octagonal superstructure, for example, Dundee was adapted to Scottish preferences by being designed to have a crown-steeple, though it is unlikely that it was ever built.

Despite the differences between Dundee and the telescoped towers of the Netherlands, I think it would be difficult to see the design of Dundee's tower having been evolved without the initial stimulus of the Low Countries examples. The case becomes even stronger on closer examination of details such as the parapets at the intake and wall-head in which — allowing for adaptation to local usages — the traceried treatment punctuated by miniature pinnacles is strikingly close to what is seen in some of the Netherlands examples. In view of this, it is also important to note the form and inter-relationship of the west window and doorway at Dundee, since these are very like what we have already seen at Haddington. (Pls XIIA and XVIIc) As at Haddington, the window is sub-divided by massive sub-arches, while the doorway has a round arch embracing two smaller round-arched openings. Taking account of the clear debts to the Low Countries in the overall design of the tower, the similarity of the doorway and window to those at Haddington is so close that this further strengthens the case for Netherlands inspiration there.

As already said, there is nothing else quite like Dundee's tower in Scotland, though it may have been at least an influence on the tower of one other burgh church. The west tower of Holy Rude Church at Stirling had been started together with the nave around the 1450s, but is unlikely to have been raised much above the level of the nave roof at that time. It was subsequently greatly heightened, however, probably as part of the later campaign that embraced the rebuilding of the choir. This second campaign followed an agreement of 1507 with Dunfermline Abbey,[27] the appropriating body, and there are indications that it was intended to heighten the nave clerestory and add transepts and a crossing tower, though these latter were never carried out. The master mason who heightened the west tower at Stirling had the problem that it was wider on its north–south axis than on its east–west axis. Despite this, it was decided to make the new top stage of the tower square in plan, which was achieved by corbelling out the east and west faces beyond those of the lower stages, while contracting the north and south faces sufficiently to allow a wall-walk on those two sides. This solution creates a silhouette partly related to that of the tower at Dundee, and could represent the further assimilation to Scottish tastes of an idea of ultimately Netherlands origin.

Yet another building in which there are reasons for suspecting debts to the Low Countries is the north chapel of the Dominican Church at St Andrews, the only remaining part of a friary built after 1516 with money left by Bishop Elphinstone of Aberdeen.[28] Its construction could also be linked with agreement being given in 1525 for new buildings to encroach on to the street. The most striking feature of the chapel is that it is a laterally-directed polygonal apse, though it is not known if it was transeptal, or if it simply projected from the flank of the church. However, at least two other Scottish churches are known already to have had such lateral apses around the early years of the sixteenth century, at Ladykirk and Arbuthnott, and in both cases they were at the junction of nave and choir and thus essentially transeptal. The existence of those earlier lateral apses, together with the construction of a characteristically Scottish ribbed tunnel vault over the St Andrews chapel, might be taken to suggest that the chapel as a whole is an inherently native product. Nevertheless, late Gothic lateral apses are to be found throughout Europe, from the chapel of St George at Windsor, in England, to the cathedral of Florence in Italy, and in the present context it is worth noting that such chapels are also fairly common in the Netherlands. Among many examples that might be cited are Zaltbommel St Michael, where a polygonal chapel was abutted against the flank of the mid-fifteenth-century nave, or Leiden St Peter, where one serves as a baptistery at the west end of the nave as rebuilt in 1512–18. Taking account of such parallels, and despite the Scottish features of the St Andrews chapel, the possibility of some element of Netherlands inspiration may be additionally worth considering because we know that the friary was built after the Scottish Dominican province had been reformed by that of Holland, and that in some sense it was an expression of the orders' renewed sense of mission in Scotland resulting from that visitation.[29]

The strongest pointer to the possibility of a Netherlands connection for St Andrews Blackfriars, however, is the type of tracery employed in the chapel, which is of uncusped loop-like forms. (Pl. XVIIIA) Tracery of this type had a limited but significant popularity in early sixteenth-century Scotland, as at Tullibardine Chapel of about 1500, at Midcalder Parish Church of about 1542, and in the transepts of Trinity Collegiate Church in Edinburgh, which was possibly completed around 1531.[30] While a tendency towards simplification of forms encouraged the production of uncusped tracery in all parts of Europe at this phase of the later middle ages, the closest parallels for the Scottish examples are certainly those to be found in the Netherlands, where in at least some cases it was the construction of the tracery in brick that encouraged the evolution of this approach. Amongst a number of possible parallels for the St Andrews Blackfriars tracery are windows in the apsidal north choir chapel of the church at Kapelle, which are datable to the late fifteenth century. (Pl. XVIIIB)

Other churches which have this type of tracery may also be shown to have been raised for cosmopolitan patrons with a likely knowledge of buildings on the continent. At Midcalder in West Lothian, for example, the church was built under terms of a contract drawn up in 1542 between the rector, Peter Sandilands, and his nephew, Sir John Sandilands, who was the local landholder.[31] Several members of that family are known to have travelled on the continent, and could have seen churches in the Netherlands. John Sandilands was a student in Paris for a while, while in 1526 his father had the dubious privilege of travelling to Rome in penance for a murder he had committed,[32] and is likely to have passed through the Netherlands. None of this could be regarded as conclusive evidence for appropriate contacts, but it is easy to understand how ideas could have been introduced into Scotland by such patrons. Without suggesting it as a specific source, could it have been tracery in a church such as Vianen which was the inspiration for that at Midcalder? Vianen coincidentally, was partly rebuilt after a fire in 1542.

The difficulty of understanding how far Low Countries influences were a factor in the design of Scottish buildings, in view of the transformations those influences underwent at the hands of Scottish masons, is nowhere more clear than at King's College Chapel in Aberdeen. The chapel was started in 1500 by Bishop William Elphinstone[33] and was ready for dedication in 1509. As one of Scotland's leading bishops, who at one stage had hopes of translation to the archiepiscopal see of St Andrews, Elphinstone was a cosmopolitan figure. He probably travelled to or through the Netherlands on several occasions, but he was certainly there in 1495, and while in Bruges at Easter-time he took the place of the Bishop of Tournai at a number of important services and ceremonies.[34]

Two years after his stay in Bruges Elphinstone was ordering carts and gunpowder from Andrew Halyburton in Middelburg when he was preparing his site in Aberdeen for the construction of his new college chapel,[35] and it is permissible to speculate if his mind was still on the churches that he must have seen in the Low Countries. The overall plan of the chapel, for example, which is an aisle-less rectangle with an eastern polygonal apse, could certainly have been taken from several buildings he may have seen; on balance, however, it is perhaps more likely that the direct inspiration had come from the similarly-planned Scottish university chapel of St Salvator at St Andrews, which had been built half a century previously by Bishop James Kennedy. Another feature that might arguably reveal a Netherlands debt is the ribbed timber wagon ceiling, since timber ceilings were widespread in those parts of the Low Countries where good building stone was scarce. But again there can be no certainty, because the flattened profile and the diagonal pattern of the ribbing in imitation of quadripartite vaulting are unlike what was most usual in the Netherlands, and I suspect that the ribbing at Aberdeen was as much influenced by the Scottish taste for ribbed stone tunnel vaults as by anything in the Low Countries. However, it may be worth pointing out that the widely-sprigged bosses which emphasize the intersections of the ribs do show parallels with those on the timber vault of the town hall at Bruges, which had been constructed by Jean de Valenciennes in 1402. Rather more significantly, related sprigged bosses are also to be seen on the wagon ceilings over the chancel chapels in the church of St Giles in Bruges, where it is known that Scottish workmen had a chapel dedicated to St Andrew. It may be added that, around the same time that King's Chapel was under construction, similar sprigged bosses were employed in the closely comparable wagon ceiling over the choir of St Nicholas' Parish Church in Aberdeen, which was started by the wright John Fendour in 1495, but which was only completed some years later.[36] Since we know that Bishop Elphinstone had a close interest in the work at St Nicholas, it seems possible that Fendour was the wright at King's College Chapel as well as at St Nicholas. It may also be mentioned here that comparable bosses were to be used in the flat ribbed ceiling over the nave of Aberdeen Cathedral, which was installed a few years later for Bishop Gavin Dunbar; this could also be a work of Fendour's, since we know that he worked on the central tower of the cathedral.[37]

There is thus a group of Aberdeen buildings using this type of sprigged boss, suggesting that a motif observed by Elphinstone in the Netherlands could have been copied in one of his projects and then spread to other buildings under construction in the city over the following years. When we move on to consider another aspect of the design of King's College Chapel, the window tracery, the case for a debt to the Low Countries seems to be even clearer, though in this case there is little evidence of the idea being copied at any other projects.[38] The most striking feature of several of the chapel windows is that they are subdivided by a heavy central mullion rising to the apex of the window arch, a motif which, although not unknown elsewhere, finds the closest reflection for this slightly ungainly variant in the Netherlands. The rather loose combination of forms flanking the central mullion, which are seen in their most expansive form in the great west window, might also reflect a fashion in the Low Countries. (Pl. XVIIIc) Unbroken central mullions are to be found in a number of churches there, including Notre Dame du Sablon in Brussels, St Jacques in Liege and 's-Hertogenbosch Cathedral. But a window that bears closer comparison with the Aberdeen window than those, both in the central mullion and in the loose combination of forms, is one in the south flank of the Domproosten chapel, off the south transept of Utrecht Cathedral. Significantly, it is also very close in date to the Aberdeen examples, having been inserted in about 1497.[39] (Pl. XVIIID) This is not to suggest, of course, that it was the Utrecht window that directly inspired those in Aberdeen, and it must be conceded that the design is handled with greater fluency in the Utrecht example. Nevertheless, in the absence of Scottish predecessors, the general similarity of approach seen at Aberdeen and Utrecht, together with the closeness of dating does support the likelihood of the Aberdeen windows having some debt to examples in the Low Countries.

Further examples could be cited from which it might reasonably be argued that elements employed in Scottish churches are traceable back to buildings in the Netherlands, though to do so would largely involve the reiteration of similar points to those already made in the course of this paper. The fundamental problem in this area of research is, of course, that there can be no certainty. Although Scottish patrons did occasionally state the models from which parts of their churches were to be copied,[40] the only case known to the author of a patron citing models in the Low Countries is that of the Melrose choir stalls, which were to be based on those of Ter Duinen and Thosan.[41] In the absence of firmer evidence we can only speculate how far the Low Countries were looked to for new architectural stimuli. In the cases of the overall design of Dundee's tower or of the window tracery types employed at St Andrew's Blackfriars Chapel and Aberdeen King's College Chapel, it is so difficult to find acceptable alternative sources for the underlying ideas that a Netherlands source seems most reasonable.

Taking consideration of those elements further, the case is also strengthened for suspecting a significant degree of Netherlands inspiration behind Haddington's west front, St Andrew's Blackfriars Church's lateral apse and the Aberdeen King's College Chapel's sprigged roof bosses. In other cases, however, the possibility that ideas taken up in Scotland had some basis in what patrons or masons had seen in the Low Countries might seem to have a slightly *faute de mieux* feel to it. It must be admitted, for example, that the revived use of cylindrical piers might be seen as essentially a Scottish expression of a wider European fashion, though even there the particular form of the Aberdeen crossing piers would seem to strengthen the case for specifically Netherlands inspiration in that case at least. Despite these caveats, I would suggest that, on balance, it is reasonable to accept from the architectural evidence that, at a time when Scotland was in need of a new range of architectural stimuli and when its relationships with the Low Countries were stronger than those with any other area, at least some of the ideas that found fertile ground for reinterpretation in Scotland had their origins in the Low Countries.

REFERENCES

1. The author's views on the architectural links between Scotland and the Low Countries are also discussed in 'Late Gothic architecture in Scotland: considerations on the influence of the Low Countries',

Proceedings of the Society of Antiquaries of Scotland, vol. 112 (1982), 477–96, and in *Scottish architecture from the accession of the Stewarts to the Reformation, 1371–1560*, The architectural history of Scotland (Edinburgh 1994).

2. G. W. S. Barrow, 'The beginning of military feudalism', in *The kingdom of the Scots* (London 1973), 289–90; A. A. M. Duncan, *Scotland, the making of the kingdom*, The Edinburgh history of Scotland (Edinburgh 1975), 475–78.

3. *Liber Sancte Marie de Melros*, ed. Cosmo Innes, Bannatyne Club (Edinburgh 1837), nos 14–15.

4. J. T. Fowler, *The rites of Durham*, Surtees Society, (Durham, London and Edinburgh 1903), 24–25.

5. G. W. S. Barrow, op. cit. note 2, 'The royal house and the religious orders', 165–87.

6. On trading links with the Low Countries see: John Davidson and Alexander Gray, *The Scottish staple at Veere*, London, 1909; M. P. Rooseboom, *The Scottish staple in the Netherlands* (The Hague 1910); Alexander Stevenson, *Trade between Scotland and the Low Countries in the later middle ages*, unpublished PhD thesis, Aberdeen University, 1982; idem 'Trade with the south', *The Scottish medieval town*, eds Michael Lynch, Michael Spearman and Geoffrey Stell (Edinburgh 1988), 180–206.

7. *The ledger of Andrew Halyburton, 1492–1503*, ed. Cosmo Innes (Edinburgh 1867).

8. Colin Thompson and Lorne Campbell, *Hugo van der Goes and the Trinity panels in Edinburgh* (Edinburgh 1974).

9. O. Delepierre, 'Documents from the records of West Flanders relative to the stalls of Melrose Abbey, *Archaeologia*, vol. 31 (1846), 346–49; G. G. Coulton, *Scottish abbeys and social life* (Cambridge 1933), 194–95.

10. *Accounts of the Masters of Works for building and repairing royal palaces and castles*, ed. Henry M. Paton, vol. 1 (Edinburgh 1957) 76, 99 and 256.

11. R. J. Lyall, 'Scottish students and masters at the universities of Cologne and Louvain', *Innes review*, vol. 36 (1985), 55–73.

12. Hector Boece, *Murthlacensium et Aberdonensium episcoporum vitae*, New Spalding Club (Aberdeen 1894), 24; Alexander Myln, *Vitae Dunkeldensis ecclesiae episcoporum*, Bannatyne Club (Edinburgh 1831), 16; *Scotichronicon*, ed. D. E. R. Watt, vol. 8 (Aberdeen 1987), 74.

13. Since this paper was first written a study of the possibility of there having been a late medieval Romanesque revival has been published by Ian Campbell in 'A Romanesque revival and the early Renaissance in Scotland', *Journal of the Society of Architectural Historians*, vol. 54 (1995), 302–25.

14. R. M. Lemaire, *Les origines du style Gothique en Brabant*, vol. 2 (Antwerp and Zwolle 1949).

15. Unless otherwise stated, dating of churches in the modern Netherlands is generally taken from *Kunstreisboek voor Nederland*, Rijkscommissie voor de Monumentenbeschrijving, 7th ed. (Amsterdam 1977).

16. Christopher Wilson, *The Gothic cathedral* (London 1990), 240.

17. John Dowden, *The bishops of Scotland* (Glasgow 1912), 114.

18. J. Cant, *Memorabilia of the city of Perth* (Perth 1806).

19. T. Dickinson and J. Balfour Paul, *Accounts of the Lord High Treasurer of Scotland*, vol. 1 (Edinburgh 1877), 133.

20. Christopher Wilson, in John Gifford, Colin McWilliam and David Walker, *The buildings of Scotland, Edinburgh* (Harmondsworth 1984), 109.

21. *Illustrations of Scottish history*, ed. Joseph Stevenson, Maitland Club (Glasgow 1834), 75–76.

22. I am grateful to Dr Alexander Stevenson for pointing out to me the importance of Gheeraerts' map.

23. Semicircular-arched doorways were to be common in Scottish late Gothic architecture from the late fourteenth century onwards, as in the doorway from the north nave aisle into the cloister at Melrose Abbey; the particular combination of elements as seen at Haddington, however, is more remarkable, and is only found in this form elsewhere at Dundee (see below).

24. Monique Dewulf, 'De kerkelijke architektuur van de Dominikanen te Brugge', *Gentse Bijdragen tot de kunstgeschiedenis en de oudheikunde*, vol. 18 (1959–60), 107–57.

25. *Charters, writs and public documents of the royal burgh of Dundee*, ed. W. Hay, Scottish Burgh Records Society (Dundee 1880), 19–23.

26. E. J. Haslinghuis and C. J. A. Peeters, *De dom van Utrecht*, De Nederlandse monumenten van geschiedenis en kunst (The Hague 1965), 404–47.

27. *Extracts from the records of the royal burgh of Stirling*, ed. R. Renwick, Scottish Burgh Records Society (Glasgow 1884), no. xxxvii.

28. *Registrum episcopatus Aberdonensis*, ed. Cosmo Innes, Maitland Club (Edinburgh 1845), vol. 2, 311–12.

29. Anthony Ross, *Dogs of the Lord*, Exhibition booklet (Edinburgh 1981), 5–7.

30. Richard Fawcett, 'Scottish medieval window tracery', in *Studies in Scottish antiquity*, ed. D. J. Breeze (Edinburgh 1984), 181–82.

31. Joseph Robertson, 'Notice of a deed by which Sir John Sandilands . . . binds himself and his heir to complete the vestry and build the nave, steeple and porch of the parish church of Mid-Calder', *Proceedings of the Society of Antiquaries of Scotland*, vol. 3 (1857–60), 160–71.

32. Ian Cowan, *The Scottish Reformation* (London 1982), 8; Margaret H. B. Sanderson, *Cardinal of Scotland* (Edinburgh 1986), 84.

33. G. Patrick Edwards, 'William Elphinstone, his college chapel and the second of April', *Aberdeen university review*, vol. 51 (1985), 1–17; Richard Fawcett. 'The architecture of King's College Chapel and Greyfriars' Church, Aberdeen'. *Aberdeen university review*, vol. 53, 1989, 102–26.

34. Leslie J. Macfarlane, William Ephinstone and the kingdom of Scotland (Aberdeen 1985), 232.

35. *Ledger of Andrew Halyburton*, op. cit. note 7, 182–85.

36. William Kelly, 'Carved oak from St Nicholas Church, Aberdeen', *Proceedings of the Society of Antiquaries of Scotland*, vol. 68 (1933–34), 355–66.

37. There is a tradition that the Aberdeen Cathedral ceiling was the work of a wright named as James Winter (W. Orem. *A description of the chanonry, cathedral and King's College of old Aberdeen*, Aberdeen 1791), 61, though one wonders if 'Winter' might be a corruption of Fendour.

38. Fawcett, op. cit. note 30, 180–81.

39. Haslinghuis and Peeters, op. cit. note 26.

40. For example, in 1387 the vaulting of five chapels in Edinburgh St Giles was to be copied from that over St Stephen's Chapel in Holyrood Abbey, *Registrum cartarum ecclesie Sancti Egidii de Edinburgh*, ed. David Laing, Bannatyne Club (Edinburgh 1859), 24; in 1511 Bishop Elphinstone required that the central steeple of Aberdeen Cathedral was to be copied from that of Perth St John, *Records of the Sheriff Court of Aberdeenshire*, ed. David Littlejohn, New Spalding Club (Aberdeen 1904–07), vol. 1, 102; in 1542 at Midcalder Church the vaulting was to be copied from that over St Anthony's Aisle in Edinburgh St Giles (Robertson, op. cit. note 31, 162).

41. Op. cit. note 9.

The Financing of the Construction of the Gothic Cathedral in Utrecht[1]

by W. H. Vroom*

The tallest church tower in the Netherlands is found in the heart of the city of Utrecht: it used to be the tower of the Dom (cathedral), the only episcopal church in the area which later was to become the Republic of the United Provinces. Notwithstanding the large-scale urban conglomeration, the words of the art historian Frits van der Meer about French cathedrals more than fifty years ago apply to the Utrecht Dom even now: 'the cathedral appears on the horizon long before the city does'.[2]

In contrast to the situation in France, from Utrecht one had to travel quite far to see another cathedral looming up on the horizon: to Osnabrück, Münster and Cologne in eastern direction, or to Liège, Tournai and Cambrai in the south. The bishopric of Utrecht was quite a large diocese, comprising almost 1,200 parishes in the late Middle Ages; many dioceses had no more than half that number. Moreover, these parish churches were situated in one of the more highly urbanized areas of Europe.

The gothic Dom, dedicated to St Martin, is no longer complete; the nave was destroyed by a tornado in 1674. The church was built on the site of its romanesque predecessor, within the confines of the Roman *castellum*; its foundations were laid after a fire destroyed the romanesque cathedral in 1253. Real progress on the new choir was only made after 1288, when an episcopal mandate established new sources of income to pay for the building work. The enormous tower was erected between 1321 and 1382, followed by the choir clerestory and the transepts, which were almost complete by 1479. Meanwhile, the cloisters were finished along with the small and the larger chapter-houses. The nave (now lost) was begun in 1471 after the demolition of the last remaining part of the old romanesque church, which up to then had remained in use. The bishop's tribune, which connected the tower to the nave, was built two decades later. Around 1525 the building work came to a halt, and aisles, the vaults of the transepts and the central nave and its buttressing, remained unfinished.

The nearly 110 m high Dom tower represents the 'community of the faithful in the bishopric'.[3] The Dom was the main church of the diocese, the mother church, the *matrix ecclesia* of this extensive and densely populated bishopric. This is an important factor to consider when looking at how the construction of this cathedral was financed. In principle, as we shall see, the faithful all shared the responsibility for the maintenance of the building, which is why the chapter's statutes of 1345 assigned the revenues *de bonis elemosinarum* as its prime source of income.

Beside being the main church of the bishopric, the Utrecht Dom is also the bishop's own church and where he had his throne or *cathedra*; the cathedral represents his spiritual bride, dear to him above all other churches in the diocese. This is why, in accordance with the canonical rules, the bishop was honour-bound to put the proper maintenance of the Dom before everything else. It also allowed him to apply his spiritual power towards the completion of his cathedral.

Yet it was not the bishop who had overall control of the Dom and all matters relating to its construction, maintenance and church furnishings; these issues were the

*Translated from the Dutch by S. Oosterwijk MA

prerogative of the chapter of the Dom which, according to ecclesiastical law, was first of all responsible for the communal offices in the Dom and the assistance of the bishop in word and deed. It is not surprising, therefore, to find that the chapter regarded the Dom very much as its own church. In many episcopal cities, especially from the thirteenth century onwards, the cathedral chapters developed into largely autonomous and quite wealthy corporations which were financially and judicially independent, although often at the expense of the bishop's privileges. This was certainly the case in Utrecht where the Dom chapter consisted of the dean and thirty-six canons. The chapter was in charge of the Dom church and considered itself the proper guardian of the cathedral, its privileges and its venerable traditions. As in so many other episcopal cities, the Dom chapter in Utrecht did its utmost to prevent episcopal interference in the affairs of the Dom. As early as 1118, the bishop had put his prebend at the dean's disposal (who thereby enjoyed double prebends) and thus formally withdrew himself from the chapter where he thus no longer enjoyed voting rights. However, the bishop did remain an honorary member of the Dom community and was still in supreme control of the Dom, though he only seldom visited it.[4]

So it was really the chapter which managed the Dom. In the early thirteenth century, when no renovation plans had yet been conceived, the chapter instituted a separate administration called the *fabrica ecclesie Trajectensis* which was to be in charge of the construction, maintenance and furnishing of the church. Once the reconstruction of the cathedral had begun, the chapter appointed two of its canons, one to manage the funds for the old romanesque Dom and the other to take care of the funds and administration for the construction work on the new church; the two offices were united in 1464. The masters of the fabric had only limited authority; any expenditure above a certain — rather small — amount required permission from the chapter assembly. They did have the power to hire and fire workmen, but the ultimate approval of the fabric accounts lay with the chapter assembly.

The above picture corresponds to the typical canonical position of the cathedral in the late Middle Ages. Everywhere in Europe cathedrals were the principal diocesan churches and centres of episcopal sees; moreover, every cathedral chapter was *de facto* in charge of its cathedral, and all matter relating to church building were managed by the cathedral fabric.[5] The construction and financing of the Utrecht Dom may indeed be regarded as a typical model of cathedral building in the period. However, there is one circumstance which makes the Dom virtually unique: hardly any other cathedral in Europe can boast chapter and especially fabric archives as complete as those in Utrecht. There remain not only sources of an institutional nature such as cartularies, statutes and minutes of chapter assemblies, but also accounts of the Dom fabric from 1395 on, which show quite clearly how all these canonical guidelines and regulations regarding the fabric were translated into actual decisions about the construction and furnishing of the church.[6]

It will have become obvious that little could be expected from the bishop other than his indispensable support by virtue of his spiritual power in all ecclesiastical matters in his diocese, such as the issue of indulgences to all those who donated money towards the construction, or the despatch of mandates to the lower clergy regarding the collection of monies for the construction of the Dom.

Admittedly, the Dom chapter was directly responsible for the fabric and acted accordingly, but it considered its chief obligation to be the upkeep of the existing building rather than raising additional contributions for prestigious new building work. New canons had to wait for three years before they could obtain their prebends; two years' annual revenue was assigned *ad fabricam et usum ecclesie*. This arrangement, which existed among many cathedral chapters, had already been in use prior to the new building plans; the *fructus prebendae defunctoris* had been the most important source of income for the maintenance and furnishing of the romanesque cathedral, although the revenues were never very substantial. However, the contributions from the chapter increased after 1525 while donations from the faithful dropped quite dramatically and the building work thus had to be discontinued at that time. The canons were quite aware of their responsibilities for the maintenance of the building and acted accordingly by assigning often quite considerable sums of money to this purpose. Of course, some canons contributed individually to the cathedral fabric, especially in their wills, but these were voluntary — and thus incidental — donations. The bulk of the financial support was left to the members of the whole diocese: *de bonis elemosinarum*, according to the above-mentioned instructions to the fabric masters in the 1345 statutes.

In contrast to other cathedrals, such as Canterbury or Santiago de Compostela, the Utrecht Dom was never an important centre of pilgrimage. Of course, worshippers in the Dom were encouraged to offer donations in money or in kind; there were offertory-boxes for this purpose and on special feast-days there would be a member of the clergy present to receive any donations. However, the *recepta de immolacionibus et ex truncis* were always remarkably small: at best they constituted only a few per cent of the Dom's total revenue. The main reason for this must be the fact that the Utrecht Dom did not possess any relics of more than merely local interest. Proceeds only increased on those occasions when the Dom could tempt worshippers with a major papal indulgence, which temporarily turned it into a regional centre of devotion.

The construction of the gothic Dom was financially dependent, in the first place, on the episcopal mandates or *mendicatoria* in which the collections of funds for the construction of the church were arranged for the whole diocese. These mandates were all copied into the Dom fabric cartulary, which lists the holdings of the fabric. The earliest mandate dates to 1288, the last to 1518. They consist of charges addressed to all members of the diocesan clergy in which the bishop did not call on the faithful to make a pilgrimage to Utrecht but rather the reverse: he would announce the dispatch of *nuntii* or collectors on behalf of the cathedral while emphasizing at the same time his canonical power. Parish-priests were obliged to receive the bishop's messengers and any interdicts would temporarily be lifted at their arrival. In every parish two reliable laymen were supposed to collect the contributions and keep them safe until the appointed day, the *dies reportacioniss*, when, together with the parish-priests, they were to hand over the monies to special emissaries from the Dom fabric. Parish-priests were also instructed to recommend parishioners on their deathbed to bequeath money towards the construction of the Dom, while beneficiaries of the fabric were granted indulgences. On the other hand, those who opposed or obstructed the collections risked fitting punishment from the Church. Later *mendicatoria* show that this *dies reportacionis* coincided with the annual assemblies of parish-priests which were conducted by the deans in each of the deaneries. This suggests that the collection procedure followed existing channels within the ecclesiastical organization.

A highly important new element was introduced in a mandate of 1322, one year after the start of the ambitious construction of the tower: in addition to the visitations by Dom collectors to the parishes, there would also be *questores* or collectors on behalf of convents and other religious institutions who were to be received by the parish-priests, but only if they could present an official letter of introduction from the bishop and chapter. This official admission is fundamentally important as it shows that the bishop

and chapter regarded the collection of money for the construction of the cathedral —
the mother church of the bishopric — as the first and only permissible diocesan
collection. Anyone who tried to make a collection for any other cause was guilty of
infringement on the Dom's monopoly, which would have to be compensated for with
the payment of admission duties.

The other mandates basically repeat the above regulations, sometimes with further
details and elaborations. Again, these *mendicatoria* are not unique to the diocese of
Utrecht; similar episcopal prescriptions occurred in other dioceses from the thirteenth
century on, always in aid of the construction of a cathedral church. Therefore, in this
respect, Utrecht is again representative of other dioceses.

The fabric rolls after 1395, more than a century after the earliest mandate of 1288,
show how the above prescriptions were actually put into practice and what results they
had financially. They illustrate how reality often differed from the prescriptions, and it
is not difficult to see why. After all, prescribing a collection throughout twelve hundred
parishes in aid of the construction of the Dom, often many days' journey away, was
one thing, but actually collecting the money (preferably complete without deductions
or discounts) was quite another. In principle the Dom chapter found a solution to this
problem by renting out the collection of funds towards the Dom construction to the
local parishes. These collections, called *Sint Maartensbede* or *reportatio sancti Martini*,
would raise quite substantial amounts because, in return for their contributions, the
parishioners would get their shares in the indulgences and other religious favours
bestowed by the bishop. The rent was considerably lower than the amounts received so
that parishes were quite willing to cooperate.[7] In practice, however, the problem of
non-payment became more and more acute from the early fifteenth century on;
increasingly, the names of the eight hundred odd parishes (the 360 parishes in Friesland
were no longer taking part at least as early as 1395) copied each year into the accounts
would lack entries for the amounts due. The *reportationes sancti Martini* were clearly
proving to be less and less profitable.

The proceeds from collections or quests of the convents and religious orders, which
went around the diocese with permission from the bishop and chapter were very high
indeed. They apparently regarding the Utrecht diocese as a rich hunting-ground or, in
the words of a contemporary metaphor, a flock worth shearing with the shepherd's
permission.[8] The collecting convents had much to offer, such as relics of popular saints
reputed to cure various diseases, numerous indulgences and other religious benefits.
Many religious institutions therefore came to the bishop and chapter, not just in
Utrecht but also in other dioceses, to pay for permission to make collections. In some
dioceses the bishop and chapter were rather careless with their authorization,
permitting numerous quests from outside. It is to the credit of the Dom chapter in
Utrecht, which in 1344 had taken over the right to grant collections from the bishop,
that it succeeded in financing the construction of the new Dom up to around 1525 by
limiting the number of collections while at the same time claiming a large share of the
proceeds towards the building work. From 1371 the policy of granting permission for
collections is more well-defined. First and foremost among the permitted quests was
the 'Sint Maartensquest' (quite distinct from the 'Sint Maartensbede, which was the
parish contribution). This collection was carried out by the Dom itself although it was
not handled differently from the 'competitive' quests by outside convents and other
institutions, *viz*. those of the Holy Sacrament by the church at Meerssen; of St Cornelius
by the abbey of Kornelimünster near Aachen; of St Hubert by the eponymous abbey in
the Ardennes; of St Anthony by the Antonite order; of St Quirinus by the abbey of

Neuss; of Our Lady by the Regulierenklooster in Utrecht; and of St Theobald (origin unknown). For more than 150 years, between *c.* 1370 and *c.* 1525, these quests provided between fifty and eighty per cent of the Dom's revenue. In contrast to the proceeds from the Sint Maartensbede or *reportatio sancti Martini*, which were accounted for per parish but which steadily decreased from *c.* 1400 on, the income from the 'quest' money continued to rise quite spectacularly until around 1525, after which it fell to rather insignificant sums within less than ten years. There has been a great deal of speculation about the reasons for this, until rather recently.[9] The canons themselves regarded the *doctrina Martini Lutheri* as the main structural cause, besides more temporary economic and political factors, and probably with good reason. Whatever the true cause, it is important to note that the faithful did not choose to offer donations towards the construction of the Dom, but rather to express their devotion to saints whose relics or religious favours came from convents or abbeys which in some cases even lay outside the diocese. The finances of the Dom fabric were based on the agreed principle that the only permitted collection of funds within the diocese was the one which benefited the mother church and the other institutions wishing to make collections would have to indemnify the Dom fabric for that privilege.

By consistently applying this principle the Dom chapter had at its disposal an almost constant flow of funds towards the construction and furnishing of the church; in addition, the collections were rented out so that the amounts due were tied up for longer periods. Whereas so many other cathedral fabrics saw intensive building campaigns interspersed with spells of inactivity, in Utrecht the continuity of the construction work on the Dom was guaranteed, except for a few years of crisis. Although the peaks of activity were considerable they were usually caused by high expenditure on special furnishings like paraments, an organ or church bells. The cost of labour, in particular, constituted a fairly consistent sum whereas the amounts spent on building materials show greater variation. The steady increase in proceeds from the quests makes it possible to establish that the most active period in the construction of the Dom was between 1480 and 1527, followed by an almost complete and final collapse of building activity as outlined above.

Converting the sums spent on the construction and furnishing of the church from 1395 (the year of the oldest extant fabric account) up to 1527 (the end of the construction work) into the annual wages of an unskilled building worker, we find that an average of 81 annual wages were paid each year, with a peak of 212 annual wages in 1505 when the thirteen bells for the Dom tower had to be paid for. Compared to the few figures known from other cathedrals and churches, this rate of building activity seems rather high; however, the scale quite fits the general picture. Both in the organization of its cathedral fabric and the extent of its construction work, the Utrecht Dom may be regarded as a typical late-medieval cathedral.

Unlike many other episcopal cities like Cologne, however, the canons of the Utrecht Dom succeeded after almost three centuries in completing the reconstruction of their cathedral — albeit only just — before the tide turned forever and the traditional devotions fell out of favour.

REFERENCES

1. This paper is based on the author's dissertation *De financiering van de kathedraalbouw in de middeleeuwen, in het bijzonder van de dom van Utrecht*, Maarssen 1981. The footnotes in this paper only include literature not referred to in the dissertation. For a general survey, see also W. H. Vroom, 'La

construction des cathédrales au Moyen Age: une performance économique' in Roland Recht, *Les batisseurs des cathédrales gothiques* (Strasbourg 1989), 81–90.

2. F. van der Meer, *Geschiedenis ener kathedraal* (Utrecht 1940), 1.

3. Aart J. J. Mekking, *Het spel met toren en kapel; bouwen pro en contra Bourgondië van Groningen tot Maastricht* (Zutphen 1992), 5.

4. R. H. A. Rikhof, *Vikarissen en kapelaans in de dom van Utrecht (12e–16e eeuw)*, unpublished MA dissertation, University of Amsterdam (1988), 120–26.

5. On the matter of cathedral management, see Wolfgang Schöller, *Die rechtliche Organisation des Kirchenbaues im Mittelalter vornehmlich des Kathedralbaues*, dissertation (Cologne/Vienna 1989).

6. The Dom chapter archives are now in the Rijksarchief in Utrecht; see K. Heeringa, *Inventaris van het Archief van het kapittel en Dom* (Utrecht 1929). The fabric accounts for 1395–1529 have been published by N. B. Tenhaeff and W. Jappe Alberts in *Bronnen tot de bouwgeschiedenis van den Dom te Utrecht*, vol. 2, parts 1, 2 and 3, Rijks Geschiedkundige Publicatiën, large series, vols 88, 129 and 155 (The Hague 1946, 1969 and 1976).

7. For the proceeds from the *Sint Maartensbede* in the Oude Kerk, Delft, and the much lower rent for the Dom fabric, see G. Verhoeven, *Devotie en Negotie: Delft als bedevaartplaats in de late middeleeuwen* (Amsterdam 1992), 173–76.

8. See W. H. Vroom, 'Het jachtgebied van Sint-Hubertus' in: *Bouwkunst: studies in vriendschap voor Kees Peeters* (Amsterdam 1993), 571–79, quotation p. 579, no. 15.

9. Koen Goudriaan, 'Het einde van de Middeleeuwen ontdekt?', *Madoc, tijdschrift over de Middeleeuwen* vol. 8 (1994), 66–75.

Saint Margaret under Our Lord's cross:
A mural painting in the cathedral of Utrecht

by Johann-Christian Klamt

for E. S. de Jongh on his 65th birthday.

In his *Pantheon* of about 1190 Gottfried of Viterbo dedicated some commendatory verses to the diocese of Utrecht. He described her capital as an important trading centre where people from many regions met, among them merchants from London who — from Utrecht as outlet — swarmed out over the continent.[1] In the first line dealing with the political and commercial role of Utrecht and her bishops, Gottfried unfortunately fails to enter into other aspects. Unlike so many an author of a *laus urbis* he does not mention the churches of Utrecht and the relics of venerable saints there preserved, nor does he, for example, say anything about the crafts and arts executed within the walls of that town.[2]

As a member of the *capella* of Emperor Frederic I Barbarossa (1152–90) for many years, the highly educated and learned author of *Pantheon* may have got acquainted with Utrecht when he accompanied his sovereign who paid a visit to this town no less than four times.[3] Like the English merchants — named *expressis verbis* by him — Gottfried would have taken notice of many a religious building, in the first place the old cathedral and the four chapters which under the rule of Bishop Berthold (1027–54) had been erected to form the famous 'cross of churches' and thus give expression to the idea of Utrecht as an ideal community marked by the sign of redemption.[4] Those churches would have been rich in murals, stained glass, sacred vessels or other kind of *ornamenta*. But only very few artistic records of Gottfried's and earlier times have been preserved. The same is true with regard to the artistic activities of later periods. The remnants of the sculptural production of the second half of the fifteenth century permit a relatively reliable survey of this field. But still the losses are to be judged as severe, considering the many sculptors' names and commissions which are to be found listed in the archival sources of, for example, the *fabrica* of the cathedral or of that of Our Saviours' (Sint Salvator or Oudmunster). Nothing is left of the stained glass windows. Extremely scarce are the records of panel painting although the production must have been rich, however perhaps not as rich as in the *metropolis* Cologne, where important influences on Utrecht came from. We have to content ourselves with the epitaph for the canon Henrik van Rijn of St John's chapter who died in 1364.[5] Scarce are also the witnesses of mural painting. Only a few are left, ranging from ornamental decorations of the eleventh century to figurative representations of the early fourteenth to the late fifteenth centuries.[6] This is not much to go by. The many losses are partially due to developments of later periods. The religious and cultural climate of the sixteenth and following centuries has not been favourable to objects of art which put the protestant ministers and their flock in mind of a catholic, papal past.[7]

Yet, few as the medieval remnants are and faintly though the glimmer of a once productive past may shine into our times, there are enough visual traces and sources left to draw a rough sketch with regard to Utrecht as a place of artistic activity throughout the Late Middle Ages. There is evidence that in different fields important influences from Cologne — the archepiscopal see upon which the diocese of Utrecht depended — had an impact on artists active in Utrecht. This is as clear from the early designs for the gothic structure of Utrecht cathedral started in the late thirteenth century, as from a mural of about 1320/1330 in the house *De Rode Poort*, the former residence of one of the canons of the cathedral chapter.[8] Not only did the regions of the Lower Rhine or of the Maas Valley play an important role, before the so-called Burgundian period of the late fifteenth and the early sixteenth centuries, but the bishops and the developed *burgerij* of Utrecht also turned their eyes to France — as did the artists of Utrecht origin. They went south to find employment at the courts of the French King Charles V and his brothers. Obviously these men from the Northern Low Countries enjoyed the reputation of well-skilled craftsmen. One of them, was the goldsmith Willem Scerpswert of Utrecht who in 1391 emigrated to Paris and was entered on the pay-roll of Philipp the Bold as Guillaume Scarpsuet.[9] Willem was not the only son of Utrecht to go south. Here, in the French capital he could meet fellow citizens who had come the same way.[10] Nor should we forget the Limbourg Brothers of Nijmegen who entered the service of Philip the Bold and of Jean de Berry. Their uncle Jean Malouel had smoothed their path to France, and their entrance into an excellent career. Between 1397 and 1415 he himself was in the service of Philip the Bold at Dijon.[11]

As already indicated, there is evidence enough that Utrecht artists had, for a long time, stood open to influences from many regions. At least their *élite* must have been aspired to acquaintance with what was going on elsewhere. Those of higher ambition did not content themselves with vernacular traditions. With regard to the period around 1400 we have to remember Willem Scerpswert's departure for Paris which together with the princely courts at Dijon and Bourges, for example, exerted a strong fascination almost everywhere in Europe, not least by a wide range of delicate artistic production. Needless to say, the Dukes of Holland also shared in the attraction of French culture on various levels and fields. The Parisian court of Charles VI had a Europe-wide fame for being luxurious and wordly as well as impious.[12] The court of Albrecht of Bavaria in The Hague could have shared only a fraction of the roaring life of the Parisian court; however, from the entries in the archives, it is apparent that panel paintings of Parisian origin were put up in the rooms of the residence in The Hague and that many orders for jewellery of various kinds were given to Parisian goldsmiths.[13] The bishops of Utrecht and the canons of the cathedral chapter were not inferior to the princes in The Hague. They shared the same attitude to France. This is clear from a mural painting in the *Chapel of Guy d'Avesnes*[14] of Utrecht cathedral. It deserves our attention because of its uncommon iconography which must be studied against the background of contemporary devotional life. But it is not only from this point of view that this mural has to be regarded. It is also the high quality and the French flavour of the mural that draws the eye of the beholder. It was perhaps not chance that the canons of the cathedral knew how to attract a painter of such a high level of skill, though it has to be admitted that because of the almost total lack of other mural paintings of that period in Utrecht this notion cannot be proved.

The mural shows Christ crucified, with Mary and St John on the left, with St Margaret and 'her' dragon on the right side (Pl. XIX A, B and C). Situated within a deep niche in the east wall, the beautiful painting came to light not earlier than 1919 when the cathedral underwent extensive restoration. At an unknown date — presumably in the year 1580 or a little thereafter, when the cathedral and the other chapters of Utrecht fell to the protestants, after having been attacked by the iconoclasts during the *beeldenstorm* — the niche was blocked by a layer of bricks which had the oldfashioned late medieval format of the so-called *kloostermoppen*.[15] Fortunately the brick layer was not deep enough to touch the surface of the painting. Consequently it is clear that most parts of the mural were found in relatively good condition and the delicate and varied colouring of the painting still strikes the beholder of today. An examination of the technique led to results which cannot be called satisfactory in every sense. After all, it turned out that the pigments exhibit a high percentage of oil. So, with regard to the technique experts were inclined to classify this excellent piece of art as being closer to panel than to mural painting.[16] From a document in the cathedral archives we know that an altar dedicated to St Margaret existing in the *Chapel of Guy d'Avesnes* is mentioned in 1438 for the first time. Of course, the altar may have been established at an earlier date and there is no reason to link the painting with that year. G. J. Hoogewerff suggested a dating of about 1430, others of about 1420. More recently, it was A. Châtelet who drew attention to some stylistic characteristics which made him suggest the period of about 1410 even, without going into details.[17] Indeed, from further analysis this early dating can be established.

There are some general stylistic and specific iconographical features this painting shares with miniatures produced in Utrecht itself or adjacent provinces such as Gelre and Cleve in the period of about 1400 to 1415.[18] Parallels of various kinds are to be found in the physiognomies and in the attitudes of figures or in the arrangement of scenes of the crucifixion as a whole. But there are also other features. For example, the dark blue stripe with sun and moon above the cross — contrasting with the gloomy red background of the composition — can also be observed in some miniatures of a copy of Jacob van Maerlant's *Rijmbijbel* which had been made for the court of Albrecht of Bavaria at The Hague as early as in the nineties of the fourteenth century.[19]

St Margaret is presented as a small and frail princess with a pale face, with long locks of blond hair and with elongated hands. It was the artist's intention to present her as a refined young person of aristocratic origin and breed. Her costume is in the French fashion. As head-gear she wears the *bourrelet*, so fashionable at the courts for some time among courtly damsels. The female saint appears in all her beauty. And not to forget the brooch in front of the *bourrelet* which draws the beholders attention. This brooch contains a bright white stone at its centre. Taking the meaning of the latin word *margarita* into account, the artist obviously had a pearl in mind when he painted this precious piece of jewellery. And he had good reasons for it, because he was not the first to link the pearl with the saint's name. The Golden Legend of Jacopo de Voragine has it:

Margaret comes from margarita, which is the Latin name for a pearl; and this precious gem is shining white, small, and endowed with virtue. So Saint Margaret was shining white by her virginity, small by her humility, and endowed with the power to work miracles. The virtue of this stone is said to be of good effect against the outpouring of her blood by her constancy in martyrdom, and against the disturbance of the heart, that is the temptations of the Devil, by her victory, because she overcame the Devil himself, and likewise for the strengthening of the spirit by her doctrine, because by her teaching she strengthened the spirit of many, and converted them to the faith of Christ.[20]

This passage from the Golden Legend concerns just a tiny but relevant detail of the mural. We will quote from this book again when dealing with St Margaret's legend and the religious implications of the mural painting more intensively. But first we will continue to explore the field of stylistic and iconographic sources which possibly had an influence on the unknown artist active in Utrecht cathedral. Once again a glance at French art proves profitable. For example, Saint Margaret's dragon has his 'ancestors' in the many monstrous beasts of the Apocalypse Tapestries at Angers produced for

Duke Louis I of Anjou between about 1373 and about 1381 after designs of Jean de Bondol (also called: Jean de Bruges or Hennequin de Bruges).[21] Represented in, as it were, inexhaustible variations, these ferocious envoys of evil are characterized by features which are also typical of the dragon in the Utrecht mural: the heaviness of the muscular trunks supported by short and thick legs with sharp claws, wings like those of a bat, long necks and heads as if originating from a fantastic cross-breed of cat, lion and leopard, to name but a few. Some of these features are also recognizable in a drawing of Jacques Daliwe whose model-book, put together from about 1400 until about 1420, contains a — with regard to the purpose and the iconographic implications — still enigmatic *Fight against a dragon*.[22] Finally, there is the full-page miniature in the Boucicaut Hours which was illuminated by the so-called Boucicaut Master and assistants in the years 1405–08.[23] Here we encounter a corona of five virgin saints: Catherine, Margaret, Martha, Christine and Barbara (Pl. XXa). Contrasted with her sisters *in Christo*, Saint Margaret has a fashionable coiffure. She is put prominently forward as the most elegant among these heavenly ladies. It is only she who wears a *bourrelet*; it is only she who wears a fur-trimmed jerkin. And there is again her dragon with a small head, with bat-like wings and a trunk which shows the spotted skin of a leopard. The beast has much in common with the one in the Utrecht mural, though it seems more domesticated, perhaps to be regarded rather as a mere 'attribute' than a threatening antagonist to Saint Margaret. It may be clear that the artist active in Utrecht excels in a more dramatic mise-en-scène. And he knew how to add another variation to the medieval bestiary of evil creatures. He crossed a 'common' dragon with a *hystrix cristata*, i.e. with a porcupine, the quills of which enhance the impression of the ferocity of the beast. By depicting its head turned back to the saint and to the cross in her hands he succeeded in creating the tension of a struggle between two extremes: on the one side St Margaret as the personification of Christian virtue and heroism, on the other the dragon as mark of evil. Like many an other artist who had been commissioned to paint that particular episode from St Margaret's legend, the painter of the Utrecht mural must have felt himself challenged to illustrate this tension as convincingly as possible.

Here, as in so many other representations, St Margaret is depicted as stepping out of the dragon's trunk after having been devoured by the diabolical beast. This iconographical version is not the one which Jacopo de Voragine would have preferred. Well acquainted with it, he has some objections:

While in prison, Margaret besought the Lord to make manifest in visible form the enemy who was striving against her. Then there appeared to her a hideous dragon, who sought to throw himself upon her and devour her. But she made the sign of the cross, and the dragon vanished. Or again, as another legend tells it, the monster seized her by the head and drew her into his maw, and it was then that she made the sign of the cross, and caused the dragon to burst, the damsel emerging unharmed from his body. But this legend is apocryphal, and all agree to consider it a groundless fable.[24]

The more dramatic version of the legend — declassified as 'apocryphal' by the Italian author — enjoyed wide-spread popularity. Especially in the Low Countries, the Rhinelands and in France it was *en vogue* from the fourteenth until the sixteenth centuries.[25]

Numerous representations of this particular version have survived,[26] providing evidence of its popularity in those countries. Just to name a few of them, excelling by high artistic quality and executed in various media:[27] beside the miniature in the

Boucicaut Hours mentioned above, there is the less known, and until now under-estimated, brass epitaphium for the abbess Marguerite de Gavres-Escornay (Scornay) of 1464 in the Collégiale Sainte-Gértrude at Nivelles (Pl. XXI A and B)[28] or the most charming statue of Saint Margaret, sculpted at the end of the fifteenth century in Languedoc, now in a private collection in the United States.[29] With regard to these admittedly few but excellent examples mentioned here — especially to the just mentioned statue of French origin — it may become clear that many an artist of the Late Middle Ages was challenged to express the contrast between the frail maiden princess and the repulsive textures of the horrible dragon. So was the painter active in Utrecht cathedral. He knew how to master this antagonism as convincingly as he knew how to depict the suffering of the Lord crucified and the fainting Virgin held up by St John.

As one of the Fourteen Helpers, Saint Margaret enjoyed a favourite role in daily life. For example she used to be invoked by pregnant women for an easy delivery. Especially important for them is that this saint obtained favour from the Lord at the hour of her death, according to the Golden Legend: 'Finally the prefect, fearing still other conversions, ordered her to be beheaded as quickly as possible. But she sued for leave to say a prayer, and prayed for herself and her persecutors, and likewise for those who in time would invoke her aid. And she asked especially that whenever a woman in labour should call upon her name, the child might be brought forth without harm'. Probably this special prayer for women in labour is inspired by the obviously older version of the legend, which had been rejected by Jacopo de Voragine as less likely. To recall it, St Margaret finally stepped unharmed out of the 'womb' of the dragon. Popular belief has always been imaginative and inventive enough to fashion the lives and deeds of the saints according to notions of the time.

Certainly St Margaret enjoyed a high reputation as one of the much evoked Fourteen Helpers who promised to ease the troubles and griefs of daily life. But it is by no means that reputation alone which can explain the presence of St Margaret under the cross of Christ. The unusual configuration chosen for the mural painting deserves consideration under aspects of quite another order. During her martyrdom St Margaret underwent many tortures of extreme cruelty, as did thousands of other martyrs. All together they constitute the corona of the elected soldiers of Christ who in the Sermon of the Mount had promised: 'Blessed are they which are persecuted for righteousness' sake: for their's is the kingdom of heaven. Blessed are ye, when men shall revile you, and persecute you, and shall say all manner of evil against you falsely, for my sake (Matthew 5, 10–11).' St Margaret — according to the Golden Legend — very eloquently knew how to oppose her heathen persecutor by pointing to the passion of the Lord:

She answered that she was of noble estate, that her name was Margaret, and that she was a Christian. Then the prefect said: 'The first two of these three things are most seemly for thee. For all in thee is noble, and no pearl can equal thy beauty. But the third befits thee not, namely that a damsel so fair and noble should have for god one that was crucified.' And she asked: 'How knowest thou that Christ was crucified?' 'I have read it in the books of the Christians,' he answered. And Margaret said: 'Since thou hast read these books, thou hast seen both the Passion of Christ and His glory. How canst thou believe the one and deny the other?' Thereupon she expounded to him how Christ had freely accepted His death for our redemption, but that now He lived in the glory of eternal life. Angered at this, the prefect threw her into prison. On the morrow he summoned her again, and said to her: 'Foolish child, have pity on thy beauty, and adore our gods, that all may go well with thee!' But she replied: 'I adore Him Who makes the earth to tremble, Who stirs the sea to its depths, and Whom all creatures fear!' 'Unless thou yield,' said the prefect, 'I shall order thy body to be torn piecemeal!' 'No dearer wish have I,' she answered, 'than to die for Christ, Who condemned Himself to death for me!'[30]

From these words it becomes clear that for her many tortures St Margaret obtained all her strength and heroic spirit from a compassionate plunging into the passion of Christ. This idea was also expressed in an Italian poem of the fifteenth century. The anonymous author made St Margaret speak:

> O redentor del mondo, Jesù pio,
> Qual per me in croce il sangue tuo versasti,
> Tu sei quel vero e immortale Dio
> Che alla imagin tua già me creasti;
> Per tuo amore effundo il sangue mio,
> Et amo te qual me tu sempre amasti;
> Ricevi il sangue di tanto supplizio,
> Qual t' offerisco in vero sacrifizio[31]

No wonder that the Master of the St Bartholomew Altarpiece — for some time active in the Northern Netherlands, perhaps in Utrecht, before moving to Cologne — depicted St Margaret as an elegant lady with not only pearls in the hair and on her garment, but also with a small pendant cross around her neck (Pl. XXB).[32] From a microscopic look at this hanger it is beyond all doubts that this precious jewel was meant by the painter as a reliquary containing parts of the True Cross. It is as if that talisman helped St Margaret endure the pains of martyrdom. How deliberately the unknown master went at his work, can also be concluded from another detail. On no other part of her garment than exactly on the border of her *décolleté* — situated just above her heart — he 'embroidered' the words DOMINE IHESU CHRISTE,[33] no doubt to be interpreted as St Margaret's own invocation to the Lord when she had to undergo martyrdom.

Back to the mural painting in Utrecht Cathedral: Margaret, the maiden saint and early Christian heroine of Antioch, has her counterpart in the Virgin on the other side of the cross. About to faint, the Mother of the Lord is supported by St John. This part of the composition is quite conventional. It is the artistic quality of the painting which makes that scene so impressive, first of all the rendering of the Virgin who is given as sunken in and tortured by all her grief. As is known, in late medieval piety especially the role of the Virgin as co-redemptor of mankind became increasingly stressed. Her compassion formed the theme of numerous meditative interpretations which range from the twelfth to the sixteenth centuries. To give just one example among the many other relevant sources, we quote a passage from *A Meditation on the Life of Christ*, composed in the first half of the fourteenth century by an anonymous Franciscan monk who lived in Tuscany:

'And all this is said and done in the presence of His most sorrowful mother, whose great compassion adds to the Passion of her Son, and conversely. She hung with her Son on the cross and wished to die with him rather than live any longer. Everywhere are tortures and torments that can be sensed but in truth hardly described (. . .) And with her whole heart she prayed to the Father, saying, 'Father and eternal God, it pleases you that my Son should be crucified: it is not the time to ask Him back from you. But you see what anguish His soul is in now: Therefore I beg you to lessen His suffering, if it pleases you. Father, I recommend my Son to you.' And the Son similarly prayed to the Father for her and silently said, "My Father, see how afflicted my mother is. I ought to be crucified, not she, but she is with me on the cross. It is enough that I, who bear the sins of all the people, am crucified; she does not deserve the same. See how desolate she is, consumed with all her sadness all the day. I recommend her to you: make her sorrow bearable" '.[34]

Like so many other authors of the Late Middle Ages the Italian Franciscan monk stressed the Virgin's 'great compassion (which) adds to the Passion of her Son'. Of course he did not deal with the legendary passion of St Margaret as, for example, his fellow countryman of a later time did. He — in the verses quoted above — knew how to stress the 'compassio' of the princess saint, who — as opposed to the Mother of God — had to undergo real martyrdom by actual slaughter. However, both women are to be interpreted as incarnations of ideals so typical for the devotional life of the Late Middle Ages. Each of these holy women in her way answered the contemporary demands of meditation and of contemplation upon the Passion of Christ who had to shed His blood for the sake of the redemption of mankind.

Of course it has to be kept in mind that the meditation on the death and the suffering of the Lord has not been a privilege of the Late Middle Ages. Among those who warned of too simplistic a view was J. H. Marrow who once again drew attention to prominent authors of the eleventh and twelfth centuries, who in their prayers and tracts already gave witness to an hitherto unknown sensibility. In other words, the effective elements in combination with an increasing tendency to subjective experience of Christ's Passion — often claimed as typical of the devotional life of the Late Middle Ages — are based on older traditions.[35] It was only the patterns of devotion and meditation which came to change during the fourteenth and fifteenth centuries. With regard to the Northern Netherlands and the bishopric of Utrecht it is worth remembering the prominent figure of Geert Grote (1340–84) who stood in the first line to propagate what is known as the *devotio moderna*.[36] In the wake of earlier German tracts, as for example those by Henry Suso (1295–1366) and Ludolph of Saxony (died 1377), this religious movement focused on the Passion of Christ in particular. And it demanded innovations in the field of the arts, especially in the field of Passion iconography. Against the background of these new mental attitudes the mural painting in Utrecht cathedral has to be looked at. It is hard to imagine that, for example, in the eleventh or twelfth century a patron or a painter would have thought of a representation of Our Lord crucified in combination with Saint Margaret so prominently acting under His cross. Times changed, as can be concluded from the mural under discussion. In the eastern wall of the *Chapel of Guy d'Avesne* — that with one of its altars dedicated to St Margaret — the Virgin Mary was depicted on the one, and the early-Christian heroine of Antioch on the other, side of the cross: both of them — each in her specific way — as it were ideal protagonists of *contemplatio* and *compassio* and representatives of ideas which were so dear to the devotional life of the Late Middle Ages, not at least to the movement of the *devotio moderna*. So, the mural painting — in spite of all its French flavour — can be regarded as typical for the Northern Netherlands.

SHORTENED TITLES

Châtelet (1988)   A. Châtelet, *Early Dutch Painting. Painting in the Northern Netherlands in the Fifteenth Century* (Lausanne 1988).

Dehaisnes (1886)   C. Dehaisnes, *Documents et extraits divers concernants l'histoire de l'art dans la Flandre, l'Artois et le Hainaut avant le XVe siècle (Mémoires de la Commission historique du département du Nord. Documents inédits)* (Lille 1886).

Golden Age (1989)   *The Golden Age of Dutch Manuscript Painting*, Catalogue of the exhibition held in the Rijksmuseum Het Catharijneconvent Utrecht, 10.12.1989–11.2.1990, ed. H. L. M. Defoer a.o. (Stuttgart and Zurich 1989).

Golden Legend   Jacobus de Voragine, The Golden Legend, ed. G. Ryan and H. Ripperger (New York 1969).

Hoogewerff (1936)

G. J. Hoogewerff, *De Noord-Nederlandsche Schilderkunst*, vol. 1 (The Hague 1936).

Klamt (1991)

J.-Chr. Klamt, 'Sub turri nostra: Kunst und Künstler im mittelalterlichen Utrecht', *Masters and Miniatures (Proceedings of The Congress on Medieval Manuscript Illumination in the Northern Netherlands, Utrecht, 10.–13. December)*, ed. K. Van der Horst and J.-Chr. Klamt (Doornspijk 1991).

Marrow (1979)

J. H. Marrow, *Passion Iconography in Northern European Art of the Late Middle Ages and Early Renaissance (Ars Neerlandica, vol. 1)* (Kortrijk/Courtrai 1979).

Van Oostrom (1987)

F. P. Van Oostrom, *Het woord van eer. Literatuur aan het Hollandse hof omstreeks 1400* (Amsterdam 1987).

REFERENCES

1. Gottfried of Viterbo was of German origin. About his life see: *Neue Deutsche Biographie*, ed. By Historische Kommission bei der Bayerischen Akademie der Wissenschaften, (Berlin 1953–), VI, 676–77 (F.-J. Schmale). For the full text of *Pantheon* see Gotifried of Viterbo, *Gotfredi Viterbensis Pantheon (Monumenta Germaniae Historica, Scriptores, XXII)*, ed. G. Waitz, (Hannover 1872), 160 (diocese of Utrecht). With regard to the merchants from London we read:

    > Transitus ille maris datur Anglis rite parari,
    > Anglica Lindonia breviter solet inde vagari,
    > Navis iter peragit nocte dieque pari.
    > Omne solum patrie quod Renus ab equore cingit,
    > Presulis et cleri Traiecti copia stringit,
    > Et maiora satis presul honore capit.
    > Quicquid ab Angelorum regno vehit unda bonorum
    > Et fera gens Frisonum manibus deservit eorum,
    > Servit et Alsatia, Mosa, Musella, Magus.

2. About the literary *genre* of the *laudes urbium* see E. Giegler, *Das Genos der Laudes urbium im lateinischen Mittelalter. Beiträge zur Topik des Städtelobes und der Stadtschilderung*, Philosophical dissertation, University of Würzburg (1953); C. J. Classen, *Die Stadt im Spiegel der Descriptiones und Laudes urbium in der antiken und mittelalterlichen Literatur bis zum Ende des zwölften Jahrhunderts*, Beiträge zur Altertumswissenschaft, II (Hildesheim 1980); F. P. T. Slits, *Het Latijnse stededicht. Oorsprong en ontwikkeling tot in de zeventiende eeuw*, Philosophical dissertation, University of Nijmegen, Amsterdam 1990).

3. W. J. Alberts, 'De relaties van Maastricht met de Duitse koningen; een vergeten hoofdstuk uit de geschiedenis van Traiectum ad Mosam', *Campus liber. Bundel opstellen over de geschiedenis van Maastricht aangeboden aan mr. dr. H. H. E. Wouters (. . .) Bij zijn zeventigste verjaardag*, Werken, uitgegeven door Limburgs geschied- en oudheidkundig genootschap, VIII, ed. A. H. Jenniskens a. o. (Maastricht 1982), 112.

4. See the contribution of A. J. J. Mekking in this volume.

5. Antwerp, Koninklijk Museum voor Schone Kunsten, inventory nr. 519. See: M. O. Renger, 'The Calvary of Hendrik van Rijn', *Jaarboek van het Koninklijk Museum voor Schone Kunsten, Antwerpen* (1993), 9–45.

6. Of more than local importance are the remnants of a mural painting of about 1460–70 representing the *Justice of Emperor Trajanus*. The painting, which is a 'copy' of Rogier van der Weyden's lost panels of the same subject (painted for the town hall of Brussels, soon copied in the famous tapestry at Bern, Historisches Museum) came unto light in the very heart of Utrecht, and that in a house once owned by one of the canons of the chapter of Sint Salvator (actual address: Wed nr. 5–7). Detached from the original place the mural is now preserved in the Centraal Museum Utrecht. With that wall painting will deal M. van Vlierden in her dissertation in preparation.

7. See the contribution of A. de Groot in this volume.

8. M. Van Vlierden, *Het Utrechtse huis De Rode Poort en zijn piscina* (Zutphen 1989); M. W. J. de Bruijn, 'De bouwer van De Rode Poort in Utrecht', *Oud-Utrecht*, LXII (1989), 72–79; Klamt (1991), 24–25 and pls 7–9.

9. Dehaisnes (1886), 707–08; L. E. Van den Bergh-Hoogterp, *Goud- en zilversmeden te Utrecht in de late middeleeuwen* (The Hague 1990), 79–83 and 353–56.

10. E.g. Ernoul Dutrecht, Jean Dutrecht or Nicolas van Utrecht. See Dehaisnes (1886), 707–08.

11. M. Meiss, *French painting in the time of Jean de Berry. The Limbourgs and Their Contemporaries* (New York 1974), 67–68 and 99–101; F. Gorissen, 'Jan Maelwael und die Brüder Limburg. Eine Nimweger Künstlerfamilie um die Wende des 14. Jahrhunderts', *Bijdragen en Mededelingen van Gelre, Vereeniging tot de beoefening van Geldersche Geschiedenis, Oudheidkunde en Recht*, LIV (1954), 151–221; F. Gorissen, 'Jan Maelwael, die Brüder Limburg und der Herold Gelre. Nachträge und Berichtigungen', in *Bijdragen en Mededelingen (. . .)*, LVI (1957), 166–78; Châtelet (1988), 16–25.

12. Recently W. Sauerländer pointed again to the critical preachings held by the Augustin monk Jacques Legrand. See *Chronique du Religieux de Saint-Denys contenant le règne Charles VI de 1388–1422, publiée en latin et traduite par Louis Francois Bellaguet* (Paris 1842), 4 vol. (Reprint with an introduction by B. Guenée, Paris 1994); see also W. Sauerländer, 'Kinder als Nothelfer', *Das Goldene Rössl. Ein Meisterwerk der Pariser Hofkunst um 1400*, catalogue of the exhibition held in Munich, Bayerisches Nationalmuseum, 3. 3.–20. 4. 1995, ed. R. Baumstark (Munich 1995), 90–101.

13. Van Oostrom (1987), 30.

14. Named after Guy d' Avesnes, bishop of Utrecht from 1301 to 1317, who has been buried in this chapel, where his tomb is still preserved, however slightly damaged during the *beeldenstorm* of 1580.

15. Still the question has to be answered why the mural was not just simply whitewashed.

16. J. Por, 'Een olieverf-schildering van omstreeks 1420', *Oudheidkundig Jaarboek* IX (1929), 150–53; M. D. Barnard and C. C. Van Hoogevest, 'Restauratie van wandschildering, altaarretabel en cenotaaf in de domkerk te Utrecht', *Restauratie Vijf Hervormde Kerken in de binnenstad van Utrecht. (Jaarverslag 1985–1988)*, VII (1989), 122–30.

17. Hoogewerff (1936), 349–58; Châtelet (1988), 14–15 and 189 (cat.–nr. 3).

18. Golden Age (1989), 25–57; Klamt (1991), 29.

19. The Hague, Koninklijke Bibliotheek, Ms. KA XVIII. See: Hoogewerff (1936), 82–85; S. Hindman, 'Dutch Manuscript Illumination around 1400: Some Cuttings in Darmstadt (Ms. 2296)', *Miscellanea Neerlandica: opstellen voor Dr. Jan Deschamps ter gelegenheid van zijn zeventigste verjaardag*, ed. E. Cockx-Indestege and F. Hendrickx (Louvain 1987), 419–40; Van Oostrom (1987), 271; Golden Age (1989), 28.

20. Golden Legend, 351–52.

21. F. Muel a. o., *La tenture de l'Apocalypse d'Angers. Cahiers de l'Inventaire 4 (Association pour le développement de l'Inventaire Général des Monuments et des Richesses Artistiques en Région des Pays de la Loire)*, 2nd, revised and enlarged edn (Nantes 1987).

22. Berlin, Staatsbibliothek, Lib. pic. A 74, pl. VIIIb. See: U. Jenni and U. Winter, *Das Skizzenbuch des Jacques Daliwe. Faksimileausgabe des Liber picturatus A 74 aus der Deutschen Staatsbibliothek Berlin/DDR. Kommentiert von Ulrike Jenni und mit einem Beitrag von Ursula Winter*, (Leipzig and Weinheim 1987), 16 and pl. VIIIb. R. W. Scheller, *Exemplum. Model-book drawings and the practice of artistic transmission in the middle ages (ca. 900–ca. 1450)* (Amsterdam 1995), 233–40 (nr. 21).

23. Paris, Musée Jacquemart-André, Ms 2, fol. 40ᵛ. See: M. Meiss, *French Painting in the Time of Jean de Berry. The Boucicaut Master* (London 1968), 131–33 and pl. 24.

24. Golden Legend, 353. For a miniature showing St Margaret in prison and in mere confrontation with the dragon — according to the version preferred by Jacopo de Voragine — see the 'Hours of William Lord Hastings', produced probably in Ghent, in the late 1470s (London, British Library, Ms Add. 54782, fol. 62ᵛ): *Renaissance Painting in Manuscripts*, catalogue of the exhibition held in London, British Library, 25. 5.–30. 9. (1983), ed. J. Backhouse a. o. (New York and London 1983), 21–30 and fig. 3 f.

25. G. G. Van den Andel, *Die Margaretenlegende in ihren mittelalterlichen Versionen*, Groningen 1933; *Lexikon der Christlichen Ikonographie*, ed. E. Kirschbaum a. o. (Rome and Freiburg/Br. 1969–76), VII, 494–500.

26. With regard to their artistic execution it is not always a pleasure to meet Saint Margaret's dragons. There is many a malformation of that species, lame ducks as it were, haunting medieval manuscripts. See e.g. N. Rogers, 'Oxford, University College Ms 5: A Flemish Book of Hours for a Dominican Nun', *Flanders in European Perspective. Manuscript Illumination around 1400 in Flanders and abroad — Proceedings of the International Colloquium Leuven, 7–10 September 1993 (Corpus of Illuminated Manuscripts, VIII)*, ed. M. Smeyers and B. Cardon (Louvain 1995), 235, pl. 5.

27. For an ivory sculpture from about 1400 (15 cm high) representing Saint Margaret stepping out of the dragon (London, Victoria and Albert Museum) see: R. Koechlin, *Les ivoires gothiques francais* (Paris 1924), II, 257 (nr. 709). Here Koechlin also discusses other French renderings of Saint Margaret, for example the sculpture of about 1320 in the parish church at Écouis (Eure). A similar ivory is preserved in Florence, Museo Nazionale del Bargello (information kindly supplied by M. Vellekoop, Utrecht).

28. M. Norris, *Monumental Brasses. The Craft* (London 1978), Pl. 151; G. de Liedekerke, *Histoire de la Maison de Gavre et de Liedekerke* (Brussels 1957), 220.

29. *Treasures from Medieval France*, catalogue of an exhibition held in the Cleveland Museum of Art, ed. W. D. Wixom (Cleveland/Ohio 1967), 316–17 (nr. VII 12).

30. Golden Legend, 354.

31. *Le sacre rappresentazioni italiane. Raccolta di testi dal secolo XIII al secolo XVI*, ed. M. Bonfantini (Milan 1942), 448.

32. Munich, Alte Pinakothek, inv.–nr. 11863–865. See G. Goldberg and G. Scheffler, *Altdeutsche Gemälde — Köln und Nord-Westdeutschland* (Munich 1972), 232–33 and 236–37; for further information about the Master of the Saint Bartholomew Altarpiece, *Late Gothic Art from Cologne*, catalogue of the exhibition held in London, National Gallery, 5.4.–1.6.1977 (London 1977), 86–109; F. G. Zehnder, *Katalog der Altköner Malerei (Kataloge des Wallraf-Richartz-Museums, XI)* (Cologne 1990), 418–47 (with full bibliography).

33. The words in exact transcription: DOMINE IHESV XC(?)RISTE.

34. *A Meditation on the Life of Christ. An Illustrated Manuscript of the Fourteenth Century*, Paris, Bibliothèque Nationale, Ms ital. 115, Princeton Monographs in Art and Archaeology, XXXV, ed. I. Ragusa and R. B. Green (Princeton/New Jersey 1961), 335. See S. Beissel, *Geschichte der Verehrung Marias in Deutschland während des Mittelalters*, (Freiburg/Br. 1909; Marrow (1979), 11–12; D. Freedberg, *The Power of Images* (Chicago 1989), 161–91.

35. See Marrow (1979), 5–14.

36. See e.g. *Moderne Devotie — Figuren en Facetten (Catalogue of the exhibition held in Nijmegen, Volkenkundig Museum, 28.9.–23.11.1984)*, (Nijmegen 1984). See also J. H. Marrow, 'The Golden Age of Dutch Manuscript Painting', Golden Age (1989), 9–10.

Medieval and Early Modern Houses in Utrecht

by Tarquinius J. Hoekstra

INTRODUCTION

The medieval city of Utrecht boasts over 2,000 houses originating from the medieval and early modern periods. They range from very small houses of only one room, the so-called *kameren* (rooms), to the sturdy, fortified houses of the thirteenth- and fourteenth-century aristocracy. In between lies a great variety of dwellings which underwent an even greater variety of changes during the long period through which they have survived.

In order to describe this heterogenous collection in a short article, some order must be imposed upon it. Traditional stylistic classifications like romanesque, gothic, renaissance and baroque are of little help in describing common houses, which frequently have no stylistic features at all. Simple schemes of chronology similarly offer little assistance as many types of houses were built over very long periods of time and most of them were altered during their long lives.

To bring order to the apparent chaos, the typological system of Dolfin, Kylstra and Penders will be used here.[1] They divided the Utrecht houses into five main categories, two of which are subdivided into up to four further subcategories. As the authors themselves point out, their system is not flawless, but such is the case with formal categories used to classify the architecture of houses which have been used and altered over the centuries.

The supply or absence of certain building materials determines the construction and even the architecture of buildings to a great extent. Therefore this article will begin with a short description of the main materials used in Utrecht house building and of the influence they had on construction and form. The use of certain building materials may be encouraged or forbidden by the city government. This began in Utrecht during the fourteenth century. These regulations have had broad implications for house building. The article will conclude with a short description — based on a number of selected examples — of the main house types and their distribution within the city.

BUILDING MATERIALS[2]

The northern Netherlands — and their medieval 'capital' Utrecht — are almost totally devoid of building stone. This fact had a profound effect on their building tradition and architecture. Before the middle of the thirteenth century most churches and other important public buildings and even a few private houses[3] were built from tufa (Pl. XXIIA). Both this volcanic stone and quantities of red sandstone were brought to Utrecht from the Eiffel region by ship along the Rhine. However, the great majority of houses were built of timber or wattle.[4]

Bricks made from local clay appear from the beginning of the thirteenth century. During that century, the use of bricks was chiefly reserved for the building of large houses, churches and large monastic buildings. Therefore production was organized on a relatively small scale, which made it possible to shape the individual bricks carefully. The average size of a thirteenth-century Utrecht brick is 32 × 16 × 8 cm.

The fourteenth century witnessed a 'brick revolution'. Production rose dramatically, the quality of trimming sank and the average size diminished to 30 × 15 × 7 cm.[5] The reason for the expansion in production can be linked to a growth in the population of Utrecht (and that of the Netherlands as a whole). In towns the rising number of inhabitants caused greater concentration and an increase in the risk of fire to the mainly wooden and thatched houses. In response to this danger town councils encouraged the use of brick and roof tiles.

Large beams for half-timbering, floor- and roof-beams had to be imported, especially in the western part of the country, from Germany and the Baltic. Until the early fourteenth century German spruce was widely used in Utrecht. Large, flat floor beams of c. 15 × c. 50 cm and set closely together on edge are characteristic of grand thirteenth-century houses[6] (Pl. XXIIA). From c. 1300 onwards, spruce was replaced by square oak beams from the Baltic. In floors they are more widely spaced and joined by smaller secondary beams.

Originally roofs of ordinary houses were thatched with reeds or straw, which presented a great fire hazard. Large buildings had slate roofs. Slate was imported from the Rhine area in Germany and the Meuse region of France.[7]

At the same time of the development of brick production, roof tiles were first made in great quantities in response to the same stimulus. Until the middle of the sixteenth century, when pantiles were introduced, the ordinary Utrecht roof was covered with flat, rectangular roof tiles of c. 25 × 15 × 1.5 à 2 cm (Pl. XXIIB). The lower third of the more expensive tiles was lead-glazed, sometimes in various colours (red, green, blackish, yellow). The unglazed part was covered by the overlaying tiles in stretcher-bond pattern. The Utrecht tiles hung on battens by a knob and were often mortared.[8]

Mortar was mixed using lime and sand. The former was imported from Germany or Belgium or — in the case of shell-lime — from the coastal areas of Holland. Loam was used as a cheaper but somewhat unstable material for bricklaying. It was also used to cover floors.

Tiled floors appear in houses from the late thirteenth century onward. The older ones must have been fairly expensive, particularly those which employ mosaic.[9] Since the fifteenth century simple square floor tiles were used more commonly. For the covering of the upper floors planks were the rule.

Walls were whitewashed both inside and out; exterior walls were frequently brightly painted.[10]

CONSTRUCTIONS

Of the fully-timbered houses of Utrecht so little is known that they will not be dealt with here in this article.[11]

Remains of half-timbered houses are sometimes found in the fabrics of buildings under investigation. The only remaining half-timbered exterior wall is part of the fourteenth-century sidewall of Oude Gracht 133. All half-timbering found in Utrecht was filled in with mostly broken bricks.

Completely brick-built houses have relatively thick weight-bearing walls. Floor- and roof-beams bear no relation to each other as is the case in half-timbered houses.

An interesting type of construction is found in brick-built houses which have a complete timber frame supporting the floors and the roof. Curved braces connect the uprights to the horizontal beams allowing a greater span to be achieved between the walls (Pl. XXIIIA). As the timber construction takes the weight of the roof and the floors, the walls can be made thinner, creating even more space within the building. The brick walls are often laid out around the prefabricated timber construction, the form of the original timber frame can often be seen long after it has been removed in the bricked-up cavities and recesses and in the thickening of masonry to either side of the uprights. Another tell-tale mark is the indenture left by the curved brace on the lower side of the sleeper beams.

The so-called 'three-quarter house' had three brick-built walls and a wooden façade, thus combining the sturdiness of a brick house with the flexibility of a timber front[12] (Pl. XXIVA). At the front of the lower storey was often used as a shop with wooden shutters, which could be lowered to serve as counters. Although officially forbidden since the early seventeenth century, such façades survived until well into the eighteenth century.

From the middle of the thirteenth century completely brick-built houses were erected for the Utrecht aristrocracy. A number of them still exist in their original form, though the fronts of all of them were altered in the nineteenth century. During the later Middle Ages smaller houses with four brick walls also began to be built. A number of these large houses initially had no cellars. The houses stood upon numbers of submerged brick pillars connected by brick arches; this technique provided the most stable affordable foundations. Often a cellar was inserted later, and the space beneath the arches bricked-up. Where the pillars were not sufficiently deep they could be extended.

The roofs of these large houses were either tiled or slated. In the latter case the roofs had to be boarded. On open roofs the tiles were hung on battens.

FIRE PREVENTION

During the fourteenth century a process was initiated in Dutch towns, which — for want of a better word — might be called 'brickification'.[13] This process was driven by the policy of town councils, which — by prescribing and subsidizing the use of fireproof building materials — were seeking to prevent large town fires, which had brought havoc to many towns during the late thirteenth century.

The main cause of such fires were thatched roofs. Already before 1340 the Utrecht city government agreed to meet the cost of one hundred per cent of tiles or slate if householders were willing to replace their thatched roofs with tiled or slate roofs. That the city even offered to subsidize the replacement of tiles with slates may have as much to do with civic status as fire prevention. At the same time changing a tiled roof into a thatched one was expressly forbidden. During the next hundred years the conditions on which subsidies were given varied, but their main purpose remained unchanged: to prevent fires from spreading.

The changes in the 'roofscape' has been vividly described by Kipp:[15]

The best view of the changing Utrecht roofscape is perhaps that of the towns' watchman [who looked down upon the city from the top of the *Buurtoren*, the tower of the most centrally-situated parish church, the *Buurkerk*] . . . During the first half of the thirteenth century he would have seen a mass of mostly low, one-storied thatched houses, of which the reeds or straw were often 'loamed', producing an overall brownish-grey hue. Between these little houses rose the city's larger buildings, the churches, monasteries and patrician houses with their dark, blue-grey slate roofs. A fast-growing number of red tiled roofs sprang up between them from the late thirteenth century onward, mainly along the banks of the Oude Gracht, the city's main artery. Occasionally a colourful, glazed-tile roof could be seen glistening in the sun. Inside the five Closes of the collegiate churches, where town law did not apply, the canon's freestanding houses were covered with slates or tiles, while their many outbuildings were thatched. With their large kitchen gardens, orchards, stables, chicken coops etc. they presented a rather rural sight.

Gradually a greater number of taller houses rose over the mass of lowly hovels. The latter were increasingly provided with a parapet, which gave them a heightened attic, or they were enlarged with the addition of a complete extra storey. By law, all newly built roofs had to have a 'hard' cover. The greyish-brown of the thatched roofs lost its pride of place.

As the number of brick walls grew, the humble smoke vents gradually gave way to towering chimneys of brick or wood, adding to the variation of the roofscape.

Thatch did not disappear completely. It was still used for temporary roofing, even on magnificent buildings like the Cathedral (c. 1500) or Vredenburg Castle (until 1543)'.

Timbered and half-timbered houses had their own side walls. The width of the eavesdrop was laid down by law and varied according to the type of roof; thatched roofs required the widest eavesdrop.[16] Once the old sidewalls of a house had been replaced by solid brick walls, the eavesdrop lost most of its function. Often a householder was allowed to tail the beams of his house into a neighbour's previously built brick wall. In that case — and where neighbours built their own brick walls — the eavesdrop was divided between them, widening their houses. Often the division between plots behind the houses remained unchanged. On cadastral maps, a doglegged partition indicates an eavesdrop once divided between neighbours.

The fact that there are few regulations or disputes about eavesdrops in Utrecht suggests that most of them had disappeared before the end of the fourteenth century as a result of the 'brickification' of the city.[17]

TYPOLOGY

As discussed in the introduction any typology of houses is a necessarily artificial tool of classification. The typology devised by Dolfin, Kylstra and Penders has the beauty of simplicity, but does not pretend to offer a broad chronology or to be valid outside the historic centre of Utrecht. The typology was developed for the publication of a Utrecht volume of the national series of inventories of historic buildings. Classification is based on the general form of the plan and the corresponding shape of the houses. From this principle a series of types are suggested:[18]

1. the *narrow-fronted house* with its roof at a right angle to the street.
2. the *wide-fronted house* with its roof parallel to the street. This category contains two separate variations:
   a.   the so-called *chambers (kameren)*.
   b.   the *double-aisled, wide-fronted house*.
3. the *square house* which has no overall roof orientation.
4. the *composite house* the roofs of which may be aligned in various directions. This category consists of four sub-groups:
   a.   the *freestanding composite house*
   b.   the *large house with a side-annex*
   c.   the *house with aisles on both sides of a backyard*
   d.   the *gradually grown composite house.*

1. The *narrow-fronted house* (Pl. XXIIIB)

The main characteristics of the narrow-fronted house are:
   a roof at a right angle to the street

greatest length from front to back
floor beams parallel to the front

The narrow-fronted house is the most common type of house in Utrecht, especially in the more densely built-up areas. Their plan is determined by the narrow plots from 5 to 7.5 m wide, which excavations have shown to exist as early as the eleventh or twelfth century.[19]

In height they range from 'one storey plus roof' to a maximum of 'four storeys plus roof'. Cellars are not counted as storeys. At ground-floor level the narrow-fronted houses sometimes had an entresol at the back. With the addition of further storeys many single-storey houses disappeared until they were rediscovered during surveys of surviving structures.

The large narrow-fronted houses have rectangular plans. The average ones measure 5 to 7 m by 10 to 16 m. The small ones are 2.5 to 5 m wide, but they vary in depth: the largest houses are seven or more metres wide and may be more than twenty metres deep.

Sometimes a wide-fronted house may be divided into two parts, which then develop into two separate narrow-fronted houses.

Many narrow-fronted houses have gables at the front and the back. A number have heightened front gables, which conceal the triangular shape of the roof. This is particularly common in larger medieval houses where this was done in order to give the house an imposing, sometimes crenellated façade. During the eighteenth and nineteenth centuries many gables were changed into cornice-façades, as these are cheaper to maintain.

2. The *wide-fronted house* (Pl. XXIVb)

The main characteristics of the wide-fronted house are:
a roof parallel to the street
longest side parallel to the street, unless forming part of a row of houses
floor beams mostly at right angles to the front

This type was frequently the oldest part of complex dwellings, such as the canons houses within the Closes, where the plots were very wide. A large, multi-storeyed, wide-fronted house presented an impressive façade.

Wide-fronted houses are also very common in secondary streets and alleys where their plots do not stretch far from the street. These plots were often divided from larger ones behind big houses. The New Canal (*Nieuwe Gracht*) — dug from Servaashek to Plompetoren between 1391–93 — is the only main thoroughfare lined with a number of medieval wide-fronted houses.

2a. The *kameren (chambers)* (Pl. XXIVc)

These small houses consist of one room and an attic. During the Middle Ages there was a large number of these dwellings for the moderately poor in Utrecht. Groups of such houses survive in the form of almshouses: a row of *kameren* under one roof. Collectively they assume the shape and structure of a low wide-fronted house with two doors next to each other, widows, dormer windows and chimneys. The partition wall between the houses contains a fireplace.

Singly these little houses originally had no partition walls or annexes. Their groundplan measures *c*. 20 m², though they are generally slightly deeper than they are wide. The joists are laid at a right angle to the street.

Very often rows of *kameren* were built for the (deserving!) poor by wealthy citizens. In such cases a commemorative plaque was set up in the part of the *kameren* used for meetings of the trustees who took over the management of the *kamezen* after the death of their founder. The room was often somewhat larger than the average *kamer* and lavishly decorated.

2b. The *double-aisled, wide-fronted house* (Pl. XXVA)

This type of house probably originated from a one-aisled, wide-fronted house with an annex with a lean-to roof at the back. However, during the middle of the seventeenth century it occurs frequently as a type on its own. Almost ninety per cent of these houses were built in Utrecht between 1630 and 1665.

The characteristics are:

both aisles have approximately the same dimensions; they are divided by a common brick wall on which the floor beams rest.

there are two parallel saddle roofs, one behind the other. Only rarely are both aisles spanned by a single roof.

the longest side of the separate aisles is either parallel to the street (wide-fronted variety), or at right angles to it (the rare narrow-fronted variety).

the beams are either parallel to the street (narrow-fronted variety), or lie at right angles to it (wide-fronted variety).

the double-aisled, wide-fronted house may have developed as a solution to creating a large dwelling without a wide span or a complicated roof construction (see: the square house)

3. The *square house* (Pl. XXVB)

The square house originated shortly after the development of the double-aisled, wide-fronted dwelling.

Its main characteristics are:

a roughly square plan

a roof identical on all four sides (e.g. four saddleback roofs, a helm roof or a hipped roof with a short apex)

load-bearing exterior walls, enabling each room to be spanned separately, so that beams are laid both parallel and at right angles to the front.

In the context of Utrecht the square houses are fairly large, measuring about 15 × 15 m. Therefore they did not require separate annexes. Load bearing inner walls could be placed anywhere, giving the square houses internal flexibility independent of the directions of beams and joists. In accordance with classical principles, the square house was planned symmetrically, both externally and internally. Beyond the entrance hall is a corridor. On either side of the hall lies a front room. Behind one of the front rooms is the staircase, followed by a room at the back. At the other side of the corridor lies a large back room. This scheme is often repeated on the first storey and in the cellar.

4. The *composite house*

The composite house forms a separate category of which the more regularly shaped ones have already been described, e.g. the double-aisled houses. To introduce some order into this varied category, it has been divided into four subcategories.

4a. The *freestanding composite house* (Pl. XXVIA)

These houses stand on large plots. The main building takes a number of forms: tower-like, wide-fronted or narrow-fronted. In the course of time various large annexes are added to the original core, and frequently the original configuration is only rediscovered by structural survey. So more houses of this type may be found within the fabrics of large houses.

4b. The *large house with a side-annex* (Pl. XXVIB)

This type of house is typical of medieval Utrecht.[20] The very large aristocratic dwellings, the so-called 'towncastles', almost always have one or two side-annexes, which are quite separate from the main house in their use and construction. The house generally has three main storeys, measuring (from ground floor upwards) 5 to 7 m, 3 to 5 m, and 2.5 to 5 m respectively. The height and size of the floors of such houses suggest they may have been used as representative halls, commercial premises and stores, while living quarters were located in the annexes. The core building buildings of this type which survive date from the early thirteenth century to the middle of the fourteenth century. Their fabrics have been altered very little. However, the annexes were much more adaptable; initially they were probably made of wood or half-timbered.

4c. The *house with aisles on both sides of a backyard* (Pl. XXVIC)

This type is fairly rare in Utrecht. It is much more common in the south e.g. in Maastricht. The main entrance to the house is at the side of the yard, which is closed by a wall with a gate. The examples which survive in Utrecht date from the fifteenth and early sixteenth centuries.

4d. The *gradually grown composite house* (Pl. XXVID and Fig. 1)

The most common way in which this type developed is through the joining together of two or more pre-existing houses by the insertion of doors in their side walls. This practice still occurs quite frequently. Sometimes the interior of the houses is more thoroughly modified, and a new façade or roof may be added.

A fifth type, *the block of houses*, does not belong to the scope of this article as it originates during the nineteenth century in Utrecht.

DISTRIBUTION

The various house types are not spread evenly across the city of Utrecht. The narrow-fronted house is very common along the 'old' streets, i.e. those known during the twelfth century, it occurs though in practically all areas of the city. The largest concentration of wide-fronted houses is to be found in the south-eastern part of the

CELLAR

| 0 | 5 | 10 | 15M |

░░░ BEFORE 1467

▨ 1467 FIRST PHASE

▨ 1467 SECOND PHASE

▨ 1903

FIG. I.   Donkerstraat 15/19. Multi-period, composite houses. Plan of the houses gathered behind
the stone front. Due to fire of 1905 dating of the houses is no longer possible, though written
sources indicate that they belong to different phases.
Drawing by Rijksdienst voor de Monumenzorg, Zeist

city. Settlement of this area was based on plots along newly laid out streets during the
late fourteenth and early fifteenth century. Its axis is the Nieuwe Gracht (New Canal),
dug in 1391–93. The *kameren* were mainly built along alleys behind large houses in the
southern part of the city. The double-aisled, wide-fronted house is found in the eastern
part of the city, mainly inside the former Closes of St Peter's and St John's. After the
Reformation large plots became available for house-building. The same is true for the
almost contemporary square house and the freestanding composite house. The large
house with side-annex is an almost exclusive feature of the Oude Gracht, along which
the thirteenth-century patricians lived. The other composite houses are not restricted
to a specific area.

The general conclusion to be drawn from the distribution of house types is that the narrow-fronted houses and the large houses with side-annex occur on narrow plots along the 'old' streets. The other types are found in the less densely built-up areas in the east and the south of the city, and more specifically inside the Closes of St John's and St Peter's both before and after the Reformation.

REFERENCES

1. Marceline J. Dolfin, E. M. Kylstra & Jean Penders, *Utrecht. De huizen binnen de singels* ('s-Gravenhage 1989). De Nederlandse Monumenten van Geschiedenis en Kunst. Geïllustreerde Beschrijving. De Provincie Utrecht. De Gemeente Utrecht deel IIIA en IIIB. Edsard M. Kylstra, 'Typologie der Wohnbauten in Utrecht', *Hausbau in den Niederlanden*, eds Dirk J. De Vries & Gerrit Berends. *Jahrbuch für Hausforschung*, Band 39 (Marburg 1990), 233–48.

2. A particularly well-documented publication which deals with the principal building materials used in the bishopric of Utrecht (the present provinces of Utrecht, Overijssel, Drenthe and the town of Groningen) during the Middles Ages and Early Modern Times is: Dirk J. De Vries, *Bouwen in de late middeleeuwen, Stedelijke architectuur in het voormalige Over- en Nedersticht* (Utrecht 1994).

3. Remains of tufa-built houses are almost always found in the side walls of later buildings. A particularly interesting one is found at Oude Gracht 114, and dates to the twelfth century. See Dolfin, Kylstra & Penders, *Utrecht. De huizen*, 395–99, 430; H. van der Wal, 'De bouwgeschiedenis van het huis Drakenburg te Utrecht', *Bulletin van de Koninklijke Nederlandse Oudheidkundige Bond*, Vol. 74-2 (1975), 71–79.

4. Timber houses do not survive in Utrecht, their remains are rarely found even by archaeological excavation. The later brick houses with their deeply-laid foundations have obliterated almost all traces of earlier structures. The same is true for foundations made of tufa: they were mostly rather shallow, which indicates that cellars must have been rare in these houses. Wooden gables remained in use for much longer, some of them even until the middle of the eighteenth century (see Chris J. Kolman, 'Spätmittelalterliche Holzfassaden in Utrecht', *Hausbau in den Niederlanden*, eds Dirk J. De Vries & Gerrit Berends. *Jahrbuch für Hausforschung*, Band 39 (Marburg 1990), 283–92.

5. In the former County of Holland the size of bricks diminished rapidly during the Middle Ages. During the fifteenth century they measured 22 × 11 × 5 cm. In Utrecht that size was reached only in the eighteenth century (22 × 11 × 4 cm), the intermittent stages being 26 × 13 × 6 cm in the sixteenth century and 24 × 12 × 5 cm in the seventeenth century. It is needless to say that both measurements and periods are approximate. The standard work on medieval brickmaking in the Netherlands is still: J. Hollestelle, *De steenbakkerij in de Nederlanden tot omstreeks 1560* (Arnhem 1961; unchanged reprint Arnhem 1976). With summary in English.

6. A fine example from 1291 can still be seen at Oude Gracht 114; see Van der Wal, 'Bouwgeschiedenis', 79.

7. The Meuse slates are rectangular in shape; they are laid stretcher bond-wise. The Rhine slates are scalelike in shape and laid diagonally; E. J. Haslinghuis, *Bouwkundige Termen. Verklarend woordenboek der westerse architectuurgeschiedenis*. Bewerkt door F. H. M. Bosch — Kruimel, H. Janse, A. F. E. Kipp, N. C. G. M. van de Rijt & E. M. van Tienen (Utrecht/Antwerpen 1986), 230–31. This dictionary contains glossaries from Dutch into German, English and French and vice versa.

8. Holes for nailing the tiles to the battens are very seldom found in Utrecht. In 's-Hertogenbosch they occur in fourteenth-century archaeological contexts, but they disppear during the fifteenth century. The change may be due to a change in the slope of the roofs, the older and steeper ones requiring extra fixing of the tiles to prevent them from slipping. H. L. Janssen, 'Bricks, Tiles and Roofing-tiles in 's-Hertogenbosch during the Middle Ages', *Terres cuites architecturales au moyen age*, ed. D. Deroeux (Arras 1986), 73–93. (Textes du Colloque de St. Omer, 7–9 juin 1985. Mémoires de la Commission départementale d'Histoire et d'Archéologie du Pas-de-Calais 22/2); De Vries, *Bouwen*, 85–86.

9. See Van Rooijen and Hoekstra in this volume.

10. Even the masonry of the almost 100 metre high cathedral tower was originally painted red and white.

11. See however Dolfin, Kylstra and Penders, *Utrecht. De huizen*, 425–27.

12. The term 'three-quarter house' was first coined by C. L. Temminck Groll, in *Middeleeuwse stenen huizen te Utrecht en hun relatie met die van andere noordwesteuropese steden* ('s-Gravenhage 1963), 92–99. With summary in English. For the wooden gables see Kolman, 'Spätmittelalterliche Holzfassaden'.

13. This process has been described in detail for the town of Deventer in G. M. de Meyer en E. W. F. van den Elzen, *De verstening van Deventer. Huizen en mensen in de 14e eeuw* (Groningen 1982).

14.   R. Meischke, 'Huizen en keuren', *Rotterdam Papers II. A contribution to medieval archaeology*, ed. J. G. N. Renaud (Rotterdam 1975), 89–116 lists a great number of rules and regulations for fire prevention in medieval Dutch towns.

15.   Frans Kipp, 'Water en vuur. Brandpreventie en het middeleeuwse dak', *Het Vuur Beschouwd*, ed. H. L. de Groot (Utrecht 1990), 77–106. Here a somewhat shortened and slightly adapted version of pp. 99–101 is given.

16.   On eavesdrops in general see Meischke, 'Huizen en keuren', 90–92.

17.   M. W. J. de Bruijn, 'Had Utrecht een ozendrop van drie voet?' *Maandblad Oud-Utrecht* (1987–1), 6–9.

18.   Dolfin, Kylstra and Penders, *Utrecht. De huizen*, XXIV–XXV (general principles), 59 (type 1), 147 (type 2), 222 (type 2a), 255 (type 2b), 291 (type 3), 327 (types 4a–d).

19.   H. L. de Groot and T. J. Hoekstra, ' "The moving river", the 12th-century riverfront in the north of the city of Utrecht', *Conference of Waterfront Archaeology in North European Towns* No. 2 (Bergen 1983), ed. Asbjorn Herteig (Bergen 1985), 106–11, especially 108–09; Tarquinius J. Hoekstra, 'The early topography of the City of Utrecht and its Cross of Churches', *JBAA*, CXLI (1988), 1–34, especially 25–26; T. J. Hoekstra, 'De vroege topografie van Utrecht', Dolfin, Kylstra and Penders, *Utrecht. De huizen*, 1–20, especially 14–15.

20.   A. F. E. Kipp, 'Große mittelalterliche steinerne Wohnhäuser in Utrecht', *Hausbau in den Niederlanden*, ed. Dirk J. De Vries & Gerrit Berends. Jahrbuch für Hausforschung, Band 39 (Marburg 1990), 257–81.

Utrecht between Pleshey Castle (Essex) and the Hasker Convent (Friesland): The Origin and Distribution of Late Thirteenth- and Early Fourteenth-Century Decorated Floor Tiles in the Netherlands

by Cees A. M. Van Rooijen and Tarquinius J. Hoekstra

INTRODUCTION

In the nineteenth century medieval decorated mosaic tiled floors were already recorded in Utrecht. The most famous, beautiful and intricate one was found at the site of a canons house of St John's (Janskerkhof 16) in 1869, now in the Centraal Museum Utrecht.[1]

For the more common mosaic and slip decorated tiles a Utrecht origin was long supposed, but only proven in 1979 when wasters of roof tiles and floor tiles were found in the suburb of the Bemuurde Weerd[2] (Pl. XXVII). It then came as a pleasant surprise that not only monochrome mosaic tiles and slip decorated tiles had been fired there but also the much rarer painted tin glazed ones. The idea of a southerly provenance (France or even further afield) of the painted tin-glazed tiles in the existing Utrecht floors could be discarded.

In 1984 a large-scale excavation took place on a site just south of the area where the first wasters were found. There five potters' and tilers' workshops, including their waster pits, came to light. One of them was a specialist tiler, the rest were mainly potters. The results of the excavation made it clear that Utrecht had an important tile industry during the late thirteenth and the first half of the fourteenth century.

The tile industry could flourish at Utrecht for several reasons. First, the river Vecht had deposited excellent, red firing clay. It was no accident that the potters and tilers settled along a canalized part of that river, which also provided a good way of transport for fuel on the one hand and of finished products on the other.

Secondly, Utrecht was by far the largest city in the Northern Netherlands and an important ecclesiastical centre. Moreover, the first half of the fourteenth century saw an economic boom, which among other things caused great building activity.[4]

It is therefore hardly surprising that a great number of floors have been found in the city, mainly in ecclesiastical buildings (churches, monasteries, canon's houses) but also in the houses of the aristocracy.[5]

Another concentration of mosaic tiled floors was found in Friesland, mainly in former monastic buildings.[6]

The Utrecht tiles (Pl. XXVIIIA)

The Utrecht tiles were made of local red firing clay. Their initial size is 16/17 × 16/17 × 2 cm.[7] They were trimmed with a flat piece of wood the size of the tile. To prevent the tile from slipping, nails were stuck through the wood. The position of the little holes they left in the tiles seems to have been used to help to determine the scoring lines (Pl. XXVIIIA). By scoring the tiles a great number of rectilinear shapes could be made for use in mosaic floors. The smallest tiles found in floors measure 1 × 1 cm.

Apart from a few tin glazed ones, all tiles were lead glazed. The reddish brown ones had glaze only, the black ones probably had iron added to the glaze.[8] The yellow ones had glaze over a white slip, the green ones had copper added to the glaze over their white slip.

Slip decoration was applied by pressing a positive mould into the clay, pouring the white clay over the tile and scraping the surface until the white picture showed up on the body of the tile (Pl. XXVIIIA).

The somewhat odd waster on Pl. XXIXA shows two impressions askew over one another. Slip had been applied, but not scraped. The tile probably was used as a prop in the kiln and therefore was fired during the process. Part of the slip has fallen out, so that the bevelled sides of the mould can be seen. Depending on the depth of scraping this bevel causes the slight differences in size of otherwise identical decorations. However, sometimes a mould with straight sides was used, e.g. on a tile decorated with fleurs-de-lis.

The tin-glazed tiles were painted free-hand on the opaque white base (Pl. XXIXC and D). They show a great variety in their greenish-brown decoration, ranging from simple geometrical motives to portrait heads or intricate architectural tile pictures.

THE UTRECHT MOSAIC TILED FLOORS

Since the 1986 publication on Utrecht mosaic tiled floors, which contains a catalogue of the floors or fragments of floors found till then,[9] a number of other ones have been either excavated or drawings of them discovered in archives[10] (Pl. XXVIIIB). Frequently individual tiles are found out of context, which suggests that rectilinear mosaic floors were rather common in monastic buildings[11] and in the houses of the rich in Utrecht during the first half of the fourteenth century.

In 1994 and 1995 excavations in St Mary's Close brought to light a further three large fragments of mosaic floors in the remains of canon's houses (Fig. 1A and B)) The almost complete one (Fig. 1B at no. III and Pl. XXXA) will be preserved *in situ* and be visible for the public in the parking garage of the newly built houses. The long black and yellow fragment (Fig. 1B at no. V and Pl. XXXB) will adorn the stairwell of one of the apartment blocks to be built there.

By far the most puzzling floor was found in the second canon's house (Fig. 1B at no. II and Pl. XXXC). The main part of this floor consisted of normal green and yellow Utrecht tiles in diagonal checkerboard pattern. However, in its centre a diagonal square of different, slip decorated tiles was laid, which — in a small way — has thrown new light on Anglo-Dutch relations during the early fourteenth century.

FROM PLESHEY CASTLE TO UTRECHT (Fig. 2)

The square measures *c*. 125 × 125 cm and consists of 8 × 8 tiles, which for Utrecht have the unusual size of 15 × 15 cm.[12] They have a continuous decoration of sixteen quatrefoils in total, each containing eight coats of arms of two types. The lion rampant *per se* is rather common on tiles, but on Utrecht tiles it is never shown on a shield (Pl. XXVIIIA, m–o). The coat of arms with chevrons and bars — of which only halves are visible on each tile (Pl. XXVIIIA, a) is completely unknown in the Netherlands. The

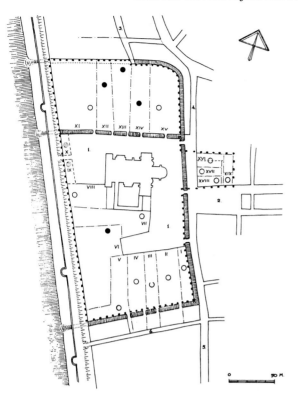

FIG. 1A. Plan of St Mary's Close
c. 1400. The plots of the canon's houses
are indicated by roman numerals.

Drawing by A. F. E. Kipp

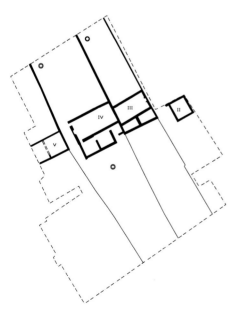

FIG. 1B: Simplified plan of the excavated houses in
St Mary's Close. The numbers are in the rooms in
which remains of tiled floors were found. In house
no. IV a completely robbed floor was found.

Drawing by C. A. M. Van Rooijen

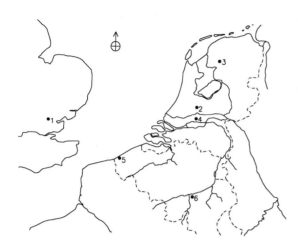

FIG. 2.   Map of the eastermost part of England and the Low Countries. 1: Pleshey Castle; 2: Utrecht; 3: Haskerdijken; 4: Heukelum; 5: Ter Duinen, Koksijde; 6: Andenne and Ciney.

Drawing by C. A. M. Van Rooijen

decoration in general has a strong English flavour, and more precisely that of the Central Essex Group found at Pleshey Castle.[13] However, the fabric of the tiles is distinctly Utrecht.[14]

Drury already saw an Anglo-Dutch connection in Central Essex type tiles found in the Dutch Reformed Church of the little village of Heukelum on the river Linge south of Leerdam[15] (Fig. 2). For the rest this floor consists of typical Utrecht plain, slip decorated and tin glazed tiles (Pl. XXXI). The problem of provenance of the Central Essex tiles, both in Heukelum and in the canon's house floor, was solved by the finds of almost identical wasters in de Bemuurde Weerd (Pl. XXVIIIA, d and c). Moreover another fragment was found there which is closely akin to finds from England.[16]

According to Drury the Central Essex tile industry stopped during the early fourteenth century.[17] The Utrecht tile industry flourished during the first half of the fourteenth century.[18] It therefore seems likely an out of work Essex tiler emigrated to Utrecht, bringing his stamps with him. He obviously found work in the Bemuurde Weerd.[19] There he made or at least decorated tiles with Essex motives, which found their way to the Close of St Mary's and to Heukelum.

FROM UTRECHT TO THE HASKER CONVENT

During the restoration of the former chapel of the Augustinian Convent at Haskerdijken (the Hasker Convent) in Friesland (Fig. 2) a number of fourteenth-century tiles were found.[20] Apart from tin-glazed fragments, slip decorated ones had come to light. A number of them were probably made locally, because their decoration does not occur outside Friesland.[21] However, a number of them are distinctly Utrecht products, among them a number of fragments with Central Essex decoration (Pl. XXIXB). Similar tiles were found at other places in Friesland.[22]

INFLUENCES FROM THE SOUTH

A small number of tiles of a fabric completely different from the red-firing Utrecht one were found at St Mary's Close and in St Paul's Abbey Utrecht[23] (Pl. XXVIIIA t–w). They were made from white firing clay and four of them scored from tiles measuring

13 × 13 cm. They are lead glazed in not very homogenous buff, drab or grey-green colours and decorated with red slip. They probably originate from the Meuse Valley, where similar tiles have been found among the wasters of Andenne and — much closer in time, size and decoration to the Utrecht ones — in St Agatha's Chapel at Hubinne, canton de Ciney[24] (Fig. 2). It remains rather enigmatic how the relatively small number of these tiles reached Utrecht. No other ceramic imports from the region are known in Utrecht at that time.

The same is true for the tin-glazed tiles found in Utrecht, both in floors and among wasters at the Bemuurde Weerd[25] (Pl. XXIXc and D). They are fairly common in Flanders, where the tiles of the Duinen Abbey at Koksijde (Fig. 2) are rightly famous.[26] In Utrecht tin-glazed tiles occur during a short period only, e.g. during the early fourteenth century. Would it be too bold to assume that a Flemish or North French tiler settled at Utrecht, made his tin-glazed tiles at the Bemuurde Weerd and died without a successor? Again, ceramic imports in Utrecht from that area during that period are extremely rare.

CONCLUSION

During the late thirteenth and the first half of the fourteenth century Utrecht boasted a large number of rectilinear mosaic tile floors. The tiles of these floors were mainly made locally in the suburb of the Bemuurde Weerd. Only the small number of tiles made from white firing clay were imported from the Meuse region in present day Belgium. However, even the local production had an international flavour. A Wessex tiler used his stamps with English heraldry to make tiles for a house of a canon of St Mary's Utrecht. Similar tiles were exported to Friesland. Moreover it might be argued that a Flemish tiler made tin-glazed tiles at Utrecht, where his products are found both in floors and among wasters in de Bemuurde Weerd.

This presents a picture of trade in tiles and travel of tilers during the first half of the fourteenth century.

ACKNOWLEDGEMENTS

The authors wish to thank Dr Christopher Norton (University of York) for his advice, Ms Beverley Nenk (British Museum) for showing the second author tiles from the reserve of the Museum, Mr H. De Jong (of the Archaeological Study Group of the Frisian Academy) for his generousness in showing us the tiles from Haskerdijken and from other sites in Friesland, Mr G. Elzinga (former Archaeologist of the Province of Friesland) for his help in visiting various sites and sharing his vast knowledge of Frisian finds with us, Dr Chris Kolman who drew our attention to the drawing of the floor of Vrouwenklooster Oostbroek, Prof. Dr Frans Verhaeghe (Free University Brussels), who provided us with a xerox of the article by Courtoy and Mr Tj. Pot (Archeologisch en Bouwhistorisch Centrum Utrecht) and Ms Ingrid van Weert (volunteer) for their impeccable restoration and mounting of the 'English' Utrecht tiles.

REFERENCES

1. Tarquinius J. Hoekstra and Hubert L. de Groot, 'Rectilinear mosaic tiled floors and tile production in Utrecht in the 14th century', *Terres cuites architecturales au moyen âge*, ed. D. Deroeux Memoires de la Commission départementale d'Histoire et d'Archéologie du Pas-de-Calais, tome XXII/2 (Arras 1986), 241–55, especially 246.

2. T. J. Hoekstra, 'Kaatstraat', *Archeologische Kroniek van de gemeente Utrecht over 1978–1979–1980* (Maandblad Oud-Utrecht 1981–3), 54–57.

3. H. L. de Groot and T. J. Hoekstra, 'Baksels en Misbaksels. Resten van een middeleeuws industriegebied', *Natuur & Techniek* (1985–5), 363–77. H. L. de Groot and Tj. Pot, 'Oudenoord', *Archeologische en Bouwhistorische Kroniek van de gemeente Utrecht over 1984* (Maandblad Oud-Utrecht 1985–5), 154–62. Huib de Groot and Cees van Rooijen, 'Door het vuur en voor het vuur. De Utrechtse aardewerk-industrie in de Bemuurde Weerd', *Het Vuur Beschouwd*, ed. H. L. de Groot (Utrecht 1990), 11–33. C. A. M. van Rooijen, 'Domplein 4' *Archeologische en Bouwhistorische Kroniek van de gemeente Utrecht. Over 1991–1992* (Utrecht 1994), 68–74.

4. Hoekstra in this volume.

5. Hoekstra and de Groot (1986).

6. H. M. van den Berg, *De Nederlandse Monumenten van Geschiedenis en Kunst. De provincie Friesland. Noordelijk Oostergo* ('s-Gravenhage 1981–1989), 4 vols. H. M. van den Berg, 'Middeleeuwse tegelvloeren in Friesland en omgeving'. *Publicatieband van de Stichting Âlde Fryske Tsjerken* III (1981), 21–28.

7. The distance between the bridges found in the extensive remains of the tile kiln in the Bemuurde Weerd was 15 cm, which is identical with the header of the bricks used in the kiln. So the size of the tiles may have been determined by the construction of the kiln.

8. Because of the high content of iron in the clay, which was also used for making the glaze, it is difficult to trace iron in the glaze.

9. Hoekstra and de Groot, 'Rectilinear mosaic tiled floors' (1986).

10. On the site of a former canon's house of the Cathedral, Domplein 4: C. A. M. van Rooijen, 'Domplein'. Vrouwenklooster at Oostbroek near Utrecht: Rijksarchief in Utrecht, Topografische Atlas, no. 1932.

11. Tin glazed and slip decorated fragments in the Convent of the Black Friars and a slip decorated one of the type of Pl. XXVIII, h at the House of the Teutonic Order.

12. The square has been preserved. Ingrid van Weert and Tjeerd Pot, *Met voeten getreden. Restauratie en reconstructie van een tableau van vroeg veertiende-eeuwse slibversierde plavuizen*. Private edition (Utrecht 1995).

13. P. J. Drury, 'Floor tiles', *Excavations at Pleshey Castle*, ed. F. Williams (Oxford 1977), 92–123. British Archaeological Reports 42. He supposes that the coat of arms is that of the East-Anglian Fitzwalter family.

14. Examination of tile type Eames no. 1725 in the British Museum by the second author on 27 October 1995, showed that this tile has a completely different fabric compared with the Utrecht ones, mainly because of its inclusions of small pebbles. E. S. Eames, *Catalogue of Medieval Lead-Glazed Earthenware Tiles in the Department of Medieval and Later Antiquities* (London 1980), 2 vols.

15. P. J. Drury, 'De l'Est-Anglie aux Pays-Bas', 'De la couleur dans l'édifice médiévale: carreaux et carrelages gothiques', ed. M.-M. Gauthier. *(Revenue de l'Art 1984), 74*. For the Heukelum floor: G. Berends and Th. Van Straalen, 'Een tegelvloer in Heukelum'. *Nieuwsbulletin van de Koninklijke Nederlandse Oudheikundige Bond* (1965), 17*–18*. It remains an enigma why such a richly decorated floor was made in a simple village church. It differs from the floors found in Utrecht by its circular panels. Circles also occur in Friesland: H. M. van den Berg, *Noordelijk Oostergo*. H. M. van den Berg, 'Middeleeuwse tegelvloeren in Friesland'.

16. E. S. Eames, *Catalogue*, types nos 1720 and 1721.

17. P. J. Drury, 'Floor tiles', 102.

18. Hoekstra and de Groot, 'Rectilinear mosaic tiled floors' (1986).

19. As the potters and tilers were not subject to the regulations of a guild, there were no official bars to the employment of foreigners.

20. Now Dutch Reformed Church of Haskerdijken.

21. H. M. van den Berg, 'Middeleeuwse tegelvloeren in Friesland' and unpublished ones from the church of Longerhouw.

22. They will be published shortly by Mr H. de Jong. A tile fragment found over sixty-five years ago on the site of the former monastery of Klaarkamp at Rinsumageest in Friesland and now in the Frisian Museum at Leeuwarden is identical with the 'Essex' tiles from Utrecht (Pl. XXXc) and the one from Pleshey Castle. H. M. van den Berg, *Noordelijk Oostergo*, III, 150; Pl. 228.

23. St Paul's: *Catalogus van het historisch museum der stad* (Utrecht 1928), no. 1555. The floor from Janskerkhof 16 (Canon's House of St John's) also contains a number of white firing tiles. However, it is doubtful whether they belong to this floor: they might have added during the reconstruction in the museum.

24. R. Borremans and R. Warginaire, *La céramique d'Andenne. Recherches de 1956–1965* (Rotterdam 1966), passim, but especially group A49 (undated) which shows decorations similar to those found in Utrecht.

However, these Andenne tiles are smaller in size. The tiles mentioned in F. Courtoy, 'La fabrication de carreaux en terre cuite à Andenne au moyen âge', *Namurcum. Chronique de la Société archéologique de Namur* (1956–63), 43–49, come much closer to the Utrecht ones. Not only does Courtoy present written evidence for tilers in Andenne in 1363 (p. 44), but he also describes tiles in St Agatha's Chapel at Hubinne, canton de Ciney, during excavations in 1912, which are very similar both in size and in decoration to those found in Utrecht. They have a *datum ante quem* of the (early) fifteenth century, when the chapel was destroyed.

25.   Hoekstra and de Groot, 'Rectilinear mosaic tiled floors' (1986).

26.   See on medieval tin-glazed tiles in general: Christopher Norton, 'Medieval Tin-Glazed Painted Tiles in North-West Europe'. *Medieval Archaeology*, XXVIII (1984), 133–72, on those of the Abbey of Ter Duinen: *ibidem*, 148–49 (with relevant references).

A Glazier from the Bishopric of Utrecht in Fifteenth-Century Norwich

by David J. King

When the Treaty of Arras was concluded on 21 September 1435 between Philip, Duke of Burgundy and King Charles VII of France, with the consequent loss of Burgundian support for England in the long struggle against the King of France, many countries in the Netherlands under Philip's rule, including Holland, came to be considered as enemies of the English throne. As a result of this, aliens from those parts who were residing in England were invited to swear an oath of fealty to Henry VI to secure their support and protect them from hostility in this country. In 1436, 'William de Mountford, born in the bishopric of Utrig' was recorded as one of the aliens resident in Norwich who chose to take the oath of allegiance.[1] The purpose of this article is to demonstrate that William was a glazier of Dutch origin who settled in Norwich, carried on his craft and raised a family. The workshop in which he worked is discussed and an attempt made to attribute some extant glass painting in Norwich and the county to this workshop, some of which, it will be suggested was painted by him and his wife.

In the same year that William took his oath, a man called William Mountford was left a legacy in the will of Robert Sylveryn, probably the same person as Robert Sylverne who was made free of the city as a painter in 1415, suggesting perhaps that William himself may have been associated with painting of some kind. In 1439–40 a 'William Duchman glasier' is mentioned as dwelling in Norwich and having paid the levy on aliens imposed by parliament in that year and renewed intermittently up to 1483. In the same accounts for the next two years he is referred to as 'William Glasyer' and 'William Glaswright' respectively, but in the 1450–51 list he is called 'William Fflemyng'. He makes a final appearance in the same class of documents in 1468–70, when he is called 'William Mounford'.[2]

Any lingering doubts as to whether 'William de Montfoort', 'William Mounford' and 'William Duchman glasier' were the same person are dispelled when two other documentary references to him are examined. The first is in the will of John Wighton. He seems to have been the leading glazier in the city in the mid fifteenth century, and in his will written on 11th February and proved on the 16th of the same month in 1457 he calls himself 'John Wyghton, alias Harrowe, glasier and citizen and alderman of Norwich'.[3] One of the legacies which he stipulates is for 40s. To William Mundeford 'who works for me' (*meo servienti*). He also provides for 10s. to be given to William's wife, Helen, and 10s. to his godson John Mundeford and 6s. 8d. to Henry Mundeford, both sons of William. John became free of the city as a glazier in 1453 having been apprenticed to John Wighton; this would indicate that William had arrived in Norwich by about 1432 at the latest, if Helen was, as would seem most likely, English. Henry was granted his freedom in 1465, having fulfilled his indentures with another glazier, Henry Piers, of whom more anon.[4] This document provides a firm link between the name William Mounford and the craft of glazing, and also provides details of his family.

The second document is the will of Helen Mounford, William's wife, who died the following year. She calls herself 'Helena Moundeforde of Norwich Glazier . . . by the assent of my husband William' and asks to be buried in the cemetery of the church of

St Mary Coslany in Norwich.[5] She leaves legacies of property, goods and money to William, John and Henry. The phrase 'by the assent of my husband' implies that it was necessary for women to have such permission in order to carry out a craft or trade.[6] The will was written only a year after the death of William's employer which may have placed him in a difficult position because of the fact that he was an alien. One wonders whether Helen, who was presumably English and probably a native of Norwich, had trained as a glazier in order to further her husband's career, or perhaps, since this is the only reference in the Norwich records to a female glazier, whether wives who worked in the family workshop were usually taken for granted and not officially recorded as craftswomen, except when, as here, there was a special reason for doing so.

One reason for William having been in difficulty after his employer's death could have been the fact that he was not enrolled as a freeman of the city, but this is a problematical question. Aliens and other 'foreigners' (i.e. people not from Norwich) could take up the freedom on payment of a fee. The 1415 composition had ruled on this question, and the matter was dealt with at greater length in the 1449 craft ordinances.[7] William is not recorded as having enrolled as a glazier, but in 1446, 'William Mountford' did enroll as a 'currier'.[8] There are many cases of people changing crafts in late medieval Norwich, so it is possible that our William was exercising the craft of leather-dressing in a city with a long tradition of leather working, that he had not been able to find work as a glazier at this time, and that his taking up the freedom in that year may have had something to do with his son John, who became free as a glazier in 1453, beginning his seven-year apprenticeship at this time. The lay subsidy rolls referred to above call William a glazier from 1439/40 to 1441/42, but not in 1450/51, when his occupation is not given, so that it could have been possible for him to have been working at another trade at the time of taking up his freedom in 1446, only to have resumed it again when he was recorded as working for John Wighton in 1457. Alternatively, there could have been another William Mountfort working in the city, as there had been in the fourteenth century.[9]

William's name occurs twice in a muster of armed men carried out in 1457 for both Berstrete and Ultra Aquam wards of the city.[10] This is interesting in the light of his will, the only other documentary reference to him, in which he leaves some items of armour and weaponry to his son John (a sallet, gorget, sword and pole-axe). The will itself was written on 20 December 1457 and proved on 4 October 1478.[11] He calls himself William Mounford of Norwich, glazier, and like his first wife Helen, asks to be buried in the cemetery of St Mary Coslany. He makes ecclesiastical bequests totalling only 6s. 8d., leaves 5 marks to his wife Matilda and also a silver-gilt mazer, six silver spoons and a bronze pot which was in the possession of his son John, who must give it up when asked. She also receives one half of his personal belongings, the residue to be disposed of for the benefit of his soul. His son John receives only the armour and weapons, and not only has to give up the bronze pot, but also pay 26s. 8d. to his father's executors. The implications of this are that William was not a rich man, and that there was some coolness in his feelings towards his son, perhaps over an outstanding debt. Of Henry the other son there is no mention; perhaps he had died by this time. His will is not extant and he does not appear in any other records as far as is known.

It is not easy to assess William's status as a craftsman in the city. On the one hand, he did not succeed as far as is known in establishing himself as an independent glazier and certainly on the evidence of his will did not become a wealthy man, nor does his name appear, as do those of several Norwich glaziers, on property deeds in the city court rolls. Indeed, he may have been forced to change occupation for a time at one stage. On the other hand, he did work for a large and successful workshop led by a man who became an alderman of the city, and he did establish his wife and two sons as glaziers, probably all working within the same workshop for John Wighton. If he arrived in Norwich by at least 1432, as suggested above, and died in 1478, he would have contributed considerably to the production of painted glass in the city, although of course it could have been as a designer, painter, or the craftsman who leaded-up the windows.

His son John bought a property with his wife Alice in the parish of St Andrew's in 1475/76, perhaps implying some degree of prosperity, and was a member of the influential Guild of St George, being mentioned in its proceedings from 1473 to 1477, in which year he was elected one of its supervisors, which suggests that he had a certain political status, but he outlived his father by only three years, according to Kirkpatrick's transcription of the inscription on his monumental brass which puts his death in 1481.[12] It may be significant in view of the possible problems with his father that he chose not to be buried in the same church as his parents, but in the nearby church of St George Colegate.

Henry, the younger son, is not heard of after becoming free in 1464/65. The main interest in him is that he was apprenticed to Henry Pers, glazier, himself made free of the city in 1427, but also recorded as an alien in the lay subsidy rolls.[13] His is first mentioned in 1442/44 as 'Henry Piers, Glazier'; in 1450/51 he is 'Henry Piers glasier Flemyng' and in the next year, 'Henry Pers glasier', but in the year after he is recorded as' Henry Piers Glazier Frenchman'. The designation as both Fleming and Frenchman suggests that Henry was a French speaking native of Flanders. He does not appear in the records after the mention of Henry Mundeford's apprenticeship to him in 1464/65. One possibility is that he went back to Flanders to set up business, but it does need to be borne in mind when considering as we shall do later what William's influence was on Norwich glass that as well as a Dutch glazier there was also a Flemish one in the city.

Another person mentioned in the lay subsidy rolls but not until 1483 as being an alien in Norwich was Robert Mundford, perhaps another member of the family. His occupation is not given in that source, but he became a freeman in 1455 as 'Robert Montiforde, graver' and in 1475/76 he sold a property with his wife in the parish of St Gregory in Norwich, being here called a 'gravor'.[14] There were close links between the arts of glass-painting, carving and engraving in fifteenth-century Norwich, but there is no evidence of whether or how Robert was related to William.

Having discussed the various members of the Mounford family, it is now necessary to examine in more detail what is known of the career of John Wighton, as it is important before going on to other matters to demonstrate the truth of the claim that he was the leading Norwich glazier at that time. The earliest mention of him is his enrolment as a freeman in 1411/12, suggesting a possible birth date of c. 1390. In 1416/17 he was acting as an executor to the estate of Adam Hadesco, glazier, together with Isabel, late wife of Adam, who was dead by 1397, having been active around the middle of the century as a glazier. John was clearly not his original executor, but must have been co-opted to replace one who had died. In 1425 he is mentioned in the city records and in 1428/29 he is recorded under his other name, John Harrowe, glazier, as the joint purchaser of a property in the parish of St Martin's Coslany. By 1435 his status had risen sufficiently for him to be elected Treasurer of the City of Norwich and in 1445–46 and 1447–48 he was the warden of the glazier's craft, responsible first of all with Thomas Felipp and then with John Roo for the quality control of the glass painting being carried on in the city. In 1451 he was assessed with an income of £2 in a taxation list for that year. In 1453 the first of a number of his apprentices was made free, being William's son John. Others followed in 1458 (John Bemond) and, after his death, in 1462 (William Baxter). John Tasburgh was mentioned in his will as an apprentice with three more years to serve, but there is no record of him becoming a freeman. In the same year as his first recorded apprentice became free, 1453, he was also elected as an alderman of the city for Colegate or Fyebridge, both 'Ultra Aquam', on the north side of the river. Only one other glazier, William Heyward, achieved that honour, and that was not until 1505. In the freeman's list for 1453 he is described as 'Gentleman and Alderman'. In 1455/56 he was paid 20s. for glazing two windows in the chancel of the parish church at Wighton in North Norfolk from where he originally came (his will tells us that his sister lived there).

Unfortunately, the extant glass there, mainly tracery-light figures of saints and angels, is in the nave, but it is interesting in view of what will be said below that some of it is in a style compatible with some of the glass in the church of St Peter Mancroft in Norwich.[15] John Wighton's will has already been mentioned in connection with the bequests to the Mounford family and with one of his apprentices. He too asks to be buried in the church St Mary Coslany, indicating that his workshop or residence was probably located in that parish. He makes bequests to eleven religious institutions, nearly all in Norwich, and to twenty-seven named individuals, mainly relations. His cash bequests total nearly £50, and there is also mention of some property. The largest legacy to an institution was £11 to his own church, and to an individual was £10 to John Wighton his nephew, son of Robert Wighton, presumably a brother of his who was dead at the time. John was to get the money when he came of age, and is known in later documents as a fairly prosperous glazier himself.

The overall impression gained from what is known about John Wighton senior is that he was a successful, respected, generous and moderately wealthy member of the Norwich citizenry and if one compares him with other known glaziers of this period in terms of the numbers of apprentices he had and the offices which he held, he is easily the most important figure amongst the members of that craft.

Although the names of about seventy glaziers are known in Norwich in the medieval period, and there are a few documents in which some of them are paid for specific pieces of work, in no case before the mid-sixteenth century is it possible to link the name of a glazier to an extant panel of glass using documentary evidence. However, with regard to the Wighton workshop, it is now possible to make out, if not an absolutely cast-iron case, at least one based on reasonably convincing circumstantial evidence for attributing a range of glass to that workshop. The glass which will mainly occupy our attention is the largest collection of medieval glass in the county, that in the church of St Peter Mancroft, Norwich.[16] This was and still is the leading parish church in the city. It was rebuilt from about 1390 to about 1475, but the eastern arm of the church was completed by 1455 when it was dedicated, several windows having also been finished by that time. Extant glass from these windows includes several panels from the east window of the north chancel chapel, beneath which the Mass of the Name of Jesus was held. This window had an Infancy series and a cycle of the Death, Funeral and Assumption of the Virgin Mary, with English Kings, Bishops and Archbishops in the tracery. There was also heraldry relating to Robert Toppes and his wife Joan. It will be referred to as the Name of Jesus window. Two painters appear to have worked on it. One, who was the master, did the heads and drapery in the main lights and some of those in the tracery. His drapery is characterized by rounded folds with hooks at the end of the trace-lines and modelling done with thin, delicate hatching, a thin matt wash and some relieving of the paint. The second hand, who looks like an apprentice of the master, painted some of the heads in the tracery in a similar and slightly cruder and more linear style, and his drapery painting is also similar, but noticeably more angular. The same workshop was also responsible for the east window of the south chancel chapel, which had a genealogy of Christ in the tracery, and probably for the adjacent window in the chapel which had a Holy Kindred representation in the tracery. The Life of St Peter window, almost certainly from one of the chancel side windows, looks at first sight to be later work from the same workshop, since the drapery is more angular than that in the main lights of the Name of Jesus window. However, some of the heads are so similar that a more probable explanation is that this window, whose subject was the saint to whom the church was dedicated, was also made ready for the dedication in 1455, but was entrusted largely to the same apprentice as worked on the Name of Jesus window, with the exception of the heads, which were painted by the head of the workshop, a practice which is thought to have been common.

A window depicting the Passion of Christ, probably from the north transept, was also by this workshop, but included some panels by a different painter called the Passion Master who was also responsible for two panels depicting seated female saints, perhaps from the clerestory. Another window in the south chancel chapel which contained glass relating to female saints shared a common cartoon with the Name of Jesus window but was by another painter again. It is designated here as the St Margaret window. So, although at least three main painters are involved in these windows, it would appear that they worked together and were probably in the same workshop.

The St Margaret window can be dated on internal evidence to 1453 and the Name of Jesus window to about the same year. The Passion window and the seated female saints may be a little earlier. In 1453 there was a royal visit to the city which may be connected with at least one of the windows and in the same year the windows of the council chamber in the Guildhall on the other side of the market place were glazed.[17] In this chamber would have met the mayor with the aldermen of the city, and in that very year, John Wighton was elected as an alderman. It would seem highly probable to say the least that the occurrence of all these events within the same year or two was not just coincidence, but that John Wighton was receiving recognition for the work which his glazing workshop had done in the city's administrative headquarters, the largest such building in the country outside London, and in the leading parish church in the city which counted many of the most influential citizens amongst its congregation. The idea is supported by the facts that the council chamber in the Guildhall still retains a collection of glass, which includes figures by both hands of the Name of Jesus and Life of St Peter windows and that the Name of Jesus window, completed in or around 1453, was given by Robert Toppes, alderman, who had been elected mayor in 1452 and who would have been in a strong position to support the election as alderman of John Wighton.

This of course must remain an hypothesis, but if one accepts it as a possibility, then the next question to consider is the identity of the various hands detectable. The leading figure would seem to be the main painter of the Name of Jesus window who also did the heads of the St Peter window and of the Guildhall glass. With the obvious exception of the east chancel window, about which nothing is known as far as its glazing is concerned, the two east facing chancel chapel windows were the most visible and most important in the church, and it would have been not at all surprising for the painting of these windows to have been confided to the leading painter of the workshop, and it therefore follows that this work must be attributed to John Wighton. It is possible to trace the development of the style of these windows from the early fifteenth century to the 1450s in Norfolk glass, part of the recognizable quality of the work being the use of a range of widely repeated decorative motifs, and this would fit in with the career of a man who started work in the early years of the century. The part played by an apprentice in the painting of this glass suggests that the second hand was that of John Munford, William's son, who was apprenticed to John Wighton and became free in 1453.

The exact identity of the Name of Jesus Master is an interesting question, but of greater importance in the present context is the identity of the Passion Master. His hand is very recognizable, and not only is to be seen in the Passion window and seated female saints panels at Mancroft, but also in several other churches in the county (as indeed is that of the painter of the Name of Jesus window). He painted a set of the Twelve Apostles in Pulham St Mary the Virgin Mary church, an Old Testament cycle in Martham church, a small representation of the Holy Trinity in Thurton church, some isolated heads in Warham St Mary church, and may have worked on the glazing of the bishop's palace at Lincoln.[18] He uses many of the same decorative motifs as the Name of Jesus Master such as rod-and-leaf border and seaweed background, but his figure and drapery styles are very different. Whereas the head types of the Name of Jesus Master are based on an essentially linear drawing which is precise, vivid, but sometimes stereotyped and with a lack of emotional appropriateness, those of the Passion master are much more varied, old-fashioned, less precise and almost careless on some occasions and rather grotesque on others, but at times also achieving a nobility of expression, as in the face of Adam in the scene of the expulsion at Martham (now at Mulbarton), and the face of Christ in the Crowning of Thorns at Mancroft (Pl. XXXIIA). The drapery style is also less linear, with a soft, sketchy modelling and a greater use of relieving for highlights. Could this be our Dutch glazier? Tracing his origins in terms of English glass-painting is difficult. His style is somewhat reminiscent of John Thornton's work, with his combination of gravitas and the grotesque.[19] By 1450, however, that style had not only developed into the rather sweet and more stereotyped version seen in northern and Midlands glass of the 1420s and 1430s, but had developed beyond that again to adopt the more crisp and sharp-edged painting technique of the mid century.[20] The Name of Jesus Master (John Wighton?) is in some ways a little old-fashioned in his adherence at this time to the rounded elegancies of International Gothic draperies, but the Passion Master seems to reflect a different tradition, and it is quite possible to see in his work certain foreign characteristics such as a Germanic expressionism in his emotional range and a Dutch looseness and freedom of handling in his drawing and modelling. The fact that his style looks back to the first three decades of the fifteenth century would also be consistent with an artist who had left Holland about twenty years previously. If the Passion Master was William Mounford, his work at Mancroft would certainly fit in with his known status within the Wighton workshop as an assistant rather than a master, since he both helped in the Passion window, which probably decorated a less important window in the north transept, and also painted a series of seated female saints which were probably placed at clerestory level, while, as we have seen, his master painted much of the important windows.

In addition to the above arguments which attempt to identify the Passion Master as William Mounford, there is also an iconographic comparison which would tend to support this thesis. Of the handful of Dutch panel paintings which survive from the late medieval period, one is the Epitaph of the Lords of Montfoort, now in The Rijksmuseum, Amsterdam, and originally made for the altar-piece of the Virgin from the Sint-Janskerk at Linschoten, about five kilometers from Montfoort, William's native town. (Pl. XXXIIc) Panofsky dismisses this work as 'problematic' and dates it to *c.* 1390, but Châtelet puts it at *c.* 1375–80, pointing out that despite the weaknesses in its execution, it shows the influence of a sophisticated milieu. The large throne of the Virgin with the child is similar to those designed and painted by the sculptor André Beauneveu in the Duke de Berry's psalter. It is also to be seen in the manuscripts painted by the Master of the Parement de Narbonne and the artists who followed him in the Très Belles Heures de Notre Dame, and also in cruder form in some early fifteenth-century Dutch manuscripts.[21] (Pl. XXXIIB) The link with Mancroft is to two panels by the Passion Master which may have come from the clerestory there and which show female saints, St Faith and St Cecilia, seated in large thrones very similar to those in the Montfoort panel and the Beauneveu manuscript. (Pl. XXXIIIA) The more complete of the two panels is a very striking panel with a bold design capable of being seen from a distance. It is tempting at least to make the suggestion that William Mounford had some hand in both designing and painting this panel from his knowledge of the Monfoort panel, or some very similar painting in the area where he lived.[22]

Another window which was made ready for the dedication in 1455, and was probably started in 1453 as it appears to contain allusions to the visit of Queen Margaret in that year and to her pregnancy leading to the birth of Prince Edward in the autumn of that year, must be considered now. It contained in the main lights glass depicting St Elizabeth of Hungary and St Margaret of Antioch, a donor panel with Robert Ringman, suffragan bishop of Gathy and a Franciscan, and canopy tops. In the tracery were representations of the Annunciation and Visitation and possibly also the Virgin and Child and St John the Baptist. The window was located in the south chancel chapel, which housed the Guild of St Anne, and was clearly seen as the centre of feminine spirituality within the church. The glass of this window was recognized by Woodforde[23] as being in a style which was different to that of the other windows in the church, but which was most similar to that of the Passion Master. The two hagiological main-light panels have the same crowded composition as the Passion Master's Passion scenes, and in the case of the St Margaret panel, the same simultaneity, with two scenes shown together. Both painters also use the device of showing the teeth of unpleasant characters; compare the figures of Olybrius and the gaoler in the St Margaret panel and two of the men striking Jesus in the Mocking of Christ. However, where the Passion Master is sketchy and soft in his painting, with heavy modelling and bold highlights, the St Margaret window artist is precise and linear in drawing, with hatching and scribbling preferred to matt wash modelling and a thinner paint used. The contrast and similarities between these two painters are intriguing. That they both belonged to the Wighton workshop is suggested by the Passion Master's shared production of the Passion window with the Name of Jesus Master and his use of a similar range of decorative devices, and by the reuse in the St Margaret window of cartoons made for the Name of Jesus window (the figures of Mary and Elizabeth in the Visitation). (Pl. XXXIIIc) If a good case can be made out for the Passion Master having been William Mounford, it is at least worth raising the possibility that the St Margaret window was painted by Helen Mounford. This would explain the links with the Passion window in particular and the Wighton connection in general, and of course it would have been more than appropriate for a woman to have painted a window with such strong feminine iconography and symbolism in a part of the church which seems to have been the focus of female religious devotion. The Mancroft windows include some fascinating symbolism, double meanings and even political propaganda, which cannot be discussed here. There is one detail in the St Margaret window, however, which is worthy of mention in the present context. In the panel showing the scenes of St Margaret before Olybrius, and the saint being led into gaol, the gaoler, who stands in a prominent position bottom right, carries a pole-axe over his shoulder. (Pl. XXXIIIB) Helen's husband owned a pole-axe, as his will informs us; could the figure of the gaoler be modelled after William, and was Helen making a veiled feminist complaint when she showed him putting a woman into prison? No other work has been identified by this painter, whereas as stated above, several other panels by the Passion Master are known. This of course would be consistent with the fact that Helen died well before her husband.

There are of course other ways of apportioning the surviving Norwich fifteenth-century glass to the glaziers who are known to have worked in the city and further detailed research may change the tentative conclusions drawn here, although in the present state of knowledge the attribution of glass to glaziers is the best fit for the available evidence. More work is also needed to see if any stylistic parallels can be found between Norwich glass and the fifteenth-century Dutch work in other media such as panel painting and manuscripts which do survive. The suggestions made here are, however, consistent with the facts as known and the reader must be left to judge on their merits. At the very least, we now know something of what happened to one Dutch glazier from near Utrecht, and if the hypotheses put forward here are true, a start has been made on the task of linking the names of some of the numerous Norwich medieval glaziers to the glass which they made. The work of discovering the extent of continental influences on English art in the period 1420 to 1460 is still in its early days, and other examples are certainly to be found in Norwich art.[24] One suspects that particularly in East Anglia this field is a rich one for further research.

SHORTENED TITLES

Blomefield	F. Blomefield, continued by C. Parkin, *An Essay towards a Topographical History of the County of Norfolk* (London 1805–10), 11 vols.
L'Estrange and Rye	J. L'Estrange and W. Rye, *Calendar of the Freemen of Norwich from 1317 to 1603* (London 1888).
Hudson and Tingey	W. Hudson and J. C. Tingey, *The Records of the City of Norwich.* 2 vols. (Norwich 1906/10).
Woodforde (1950)	C. Woodforde, *The Norwich School of Glass-Painting in the Fifteenth Century* (London, 1950).
Panofsky	E. Panofsky, *Early Netherlandish Painting* (Harvard 1971).
N.A.	*Norfolk Archaeology.*
N.C.C.	Norwich Consistory Court Wills.
N.R.O.	Norfolk Record Office.
N.R.S.	*Norfolk Record Society.*
P.R.O.	Public Record Office.

REFERENCES

1. E. F. Jacob, *The Fifteenth Century 1399–1485* (Oxford 1961), 262; N. J. M. Kerling, 'Aliens in the County of Norfolk, 1436–1485', *N.A.*, XXXIII (1965), 200–15. *Calendar of Patent Rolls, Henry VI 1429–1436*, 578.

2. N.R.O., N.C.C. 213, 214 Surflete; P.R.O., Lay Subsidy Rolls E179 235/6. 149/131, 149/138, 269/42, 149/161.
3. N.R.O., N.C.C. 84, 85 Brosyard.
4. L'Estrange and Rye, 99.
5. 'Helena Moundeforde de Norwico Glasyer . . . ex assensu dicti Willielmi Mariti mei'. N.R.O., N.C.C. 109 Brosyard.
6. The Ordinances for Crafts of 1449 are silent on this matter, but do imply that women as well as men were exercising crafts in the city. Hudson and Tingey, II, 278 ff.
7. Hudson and Tingey, II, xlv; see also the case of Henry Pers in this article.
8. L'Estrange and Rye, 98.
9. Hudson and Tingey, II, 241; William Mounfort (see note above) is referred to in an extent of city property in 1397 as the former owner of four stalls on the fish market.
10. Hudson and Tingey, I, fol. 407.
11. N.R.O., N.C.C. 203b Gelour.
12. N.R.O., City Court Rolls, Roll I 19 m1; M. Grace, ed. 'Records of the Guild of St George in Norwich, 1389–1547', N.R.S., IX (1937) 73 76; Fitch Collection, shelf T150D, small 8⁰ notebook, unfoliated.
13. P.R.O., Lay Subsidy Rolls, E179, 149/138, 269/42, 149/150, 149/147.
14. P.R.O., Lay Subsidy Rolls, E179, 149/198a; N.R.O., City Court Rolls, Roll I 19 m3.
15. L'Estrange and Rye, 11, 12, 99, 154; N.R.O., F. Johnson, MS, *Calendar of Norwich Deeds Enrolled in the City Court 1413–1508* (Rolls 17 20), 9; Woodforde (1950), 10; Hudson and Tingey, I, 298; N.R.O., City Court Rolls, Roll 18 m15; T. Hawes, ed. 'An Index to Norwich City Officers', N.R.S., LII (1986), 165; R. Virgoe, 'A Norwich Taxation List of 1451', N.A., XL (1988), 150; N.R.O., City Muniments, Court Book 1425–1510, 43, 46. P. Cattermole and S. Cotton, 'Medieval Parish Church Building in Norfolk', N.A., XXXVIII (1983), 273. John Wighton's name is not given here, but Dr Cotton has kindly given me a note of it (personal communication).
16. What follows concerning the building of the church of St Peter Mancroft and its glazing will be discussed in detail in the present writer's fascicle for the *Corpus Vitrearum* on the church, which is nearing completion. See also C. Woodforde, *The Medieval Glass of St Peter Mancroft, Norwich* (Norwich, N. D.) and Woodforde (1950), D. J. King, 'New Light on the Medieval Glazing of the Church of St Peter Mancroft, Norwich', *Crown in Glory* (Norwich 1982), 18–19, 22.
17. Blomefield, III, 158 (given as 1452); B. Wolffe, *Henry VI* (London 1981), 370; E. A. Kent, 'The Stained Glass in the Guildhall', Norwich, N.A. (1923), XXIII, 1–10; I. Dunn and H. Sutermeister, *The Norwich Guildhall* (Norwich, N. D.), 2, 20. E. S. Taylor, 'Notices of the Church of Martham Norfolk, Previous to its Restoration', N.A. (1859), V, 168–79; Woodforde (1950), 169, 174; H. Read, J. Baker, A. Lammer, *English Stained Glass* (London 1960), pls 75, 77, 78. D. J. King, *Stained Glass Tours around Norfolk Churches* (Woodbridge 1974), 11, 24. Some of the Martham glass is now at Mulbarton; the Thurton glass is unpublished. For the Lincoln Bishop's Palace Glass, see an unpublished report by the present writer commissioned by the City of Lincoln Archaeological Unit.
19. T. French, *York Minster, The Great East Window*, Corpus Vitrearum Medii Aevi, Great Britain, Summary Catalogue 2 (Oxford 1995).
20. For an excellent general survey of style developments in English fifteenth-century glass up to this period, see: R. Marks, *Stained Glass in England during the Middle Ages* (London 1993), chapters 8 and 9.
21. Panofsky, 92 and figs. 116, 119; A. Châtelet, *Early Dutch Paintings* (Lausanne 1988), 13–14; M. Meiss, *French Painting in the Time of Jean de Berry — The Late XIVth Century and the Patronage of the Duke* (London 1967), figs 36, 50, 51–74, 180.
22. Figures in large thrones also appear in the pasted-in miniatures of c. 1400–1410 by a Flemish artist in the Beaufort/Beauchamp Hours, British Library Ms Royal 2. A, XVIII, fols 7ᵛ, 13ᵛ. R. Marks and N. J. Morgan, *The Golden Age of English Manuscript Painting 1200–1500* (New York 1981), 101, pl. 31.
23. Woodforde (1950), 169.
24. For example, there are distant but perceivable echoes of the design of the Dijon Altarpiece of Melchior Broederlam in the Annunciation and Visitation panel painting of c. 1420–30 now in Norwich Cathedral but originally from the church of St Michael at Plea (Panofsky, pl. 51 and A. A. G. Thurlow, Norwich Cathedral, [Pitkin Guide, Eastleigh, 1990], 10.); this in turn influenced the Annunciation of the Mancroft Name of Jesus window, and other panels in this window have iconographic details which are more easily derived from continental sources than English art. The clearest case of this is the detail in the Nativity scene which shows angels repairing the stable roof with bundles of thatch; this occurs in a panel painting of 1410–1415 attributed by Panofsky to North Guelders or Cleves (Panofsky, 94–95, fig. 110). A final example points in another direction. A tracery light of Norwich workmanship of c. 1460 in the Victoria and Albert Museum depicting a scene from the Life of St Benedict is very similar in its basic design to the

same scene in the Bedford Breviary, fol. 438ʳ illuminated in France 1424–35 (London, Victoria and Albert Museum Inv. No. C. 351. 1937; P. Lasko and N. J. Morgan, *Medieval Art in East Anglia 1300–1520* [Norwich 1973], 60–62. The most probable explanation for this is that the panel comes from the chapel in the south aisle of the church of the monastery of St Benet at Hulme and was provided by Sir John Fastolf, who was buried there in 1459 in the chapel which he had rebuilt. He was a patron of both manuscript painting and stained glass and as Steward to the Household of the Duke of Bedford earlier in his career he would no doubt have seen the manuscript from which this design comes and may have known the artists. He himself used the services of a French illuminator in England and is known to have had stained glass in the windows of his house in Norwich (*Dictionary of National Biography*, VI, fol. 1099; R. Tuve, 'Notes on the Virtues and Vices', *Journal of the Warburg and Courtauld Institutes*, XXVI, 284; Blomefield, XI, 207, 208).

Medieval Roof Construction in Utrecht and the Netherlands

by Dirk J. de Vries[1]

INTRODUCTION

In the Netherlands, the value of historic timberwork has only been recognized in the last three decades while much has been lost in the course of restoration.

The BAA has visited the romanesque church of Lebuinus in Deventer where a new roof was built during the first half of this century at the expense of a number of medieval structures. Other victims of restoration include the fourteenth-century roofs over the nave of the Reformed Church in Hellendoorn and Our Lady in Maastricht. For the purpose of this study I examined the early fourteenth-century roof of the Dean's chapel of St Peter's in Utrecht. It was a surprise for me and the restoration architect to discover that the former common rafter roof of fir wood had been almost entirely replaced by a firm oak construction, even including the application of rustic chiselled 'Roman' assembly marks. By chance, the shape of the old construction had been copied. However, information about the exact dimensions of the beams, the type of wood, the joints, techniques of manufacture and assembly-marks had disappeared or become very uncertain. Dendrochronological dating is no longer possible once the old timber has been replaced.

The first studies of carpentry appeared in Germany in 1908 (Ostendorf) and in France in 1875 (Viollet-le-Duc) and 1926 (Deneux). Herman Janse, an active member of the Dutch Department for Conservation (Rijksdienst voor de Monunumentenzorg -RDMZ- at Zeist NL) until 1991, published his main work, 'Wooden roof framing in the Netherlands' in 1989.[2] Previously, in collaboration with the Belgian Luc Devlegher, Janse had presented an important article about shared timber heritage (1963).[3] Janse's elaborate typological investigation, comparable with those formulated by C. Hewett, can now be better dated thanks to a series of dendrochronological investigations which I have carried out for the RDMZ since 1984.[4] Now it may be useful to give roof construction a relational context, and to consider roofing-materials and the connections with floor and wall structures. In this study I will consider a score of examples situated in the province and the town of Utrecht, the oldest and only diocese in the north of the Netherlands with secular power until the year 1528.

THE SHAPE OF ROOF CONSTRUCTIONS

The Common Rafter Roof

In Utrecht and throughout the Netherlands, no evidence of timber roof construction prior to the thirteenth century has yet been found. The most basic form, the pure single rafter roof, is practically timeless: this type of roof occurred in towns up until the fourteenth century and in the countryside in the following centuries. In a small country like the Netherlands there are remarkable differences in the 'development' and 'geographical spread' (as far as this might be considered an autonomous process) of roof construction in particular periods and in buildings of comparable scale.

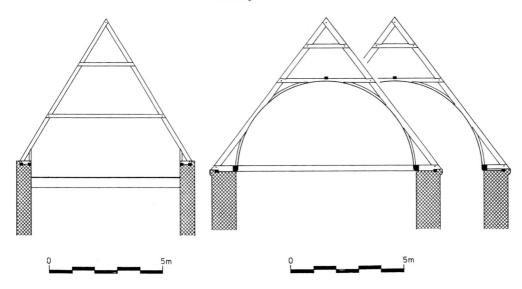

FIG. 1.   House Te Putte, Oude
Gracht 187 Utrecht, cross-section of
the common rafter roof, 1309 d
Drawing: L. M. de Klein RDMZ

FIG. 2.   Saint John's church Utrecht, with firwood rafters
and boarded ceiling, XXIId?
Drawing: L. M. de Klein RDMZ

Utrecht has a number of houses and churches with common rafter roofs, built around 1300. Carpenters used South-German fir (Abies Alba) timber for rafters and collars in addition to smaller pieces of oak at the bases and for curved parts. Drakenburg House (1291 d)[5] and Te Putte House (Fig. 1 1309 d) both situated on the Oude Gracht have roofs built in this way, as does the structure at Maria Plaats 50, with three collars, and one with two collars, and the Dean's chapel of St Peter's; the two later structures have so far not been dated dendrochronologically. The frames are erected on double wall plates and, at a right angle to them, on a sole-piece in which each rafter and a vertical post, the ashlar-piece, are joined with a mortice-and-tenon.

A variation of the common rafter roof with braces is the boarded ceiling, giving the effect of a barrel vault. Examples of this type of ceiling can be seen in the churches of St John's (Fig. 2) and St Nicolas' in Utrecht. However, without dendrochronological dating, the roof covering St John's church in Utrecht is presumably older (± 1280) as fir is used for the rafters and collars. Tie-beams only occur on every fifth or sixth pair of rafters; presumably to save on wood. The sole-pieces of the rafters in between are joined by a horizontally tenoned piece. One could also call this beam an inner wall plate but the trimming is bigger and lies not, or only partly, on the wall. Due to the apparent economy in the use of timber these sole-pieces have the appearance of reduced tie- or foot-beams. Every couple of rafters had its own tie-beam in the oldest (church) frames.[6] In Drakenburg House they look like redundant tail-ends. The use of truncated or interrupted tie beams is discussed by Brunskill.[7]

It was generally accepted that the carpentry of St Nicolas' church was the oldest in Utrecht, thought to date back approximately to the year 1100. However, recent dendrochronological research ascertained that the oak carpentry on the nave dates to

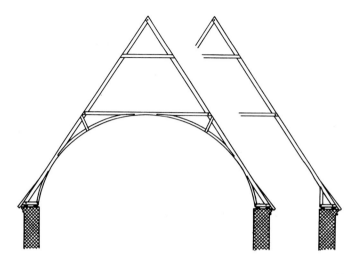

Fig. 3.   Main building of the Teutonic Knights with a roof built in or shortly after autumn/winter 1347 (d)

Drawing: after K. Rampart Utrecht

0 ⊏⊐⊏⊐⊏⊐ 5m

1338, the reused rafters of the choir to 1345, and it shows that the wood of the rafters in the high-choir was cut in the winter of 1364–65.

The construction on the main building of the Teutonic Knights in Utrecht is of a comparable age and set-up (Fig. 3). Here the oak which provided the timber was cut down in 1347 (d). Documents affirm this date since the knights bought their parcel in 1346 and began building on Wednesday, 2 May 1347.[8] The sole-pieces of the huge rafter 'trusses' at the Teutonic Knights' House contain holes on one side. The Utrecht architectural historian Bart Klück interpreted these as pegholes to hold the two sole-pieces together when they were pulled up. Once vertically fixed, the temporal tie-beam was disconnected and used for the next pair of rafters. These pegholes may be the same as the holes that Brunskill calls 'problem holes'.[9]

In about 1300 the saving of tie-beams and additional braces led to a more complex system of trusses. In this phase timber roofs are characterized by both single and double wallplates and developed longitudinal members. Longitudinal members occur in the middle of the roof, under or above the collars. Primarily these longitudinal beams (plates or purlins) seem to have had a coupling function in the oldest roof constructions. The beams are later employed as stiff plates, and combined with king posts to brace the roof longitudinally. However, this solution is well known in different forms in neighbouring countries, including Britain, from the twelfth century. In the Netherlands, however, there was only a short and limited experiment with this method or technique during the fourteenth century. In the east, for instance in the town of Zutphen, a number of great examples with central plates are preserved.[10] From the fourteenth century the longitudinal beam is retained as a collar purlin in combination with and on top of the trusses. In Germany, for centuries carpenters continued to install longitudinal plates, both central and double, under the 'arm-pits' of the rafter-collar joints in place of queen posts.

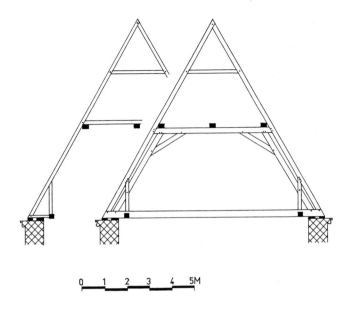

FIG. 4.   Choir of the
Dominican's Church in
Maastricht, 1277

*Drawing: L. M. de Klein after
H. Janse RDMZ*

0   1   2   3   4   5M

The carving of assembly marks is interesting. At Drakenburg House the beams are numbered using a system of symbols and strokes incised into the timber: tens are denoted by the symbols + and ×; single units are indicated by simple strokes. A refinement took place by adding symbols for the number five (V, Y, half tens) in Te Putte House (1309 d) and also in the (not accurately dated) roof of St John's in Utrecht, both of which are built from fir. In the roof above the nave of St Nicolas' church are rafters with numbers like ×//////// for eighteen in 1338 (d). Later examples of this system of numbering (without a symbol for five) are found in eastern areas, as in the roof of the Pelsterhome in Groningen (1385 d)[11] and in the roof of the (Catholic) church in Ootmarsum (± 1400 d) both of which have rafters with a rectangular and a square cross-section.

There is another type of incised mark which Brunskill calls a 'carpenter's mark' but which I prefer to call an 'owner's mark' because it had a function to indicate ownership after buying wood in a market place and during transportation to the building site. Not only carpenters or commissioners had their personal marks to refer to the ownership, but also towns, as we know from accounts and from timberwork in Kampen and Zwolle.[12] Certain towns had their own timber marks.

The appearance of trusses

The oldest roofs with trusses date to the last quarter of the thirteenth century and are only present in the very south of the Netherlands. Examples of these are found in the choirs of the Dominican (Fig. 4) and Franciscan churches in Maastricht, which date to 1277 (d) and 1305 (d) respectively. In Utrecht, the oldest dated truss is found in Leeuwenberch House, Oude Gracht 307, and dates to between 1319 and 1325 (d). It is worth mentioning here the use of both fir and oak for the sole-pieces and the curved parts. As in the choir of the Franciscan church in Maastricht, the horizontal truss-beams are joined with pegs to the rafters under they are placed, and bear similar number/assembly-marks.[13] Only in the course of the fourteenth century did carpenters start to number the trusses separately from the rafters. The earliest surviving instance of the separate numbering of trusses and rafters occurs in the roof of the tower at Oudewater, dated to between 1336 and 1343 (d). The trusses along the west display a further assembly mark, '⟨' (Fig. 5). Halfway between the trusses are three rafter trusses with braces, the outer members supporting two kingposts, of which the ashlar-pieces stand on brick cantilevers. Due to the kingposts, the roof at Oudewater contains a longitudinal plate under the lowest and the middle of the three rows of collars. The lower longitudinal plate is braced against the side walls by means of wallposts and curved braces. The placing of the windows in each façade reveals that the brick layers respected the position of the longitudinal timber plate.[14] Other features of the fourteenth-century roof construction can be seen in the coupling of the principal and the wall plate via a short beam with a mortice-and-tenon in the principal; the same is done with the windbraces in the principals,[15] and a solid connection between collar and rafter by means of a dovetail, notched lap joint or with mortice-and-tenon. The arrival of trusses brought with it the practice of adding a separate mark to the assembly marks on one side of the construction. This extra mark can come in the shape of a '⟨', a 'fish', an 'arrow', a semi-circle or an added square stripe (also called a Flemish mark). During the fourteenth century a uniform system came into being by which the two opposite sides of the rafter could be distinguished for instance, number three on one side was written as /// and on the other side as //⟨ or ⟨⟨⟨.[16] Early examples of this system can be seen in the roof of the nave of the Bethlehemkerk in Zwolle (built between 1333 and 1369) and in the carpentry of the choir of the Domkerk in Utrecht (Fig. 6, 1386 d). This type of assembly mark (made with a special V-shaped blade)[17] was replaced between 1500–50 by smaller marks cut with a chisel and gouge. This change first took place in the west and Utrecht, and later in the east.[18] Apart from the marks, the Zwolish carpentry bears many features common to mid-fourteenth-century construction. The Domkerk however, has double trusses and a collar-purlin in a form which remains unchanged for a hundred and fifty to two hundred years. Rafters and trusses are separately numbered with broken assembly marks on the north side, from east to west and ending with the transept with truss V//. This truss contains the remnants of a timber frame that served as a temporary covering when the choir was ready. Some shelves of the wainscotting gave a dendrochronological date of approximately 1395. The rafters have a regular square profile after ± 1375–1425. Before that carpenters economized on tie-beams at the foot of the roof construction. Later they left out the lower collars at the level of the roof/truss plates. Large ambitious constructions, like those of the Domkerk, have double plates on the lower trusses.[19] Mounting the trusses and rafters on solepieces remained customary in roofs with large spans, however this principle was not followed for smaller roofs of houses after the fourteenth century. An example with an extended system of trusses is found dating to around 1446 under the very high roof of the Buurkerk in Utrecht.

The application of purlins

So far I have described trusses which all have plates (arcade plates). These longitudinal, horizontal beams are different from inclined purlins which lay in the line of the roof on the trusses, or in the principals. These purlins appear relatively early in Great Britain (e.g. in early fourteenth-century Great Coxwell Barn) and in France. The use of the purlin apparently spread from the south. The first purlins, with a mortice-and-tenon

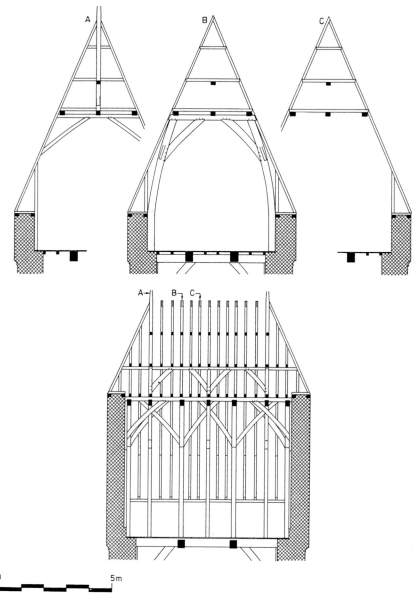

FIG. 5.   Tower carpentry of Oudewater Church, about 1340
Drawing: L. M. de Klein RDMZ, after R. H. Nijkamp 1961

joined to the principals and placed on kingposts to support the ridge, can be traced to
Maastricht just before 1400.[20] This carpentry exhibits a combination of trusses with
both plates and purlins (Fig. 7). The earliest known example of this type was used in
the transept of the Domkerk in Utrecht in 1477, true purlin roofs without plates, can be

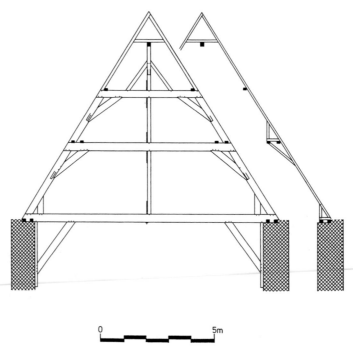

FIG. 6.   Choir of the Domkerk in Utrecht, erected in or shortly
after 1386

Drawing: L. M. de Klein RDMZ 1983

found in the south from the last quarter of the fifteenth century[21] and surprisingly, in a number of choir chapels of the Nieuwe Kerk in Amsterdam.[22]

Roof construction in relation to other parts of the building

A common rafter roof goes together with a single flooring with a distance from centre to centre of 60–90 cm, comparable with the distance between the rafters. However, on account of the side walls they are not directly joined in houses. Sometimes the joists lie on a side-beam supported by stone corbels.[23] The walls of these houses are thick, between 60 to 100 cm, and sometimes even thicker. The load that the rafters and beams put on the walls is more or less regularly divided, and windows are small. This is a romanesque scheme of building. However, from a consideration of the roof, in isolation from the structure of the walls, it may be possible to make suggestions for the framework construction in the period 700–1200. Posts for supporting the roof are positioned opposite each other in the sidewalls; pairs of posts were connected by tie-beams. This tie-beam was essential in framed buildings to counterbalance lateral stress and to avoid the sidewalls being pushed outwards. The system is called a couple-close rafter-roof. From this system a (theoretical) model of the house appears in which, on the basis of the arrangement of the oldest roof constructions, there is no place for trusses or a three-way bracing, or frames on stone bases with curved braces and windbraces.[24] The earth-fast post disappeared when trusses on stone bases appear;

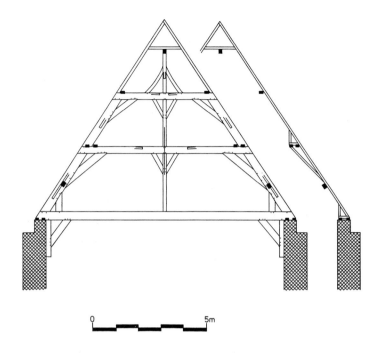

FIG. 7.   Transept roof with plates and purlins, Domkerk Utrecht 1477
Drawing: L. M. de Klein RDMZ 1983

durable lasting structures could then be built. In about 1300 monks erected structurally modern (gothic) timberwork in barns such as Great Cowwell and Ter Doest in Belgium. The gothic constructional method tends to place great stress upon skeletons of either stone or timber. Regarding timberframes, the improvement seems to start with the reduction of long beams. In carpentry, this was achieved when smaller, shorter, square rafters distribute their weight via plates to the trusses which in turn were laid on piers with buttresses and which were often supported by curved braces on the inside. Gothic joisting, comprising sleepers and secondary beams, appears in the Netherlands between about 1300 and 1600 and continues to be employed in Utrecht until around 1675. The binders can be supported by sole pieces, curved braces (corbels) and wallpieces (off the floor or on a cantilever); this arrangement occurs frequently from the fourteenth century onwards. Curved braces and sole pieces reduce the tension on the sleeper, increasing the stability of the building and in combination with the wall piece, allowing a reduction in the wall thickness. It is striking that all pine has a rectangular profile and that these characteristics were also used in oak timberwork during the thirteenth and fourteenth century. By the fifteenth-century carpentary beams are square in cross-section, more appropriately for this type of wood. Between 1600 and 1625 Scandinavian softwood took over the market from German and southern wood because of the war with Spain. Therefore, seventeenth-century (softwood) beams usually have a rectangular cross-section, and in the first half of the century ceilings were elaborately painted in order to cober the 'inferior' timber.

Other considerations are the pitch of the roof and roofing materials. Gothic roofs are generally sharply pitched; most roofs were traditionally covered with straw or thatch for which a pitch of between 45 and 60 degrees is most effective. Lack of longitudinal stability was compensated for by a firm layer of organic material. However, the common rafter roof is less suitable for flat tiles or so called over- and under-tiles (monk and nun, hollow tiles). Due to frequent fires, tiled roofs became more common during the fourteenth and fifteenth centuries. A fifteenth century law in the town of Kleve (Germany) advised the demolition of straw-rafters in order for them to be rebuilt solidly, ready for the application of slates or (hollow) tiles.[25] Structural survey of medieval houses confirms the evidence of the written sources; the common rafter roof was unsuited to heavy roofing materials. The experiments with longitudinal plates and trusses is part of the formulation of a roof design stable enough to take heavy overlapping tiles.[26] The appearance of the lighter, single covering (Dutch) pantile in the first half of the sixteenth century (which came after the introduction of the Zwolish 'quackpan' of 1466) made it possible to make timbers lighter, as occurs from the seventeenth century onwards.

CONCLUSION

The starting point for all roof construction was the common rafter roof, with examples in the Netherlands that date back to the thirteenth century. The first trusses are present in monasteries in Maastricht, and Utrecht followed some decades later. The arrival of trusses led to a revolution in building practices. Farmhouses with dug-in posts lasted only a few decades, whereas some of those with trusses on stone pads have survived over several centuries. In the spread and application of trusses there are no noticeable differences between secular buildings and churches. The pure common rafter roof holds out longer in the north-east of the Netherlands and the corresponding lowlands in the north of Germany. Trusses and longitudinal plates arrive simultaneously with the use of tiles or over- and under-tiles, and the need to build firm and stable roofs. Changes in the timberwork or building materials are less spectacular after the fourteenth century, apart from the invention of the Dutch pantile. A striking advance such as that represented by the purlin arrives in the northern town Groningen a few centuries later than in the most southern town of Maastricht. The very gradual introduction offers, in connection with the location, a useful model for the dating of carpentry.[27]

REFERENCES

1. Dr De Vries is working at the Rijksdienst voor de Monumentenzorg, PO Box 1001, NL 3700 BA Zeist.
2. H. Janse, *Houten kappen in Nederland 1000–1940* (Delft/Zeist 1989).
3. H. Janse en L. Devliegher, 'Middeleeuwse bekappingen in het vroegere graafschap Vlaanderen', in *Bulletin van de Koninklijke Commissie voor Monumenten en Landschappen* 13 (1962), 299–380.
4. Executed with the help of a hollow drill (system H. Tisje at Neu Isenberg, Germany) and a computer programme as from 1981.
5. d stands for dendro-dating.
6. e.g. John Fletcher, 'Medieval Timberwork at Ely', in *BAA CT, II* (Leeds 1979), 61.
7. R. W. Brunskill, *Timber Building in Britain* (London 1985).
8. C. A. Rutgers, *Jan van Arkel, Bisschop van Utrecht* (Groningen 1970), 195.
9. Brunskill, op. cit., p. 172: 'Rafter holes (problem holes): holes found sometimes in the sides of common rafters just above the wall plate. The holes do not, as a rule, pass right through the rafter. They may have been intended for spockets or intended to help in some way in the alignment of pairs of rafters'.

10. For instance on the house Zaadmarkt 85, Zutphen, dating back to 1325 (d).
11. Recently Frank van der Waard in Groningen found the same system on Turftorenstraat 8, dendrochronologically dating 1379.
12. D. J. de Vries, *Bouwen in de late middeleeuwen. Stedelijke architectuur in het voormalige Over- en Nedersticht*, Utrecht 1994, 99–102.
13. The latest example with assembly marks using this system is in Deventer in the Kleine Overstraat 46–54, dating back to 1392 (d).
14. For instance in the other way around, the longitudinal plate is placed eccentrically in the roof. The plate (± 1400) is older than the façade of the transept, see Janse (1989), 86.
15. Later on this joint was nailed, but the top of the windbrace and both sides of the curved brace had a mortice-and-tenon joint.
16. Usually this form appears later. This suggestion comes from F. J. van der Waard in Groningen.
17. Also the personal marks have to do with the ownership during transport.
18. In the 'House of the Commandeur II' of the Teutonic Knights house in 1474 (d) already (with the gouge) cut assembly marks but also in Langedijk 14/16 at Vianen from 1464 (d) and Haarlemmerstraat 174 at Leiden from 1477 (d).
19. Truss construction like hammer beams, scissor trusses and the so-called arch braced truss scarcely exist in the Netherlands. There is one great example of the latest type left (reconstructed, late thirteenth century), namely the roof covering the Knights Hall (Ridderzaal) in The Hague.
20. On the nave of the Franciscans church in 1392 (d), the nave of the Dominican church that was built about 1392–97 (d), and the choir of Our Lady at Maastricht which dates from 1436 ± 6 (d).
21. Maastricht, choir of St Mathiuschurch from 1495 (d) for instance.
22. See Janse (1989), 127; possibly to be regarded as the influence of southern carpenters.
23. More over it is proven at Ganzenmarkt 8 in Utrecht that the single floorbeams probably were anchored on a horizontal beam in the middle of the wall.
24. See for more D. J. de Vries, 'Middeleeuwse boerderijplattegronden en de oudste bekende kapconstructies. Vraagtekens bij het onderzoek naar vroege kapconstructies', *Stichting Historisch Boerderij-onderzoek. Jaarverslag 1983*, 45–61.
25. De Vries (1994), 81.
26. See De Vries (1994), 78–81.
27. I thank Sarah Chambers (Utrecht/London) and Julian Munby for correcting this text.

Chimney Friezes in Late-Medieval Utrecht

by H. Defoer

During the medieval period, Utrecht as the only episcopal see was not just the ecclesiastical but also the cultural centre of the northern Netherlands. The arts flourished and artistic production was extensive and of high quality. Sculpture, both in stone and wood, is particularly prominent. In addition, there was a mass-production of the well-known pipeclay figurines. Though much has been lost in the course of time, a number of remarkable sculptured stone chimney friezes survive, albeit often in fragmentary form.

Most of these Utrecht friezes were carved between *c.* 1475 and *c.* 1575, a period when almost every town house would have boasted at least one fireplace. In large rooms such fireplaces could be of monumental proportions. The chimney hood would have had a frieze supported by two consoles reaching down to the floor. Elsewhere in the country such friezes were generally plain, but in Utrecht they tended to have sculptural decoration. The most impressive example can be found in the House St. Hieronymus on the Maliesingel; the fireplace in this house originally came from the Zoudenbalch House on Donkerstraat which had been built between 1467 and 1468 by one of the canons of the Dom, Evert Zoudenbalch.[1] The Centraal Museum in Utrecht houses two reconstructed fireplaces, in addition to a large number of dismantled chimney friezes and fragments.[2] The Catharijneconvent Museum in Utrecht also possesses some chimney friezes, and there is one other in the Rijksmuseum Twenthe in Enschede and two complete and two fragmentary examples in the Rijksmuseum in Amsterdam.[3]

As early as 1948, Bouvy distinguished a link between the remarkable fact that this particular type of chimney frieze with sculptural decoration seems to have been unique to Utrecht, and the building work at the Dom.[4] The period between 1460 and 1520 witnessed a pronounced increase in building activity; the transepts of the church were completed, as was the nave and its side chapels. This building campaign largely coincided with David of Burgundy's episcopate (1456–96). Jacob van der Borch and Cornelis de Wael were, successively, in charge of the building work.[5] The style in which the new parts of the church were constructed was flamboyant, with special emphasis on decorative and figurative sculpture. Unfortunately, most of the figurative sculpture of the Dom was lost, due to the outburst of iconoclasm in 1566, the subsequent purge, and the tornado which hit Utrecht in 1674 and which swept away the nave. Little sculpture now remains *in situ*, and most of that consists of consoles, spandrels and roof bosses.[6] Some sculpture from the Dom is now in the Cathedraal Museum in Utrecht,[7] and recently four roof bosses carved with the evangelist symbols in the Victoria and Albert Museum in London were identified as once belonging to the Dom.[8] Building activity at the Dom must have stimulated the rise of sculptors' workshops, and clearly these cannot have been solely occupied by the work at the Dom. Indeed, the workshops seem to have supplied sculpture to a number of other churches and convents in and around Utrecht. Many remains can still be found in the Centraal Museum. Sculpture was not commissioned solely for church purposes, by chapters, church-wardens and monastic orders, by guilds and religious communities; there were also private secular

*Translated from the Dutch by S. Oostenwyk

patrons, who in particular commissioned memorial tablets to be hung above their tombs as a reminder to relatives to pray for the salvation of their souls. Elsewhere in the country, such memorial tablets take the form of panel paintings, particularly triptychs, now often incorrectly referred to as altar-pieces. Some memorial tablets were made of brass although very few of this kind have survived.[9] Utrecht possesses a large number of memorial tablets carved in stone, some preserved almost intact in spite of the outbreak of iconoclasm which preceded the reformation; among them those salvaged during the demolition of the Mariakerk in the last century and now housed in the Centraal Museum.[10] Most of the memorial tablets discovered during restoration work in churches at Utrecht since the late nineteenth century tend to be rather damaged, like the one for Anthonis Pot in the Van Arkel chapel in the Dom; dating from the early sixteenth century, it served a dual function both as a memorial tablet and an altar-piece.[11]

While these private commissions were still destined for use in churches, the many chimney friezes carved in Utrecht during the fifteenth and sixteenth centuries served a distinctly mundane purpose though they often featured religious iconography; for example, one frieze in the Centraal Museum is decorated with three medallions showing Christ as the Man of Sorrows flanked by angels bearing the instruments of Christ's Passion (Pl. XXXIVa).[12] More commonly, the central medallion contains an image of a saint while the two outer medallions show coats of arms either carried by fantastically dressed attendants or suspended from a hook by a belt.[13] The Virgin and Child is the most popular image (Pl. XXXIVb),[14] often accompanied by St Anne (Pl. XXXIVc.[15] Other saints found on chimney friezes are St Martin, the patron saint of Utrecht,[16] and St Antony Abbot who occurs on two surviving friezes: one fragment in the Centraal Museum is carved with a medallion containing a half-length image of the saint,[17] while a larger piece in the Catharijneconvent Museum features a shallow niche with a scene of the Temptation of St Antony. This niche would originally have been in the middle of the frieze; on the right of the fragment is a carved image of a wildwose and his wife holding a coat of arms, and there would presumably have been a matching pair on the left (Pl. XXXVa).[18]

The depictions of saints on chimney friezes do not merely have a simple devotional purpose; they served as exemplars, exhorting the viewer to a virtuous life. This was certainly true in the case of St Anne who was particularly popular amongst the rising middle classes; she was above all the patron saint of marriage, family and kinship, and her name would have been invoked against infertility and by women eager to bear children. It is therefore not surprising to find so many examples of St Anne above the fireplace where the housewife would prepare the daily meals and thus have been continually reminded of St Anne's virtuous life as wife and mother.[19]

The motive behind the representations of St Antony would also have been more than simply devotional. St Antony was born in Egypt in AD 215; he is generally regarded as the founder of Christian monasticism, though it is not so relevant here. In the west, the veneration of St Antony started to develop under the influence of the order of the Antonites founded in 1095 by a French nobleman whose son had been cured by the saint from a disease known as St Antony's fire. The Antonites concerned themselves above all with caring for the sick, and St Antony himself was regarded as a protector against the plague and other contagious diseases. This explains the frequent occurrence in churches and houses of images of St Antony and other saints such as St Sebastian and St Roch, who were believed to offer effective protection against the plague and other contagious diseases.

On the other hand, pictures of St Antony also served to remind the viewer of the saint's exemplary life of abstinence and steadfastness against the devices of the devil. He spent most of his long life as a hermit in the desert where he is said to have been frequently tempted by devils who harassed and tortured him in various ways. They often appeared to him in the likeness of an attractive woman but Antony was not to be deceived and he continued to live piously and ascetically. There are countless representations of the Temptation of St Antony, which became a particularly popular subject in the later Middle Ages.[20] The familiar image of St Antony on chimney friezes would no doubt have served a dual purpose, both as a protection from contagious diseases and as a warning against lust and fornication. This second aspect is especially prominent in the Catharijneconvent fragment which, in addition to the scene of the saint's Temptation, shows a wildman and his wife holding a tankard. The wildwose couple serve as a contrast to the hermit: to the medieval imagination the figures would have appeared as primitive wild creatures of unbridled lust living an almost animal-like existence.[21] Like St Anne, St Antony was an example to the emancipated middle classes who valued modesty and chastity greatly, as virtues conducive to stability and security. Order and tranquillity were beneficial to trade and industry, and clearly defined family ties were important when it came to negotiating a marriage or settling an inheritance.

The sixteenth century saw the gradual disappearance of the type of chimney frieze showing an image of a saint flanked by coats of arms, often carried by attendants. Instead one finds renaissance ornaments with satyrs and garlands inspired by classical art.[22] New exemplars were chosen in accordance with the spirit of the times; images of the Judgement of Solomon and the chaste Susanna were preferred to the previously popular saints who began to occur less and less frequently.[23] However, two examples of chimney friezes featuring images of saints are known to have come from the Catharijneconvent in Utrecht, which was at one time a convent of the Order of the Knights of St John before the Reformation: one shows the severed head of St John the Baptist on a salver amidst cartouches in the renaissance style, while the other is carved with images of St John the Baptist and St Catherine, the patron saints of the Order.[24]

Like all other medieval sculpture in Utrecht, the chimney friezes were never signed and rarely dated. Only by stylistic analysis is it occasionally possible to date a piece or link it to work by a known master. Obviously, stone carving offers the best comparison but it is also useful to include wood sculpture in the analysis as sculptors commissioned by the Utrecht Guild of Saddlers are known to have worked both in stone and wood.[25]

However, it is not easy to obtain a clear insight into the range of sculpture produced in Utrecht in the late fifteenth and early sixteenth centuries; evidence is simply too fragmentary. The names of many sculptors are known to us through archival research, but the iconoclastic destruction and the stripping of the altars following the reformation make it very hard to link these names to any of the surviving pieces. Attempts have been made to recover the names of artists responsible for sculpture known to have come from the Dom or still *in situ* there, but these are not always successful. Nor has it been possible to compile a clear and coherent book of work for any sculptor known by name,[26] with the exception of Adriaen van Wesel (*c.* 1420–90). The core of this artist's oeuvre consisted of the statues originating from or stylistically connected with the figures from the altarpiece of the Brotherhood of Our Lady at Bois-le-Duc, which was completed by Van Wesel in 1477.[27] Part of the sculpture from this altar has survived and is now for the most part in the Rijksmuseum in Amsterdam (Pl. XXXVb). Van Wesel's figures are recognizable on account of their typically tranquil modest expressions; his saints are gentle rather than harshly ascetic. The lower eyelids are often quite pronounced and their straight, wavy or curly hair often resembles a wig. Van Wesel clearly preferred complicated drapery with shallow folds falling across each other in flat bundles; the folds have soft curves and edges, which rather suggests that the figures are wearing garments made of wool. Besides wood carvings, there are also a number of stone statues which can stylistically be associated with Van Wesel's work although as a group these are less coherent in style and quality. It is often unclear whether these works in stone were actually produced by his own workshop or merely influenced by his style.

We do not know the name of the second sculptor in Utrecht of whose oeuvre we now have a more or less complete picture; he is simply referred to as the Master of the Utrechtse Stenen Vrouwenkop, after the upper part of a figure of the Virgin which originally formed part of a large Annunciation group (Pl. XXXVc.[28] The compilation of this Master's oeuvre, for which J. Leeuwenberg has been largely responsible, evolved from the stone bust, now in the Catharijneconvent Museum.[29] The Master, who was active in the first quarter of the sixteenth century, appears to have inherited Adriaen van Wesel's workshop. He was clearly open to renaissance influences as can be observed in his female figures with their egg-shaped heads, which are rather wide and somewhat bulging at the top and which taper downwards to a pronounced chin. The eyes are pinched and the upper eyelids often arched. The figures regularly displayed quite intricate hairstyles with fashionable head-gear and elaborately enriched clothes. The Master's workshop must have been accomplished and rather specialized in order to produce sculptures of such distinct quality.

A number of chimney friezes can actually be ascribed to Adriaen van Wesel's workshop and to that of the Master of the Utrechtse Stenen Vrouwenkop. The former was probably responsible for the chimney frieze showing the Man of Sorrows with two angels in the Centraal Museum (Pl. XXXIVa) and the fragment with the Temptation of St Antony in the Catharijneconvent Museum (Pl. XXXVa). Both the shallow folds with their soft curves and the faces of the angels and the wildwose's wife with their small almond-shaped eyes are very reminiscent of Van Wesel's other known work; the hair of the wildwose, too, is very similar to that of some of the male figures from the Bois-le-Duc altar.

The Master of the Utrechtse Stenen Vrouwenkop is likely to have been responsible for a chimney frieze from a house that was subsequently incorporated into the city hall. The frieze, which is now in the Centraal Museum (Pl. XXXIVb), shows a central medallion of the Virgin and Child flanked by two attendants in elaborate dress carrying the coats of arms of the Van Asch and Van Gruenenborch families on the left and those of the Van Vianen and Gerstman families on the right.[30] The half-length figure of the Virgin is virtually identical to that on a memorial tablet from the Mariakerk which has been ascribed to the same Master.[31] However, the workmanship on the chimney frieze is much more delicate and detailed, which serves to illustrate the differences in quality within the workshop of this most prolific sculptor.

REFERENCES

1. For the Zoudenbalch House, see 'Archeologische en bouwhistorische kroniek van de gemeente Utrecht', *Maandblad Oud Utrecht*, LV (1982) 2, 27–30. For the chimney from the Zoudenbalch House, see D. P. R. A. Bouvy, *Middeleeuwse beeldhouwkunst in de Noordelijke Nederlanden* (Amsterdam 1948), 77, 78.
2. *Catalogus van het Historisch Museum der Stad* (Utrecht 1928), nos 348, 624, 630, 633, 634, 635, 637, 638, 639, 640, 641, 642, 643, 644, 646, 647, 648, 649, 650, 651, 652, 653, 654, 655, 657, 658, 1241, 1261, 1384, 1535, 3221, 3248. Not included in this catalogue are nos 11177 (frieze with three medallions, the middle

one showing St Martin dividing his cloak and the other two featuring two angels with Philip of Burgundy's coat of arms) and 14748 (frieze showing St Anne with the Virgin and Child).

3. For the Rijksmuseum Het Catharijneconvent, see D. P. R. A. Bouvy, *Beeldhouwkunst Aartsbisschoppelijk Museum Utrecht* (The Hague/Leiden 1962), nos 258 and 263. Also inv. no. BMH bs. 1114, an unpublished fragment featuring a medallion of the Virgin Mary. For the frieze in the Rijksmuseum Twenthe in Enschede, see Bouvy (1948), 93. For the friezes in Amsterdam, see J. Leeuwenberg and W. Halsema-Kubes, *Beeldhouwkunst in the Rijksmuseum* (Amsterdam/The Hague 1973), nos 32, 33, 34, 35.

4. Bouvy (1948), 78.

5. E. J. Haslinghuis and C. J. A. C. Peeters, *De Dom van Utrecht* (The Hague 1965), 341–44. See W. H. Vroom in this volume for the financing of the construction of the Dom in the late Middle Ages. Also W. H. Vroom, *De financiering van de kathedraalbouw in de middeleeuwen; in het bijzonder van de Dom van Utrecht*, Maarssen (1981), 359–60, diagram 2 and 3.

6. Bouvy (1948), fols 94–95, 124, 140–44, 148. Haslinghuis and Peeters 1965, profiles 258–67, 289–91, 354–60.

7. *Catalogus* 1928, 1265, 1271, 1273, 1496, 1497.

8. P. Williamson, 'Roof bosses from Utrecht and Jan van Schayk, Beeldensnijder', *Oud Holland* CV (1991), 140–51.

9. A fine example from *c.* 1500 is the memorial tablet of Henrick van Elverick (d. 1456) and his wife Yda Greve (d. 1446) in the Andreaskerk in Zevenaar. See E. H. Ter Kuile, *De Nederlandse monumenten van geschiedenis en kunst*, vol. III, *De Provincie Gelderland, 2de stuk, het Kwartier van Zutpen* (The Hague 1958), 186–87. The Rijksmuseum Het Catharijneconvent possesses a memorial tablet for Joost van Amstel van Mijnden (d. 1553) and his posthumously born son. See J. Belonje and F. A. Greenhill, 'Some Brasses in Germany and the Low Countries (III)', *Monumental Brass Society Transactions* VII (1960), 379–82. Also F. H. C. Weytens, 'De zwerftocht van een koperen plaat', *Jaarboek Oud-Utrecht* (1965), 57–63 and *Catharijnebrief* II (1983), 3–4.

10. *Catalogue* (1928), nos 1385–89; Bouvy (1948), 92, 144. Also M. van Vlierden, *Utrecht een hemel op aarde*, exhibition catalogue, Rijksmuseum Het Catarijneconvent Utrecht, Zutphen (1988), nos 83, 85–86.

11. The relief has been ascribed to the Master of the Utrecht Stone Female Head; see Bouvy (1948), 142–43; J. Leeuwenberg, 'Een nieuw facet aan de Utrechtse beeldhouwkunst I', *Oud Holland*, LXX (1955), 82–95; Haslinghuis and Peeters (1965), 354–58.

12. *Catalogue* (1928), no. 3248; Bouvy (1948), 93–94; *Middeleeuwse kunst der Noordelijke Nederlanden*, exhibition catalogue, Rijksmuseum Amsterdam, Amsterdam (1958), no. 308; W. Halsema-Kubes, G. Lemmens, G. de Werd, *Adriaen van Wesel, een Utrechts beeldhouwer uit de late middeleleeuwen*, exhibition catalogue, Rijksmuseum Amsterdam (The Hague 1980), no. 50.

13. *Catalogus* (1928), nos 633, 634, 639, 641, 644, 647, 648, 652, 657; D. P. R. A. Bouvy, *Beeldhouwkunst Aartsbisschoppelijk Museum Utrecht* (The Hague/Leiden 1962), no. 258; Leeuwenberg and Halsema (1973), nos 32, 33, 34.

14. *Catalogus* (1928), nos 630, 633, 634, 635, 638, 641, 644; Bouvy (1962), 258; Leeuwenberg and Halsema (1973), nos 32, 33, 35. The Catharijneconvent has two stone tondi of the Virgin, which were once believed to be fragments of chimney friezes (inv. nos ABM bs.603a and 603b; Bouvy (1962) nos 244–45). It is much more likely, however, that these are actually roof bosses, as Williamson already showed for inv. no. ABM bs.603b; see Williamson (1991), esp. 114.

15. The Centraal Museum possesses three examples of friezes showing St Anne with the Virgin and Child; besides inv. nos 647, 657 listed in *Catalogus* (1928), there is a third one which has not been listed, *viz.* inv. no. 14748. The Rijksmuseum Het Catharijneconvent also has a fragment with the figure of St Anne with the Virgin and Child; see Bouvy (1962), no. 263.

16. Two examples with St Martin can be found in the Centraal Museum; see *Catalogus* (1928), no. 642, and inv. no. 11177 which was not included in the catalogue.

17. *Catalogus* (1928), no. 3221; H. L. M. Defoer, 'Een laat-middeleeuws schoorsteenfries uit Utrecht met de bekoring van Antonius', *Nederlands Kunsthistorisch Jaarboek 1994*, vol. 45, Zwolle (1994), 306.

18. Defoer, *ibid.*, passim. This fragment was found broken in two by two city dustmen in 1991; it had been thrown into a rubbish container on the Oudegracht in Utrecht as building waste during the conversion of the medieval cellar of the former Leeuwenberg House (Oudegracht 147), which was demolished in the nineteenth century. Fortunately, the finders realized the potential importance of these two pieces and took them to the Archeologisch and Bouwhistorisch Centrum of the city of Utrecht, which in its turn contacted the Rijksmuseum Het Catharijneconvent where the relief was restored and included in the collection.

19. T. Brandenbarg, 'St. Anna en haar familie. De Annaverering in verband met opvattingen over huwelijk en gezin in de vroeg-moderne tijd', *Tussen heks en heilige*, exhibition catalogue, Commanderie van St Jan

Nijmegen (1985), 101–27; T. Brandenbarg, 'Heilig familieleven in de late middeleeuwen', *Helse en hemelse vrouwen*, exhibition catalogue, Rijksmuseum Het Catharijneconvent (Utrecht 1988), 52–64; T. Brandenbarg, *Heilig familieleven*, Nijmegen (1990), 140–44; T. Brandenbarg, *Heilige Anna, grote moeder*, exhibition catalogue, Museum voor Religieuze Kunst Uden, Nijmegen (1992), 32.

20. For the iconography of St Antony [the Great], see a.o. Louis Réau, *Iconographie de l'art chrétien*, III, Paris (1958), 101–15; also *Lexikon der christlichen Ikonographie*, V, W. Braunfels ed. (Rome/Freiburg/Basle/Vienna 1973), 205–17. For the Temptation of St Antony and its moralistic significance in the late Middle Ages, see L. Dressen-Coenders, 'De heks als duivelsboel. Over het ontstaan van de angst voor heksen en de bescherming tegen beheksing', *Tussen heks en heilige*, 59–82; B. J. C. Ettes, 'De vleescelike becoringhe van Antonius de kluizenaar', *Helse en hemelse vrouwen*, 21–39.

21. R. Bernheimer, *Wildman in the Middle Ages: A Study in Art, Sentiment and Demonology* (Cambridge, Mass. 1952), 47–48; J. P. Filedt Kok *et al.*, *'s Levens felheid: de Meester van het Amsterdamse Kabinet of de Hausbuch-meester*, exhibition catalogue (Rijksmuseum Amsterdam, Maarssen (1985), 144–45.

22. *Catalogus* (1928), nos 624, 640, 643, 646.

23. *Ibid.* nos 348, 650, 1261, 1384.

24. The fragment with St John the Baptist's head on a salver originally came from the former house of the last 'balijer' [bailiff], Hendrick Barck (1561–1602) and is now in the Rijksmuseum Het Catharijneconvent. The second frieze, now in the Centraal Museum, was found in a house on the Hamburgerstraat but must originally have come from the nearby Catharijneconvent. See Paul Dirkse, 'Nieuw beeldmateriaal over Hendrick Barck, Balijer van het Utrechtse Catharijneconvent', *Jaarboek Oud-Utrecht* (1986), 78–92; Defoer, 308–9.

25. This sometimes caused conflicts between the saddlers' and the stone-masons' guilds; see 'De gilden van Utrecht tot 1528. Verzameling van Rechtsbronnen uitgegeven door Mrs J.C. Overvoorde en J.G.Ch. Joosting I', *Werken der vereeniging tot uitgave der bronnen van het oude vaderlandsche recht, gevestigd te Utrecht*, first series, XIX (The Hague, 1897), 312–14. For the regulations within the saddlers' guild in the sixteenth century, see 'Schildersvereeningingen te Utrecht. Bescheiden uit het Gemeentearchief' in *De Utrechtse archieven II*, ed. S. Muller Fz (Utrecht 1880), 44–49.

26. For example, the five stone figures from the Dom, which are now in the Centraal Museum, have often been attributed to Jan Nude, Bude, Uude or Vude who, according to documents in the Dom archives, supplied five statues for the tabernacle (not the rood-loft) in 1450; see Haslinghuis and Peeters (1965), 360–62 and Halsema *et al.*, 22. However, this attribution has been challenged, quite rightly in my opinion, J. van Cauteren, *Utrecht een hemel op aarde*, no. 72. Also A. de Groot, 'Beelden in de Dom van Utrecht in dezestiende eeuw', *Nederlands Kunsthistorische Jaarboek*, 1994, vol. 45, Zwolle (1994), 48–51. Convincing is P. Williamson's attribution (1991) to Jan van Schayck of eight roof bosses featuring four church-fathers and the four evangelist symbols, of which the former are now in the Centraal Museum in Utrecht and the latter in the Victoria and Albert Museum, London. Also plausible is P. van Vlijmen's attribution of the Holy Sepulchre in the Dom and the Holy Sepulchre in the Petruskerk in Woerden to Gherit Splintersz.; see P. van Vlijmen, *De graflegging te Woerden*, Woerden (1982), typescript p. 45.

27. The name of the artist responsible for the altar from Bois-le-Duc was not known initially until Swillens revealed his identity in 1948. Previously, the then anonymous sculptor had been generally referred to as the Master of the Musical Angels. See W. Vogelsang, 'Noord-Nederlandsche beeldhouwwerken', *Oudheidkundig Jaarboek*, V (1925), 185–200; Bouvy (1948), 72–75; J. Leeuwenberg, 'Het werk van de Meester der Musicerende Engelen en het vraagstuk van Jacob van der Borch opnieuw beschouwd', *Oud Holland*, LXIII (1948), 164–79; P. T. A. Swillens, 'De Utrechtse beeldhouwer Adriaen van Wesel, ca 1420–(na 1489)', *Oud Holland* LXIII (1948), 149–63; P. T. A. Swillens, 'De Utrechtse beeldhouwer Adriaen van Wesel. Enige aanvullende mededelingen', *Oud Holland*, LXVI (1951), 228–33; Halsema *et al.*; *In Buscoducis*, exhibition catalogue, Noordbrabants Museum 's-Hertogenbosch (Maarssen 1990), 29 and nos 133–38.

28. Inv. no. ABM bs. 604; Bouvy (1962), no. 268.

29. For the main literature on the oeuvre of this sculptor see Bouvy (1948), 143–45; Leeuwenberg (1955), 82–95; J. Leeuwenberg, 'Eeen nieuw facet aan de Utrechtse beeldhouwkunst II', *Oud Holland*, LXXII (1957), 56–58; *Middeleeuwse Kunst der Noordelijke Nederlanden* 210–15; J. Leeuwenberg, 'Een nieuw facet aan de Utrechtse beeldhouwkunst III', *Oud Holland* LXXIV (1959), 79–102; J. Leeuwenberg, 'Een nieuw facet aan de Utrechtse beeldhouwkunst IV', *Oud Holland* LXXV (1960), 195–204; J. Leeuwenberg, 'Een nieuw facet aan de Utrechtse beeldhouwkunst V', *Oud Holland*, LXXVII (1962), 79–99; Bouvy (1962) nos 109, 257, 267, 268.

30. *Catalogus* 1928, no. 644; Bouvy (1948), 145; Leeuwenberg (1957), 58.

31. *Catalogus* 1928, no. 1389; Bouvy (1948), 145; Leeuwenberg (1955), 91–92; Van Vlierden, no. 86.

Adriaen van Wesel and the Sculpture of the Mariakerk in Utrecht

by Jan W. Klinckaert

A delicately sculpted stone console, representing two angels, bearing a coat of arms, was recently shown at a exhibition in Utrecht. (Pl. XXXVI)[1] The angels, barefooted but fully dressed in feather coats, with two pairs of wings can be recognized as cherubim.[2] The coat of arms is quartered and bears three violins, an inverted point, a beam and an eight-pointed star. At the bottom of the console, clouds are indicated by a few curly lines, composed around a hexagon, which clearly formed the connection point to a hexagonal column or a decorative element. The console has been extensively restored, especially the faces of the two cherubim.

The cherubim console was one of the first objects acquired by the Centraal Museum Utrecht at the time of its first opening in 1838.[3] In the first catalogue of 1838, the console is described as a 'kapiteel stuk à console, met wapen', originating from the Mariakerk in Utrecht, demolished in 1813.[4] This monumental romanesque church was built in the eleventh and twelfth centuries under Bishop Conrad and King (and later Emperor) Henry IV. In 1813 it was sold by order of Napoleon, shortly after the abolition of the chapters in Utrecht. Between 1813 and 1816 both nave and transept of the church were pulled down; the choir only in 1844–45.[5] Fortunately, the church inspired several artists to make drawings. One of Pieter Saenredam's (1597–1665) series of drawings of the church shows the interior of the nave with a sculpted console above each column, similar to the cherubim console, now preserved at the Centraal Museum.[6] Each console carried a statue, crowned by a sculpted canopy. At the end of the eighteenth century another artist, C. van Hardenbergh, made a sketch of the central part of the nave, seen from the south — an angle not shown in the drawings of Saenredam (Pl. XXXVIIA).[7] In the left-hand margin, Van Hardenbergh made an enlarged and more detailed sketch of the console, seen in the general view on the right. It is beyond any doubt that this is identical to the cherubim console, now at the Centraal Museum.

As usual in medieval churches, the making and installing of statues was paid for by important and wealthy people, who often illustrated their donation by having their coats of arms shown on the console of the statue.[8] In the collegiate churches in Utrecht, these donators were usually canons. In this respect, however, the cherubim console forms a remarkable exception. The coat of arms shown can be traced and identified via the 'Monumenta passim in templis . . .', an important heraldic work, composed c. 1600 by the Utrecht lawyer Arnold van Buchell.[9] This manuscript, gives a detailed inventory of all heraldic monuments to be found in Utrecht churches at that time. Van Buchell made a full-colour drawing of the coat of arms of our cherubim console, which he had found on a column in the Mariakerk, together with the accompanying commemorative text of Petrus Ramp 'canonicus', who died on 24 September 1488. The tombstone of this canon, decorated with the same coat of arms, was found in the pavement near this column (Pl. XXXVIIB).[9] According to the protocols of the Chapter of Our Lady, the canon Petrus Ramp, master of arts and medicine, indeed died in the night of 24 September 1488. His executors had him buried in the Mariakerk in Utrecht 'subtus imaginem Sancti Jacobi'.[10] In other words, the cherubim console, with the coat of arms of Petrus Ramp, originally carried a statue of St James, which obviously already existed at the time of Ramp's death in 1488. In fact, the making of this statue and console must be related to a chapter sentence of 24 April 1475 in a case between Petrus Ramp and Johannes Thiderici. In a fight this Johannes Thiderici had seriously injured Petrus Ramp. The Chapter of the Mariakerk, in council with representatives of the town of Utrecht, therefore sentenced Johannes Thiderici, not only to implore forgiveness and to compensate the medical costs made by Petrus Ramp, but also to have placed, within two years, a stone statue in a place in the church designated by the Chapter. This statue had to be similar to certain statues in the choir of the church. It should be painted just like the statue of St Ursula, standing in the same choir, and decorated with the coat of arms of the canon Petrus Ramp.[11] It is beyond reasonable doubt that this statue, made for Petrus Ramp between 1475 and 1477, is the same as the statue of St James, at the foot of which Petrus Ramp was buried in 1488. As a result, the preserved cherubim console, which originally carried this statue, can be dated between 1475 and 1477.

The cherubim console is a most delicate piece of sculpture. Though restricted by the almost cubistic outline of the console, the angels are represented in a natural and elegant posture, holding a great coat of arms in both hands, the legs and wings interlaced in a comfortable sitting position. The figures have been sculpted with great care and eye for detail, e.g. in the representation of the structure of each feather. Although partly restored with a plasterlike material, both heads of the cherubim, in their delicacy and sensitive freshness, still bear witness to the great skill of the sculptor. This is best shown in the head of the left-hand and least restored figure. In the broad oval face, the almond-shaped eyes are bordered by lightly indicated eyelids and placed under high eyebrows. The restored nose is sharp and long, the mouth small and slightly opened. Most characteristic are the high convex forehead and the lightly swollen cheeks ending in a small pointed chin. The long, almost wig-like hair of the figure is parted in the middle of the head and falls onto the shoulders in long and curly locks. This facial type and hair-dress is often found in the Utrecht sculpture of the third quarter of the fifteenth century. Examples can be found in the elegant statue of St Agnes (c. 1455) (Centraal Museum Utrecht, inv. nr. C 1928/1271), attributed to the Utrecht sculptor Jan Uude, or in the wild woman bearing a coat of arms beneath the statue of St Martin in the porch sculpture (c. 1468), now in the Hieronymus House in Utrecht but originally from the House of Zoudenbalch. The cherubim figures of the Utrecht console, however, show closest affinity to a zetable fragment, representing three musician angels and a male figure (St Joseph), preserved at the Rijksmuseum Amsterdam (inv. nr. N.M. 11647). (Pl. XXXVB).

The resemblance of the facial features of the left-hand and, especially of the right-hand cherub of the Utrecht console — though heavily restored — to that of the angel playing the clavichord of the retable fragment is striking indeed. The fragment, undoubtedly part of a Nativity scene, was made by the famous Utrecht sculptor Adriaen van Wessel (c. 1417–c. 1490).[12] It is assumed that this fragment formed part of the great altarpiece, which Adriaen van Wesel made in 1475–77 for the Brotherhood of Our Lady at 's-Hertogenbosch. The kinship between the cherubim console and the retable fragment is so close that one might attribute the cherubim console to master Adriaen himself. However, the less vivid expression and the more graphically sculpted features of the figures on the console, point to an attribution to the workshop of Adriaen van Wesel or at least to a sculptor, who was directly inspired and greatly influenced by the art of Adriaen van Wesel.

Adriaen van Wesel was not only an important sculptor, who is especially known for his large altarpieces in the region of Utrecht and beyond, he also was a respected citizen of Utrecht, who more than once during his career held important guild and municipal offices.[13] The chapter of the Mariakerk in Utrecht was certainly acquainted with the person and the art of Adriaen van Wesel. Moreover, Adriaen van Wesel is even said to be the maker of the sculpted altarpiece for the high altar of the collegiate church of this chapter. This statement is based on a reference in an old record concerning the commissioning of a high altar for the New Church of Delft to Adriaen van Wesel, quoted in 1667 by Dirck van Bleyswijck in his 'Beschryvinge der stadt Delft'.[14] According to this reference, Adriaen van Wesel, in 1484, received the commission for making a high altar for the New Church of Delft, similar to the one he had made before 'tot Sinte Marien upt hoech Outair'. It has been assumed, until the present, that nothing more is known about the high altar made by Adriaen van Wesel for the Mariakerk in Utrecht. However, the amateur historian G. G. Calkoen (1857–1935), who, in the first quarter of the twentieth century gathered valuable record annotations on the five collegiate churches of Utrecht, already in 1916–17 mentioned the commissioning of an altarpiece by the chapter of the Mariakerk to Adriaen van Wesel in 1471.[15] G. G. Calkoen referred to the protocols of the chapter of the Mariakerk, already mentioned. According to this document, an agreement was made on 16 December 1471 by the chapter of the Mariakerk with Adriaen van Wesel for the making of a 'tabula' for the high altar of the collegiate church (Appendix, fig. 6). For this work, the sculptor would receive 400 rhenish guilders, upon inspection of the piece by two 'expertos in illa arte'. The amount of money, which Van Wesel earned for this commission, is comparable to that of other commissions. For the altarpiece, made for the Brotherhood of Our Lady in 's-Hertogenbosch between 1475–77, he was finally paid 386 rhenish guilders. For another altarpiece, made by order of Bishop David of Burgundy for the monastery St Agnietenberg near Zwolle in 1487, 325 rhenish guilders were paid.[16] In view of their comparable price, the high altar of the Mariakerk in Utrecht probably was about the same size as the other two altarpieces. The hypothetical reconstruction of the altarpiece for the Brotherhood of Our Lady in 's-Hertogenbosch, recently made by W. Halsema-Kubes, integrating some preserved fragments of this altarpiece, gives a good impression of the size of the altar, made for the Mariakerk in Utrecht.[17] Because it was destined for a church dedicated to Our Lady, the Utrecht altarpiece probably represented scenes of the life of Our Lady, just as the altarpiece in 's-Hertogenbosch.

The rediscovery of the document, concerning the commissioning of an altarpiece for the Mariakerk in Utrecht to Adriaen van Wesel considerably extends our knowledge of the life and work of this important and influential Utrecht sculptor. It reveals at the same time the oldest reference to his work as a sculptor.

APPENDIX

Anno lxxi-o

de tabula altarum

Summum
altare
locatur
faciendum
400 flor.

xvi-a decembris conventum est inter capitulum et Adrianum de Wesel super tabula per Adrianum predictum ad altare maius ecclesie nostre facienda

Tantum modo que ipse Adrianus dictam tabulam faciet ac suis expensis totam in ligno et ferro ac reliquis necessariis deliberabit in altari predicto pro quo et quibus habebit a capitulo iiii-c flor. Renen. xx stuf. pro flor. computum. Salvo que extunc capitulum eliget duos magistros expertos in illa arte et ipse duos qui huiusmodi tabulam mature inspicient ac se iuxta dictamen plus vel minus de predicta somma mervent plus vel minus quantum illi iiii-or dictaverunt habebit. Actum in domo capitulari presentes magistro Roberto Thiderici et Wilhelmo Tonss.

(Rijksarchief Utrecht, Archief van het kapittel van Sint Marie inv. nr. 40–6)

REFERENCES

1. *Beelden uit een bisschopsstad. Utrechtse beeldhouwkunst uit de middeleeuwen en de renaissance*, exhib. Centraal Museum Utrecht, 10 December 1994–19 February 1995, no. 58. Centraal Museum Utrecht, inv. no. C 1928/1385; limestone, traces of polychromy and gilding; 42.0 × 43.5 × 28.5 cm; both faces and the left arm of the right-hand figure restored.

2. L. Réau, *Iconographie de l'Art Chrétien*, t. II, 1 (Paris, 1956), 40–41.

3. The cherubim console was acquired in August 1838 from the Utrecht architect Christian Kramm, who earlier that year bought it from M. L. M. van Hangest Baron d'Yvoy (Gemeentelijke Archiefdienst Utrecht, Archief van de Gemeentelijke Fotodienst, inv. no. 246; Rijksprentenkabinet Amsterdam, coll. autografen, M. L. M. d'Yvoy).

4. *Verzameling van Oud Beeldwerk en andere Oudheden Schilderijen en Teekeningen, meestal tot de Stad Utrecht betrekking hebbende, behoorende tot het archief derzelver stad*, (Utrecht, [1838]), p. 4, no. 7.

5. H. M. Haverkate and C. J. van der Peet, *Een kerk van papier. De geschiedenis van de voormalige Mariakerk te Utrecht* (Zutphen–Utrecht 1985).

6. Cf. the drawings at the Museen Preussischer Kulturbesitz, Kupferstichkabinett in Berlin or at the Gemeentelijke Archiefdienst Utrecht, Topografische Atlas Utrecht (cat. no. TA, Id 4.18).

7. Gemeentelijke Archiefdienst Utrecht, Topografische Atlas Utrecht, cat. no. TA Id 4.34.

8. See A. de Groot, 'Beelden in de Dom van Utrecht in de zestiende eeuw', *Nederlands Kunsthistorsch Jaarboek*, 45 (1994), 38–97.

9. A. Buchelius, *Monumenta passim in templis ac monasteriis Trajectinae Urbis atque agri inventa*, Ms Utrecht *c.* 1600 (G.A.U., Bibl. XXVIII–LI), fol. 64.

10. Rijksarchief Utrecht, Archief van het kapittel van Sint Marie, inv. no. 40–6, fol. 92$^{\rm v}$.

11. R. A. U., Archief van het Kapittel van Sint Marie, inv. no. 40–46, fol. 31. See also G. G. Calkoen, *De kapittelkerk van St. Marie te Utrecht*, II (Utrecht 1916–17) [uned. Ms Gemeentelijke Archiefdienst Utrecht], p. 39, who concludes that this Johannes Thiderici might have been a sculptor himself.

12. *Adriaen van Wesel* (1980–81) *Adriaen van Wesel (ca 1417/ca 1490). Een Utrechtse beeldhouwer uit de late middeleeuwen*, exh. cat. Amsterdam Rijksmuseum (1980–81). p. 16, no. 1.

13. Adriaen van Wesel made altarpieces for the Brotherhood of Our Lady in 's-Hertogenbosch (1475–77), the New Church in Delft (1484), the monastery of St Agnietenberg near Zwolle (1487), three statues for the high altar of the Buurkerk in Utrecht (1487) and a sculpted predella for the high altar of the Utrecht Dom (1489). Nine times, he was chosen to be one of the two aldermen or chairmen of the Saddlers' Guild in Utrecht, to which the painters and sculptors also belonged. Several times he also was a member of the Municipal Council. In 1481 he even became the head of one of the districts of Utrecht. (see e.g. *Adriaen van Wesel* (1980–81), 11–13).

14. D. van Bleyswijck, *Beschryvinge der stadt Delft* (Delft 1667), 209. (see also *Adriaen van Wesel* (1980–81), 60).

15. G. G. Calkoen (1916–17), 60.

16. *Adriaen van Wesel* (1980–81), 11, 34–43, 55–61.

17. W. Halsema-Kubes, 'Der Altar Adriaen van Wesels aus 's-Hertogenbosch. Rekonstruktion und kunstgeschichtliche Bedeutung', *Flügelaltäre des späten Mittelalters* ed. H. Krohm and Oellerman (Berlin 1991), 144–56.

The Treasury of the Utrecht *Dom* Cathedral, a Review of the Treasures from extant Sacristy Inventories

by Louise E. van den Bergh-Hoogterp

Virtually nothing has survived of the medieval treasure which once belonged to the largest and for a long time the only cathedral of the Northern Netherlands, the *Maartensdom* in Utrecht (Pl. XXXVIIB). However, sacristy inventories, building accounts from 1395 onwards and a few deeds of donation provide enough facts and clues for a reconstruction.[1] The treasure consisted partly of silver objects, most of which were made in Utrecht: the city was an important centre for the production of secular silver and church plate in the late Middle Ages. Recent research has shown that in most cases the 'clenodia' of the Utrecht churches were commissioned from local gold and silversmiths.

The sacristy inventories, written in Latin, date from 1498/99, 1504 (two copies), 1530, 1543 and 1571 (four copies). One copy of the 1571 inventory bears comments written in the margin in 1574 and an additional text dating from 1578/79. Only a partial copy of an earlier inventory dating from 1497 has survived, made by the Utrecht historian Aernout van Buchel (1565–1641).[2] The inventories of the *Dom* derive their importance from the comprehensive nature of the series and the detail in which they are recorded. They give us a near-complete picture of the treasure, which remained intact until the last quarter of the sixteenth century. In 1578, seven years after the inventory of 1571 was drawn up, all the gold and silver objects were lost to the smelting furnaces of Utrecht Mint. Not a single chalice or candlestick, reliquary chest or bust survived. The annotated copy of the final inventory records these tragic events (Pl. XXXVIIIA).

Yet the sixteenth century had begun prosperously for the Utrecht *Dom*. The large cathedral building was almost finished by the start of the century. A large silver chest for the relics of St Pontian, in the cathedral's possession since the tenth century, was completed in 1502.[3] The commission for the chest had been awarded around 1460 to the Utrecht craftsman Tyman IJsbrantsz, the regular goldsmith of the chapter. For various reasons he was unable to complete the work. His successor, the goldsmith Abell Wernersz van der Vechte (active 1493–1540) finally delivered the large reliquary chest, with its many silver figures, after more than forty years.[4] In 1502 he took the various separate sections from his workshop to the cathedral, where each was carefully weighed in the presence of chapter representatives. Then the chest was assembled for the relics to be placed inside.[5] In the early decades of the sixteenth century several other interesting silver reliquaries were added to the treasure, such as the busts of St Adrian and St Blasius and a rock-crystal holder for the relic of St Martin which had been acquired in France in 1520.[6] The chapter put out these commissions to its regular goldsmith 'Abell the goldsmith', who also made for the chapter seven silver altar candlesticks, carrying poles for processional crosses and a reliquary for an arm of St Martin which the chapter planned to donate to the cloister of Cognac.

After 1530 the number of commissions awarded to Utrecht goldsmiths fell. Around this time the chapter's income dropped sharply as a result of the general economic malaise.[7] The interior of the cathedral was stripped at the end of the sixteenth century.[8] In order to free its assets, the chapter had its precious metal objects melted down. The Utrecht *Dom* treasures thus suffered the same fate as most other medieval church treasures in Europe.

THE CHAPTER TREASURES AND THEIR IMPORTANCE

The valuables of the Cathedral had been amassed over the course of many centuries. Such a collection of precious objects had more than a purely religious function — it also played an important role as a financial reserve. The term *thesaurus*, which recurs in many documents must therefore be taken literally to mean an emergency capital reserve.[9] The inventories of the cathedral treasure rooms, usually drawn up for the *custos camere* or sacristan, had a primarily practical, financial purpose: they recorded the monetary value of unminted precious metals. The value was indicated by listing their weight. Similarly, the precious stones set into each object were carefully counted to complete its valuation. Such 'checklists' were drawn up when a new administrator took up his post. Alternatively, notes could be added in the margins of an old list.

Most ecclesiastical inventories do not focus on collections of relics. These are recorded in other sources, such as the instructions on the order in which relics should be displayed or reports of processions.[10] Even so, we do find a number of relics recorded on the list of objects in the charge of the *custos indulgenciarum* (the administrator of indulgencies).[11] Despite several attempts, the *Dom* never really managed to attract many pilgrims. It may be that the prelates were not business-minded enough to make the most of their sacred treasures in the city of Utrecht itself.

Most of the objects described in the inventories had a functional character. They were intended for the service (the 'officium') or for the decoration of the building (the 'ornamentum').[12]

SACRISTY AND TREASURE ROOM

The introduction to all sacristy inventories reads: *Inventarium clenodiorum et ornamentorum que reservantur in sacristia seu thesauraria ecclesie Trajectensis.*[13] Two categories of objects are mentioned, the 'clenodia' and the 'ornamenta'. The first of these refers to the precious metals held by the chapter, the second to its other valuable objects. The fine damask altar cloths and priestly robes embroidered with gold thread belonged to the class of ornaments.[14]

The same introductory sentence also mentions a place in which the valuable objects were stored: 'in the sacristy or treasure room' (*thesauraria*). As the inventory continues it becomes clear that the room — or complex of rooms — served both as a storage place for objects which needed to be kept within reach and as a kind of safe for the chapter's valuables.

The objects which were reckoned to be the most valuable were kept behind an 'iron door', as may be concluded from the introduction to the following section.[15] In view of the many objects it contained, some of them impressive in size, this secure room must itself have been quite large.

According to the accounts of the rebuilding of the gothic cathedral, the 'new' sacristy was not taken into use until a late stage.[16] A 'treasure room' as such is not mentioned in these accounts, but it is probable that a separate room which could be locked was built as part of the sacristy complex.[17] Originally, this 'new sacristy' could only be reached through a rectangular passageway in the burial chapel of Frederik van Sierck (Bishop 1318–22). In the mid-fifteenth century a new entrance to the sacristy was established through the northern choir aisle, linking it to the burial chapel of *Dom* provost Florens van Jutfaas.[18] In 1497 the new entrance was enhanced with the addition of a wooden door carved by Jan van Schayck (Pl. XXXVIIIB). Between 1496 and 1498 the complete interior of the enlarged sacristy was embellished with figures and capitals. It is this room which functioned as the storage room for the cathedral treasure.

THE INVENTORIES

In all the inventories, with the exception of the 1530 document, we find the objects arranged in the same order according to type. The drafter of the inventory regularly adds the word *antiquus* (old) to his brief descriptions. In a few cases he notes that an object is of recent date by adding the words *noviter factum*. The inventories begin with a summary of the paraments, consisting of valuable priestly robes, often with *aurifrisia* embroidered in gold.[19] Some of the copes were then already hundreds of years old, for instance the *cappa* 'once worn by Bishop Gwijde of Avesnes, embroidered with scenes in needlework'. Bishop Gwijde died in 1317; one of the shoes which belonged to his episcopal costume has survived (Pl. XXXVIIIc).[20]

The next section '*de mappis*' concerns the (altar) cloths and cushions embroidered with coats of arms, which items are followed by the chapter's collection of books. Under *De libris in sacristia* we find 'firstly the evangelistary written in gold letters, with a binding of gilded silver showing scenes of the Crucifixion, of Mary and John the Evangelist, surrounded with [precious] stones and gems'. We also learn that the book was newly made and that the whole was kept in a wooden box.[21]

The next section is about the precious objects of gold and silver.[22] The first to be listed is the 'Small Stall of Bethlehem', a gift made by David of Burgundy in 1489. The highly detailed description, copied from David's own *Diversorium*, recurs in all the inventories from 1504 onwards. A priceless small devotional altar, made of enamelled gold and encrusted with precious stones and pearls, contained relics of the Virgin.[23] It stood in the sacristy along with the accompanying lined and fitted chest, possibly in the wall cabinet (the *armarium* which is mentioned repeatedly). There were also various crucifixes in the room. The fourth item to be listed is a cross which 'was once donated by Bishop Jan van Arkel', who held the post between 1342 and 1364, The name of the donor is still mentioned in the inventory of 1571. Among other objects, the cross contained the relics of St Thomas Becket, which could also be displayed separately.[24] It is not known how or when the Utrecht cathedral came into possession of the relics of Thomas of Canterbury (1117–70), who was canonized in 1172. However, it is interesting that the church of St Thomas, one of the oldest in Utrecht, derives its patronage from the so-called *Dom* tablets which date from shortly after 1174.[25] According to tradition, two crosses set with precious stones were donated to the cathedral by Bishop Burkhard (1100–12). They are still to be found in the inventories, described as a pair, although the bishop's name is no longer mentioned.[26] Also listed are five (processional) crosses with their carrying poles (*baculi*), two of which were fitted with silver in 1513 by Abell van der Vechte. Other objects recorded are chalices with patens, censers, including one of copper, and altar cruets with their basins.

De argento in summo altari

The next items on the inventories are the silver objects on the high altar. According to the description of 1504, the altar was adorned with a crucifixion group. Silver figures of Mary and John the Evangelist stood on either side of the Christ figure on the cross. Beside them were placed the silver figures of St Martin and St Jerome — the latter, according to the inventory, donated by canon Willem Paedse — and the figures of Mary Magdalene and St Agnes. The figure of Agnes was bequeathed by Johannes van Drakenborch in 1498. The figures of Mary, John and Mary Magdalene no longer appear on the inventory of 1571. By this stage we find only the figure of St Margaret made in 1523 in the 'safe'.[27]

In janua ferrea

Finally, each of the inventories lists what are presumably the most precious possessions of the chapter, under the heading *Sequuntur ea, que adhuc sunt de auro et argento in janua ferrea*.[28] The first to be named is the golden cross with precious stones (of the type *crux gemmata*), which we can identify as the *Crux optima* from the twelfth century. It may have been donated personally by Emperor Henry II when the cathedral was consecrated in 1023.[29] This section also includes the chapter's golden chalice. The chapter had been able to commission the piece from goldsmith Willem van der Meer in 1485 after a donation of money.[30] In all the inventories the chalice is linked to the name of Vrouwe van der Eem, possibly the same person as Margaretha van Arkel.[31] Also mentioned here is the large tower monstrance which held a relic of cathedral patron St Martin which was acquired in Cognac in 1520.[32] There follows a rather older but no less important piece dating from the fourteenth century.[33] From a deed of donation dating from 1375, in which the piece is referred to as a *jocale seu clenogium* — a jewel or precious object — we know that it was a host monstrance of great value, decorated with precious stones.[34] The inventory of 1571 notes that this '*cyborium* for the holy Sacrament' was mostly 'taken outside the city', possibly for indulgence processions or processions. Bishop Gwijde's staff and mitre set with precious stones which date from the early fourteenth century were also kept 'behind the iron door'. The last inventory of 1571 shows that the room also contained the silver reliquary 'heads' of St Adrian and St Blasius, dated 1504 and 1512, respectively, as well as the large silver chests of St Agnes (completed in 1409) and St Pontian (completed in 1502).

THE HISTORICAL COMPONENTS

From the final inventory of 1571 we can conclude that at that time the *Dom* still possessed objects from the Romanesque period. Objects dating from after the gothic rebuilding of the cathedral (1254) can also be identified as such in the inventories. The pieces produced after 1395 can be traced using the church accounts which have survived; these include the (fifteenth-century) commissions for the shrines of St Agnes and St Pontian. The objects dating from the early sixteenth century appear in the inventories after 1530; they can also be found in the church accounts. As we have seen, the commissions awarded before that date went to the Utrecht goldsmith Abell van der Vechte. From the 1547 and 1571 inventories it is clear that personal communion cups bequeathed to the chapter were virtually the only objects to be added to the cathedral's treasure after 1530.[35]

THE FUNCTION OF THE CATHEDRAL TREASURE IN THE SIXTEENTH CENTURY

Upon study of the final inventory of 1571, the question arises how the treasure was used in the sixteenth century. From the sparse details available it can be deduced that the relics in their silver casings, including the large chests, were regularly paraded through the city, for instance during the regular processions held on the feast days of Mary Magdalene, St Agnes and St Pontian. There were also special processions such as the one held in 1501 after 'signs [omens] that great plagues are to be feared' or another held in 1535 during the ascendancy of the Anabaptists in Munster in order to 'preserve the Christian religion'.[36] Van Buchel reports much later that the silver chests containing St Pontian's relics could barely be carried by four men.[37] Although the financial position of the chapter deteriorated rapidly after 1530, it is still my impression that efforts were made to keep the objects in the treasure room and the sacristy in good order. In the years from 1560 to 1565, for example, many repairs were made to the sacristy objects on site. Almost all the objects there at the time are recorded on the invoices of goldsmith Vincent Willemsz.[38] In view of the care devoted to the conservation of the objects in those years, it is all the more remarkable that the chapter should so systematically melt everything down barely twelve years later. The immediate reason, according to the resolutions, was to reasonably cover the chapter's own debts; later the destruction of the treasure was carried out by order of the state authorities.

THE END OF THE UTRECHT *DOM* TREASURES

At the top left-hand corner of the copies of the 1571 inventory — the version which was annotated in 1574 — is a brief account of the fate of the *Dom*'s treasure. The writer, whose identity is unknown, reports that 'In 1578, all the treasures were brought to the Mint and there melted down.' On 28 February 1578 the order had arrived from the States-General in Brussels that all non-consecrated precious objects owned by the Utrecht churches, church institutions such as monasteries and fraternities and the silver held by the guilds must be handed over. The churches would be allowed to keep a third of their value, with the rest to be used to finance the war. The *Dom* chapter itself ordered that virtually everything be melted down in the months before the actual confiscation. Day after day objects were taken from the sacristy and taken to the Mint. Presumably the debts had mounted beyond the chapter's control and this was seen as the only way to alleviate its precarious financial position. The resolutions of the chapter are full of comments to this effect. Willem van Lamsweerde, secretary of the chapter, played a central role in these events.[39] He did not obstruct the process of melting down valuable objects, as the chapter of *Oudmunster* did. The various church bodies did not respond uniformly; each church seems to have taken a different decision. Presumably, much depended on the individuals responsible for administering the church and its possessions and personal motives may have played a role in their decisions. An analysis of the surviving written records allows us to form a picture of the Utrecht *Dom* treasure which was melted down. What emerges from these sources is a body of different objects of varying provenance which, though not extremely important, was carefully conserved. The large reliquary chests from the fifteenth century would have been the most valuable objects. From the inventories it appears that the treasure of Utrecht cathedral did not differ in any important respects from those of other medium-sized cathedrals in Europe.

ABBREVIATIONS

RAU   Rijksarchief Utrecht; the numbers refer to K. Heeringa, *Inventaris van het Archief van het Kapittel ten Dom* (Utrecht 1929).

RAU, dom   Rijksarchief Utrecht, Archief van het Domkapittel.

SHORTENED TITLES USED

Van Asch van Wijck (1837)   A. M. C. van Asch van Wijck, 'De intrede van Philips II in Utrecht oct. 1549', in *Van der Monde Tijdschrift voor geschiedenis, oudheden en statistiek van Utrecht*, III (1837), 109–40.

Van Asch van Wijck (1838)   A. M. C. van Asch van Wijck, *Plegtige intrede van keizer Karel den Vijfden in Utrecht in den jare 1540* (Utrecht 1838).

Van den Bergh-Hoogterp (1990)   L. E. van den Bergh-Hoogterp, *Goud- en zilversmeden te Utrecht in de late middeleeuwen* ('s-Gravenhage/Maarssen 1990).

Brom (1900)   G. Brom, 'Middeleeuwse kerksieraden', in *Archief voor de geschiedenis van het aartsbisdom Utrecht* (Utrecht 1900).

De Groot (1994)   A. de Groot, 'Beelden in de Dom van Utrecht in de zestiende eeuw', in *Beelden in de late middeleeuwen en renaissance/Late gothic and renaissance sculpture in The Netherlands. Nederlands Kunsthistorisch Jaarboek/Netherland Yearbook for History of Art*, vol. 45 (1994), 39–97.

Haslinghuis and Peeters (1965)   E. J. Haslinghuis and C. J. A. C. Peeters, *De Nederlandse monumenten van geschiedenis en kunst, deel II — de provincie Utrecht, eerste stuk — de gemeente Utrecht, tweede aflevering — De Dom van Utrecht* ('s-Gravenhage 1965).

Sejourné (1919–21)   Ed., P. Sejourné, *L'Ordinaire de Saint Martin d'Utrecht* (Utrecht 1919–21).

Exhib. Cat. *Ornamenta* (1985)   exhib. Cat. *Ornamenta Ecclesiae, Kunst und Künstler der Romanik*, Schnütgen-Museum in der Josef-Haubrich Kunsthalle (Köln 1985).

REFERENCES

1. RAU, dom, inv. no. 2505; the sacristy inventory of 1504, Brom (1900), 251–71; Van den Bergh-Hoogterp (1990), 211–72 (commissions of the cathedral chapter) and 377–90 (donations).
2. This abstract makes clear that Van Buchel was more interested in the donors than in the objects described. The document, dating from the first part of the seventeenth century, was probably composed for his *Monumenta Passim in Templis ac Monasteris Traiectinae Urbis atque Agri Inventa*, MS, Gemeente Archief Utrecht (GAU), bibl. XXVIII L 1 (old sign. 1840 *). On the historical interest of Van Buchel: De Groot (1994), 87.
3. Donated by Bishop Balderik (918–76) to his church, Haslinghuis and Peeters (1965), 160.
4. Van de Bergh-Hoogterp (1990), 219–39 and biography no. 89.
5. RAU, dom, inv. no. 2508 (16 November 1502); Brom (1900), 250; on the commission and the proceedings of the work see: Van den Bergh-Hoogterp 1990, 219–39; dean Ludolph van Veen and former treasurers Evert Zoudenbalch and Gerloff van der Donck were present when the work was delivered.
6. Van den Bergh-Hoogterp (1990), 246–47 and 249–51.
7. W. H. Vroom, *De Financiering van de Kathedraalbouw in de Middeleeuwen, in het bijzonder van de Dom van Utrecht* (Maarssen 1981), 360–62 and in this volume 'The financing of the construction of the gothic Cathedral'.
8. De Groot (1994), 39.
9. M. Groten, 'Schatzverzeichnisse des Mittelalters' in exhib. Cat. *Ornamenta* (1985), 149; B. Bisschoff, *Mittelalterliche Schatzverzeichnisse*, Veröffentlichungen des Zentralinstituts für Kunstgeschichte in München, IV (München 1967).
10. Van Asch van Wijck (1837), with a reference to Henrica de Erp (see note 36).
11. RAU, dom, inv. no. 2505, fols 22–23^v (version 1571 d); Brom (1900), inventory of 1504, 270–71. One of the objects mentioned is the hammer that as a relic is put in relation with Saint Martin of Tours, the patron of the Utrecht cathedral (Rijksmuseum Het Catharijneconvent, inv. no. OKM m. 38).
12. Exhib. Cat. *Ornamenta* (1985), passim.

13. 'Inventory of valuables and ornaments kept in custody in the sacristy or in the treasury of the church of Utrecht'.

14. In old documents, written in the Dutch language, the sacristy is often called 'gherf-', 'gheru'- or 'gheercamer'. The use of this term 'gheren' (to prepare) points to the function of this room; the priests prepared and dressed themselves there before celebrating mass.

15. In all inventories the opening sentence is the same, as is the formulation: *Sequuntur ea, que adhuc sunt de auro et argento in janua ferrea.*

16. N. B. Tenhaeff, *Bronnen tot de Bouwgeschiedenis van den Dom te Utrecht*, Vol. 2, part 1 (accounts 1395–1480). Rijksgeschiedkundige Publicatiën, grote serie, 88, ('s-Gravenhage 1946); Haslinghuis and Peeters (1965), 297.

17. Haslinghuis and Peeters (1965), 299, note 2.

18. Haslinghuis and Peeters (1965), 292.

19. '*In primis sunt in dicta sacristia sex cappe deurate* [. . .]' (In the first place, six golden caps are in the sacristy referred to [above]); Brom (1900), 252 (1504); RAU, dom, inv. no. 2505, fol. 1 (1571).

20. The sacerdotal dress of David of Burgundy (Bishop of Utrecht 1456–96) hung beside the robes of his opponent, the dean of Utrecht *Dom*, Gijsbert van Brederode (*c.* 1460).

21. Brom (1900), 260 (1504); RAU, dom, inv. no. 2505, fol. 9ᵛ (1571); on the evangelistary Van den Bergh-Hoogterp (1990), 260; the remark 'newly made' (*noviter factum*) is indeed correct for the inventory of 1504, but is wrongly used in the inventory of 1571.

22. *Sequuntur ea, que sunt de auro et argento in clenodiis in sacristia predicta* (Listed below are the [objects] of gold and silver in the sacristy referred to [above]).

23. Diversorium Davidis de Burgundia, RAU, bisschoppelijk archief, inv. no. 4 (the years 1457–96), fols 249–50ᵛ; the description has literally been copied into the sacristy inventories, for example: RAU, dom, inv. no. 2505, fols 19ᵛ–22 (1571); Brom (1900), 267–69 (1504); see for the provenance of this object: Van den Bergh-Hoogterp, 'Een Vorstelijk Geschenk van David van Bourgondië aan de Domkerk te Utrecht', *Antiek* 21 (April 1987), 510–34.

24. Van Asch van Wijck (1838), 14, note 28.

25. See Haslinghuis and Peeters (1965), 159, especially the discussion on Thomas of Canterbury as patron saint of European churches. For the latest discussion on the oldest churches of Utrecht C. J. C. Broer and M. W. J. de Bruijn, *De eerste kerken in Utrecht: Sint Thomas, Sint Salvator, Sint Maarten* (Utrecht 1995).

26. This conclusion can be drawn from the function of the two crosses in the manual of around 1200 (Séjourné 1919–21) and as given in all inventories of the sixteenth century.

27. Brom (1900), 265 (1504); RAU, dom, inv. no. 2505 (1571 d), fols 15ᵛ–16; De Groot (1994), 48. The statue of Saint Margaret had been commissioned by the executors of Abraham van Leeuwenbergh, to be placed on the altar dedicated to this saint in the cathedral, see Van den Bergh-Hoogterp (1990), 388–89.

28. The objects of gold and silver behind the iron door are listed below.

29. Compare Mekking, in this volume.

30. Van den Bergh-Hoogterp (1990), 693–95 (Appendix IV) and biography no. 74.

31. See for the Both van der Eem family Haslinghuis and Peeters (1965), 347, 393.

32. RAU, dom, inv. no. 2505, fol. 17; Brom (1990), 266; for the acquisition of the relic (a small part of the arm bone): Van den Bergh-Hoogterp (1990), 248–51; in 1571 the piece comes in sequence as no. 8.

33. In 1504 those pieces came in sequence as no. 7 and no. 8, Brom (1900), 266.

34. RAU, dom, inv. no. 2512, Brom (1900), 236–38; Van den Bergh-Hoogterp (1990), 384–85; concerning a donation 'inter vivos' of dean Zweder van Uterloe (he died in 1378).

35. As the chalice of dean Marcus van Weeze; De Groot (1994), 77.

36. Van Asch van Wijck (1837), Philips II, with assimilation of the *Annales de Henricae de Erp* [8 December 1545, ed. A. Matthaeus, *Analecta . . .* , tom. III, 120], ('s-Gravenhage 1738) and Van Asch van Wijck (1838), Karel V, from the *Triumphus Caroli V Caesaris* of Cornelius Valerius. The variety of processions also in B. van den Hoven van Genderen, *Het kapittel-Generaal en de Staten van het Nedersticht in de 15e eeuw* (Zutphen 1988), 111.

37. In his *Traiecti descriptio*, 77, see Van den Bergh-Hoogterp (1990), 767, note 81.

38. Van den Bergh-Hoogterp (1990), 701–05 (Appendix VI).

39. RAU, dom, inv. no. 1–20 (Chapter resolutions 1574–1581), without fol. 'noot van gelde'; RAU, dom, inv. no. 2148; *Rekening van W. Van Lamsweerde wegens de verkoop van versmolten kerkschatten 1578* (17 February), ed. J. J. Dodt van Flensburg in *Archief voor Kerkelijke en Wereldsche Geschiedenissen van Utrecht*, I (1838), 260–61; Van den Bergh-Hoogterp (1990), 391–97.

Internal Arrangements in the Utrecht Cathedral Before and After the Reformation

by Arie de Groot

This article discusses the changes within the Utrecht Cathedral, the Dom, at the time of the Reformation, which in Utrecht took place in 1580.

SOURCES[1]

As a result of the events in 1580 and later developments, the present building fabric yields relatively little information about the arrangements in the sixteenth and seventeenth centuries. With the iconoclast riots of 1580 and later the more regular expurgation, nearly all the statues and altars and most of the other objects of the catholic interior disappeared. The new protestant arrangements in their turn were removed in June 1672, when the French troops of Louis XIV entered Utrecht and the Dom became once more a Catholic cathedral. By November 1673 the French had left and the Dom was again a Reformed church. In July 1674, however, a hurricane destroyed the nave, that in the sixteenth century was left unfinished. Since then new arrangements in the remaining half of the building have been realized. Restorations in the nineteenth and twentieth centuries, the last of which was finished in 1988, have brought to light some remains of sculptures and wallpaintings, but apart from these, a number of funeral monuments and some brass candelabra, little is left of the furnishing from before 1674 or even 1800.[2]

No reliable representations of the Dom interior before 1580 are known, but three drawings by Pieter Saenredam from 1636 not only give a clear view of the interior during the first half of the seventeenth century, but also contain some information about the situation before 1580 (Pl. XXXIXA, B–XL).[3] The high extent of their reliability emerges from comparison with those parts of the interior that have been preserved, and also compared to documentary evidence.

A large degree of information can be extracted from written sources: the Dom chapter records, in particular the *Acta Capitularia* and the fabric rolls, which have been preserved practically in full from *c.* 1460.[4] Through these the construction of transepts and nave can be followed almost step by step, as can the expenditure on the internal arrangements from 1460 as far as this was made by the chapter. Several descriptions in manuscripts provide valuable additional information, the most important of these being the *Monumenta passim in templis ac monasteriis Traiectinae urbis atque agri inventa* by the Utrecht lawyer and historian Arnoldus Buchelius (1565–1641).[5]

THE INTERNAL ARRANGEMENTS OF THE CATHOLIC CATHEDRAL

The Dom was the principal church of the diocese of Utrecht, which in 1559 became an archbishopric. It was the (arch)bishop's church, but in fact, most of all it was the church of the chapter. There was no parish associated with the Dom besides the people directly connected: the canons, the vicars, the personnel. Although on certain days sermons for the common burghers were held, it was principally a place for the daily divine offices, memorial masses etc. of the Dom clergy.[6]

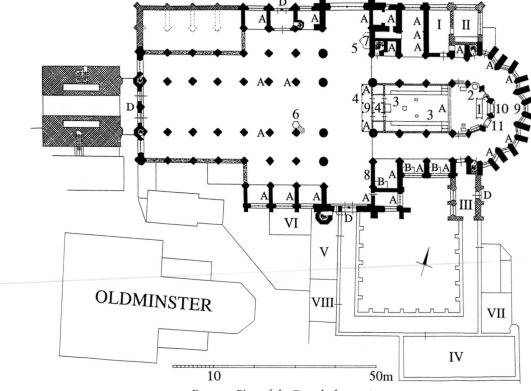

FIG. I. Plan of the Dom before 1580

1.	High altar	A.	Altar
2.	Tabernacle	B.	Bishop's tomb
3.	Choir stalls	D.	Doorway
4.	Pulpitum		
5.	Organ	I.	Vestry
6.	Pulpit	II.	Library
7.	Altar of St Martin	III.	Archives (upper floor)
8.	Altar of St Mary	IV.	Great chapter house
9.	Altars of the Holy Cross	V.	Small chapter house
10.	Easter Sepulchre	VI.	Secretary's office
11.	Cenotaph of George of	VII.	Choristers house
	Egmond	VIII.	Cathedral school

This implies that, much more than in the parish churches, the internal arrangements and decorations were centred in the choir (Fig. 1), and that everything was accomplished by either the chapter as a whole, or by individual canons, prelates and bishops and their relations. Almost nothing was founded or donated by non-clerical institutions (authorities, guilds, fraternities, etc.) or by private individuals.[7]

Thus the nave was in principal empty, except for the pulpit, one or two confessional boxes, a few altars and sepulchral monuments. The chancel was the true heart of the church. It was completely enclosed within walls and railings between the pillars, and separated from the transepts by a gothic *pulpitum*. The chancel was arranged in the usual manner: the high altar in the apse, the tabernacle on the northern side, choir stalls on both sides up to the *pulpitum*, with special seats for the bishop, the provost and the dean, and a second, smaller altar in the middle of the presbitery, between the stalls. Also, the necessary lecterns, reliquaries, statues of the Apostles against the pillars and a calvary group on top of the *pulpitum*, etc., etc.

Of all this almost nothing remains. Some stone canopies and wall paintings (painted imitations of tapestries) of the mid-fourteenth century are all that is left to remind us of the statues against the pillars. A number of fifteenth century statues, now in the Central Museum, may originate from the tabernacle.[8] Some parts of the renaissance choir stalls, dating from 1562, escaped relatively unscathed: the dorsal panels and some bench-ends of the present pews in the northern transept originate from them.

Apart from the altars in the chancel the Dom boasted some thirty side altars (served by the vicars), situated above all in the eastern half of the church, that is, in the ambulatory and the choir chapels, against the eastern walls of the transepts and under the *pulpitum*. The two most important of these altars were that of St Martin (the patron saint of both the city and the cathedral) in the northern transept and that of St Mary in the southern transept. Two other altars were devoted to the Holy Cross, one situated under the *pulpitum* and the second in the middle choir chapel. Opposite the latter (that is, behind the high altar) was the Easter Sepulchre, still *in situ*, although badly damaged. A gothic spiral staircase depicted by Saenredam (Pl. XL) led to a platform over this sepulchre. Over the altar of St Martin hung the organ of 1571, well known from drawings by Saenredam (Pl. XL) and others. It was situated in the northern transept till the present organ was built after 1826.[9]

With the above sketched general outline of the internal arrangements in mind, we will now discuss some aspects in more detail.

Saenredam's drawings show a series of escutcheons over the choir stalls. Decorated with the coats of arms of Charles V and the members of the Golden Fleece, the Burgundian order of knights, they commemorated a meeting of the order called together by Charles in Utrecht in 1546, less than twenty years after the centralizing government of the Habsburgs took over the secular power of the bishops. Before 1546 the portraits of the Utrecht bishops hung over the (then gothic) choir stalls; the series dated from the fifteenth century and was continued over the years. A similar series, with the bishops before 1300, hung in the ambulatory. These series designated the Dom as an episcopal church.

The most important of the sepulchral monuments were also connected to the bishops. The earliest bishops' graves, which were transferred from the romanesque cathedral, just had modest stones. The first new sepulchral monument that was placed in the gothic church, was the tomb of Guy of Avesnes, who died in 1317, in the middle choir chapel on the southern side. This monument is still to be seen *in situ*. Similar tombs were erected in other chapels, but they have all disappeared. The only other bishop's monument still partly in existence is the cenotaph of Bishop George of Egmond, built in 1549, ten years before his death. The renaissance triumphal arch between the apse pillars commemorates the foundation by the bishop of the Mass of the Holy Sacrament, one year earlier. The monument probably included a statue of the bishop, kneeling, and (after 1559) a shrine in which his heart was placed.

All other tombs in the Dom were marked by stones only. These were the graves of the prelates (i.e. the dean, the provost/archdeacon, the treasurer), of the other canons, of the vicars and in a few cases of members of the Dom personnel. A considerable number of these stones remain. However most of the other objects that had to keep the memory of the dead alive have largely disappeared: the epitaphs, statues, memorial paintings or altarpieces and the so-called *pallia* (tapestries that were hung near the grave after the funeral). Only a few examples remain, such as the epitaphs of the Ram canons (+ 1518 and 1550), to be found on the north-eastern crossing-pillar, the Anthony Pott reredos of *c.* 1500 in one of the southern choir chapels, and Jan van Scorel's Lockhorst triptych of 1526, now in the Central Museum. The Dom was the burial church of and for the Dom chapter, the bishops and others that were connected with the cathedral. The Utrecht common citizens were buried in the parish churches.

The last material category which needs mentioning is the glazing, of which unfortunately nothing remains.[10] In 1580 all glass windows had some form of painted decoration, dating from the beginning of the fifteenth century (one or two perhaps from the fourteenth) in the choir to the mid-sixteenth century on the west side of the nave. The glazing in the clerestories was largely installed by the chapter itself and on the whole modestly decorated with coats of arms (partly by using old glass from the romanesque cathedral), in anticipation of richer glass windows donated by individual benefactors. These, however, favoured the lower ones; in 1580 all windows in the ambulatory, aisles and chapels had donated glass. Benefactors were bishops, prelates, canons and noblemen and rulers related to them, amongst others the Duke of Cleves and Philip of Burgundy. Again: no non-clerical organizations or individuals were involved.

THE EXPURGATION OF THE INTERIOR

The Dom escaped the iconoclast riots that scourged the Netherlands during 1566, but was damaged in a further wave of furies in March 1580 after the governor of Groningen, Rennenberg, had defected to the Spanish. It was because of this event that the Catholic religion was for the first time banned in Utrecht.[11]

While information about the iconoclast riot of Monday 7 March 1580, is scanty, it is clear that the Dom altars and statues sustained severe damage. The choir, together with the books that were kept there, and the vestry (with the treasures) seem to have escaped the violence, as their keepers were richly rewarded. Afterwards the church was permanently guarded by the Dom's own personnel. The same people also helped to patch up the interior, an operation which took several weeks. The Dom, along with the four other collegiate churches in the city, had subsequently to close down by order of the governor, William of Orange; the daily divine offices ceased.

This iconoclast riot did not imply, as is often thought, a complete cleansing of the Cathedral interior. Nor did the second outbreak on the Monday of 18 July. What followed, however, accomplished a thorough job.

The second iconoclast riot arose when radicals amongst the Reformed demanded that the Dom should be opened for their religious worship and the chapter refused. The Reformed campaign was very clear-cut. After the riot they put an ultimatum to the chapter. By threatening new attacks they forced the chapter to take the expurgation of the church in its own hands. To this purpose some twenty labourers were hired, who worked non-stop for several days and nights in order to take down altars and statues; the Dom personnel supervised this operation. On Friday 22 July (Church Consecration Day) the tearing down was finished. However it took the Dom personnel several more weeks to take away altar stones and rubble, and clean up. Many statues were lying on the floor for months. During all this time the church was kept closed and remained so till 1581, when it was reopened for the Reformed service.[12]

Not all altars and statues had disappeared from the Dom during this period. In the spring of 1586, when the Earl of Leicester was to come to Utrecht as governor, a new great expurgation campaign was set up. On 8 March 1586 the magistrates ordered the five chapters to remove forthwith all that remained of altars, statues and tabernacles and to whitewash the vacated spaces. In the Dom this work took no less than five weeks. Again statues were removed, altarbases broken down. It is assumed that up until then the gothic tabernacle in the choir had been left in place and that it was only taken down on this occasion. A whitewashed wall was erected and elsewhere niches and gaps disappeared behind walls, too: the Easter Sepulchre, the cenotaph of George of Egmond, the reredos in the southern choir chapels. Later in that same year, 1586, the gothic *pulpitum* was taken down as well. This event was linked to the new internal arrangements that were effected at that time. I will return to this later.

However one by now 'forbidden' object was still present after 1586: the high altar, although it probably was incomplete. The Reformed city magistrates had ordered a wall to be raised in front of it in 1586, but the chapter had this pulled down again a couple of years later. The presence of the high altar was protracted for as long as possible, although we do not know if it was still secretly in use, as was the case elsewhere in Utrecht. Finally, in the nineties the chapter proceeded to take it down — gradually: in 1595 the last remains were cleared.

With the pulling down of the high altar the expurgation of the Dom may be regarded as accomplished, Later more objects still disappeared, usually not the result of 'expurgation', but due to ordinary wear and tear, economies and changes in taste etc. This applies to the glazing, for instance. The stained glass escaped the furies and expurgations entirely intact. In the course of extensive repairs in the nineties a couple of stained glass windows were replaced by uncoloured glass for financial reasons. In due course the stained glass disappeared from the church in similar way. In the period immediately following the Reformation, however, practically all of the old glazing was still in its place. We should not, therefore, think of the Reformed interior of the early period as a colourless space.

THE NEW INTERNAL ARRANGEMENTS

In January 1581 the chapter finally agreed to the use of the Dom for divine service by the Reformed Church authorities. This permission was granted on the condition, conceded by the city magistrates, that no costs or prejudice to the chapter would ensue from these Reformed services. The agreement is of great importance for the further history of the internal arrangements, for in later disputes about the Reformed use of the Dom the chapter would invariably refer to it.

In 1581 the city kept its promise and provided a temporary arrangement in the nave with pulpit, pews, etc., all at the expense of the city and all as cheaply as possible. For instance the pew installed for the governor, William of Orange, was not entirely new, but constructed from second-hand materials.

These internal arrangements were changed in 1586 (Fig. 2, Pl. XXXIX–XL). Several circumstances contributed to this. First, the Reformed city magistrates were by this time dominated by a radical tendency that was highly critical of the strong position held by the still partly Catholic chapters in Utrecht. Secondly, by the middle of 1586 under the pressure of Leicester the various Reformed factions had been united to one single Utrecht Reformed Congregation.

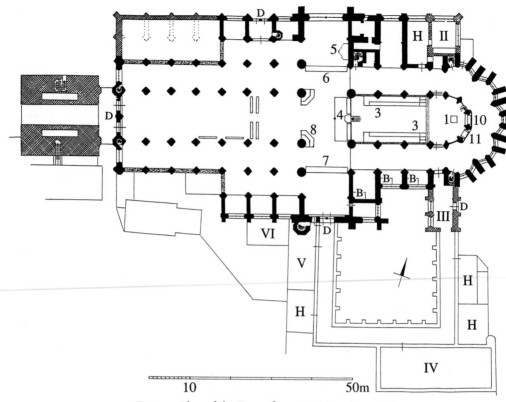

FIG. 2.   Plan of the Dom after 1586 (situation 1636)

1.	Choir pulpit; 1636: Academy lectern
3.	Choir stalls
4.	Choir screen and baptismal enclosure with pulpit, lectern and pews of the consistory and the ministers
5.	Organ
6.	Pew of the City government
7.	Pew of the States of Utrecht
8.	Pew of the Provincial Governor
10.	Easter Sepulchre

11.	Cenotaph of George of Egmond
B.	Bishop's tomb
D.	Doorway
H.	Houses of employees of the chapter
II.	Consistory
III.	Archives (upper floor)
IV.	Academy
V.	Small chapter house
VI.	Secretary's office

Also, by the time long existing plans to sell or pull down a number of churches were finally carried out. Thus in 1587 the collegiate church of Oldminster, situated next to the Dom, disappeared in order to raise money for the new fortifications. The choir of the Buurkerk had already been pulled down in 1586 to make room for a new street. The Buurkerk had always been the most important of the four parish churches in Utrecht. In 1586, however, the city magistrates set out to make the Dom the principle church of Reformed Utrecht. That would make the Dom the church where the entire body of magistrates would convene for divine service each year at the beginning of its term of office (in the beginning of October).

Several provisions had to be made for this. Seats for the magistrates had to be installed and to this end in October 1586 the city had the choir stalls from the neighbouring church of Oldminster, which was down for demolition, transferred to the Dom. The next step was that the magistrates — without consulting the chapter — ordered the gothic *pulpitum* to be pulled down and to be replaced by a choirscreen with the pulpit in front of it. This was probably done for practical reasons. Before the installation of the magistrates' benches the transepts offered the best prospects, but the *pulpitum*, that jutted out into the crossing, did not fit in very well with this arrangement. The new choirscreen, erected more to the East, allowed sufficient space for the customary baptismal enclosure (with a pew and lectern for the reader/precentor in front of the pulpit and pews for the consistory and ministers on either side) and did not obstruct the view of the pulpit. But there was more to it than that. By placing the new liturgical centre on the longitudinal axis with the pulpit in the centre of the axial perspective prospect, the architectural splendour of the building was now turned to full advantage: the imperfection of the nave was exchanged for the magnificence of the choir. The choir, less cut off by the new choirscreen than it used to be by the *pulpitum*, was now actually used in the Reformed service, to wit for the celebration of the Holy Communion; hence the wall in front of the high altar. As a result of this drastic operation from now on the entire church instead of just the nave was available for Reformed service. Thus it was a decisive step in the architectural transformation of the Dom from Catholic cathedral to Reformed 'parish church'.

To conclude, some remarks can be made on these formal aspects and the influence they had on the church interior.

In the Reformation period a medieval cathedral in the Netherlands underwent a bigger change in position than one in Anglican England or in Lutheran Germany. The Reformed Church in the Republic was a Calvinistic church in which central government and hierarchy had been abolished: there were no more bishops, so no more cathedrals either. All that was left were Reformed 'parish churches' (to stick to this Catholic term), which in principle were all equal. In the seventeenth century Republic the Dom had exactly the same ecclesiastical status as any provincial 'parish church'.

Since 1559 the Dom had no longer been the only cathedral in the Northern Netherlands, for in that year a reshuffle took place of ecclesiastical provinces which led to the institution of new cathedrals: Haarlem, 's-Hertogenbosch and others. However, a fundamental difference existed between the Utrecht Cathedral and these new cathedrals, which originally had been the big local parish churches. Once raised to cathedral status, their old functions and organizations were augmented by new functions and organizations which went with the cathedral. As a result of the Reformation they lost these again, but their old parish functions were basically continued, albeit adapted to the Reformed principles.

For the Dom the 'parish' function was truly new, and the old organization was not geared to it. The Dom had since many centuries only been a cathedral, as the four other collegiate churches had only been collegiate churches. While their churches were given new functions during the Reformation, or were pulled down (like the Oldminster), the five chapters, thanks to their size, wealth and power, largely managed to maintain their positions (till they were finally abolished by Napoleon in 1811). Admittedly, new canons were required to be of the Reformed denomination, but the chapters themselves were not reformed. They were not given a new organization, nor new tasks in the religious or educational field, as did happen elsewhere in some cases. They retained their position as independent boards and retained their old, though curtailed functions. Apart from their participation in national politics, this implied especially the administration of the property in their possession: estates, houses and also their churches.

Thus the Dom chapter remained governor of the cathedral fabric and therefore responsible for the maintenance of the Dom. It took care of repairs, and as late as 1602 it ordered the painting of the organ panels, something that had been left undone in 1571. However, the chapter, referring to the agreement of 1581, did not see it as part of its task to make provisions for the Reformed religious service. The city magistrates, on the other hand, as protectors of the Reformed congregation, thought otherwise. This situation caused a lot of friction over the years. Whenever the city magistrates ordered the chapter to have certain objects for the Reformed service (such as chandeliers or communion wine) made or paid for, the chapter, as a rule, refused, and in this way it managed to prevent certain matters and to delay others. That is why in 1586 the city magistrates took the rearrangement of the interior into its own hands. The chapter could never have been persuaded to pull down the pulpitum. The operation of 1586 caused a strong protest: in the eyes of the chapter it constituted a flagrant infringement of its rights. In later years relations between the chapter and the city magistrates improved somewhat, but whenever great costs were involved, problems were sure to arise.

Such problems were unknown in the old parish churches. There the maintenance of the building had of old been a task of the community, that is, of the town or city magistrates, who to this end appointed a number of church wardens for each church. The Reformation left this system unchanged. The church wardens ordered the necessary works to be carried out and the city paid. In addition, all sorts of non-clerical institutions such as the guilds spent money on the decoration of the church both before and after the Reformation. Thus, the big medieval parish churches, in Amsterdam, Haarlem, Gouda, Dordrecht, Kampen or anywhere else in the Netherlands had in the seventeenth century a rich protestant interior: costly furnishings, magnificent organs, panels painted with Bible passages; escutcheons, paintings and stained glass windows of the guilds; glass donated by neighbouring towns.[13] The Utrecht parish churches had such protestant furnishings and decorations too, although not quite as rich.

In the Dom, nothing of the sort existed. Virtually no costly object can be associated with the new function. Whatever stood out in richness or beauty was either left over from before the Reformation, like the stained glass windows, the choir stalls and the organ, or was a sepulchral monument of a canon, like the one of the Dom canon and navy admiral Willem Joseph van Gendt (1676). The protestant furnishings were simple and modest and sometimes they were not even newly made but second-hand. Decorations with a protestant religious content were completely lacking. Obviously, this modesty was not a result of Calvinistic views on the part of the ministers, but had everything to do with the particular situation as regards the administration. In the Dom there was not a chance that the chapter was going to pay for all sorts of decorations for the benefit of the Reformed or common good, and the city magistrates themselves wanted to spend as little on the Dom as possible. Nor were there any guilds or other corporations in the Dom to make their contributions to the interior.

As a result of all this, the Utrecht Dom, which as a cathedral used to be one of the richest as well as one of the most important churches in the Netherlands, after the Reformation became the church with the simplest and cheapest protestant interior of all the big town and city churches in the Dutch Republic.

ACKNOWLEDGEMENTS

This paper is based on my doctoral research into the internal arrangements and decorations of the Utrecht Cathedral at the time of the Reformation. The investigations, which were carried out at the Department of History of Art and Archaeology of the Free University (*Vrije Universiteit*) of Amsterdam, were supported by the *Stichting voor Kunsthistorisch Onderzoek* which is subsidized by the Netherlands Organization for Scientific Research NWO.

The greater part of the text of this paper was translated from the Dutch by Miss Helen Kost, M.A.

Plate XL is reproduced with gracious permission of Her Royal Highness Princess Juliana of the Netherlands.

REFERENCES

1. A detailed index of sources and a bibliography will be included in the author's Ph.D. dissertation which will appear in due course.
2. For the present building, see especially E. J. Haslinghuis en C. J. A. C. Peeters, *De Dom van Utrecht* ('s-Gravenhage 1965) (De Nederlandse Monumenten van Geschiedenis en Kunst, II, 1.2).
3. Two drawings (the Nave and the Transepts) in the Gemeentearchief (Municipal Records Office), Utrecht, cat. nos T.A. He 1 and T.A. He 22; one drawing (the Choir) in the Koninklijk Huisarchief, 's-Gravenhage, cat. no. MCS/189 (Royal Collections, reproduced with gracious permission of Her Royal Highness Princess Juliana of the Netherlands).
4. Rijksarchief (Public Records Office), Utrecht, Archives of the Dom Chapter, inv. nos 1 and 651. Inventory: K. Heeringa, *Inventaris van het archief van het kapittel ten Dom* (Utrecht 1929). The fabric rolls of the period 1395/96–1528/29 have been published in *Bronnen tot de bouwgeschiedenis van de(n) Dom te Utrecht*, eds. N. B. Tenhaeff, W. Jappe Alberts, 3 vols ('s-Gravenhage 1946–76) (Rijks Geschiedkundige Publicatiën, grote serie, 88, 129, 155).
5. Gemeentearchief (Municipal Records Office), Utrecht, Library cat. no. XXVIII L 1.
6. About the Dom chapter, see S. F. C. Moore, *The Cathedral Chapter of St. Maarten at Utrecht before the Revolt* (unpubl. dissertation University of Southampton 1988).
7. About the financing of the works, see W. H. Vroom, *De financiering van de kathedraalbouw in de middeleeuwen, in het bijzonder van de dom van Utrecht* (Maarssen 1981). Also W. H. Vroom in this volume. About the interior arrangements and decorations of the catholic cathedral: S. Muller Fz., *De Dom van Utrecht* (Utrecht 1906); A. de Groot, 'Beelden in de Dom van Utrecht in de zestiende eeuw', *Beelden in de late middeleeuwen en renaissance*, eds. R. Falkenburg, D. Meijers e.a. (Zwolle 1994) (Nederlands Kunsthistorisch Jaarboek 45, 1994), 38–97.
8. The question of their original setting is dealt with in De Groot 1994, 49–51.
9. About the organ: M. A. Vente, *Orgels en organisten van de Dom te Utrecht van de 14e eeuw tot heden* (Utrecht 1975), 27–37.
10. Only some small pieces of fifteenth-century glass, now in the Utrecht Central Museum, survived.
11. A definitive ban was imposed in June 1580.
12. The first Reformed service was held on 24 July 1580. No permission for this had been granted, however, by the city magistrates, who forthwith banned all further services. The only exception was the funeral service on 30 August for archbishop Frederick Schenck van Toutenburch, who had died five days earlier.
13. C. A. van Swigchem, T. Brouwer, W. van Os, *Een huis voor het Woord. Het Protestantse kerkinterieur in Nederland tot 1900* ('s-Gravenhage/Zeist 1984), *passim*.

Of Gods and Shepherds: Utrecht, Rome and London

by Elisabeth de Bièvre

'. . ..*Utrecht is not to be compared to Amsterdam or Rotterdam — although they are first class towns themselves — because Utrecht, as a free town of the Empire in the same way as a Republic, could make peace or war. . ..*' (N. van der Monde, 1841)[1]

The establishment of Utrecht as a military *castellum* of the government in Rome during the first century AD was the basis for a long history of intimate relations between the two cities. Since the late seventh-century Utrecht, as the seat of the bishops of the Northern Netherlands, and later as a free town of the Holy Roman Empire, developed ever closer real and imagined ties with Rome. This situation only began to change during the sixteenth century. First the bishop was forced to surrender his military and legislative supremacy to the young Hapsburg emperor, Charles V, who had inherited domains including the Burgundian Netherlands. Later, with the introduction of the Protestant Reformation the see ceased to exist altogether. In the new Federal Union the leading role in public affairs was taken over by Amsterdam, leaving many of the Utrecht citizens to dream in private.

This sequence of political changes following the ending of Burgundian rule had implications for artistic production in Utrecht in the sixteenth- and early seventeenth-century. Throughout the period the major artists operating there reveal different interests from those working in Haarlem, Leiden or Amsterdam, and they pleased different patrons. A characteristic shared by most of these painters in Utrecht was an experience of the city of Rome, whence they returned, often after a prolonged stay, full of visual ideals to be used in their work for local patrons. The latter belonged almost exclusively to the ruling classes, which consisted of local landowners and courtly, ecclesiastical bureaucrats, not of merchants and entrepreneurs as was the case in Holland. Besides serving their local customers, Utrecht painters, more than those of any other town in the Netherlands, also worked for highly placed individuals in other parts of Europe, especially in Rome and in London. Moreover, whatever the subject matter, their compositions during the sixteenth century contained large classically inspired figures — to such an extent that many Christian saints are disguised in the bodies of pagan gods and goddesses. Then, during the first quarter of the seventeenth century, a veritable rage developed for elegant shepherds and shepherdesses. This fashion in painting within the Netherlands definitely started in Utrecht, although later the topic was taken up — to a lesser degree — by other towns in the Republic as well.[2] By the first quarter of the seventeenth century the leisured land-owning class, resident in and around Utrecht, had become quite remote from the Amsterdam merchants, who were highly active in military and commercial enterprises. The gentry's desire to identify with the idyllic shepherds and shepherdesses, who had escaped from aristocratic French and Italian romances, was mirrored in paintings made for the courts in London and The Hague. The pragmatic citizens of Amsterdam, in contrast, selected sterner material for their art production.

Historical background

Soon after his succession in 1515 Charles set out to enlarge the loose federation of the Netherlands to which the bishopric of Utrecht, with its vast secular territories extending North of the river IJssel, did not yet belong. By 1528 he had taken over the secular power of the last worldly bishop. In order to secure the newly created situation the emperor immediately had a strong military fortress constructed on the western edge of the town, which, with the ironic name of Vredeburg (Peaceburgh) (Pl. 1), served to keep the Utrecht citizenry under control.[3] After Gelderland too surrendered to Charles in 1543, Vredenburg was joined by three other bastions, Zonnenburg (Sunburgh) (1551), Manenburg (Moonburgh) (1554) and Sterrenburg (Starburgh) (1558). Confronted by this new power structure, those families, who in the past had found their social and economic fulfilment in exploiting the political and military opportunities around the bishop's court and the many ecclesiastical institutions, now had to adapt to the changed realities. An elite developed which supported the Hapsburg centralizing policies, while contacts with Rome continued on different levels. Only fifty years later, however, the Hapsburgs were themselves excluded from the Northern Netherlandish scene, when Philip II was forced to watch as Utrecht, together with other Netherlandish towns and provinces, abjured his royal and autocratic authority in 1581. In the new, highly mobile, political construction of the Union of Seven Provinces the Provincial States or Assemblies maintained an enormous degree of independence. The States of the province of Utrecht were more than half filled by members of the landed gentry, in sharp contrast to Holland or Zeeland, where only one vote was held by the aristocracy, against eighteen by the towns.[4] In 1580, with the death of the last (arch-) bishop, catholic religious services were officially forbidden by the town council,[5] although many of the former catholic institutions and practices survived in different forms. For example, the Netherlandish branch of the political and military order of the wealthy Teutonic knights continued, albeit with diminished influence, until it too became protestant.[6] The canons of the different chapters also survived in secular form, being elected by the cities and nobility alike, and continued to enjoy large unearned incomes.

UTRECHT IN THE FIRST HALF OF THE SIXTEENTH CENTURY

In 1524 the last Burgundian bishop of Utrecht, Philip, died. This knight of the Golden Fleece had maintained the life style of a Renaissance prince. In 1508 he took the young painter Jan Gossaert (1478–1532, also known as Mabuse) with him to Rome and kept him in his service on his return to Souburg, his castle near Middleburg. In 1517, as a protégé of the emperor, Charles V, Philip was elected bishop of Utrecht. Gossaert followed him to his new residence, the castle at Wijk bij Duurstede, fifteen miles east of Utrecht.[7] During these years, in collaboration with humanist poets and scholars such as Gerard Geldenhauer, the painter created for Philip pairs of full-sized Classical nudes, such as *Neptune and Amphitrite* (Pl. XLIB).[8] Van Mander already remarked on the fact that Gossaert brought from Rome to the North . . .'pictures full of nudes and all kind of allegories which things were not so common in our country before his time'.[9] For the Netherlands this was a new and unique visual programme. Nowhere, either in the many newly burgeoning towns or in the few courts, was so much emphasis laid on the godlike and heroic body. As a Burgundian, but a bastard, Philip had every reason to be passionately interested in metaphors of personal grandeur. Related to and protected by the Hapsburg emperor he displayed a taste similar to that of Charles. Gossaert, after

Philip's death in 1524, worked for other patrons of high birth, such as the Marquess of Vere, Adolph of Burgundy, Count Henry III of Nassau-Breda, King Christian of Denmark, and also for the court in Whitehall, London, but he only produced once more a painting similar to those inspired by the last Burgundian bishop of Utrecht.[10]

In 1517, the same year as Gossaert came to Utrecht with Bishop Philip, a young painter, Jan van Scorel (1495–1562), this time born in North Holland and first trained in Haarlem and Amsterdam, arrived.[11] He worked with Gossaert for two years and then travelled south, to Venice, whence he set sail for the Holy Land. Before he returned to Utrecht in 1524 he also spent time in Rome, where he was installed by Charles V's former tutor, the Utrecht Pope, Adrian VI, as Keeper of the Antiquities collection at the Belvedere. After his papal protector's death, now thoroughly imbued with the landscapes of the Middle East, the classical sculptures in Rome and the paintings by Raphael and Michelangelo, he, too, returned to Utrecht, where he received a prestigious and lucrative appointment as canon of the chapter of St Mary in 1528.[12] Even more than Gossaert, Jan van Scorel enjoyed the support of high ranking patrons, such as Henry III Nassau-Breda, close friend to Charles V, Floris van Egmond, stadholder to Charles V in Holland and Zeeland and other 'groote Heren van Nederland'.[13] Besides the Pope, he was also patronized by the kings, Francis I of France and Gustav Vasa of Sweden.

Clear Roman influences can be seen in Scorel's oeuvre of the mid-twenties, as in the imposing triptych with the *Entrance into Jerusalem* for the Lokhorst family in Utrecht (c. 1526).[14] St Agnes and St Sebastian on the side panels look in their heroic physique more like antique gods than Christian martyrs (Pl. XLIIA and B). Later he set up a studio, where a production of altarpieces ensued displaying more and more actively gesticulating, muscular nudes, testifying to the noble lives of Christian Saints. However, compared to some of his contemporaries in Holland, such as Lucas van Leiden (1498–1574) or Maarten van Heemskerk (1494–1533) of Haarlem, his figures are softer and less strapping, almost otherworldly. Unlike them he never painted secular subjects.

Anthonie Mor (c. 1520–1575/76), born in Utrecht, belonged more completely to the generation dominated by the new Hapsburg regime. At first a pupil and assistant of Jan van Scorel, he later spent time in Rome before starting a successful career in the service of the Court at Brussels. For his royal patrons he travelled extensively, mainly to make dynastic portraits, such as that of Mary Tudor in London to be sent to her future husband, Philip II.[15] His art is wholly courtly, secular and international.

What is remarkable about the lives and works of these three painters of the first three quarters of the sixteenth century in Utrecht is their common involvement with upper class clients, who often belonged to the Hapsburg clique. Gossaert and Mor's oeuvres share properties of subject matter, style and technique that are unique in the Netherlandish context of the period. These can all be ascribed to the aristocratic tastes of their patrons, both in Utrecht and abroad. Gossaert's preference for strong figures seems to be derived from the particular ambitions of one powerful patron who still exercised a nearly monopolistic authority in the bishopric and who was backed by the emperor. Scorel's gentler creations were conceived by a semi-independent cleric, who, with strong memories of papal Rome and its classical surroundings, responded to the needs of a varied group of high-class, clerical patrons. The subjects of Scorel's paintings, when compared to those of Lucas van Leiden or Maarten van Heemskerk in Haarlem are always more spiritual, less realistic in narrative detail, their execution usually softer, their landscape background more extensive, the muscularity of their nudes less accentuated. The contrast with his two great contemporaries in Holland is emphasized by the fact that he never produced prints as they did so prolifically, probably because he lacked their large middle-class market.

Utrecht was also the first city in the Northern Netherlands which developed a classical language in its commissions for sculpture and architecture. The most decisive indications of a new taste are provided by the new façade and interiors of the townhall — originally a group of three medieval houses. This project was started in 1546 on the command of Charles V. In the same year the emperor called a solemn meeting of the knights of the Golden Fleece in Utrecht Cathedral. To commemorate the occasion a series of coats of arms of the knights were produced to replace a series of portraits of bishops which had been on display over the choir stalls in the cathedral since the previous century.[16] Charles' interventions were, as so often, timely. Less than twenty years after he took over the secular power of the Utrecht bishops, and shortly after he had conquered the last independent Netherlandish territory, the moment was opportune to display in the cathedral, the former seat of worldly and ecclesiastical authority clear visual signs of the feudal, Burgundian, roots of the new Hapsburg rule. The correct application of the orders on the new façade of the townhall, obliterating the separate identities of the medieval houses, made similar centralizing claims based on reference to a quite different, classical, tradition.[17] A further example of the town hall's role in Hapsburg policies is provided by both the style and the subject matter of its sculptural decoration, as can be seen in the fragments of Van Noort's sandstone portal, which triumphantly shows in its spandrels two Roman victory goddesses, in ascendancy over 'wild men' and 'grotesque' figurines on the pilasters (Pl. XLIIc).[18]

UTRECHT IN THE LAST QUARTER OF THE SIXTEENTH CENTURY

The abjuration of King Philip II (1581) threatened, but did not at first diminish, the continuing prestige of Utrecht, as is illustrated by the decision of the second governor-general, the Earl of Leicester, to make the city his headquarters in 1586. He clearly saw in Utrecht a potential capital for the new Union.[19] This is demonstrated by the gold and silver coins he had minted in the city with the States General's motto, CONCORDIA RES PARVAE CRESCUNT TRA (iectum) surrounding his own proud profile under the coat of arms of Utrecht.[20] Leicester's inspiration for the image on the coin may have been medals made by Steven van Herwijck, which he could have seen either at the court of Queen Elizabeth or in Utrecht itself. Of the forty or so originals in silver, bronze or lead, one is of Elizabeth herself and another of George of Egmond, bishop of Utrecht (1535–59). The style of the profile portraits is based on that of the Italians Pompeo and Leone Leoni, then working at the court in Brussels, and the papal medal-maker Alessandro Cesati.[21] Whether because of his royal taste or because of his decisive reliance on the ultra-calvinist, middle-class party in Utrecht, Leicester alienated both the local landed aristocracy and the regents of the cities of Holland and was soon compelled to return to Great Britain.

During this period of change, the 1570s and 80s, Utrecht, like most other towns in the war-plagued provinces, did not harbour a large community of artists, but the few painters we do meet are still in the mould of the gentleman painters of the previous generation. The example of Anthonie Bloklandt (c. 1534–83), member of an ancient noble family and son of a burgomaster of nearby Montfoort, who, following stays in Antwerp and Rome, settled in Utrecht around 1577, allows us an insight into Utrecht society and artistic practices.[22] As a well-to-do and twice married man with children he lived in the St Catherine's Convent, which was at the time in the hands of the knights of St John and, like several of his knightly neighbours, he had his medal cast by Van Herwijck.[23] The emblem on the reverse side of the painter's profile is borrowed from Alciati.[24] It shows a young, classical nude jumping up with his arms outstretched towards the branches of a tall palm tree set in a rocky landscape. The device, 'perfer et obdura' ('persevere and endure'), borrowed from Ovid's *Ars Amatoria*, explains how the painter in pursuit of everlasting fame (the palm leaf) has to excel.[25] Blocklandt, like Scorel, attracted several pupils and his influence may be measured by the fact that one of his last paintings, the lyrical *Adoration of the Shepherds*, survives in at least five copies.[26]

UTRECHT IN THE SEVENTEENTH CENTURY

During the seventeenth century, unlike most of the towns in the province of Holland, Utrecht did not become a centre of trade or industry.[27] All economic activity was directed to domestic consumption and no capital, such as might have provided the base for further economic development, was amassed through overproduction and export. Instead, a weekly market sold local products, such as fruit from the Betuwe region. This situation of restricted growth brought its own benefits. The absence of polluting industries and the availability of annual incomes, from provincial government, from inherited landed properties, as well as from the secularized chapters — the source of livelihood for 140 individuals —, provided ideal circumstances for a comfortable life for the ruling elite.[28] Although their isolated position was highlighted by several uprisings of the local trades people, their unreal situation gave the privileged art patrons of Utrecht a different outlook from that of the art consumer in the neighbouring cities of the coastal provinces with their thriving trade and labour-intensive industries.[29] The settled landed gentry and the more internationally oriented members of the ruling class shared the same dream of a safe and ordered rural heaven and it was this which the artists with whom they associated represented on their canvases.

While Abraham Bloemaert (1566–1651) was already in 1586 involved in the decoration of the city for the ceremonial entry of Leicester, it was not until the first half of the seventeenth century that he, together with his contemporary Paulus Moreelse (1571–1638), contributed to the great expansion of painting production in Utrecht.[30] Both ran large studios and both continued the Utrecht tradition of working for and participating in the life of the ruling classes. They were also together responsible, in 1611, for taking the painters and sculptors out of the medieval craft co-operation of the Saddlers Guild into the more socially and intellectually prestigious St Luke's Guild, which would in its turn be transformed into an Academy in the late 1630s.[31] Although Bloemaert, a Catholic all his life, never made the journey to Rome himself, he appears, like Moreelse, to have encouraged his pupils to study and work there. Gerard van Honthorst (1590–1656), Cornelis van Poelenburch (1594 or 95–1667), Hendrik Ter Brugghen (1588–1629), Dirck van Baburen (1595–1624) and many other young painters all left Utrecht studios in the first quarter of the seventeenth century for Rome. Returning during the 1620s, this group, together with their teachers, made Utrecht into an artistic centre unique for the Netherlands and an important creative reservoir to draw from for the aristocracy in Rome, Utrecht and London .

Dirck van Baburen returned from Rome in 1623 and created the first of a long series of pastoral images showing the meeting between the shepherd Daifilo and the urban princess Granida, the two protagonists from Guarini's *Il Pastor Fido* (Pl. XLIIIA).[32] This canvas is, most probably, the same as that known to have been made for the titled

Jonkheer Peter van Hardenbroeck. It shows him in the role of the faithful shepherd who volunteers to quench the thirst of Granida, here presented as a portrait of Van Hardenbroeck's secret love, the Cistercian nun, Agnes van Hanxelaer.[33] Baburen's composition became a much followed prototype, a commentary on the civilizing process which can take place when an uneducated man rejects his unbridled lusts for a sincere love. Daifilo changes from herder of sheep into ruler of men under the influence of his feelings for the upright and refined damsel. Hardenbroeck, a man of influence in the Provincial States of Utrecht and on intimate terms with the Orange-Naussau court in The Hague, exemplified the pastoral taste of his Utrecht caste.

UTRECHT PAINTERS AND PATRONS IN THE HAGUE AND LONDON

An important boost to the aristocratic cultural ideals of Utrecht was the arrival in Rhenen, just east of Utrecht on the Rhine, of the household of the ex-king and -queen of Bohemia. The queen, Elizabeth Stuart, the sister of King Charles I, and a cousin-by-marriage of Prince Frederick Henry of Orange, proved instrumental in connecting the Rome-oriented Utrecht painters with the royal court in London, mainly through the princely court in The Hague. Soon after Gerard van Honthorst came back from Rome in 1620 he met the queen at the house of Sir Dudley Carleton, the ambassador of the Court of St James to The Hague. His first British commission followed at once.[34] Honthorst's work was also noticed by Amalia von Solms-Braunfels, lady-in-waiting to the queen, who married Prince Frederick Henry in 1625. One of Honthorst's first pastoral idylls, dated 1625, interpreted the intimate moment of the declaration of love between *Granida and Daifilo* — a later episode than the one rendered by Baburen. This painting probably entered the budding collection of the newly wed princely pair around the same time.[35] Their taste was shaped even more by typical Utrecht images of gods and shepherds when the Provincial States offered the princess, in 1527, four paintings by Utrecht artists: a 'banquet of the gods' by Poelenburch (Pl. 6), a 'shepherd' and a 'shepherdess' by Paulus Moreelse and a 'scene of all sorts of animals of the air and the earth' by Roelant Savery.[36] In the spring of the following year Honthorst was invited to work for Charles I in Whitehall. There he left an enormous canvas with a train of courtiers, dressed as Roman gods, processing towards Charles and Henrietta who were enthroned high on a cloud attired as Apollo and Diana.[37] If the royal couple needed to be divine in London, they appropriately became shepherds in paintings commissioned by Charles from Honthorst for a gift offered to the queen of Bohemia in rural Rhenen. Honthorst also at the same period portrayed the Bohemian royal pair themselves dressed up as Céladon and Astrée, devotees to the goddess of natural plenty, with their children playing around them as shepherds.[38]

Like Honthorst before him, Poelenburch too moved between Utrecht, Rome (1617–25) and London (1638–41). In Utrecht he introduced a type of landscape inspired by his Roman experiences, full of bright colours, transparent light, ruins and small figurines. By 1630 the Stadtholder, Frederick Henry, already owned twelve of these works. Poelenburch was also involved in the important commission which the Prince's secretary, Constantijn Huygens, negotiated in 1635 between Amalia and a group of Utrecht painters. Huygens himself had already dabbled in pastoral literature in 1618, when he wrote *Doris oft Herder-clachte* (Doris or Shepherd's lament) on a visit to London with Dudley Carleton . A few years later he translated into Dutch part of the *Il Pastor Fido* itself. He also encouraged the musical counterpart of the pastoral mode in Utrecht as the local composer and inventor, Jacob van Eyck, demonstrated when he dedicated to him *Den Fluyten Lusthof*, his large collection of popular melodies for amateur musicians to play on the treble recorder, including such themes as 'Daphne' and 'Amaryllis'.[39] The paintings for Amalia were four large pastoral scenes based upon *Il Pastor Fido*, by Bloemaert, Poelenburch, Herman van Saftleven and Dirck van der Lisse.[40] This quartet of epic idylls was accompanied by a set of landscape paintings. Such a large pictorial programme is rare in the Netherlands. It was, however, around the same period, between 1631 and 1636, that Amsterdam's town council had its new Banqueting Hall constructed, adjoining the headquarters of the local Militia, the Kloveniers Doelen. A few years later the walls of this most public reception room in Amsterdam were covered with huge paintings — including Rembrandt's Nightwatch — filled with more than a hundred life-sized men in contemporary military uniform, many stiffly marching, all ready to fight for republican independence.[41] On the walls of Amalia's quarters in Honselaerdijk, in sharp contrast, danced and played innocent young women and men, who — dressed in floating silks — attested to the godlike order established by marital love in harmony with natural surroundings. Although the painters of Utrecht could please both the local nobility and the courts of the Hague and London with unworldly images such as that of the amorous Granida and Daifilo, the pragmatic citizens of Amsterdam, proud of their newly acquired status, required more effective defences and turned to painters of a more robust mettle.

REFERENCES

1. N. van der Monde, *Utrecht en derzelver Fraaije Omstreken* (Utrecht 1841).
2. Alison McNeil Kettering, *The Dutch Arcadia, Pastoral Art and its Audience in the Golden Age* (Mont Clair 1983), chap I.
3. J. E. A. L. Struick, *Utrecht door de Eeuwen heen* (Utrecht, Amsterdam 1968 and 1984).
4. J. G. van Dillen, *Van Rijkdom en Regenten* (The Hague 1970).
5. G. Parker, *The Dutch Revolt* (Harmondsworth 1977), 202.
6. B. J. M. Klück, *De Landcommanderij van de Duitse Orde te Utrecht* (Zutphen 1995).
7. J. Sterk, *Philips van Bourgondië (1465–1524) bischop van Utrecht, als protagonist van de renaissance. Zijn leven en zijn maecenaat* (Zutphen 1980).
8. *Neptune and Amphitrite*, c. 1517, panel, 188 × 124 cm, Bode Museum, Berlin
9. K. van Mander, *Het Schilderboek* (Haarlem 1604), ed. H. Miedema (Doornspijk 1994), fol. 225v.
10. *Adam and Eve*, panel, 168.8 × 111.4 cm National Gallery, London (on loan from Hampton Court), mentioned by Van Mander in the collection of Martin Papenbrouck in the Warmoesstraat, Amsterdam.
11. J. A. L. de Meyere, *Jan van Scorel, 1495–1562. Schilder voor prinsen en prelaten* (Utrecht 1981).
12. M. A. Faries, 'Jan van Scorel', *Kunst voor de beeldenstorm* (Amsterdam 1986).
13. Mander/Miedema (1994), fol. 234r/194.
14. Jan van Scorel, *Triptych with the entrance into Jerusalem, Saints and members of the Lokhorst family*, c. 1526, central panel, 79 × 146.8 cm, wing panels 81.5 × 65,5 cm, Centraal Museum, Utrecht.
15. E. E. H. Groeneveld, 'Een herziene biografie van Anthonis Mor', *Jaarboek Koninklijk Museum voor Schoone Kunsten* (Antwerpen 1981), 97–117; J. Woodall, 'Anthonie Mor van Dashorst', *Kunst voor de Beeldenstorm* (Amsterdam 1986), 334.
16. see A. de Groot in this volume.
17. E. de Bièvre, 'Public Order in the Low Countries', *L'emploi des Ordres a la Renaissance* (Paris 1992), 285–93
18. Willem van Noort, *Portal from the former townhall in Utrecht*, 1546, sandstone, height c. 205 cm, Centraal Museum Utrecht. Cf. *Kunst voor de Beeldenstorm* (Amsterdam 1986), pl. 178. Two entries in the catalogue deal with the remains of the sculpture belonging to the former townhall.
19. S. Groeneveld et al., *De Kogel door de kerk* (Zutphen 1979), pl. 119 a, b, c.
20. Transl.: through concord small things grow, Utrecht.
21. G. van der Meer, 'Steven van Herwijck', *Kunst voor de Beeldenstorm* (Amsterdam 1986), 338–41.

22. J. A. L. de Meyere, 'Utrechse schilderkunst in de tweede helft van de 16de eeuw', *Jaarboek Oud Utrecht* 1978, 106–91.
23. Van der Meer, 1986, see Pl. 221.1 and Pl. 221.2.
24. A. Alciatus, *Emblematum Libellus* (Paris 1542), 64–65, 24, cf. Van der Meer, 1986, 221.
25. Van der Meer, 1986, 341.
26. On Blocklandt and the different copies: Chr. Lucassen-Mackert, 'Antonie Blocklandt', *Kunst voor de beeldenstorm* (Amsterdam 1986), 426.
27. C. P. Geyl, *Geschiedenis van de Nederlandse Stam*, II, (Amsterdam 1934), 363–64.
28. See I. Vijlbrief *Van anti-aristocratie tot democratie; een bijdrage tot de politieke en sociale geschiedenis der stad Utrecht* (Amsterdam 1950); C. L. Temminck Groll *et al.* 'Utrecht in de zeventiende eeuw', *Jaarboek Oud Utrecht* (1972), 115–43.
29. See for example for the uproar of 1610: D. A. Felix, *Het Oproer te Utrecht in 1610* (Utrecht 1919).
30. See for Bloemaert: M. G. Roethlisberger and M. J. Bok, *Abraham Bloemaert and his Sons. Paintings and Prints*, 2 vols, Doornspijk, 1993, and for Moreelse: ed. A. Blankert, M. J. Bok *et al.*, *Nieuw Licht op de Gouden Eeuw. Hendrik Ter Brugghen en Tijdgenoten* (Utrecht, Brausweig 1986)
31. P. Huys Janssen, *Schilders in Utrecht, 1600–1700* (Utrecht 1990), XII. Foundation of Collegium Musicum Ultrjectinum in 1632; in 1633 foundation of the Illustrious School, which became the University in 1636, while the painters elevated themselves in 1639.
32. The theme had been adapted and made popular in a theater play by Pieter Cornelisz Hooft, published in 1615 after the work of Battista Guarini *Il Pastor Fido* (Venetia/Ferrara 1589).
33. Dirck van Baburen, *Granida and Daifilo*, canvas, 165.7 × 211.5 cm, Private Collection. Cf.: Peter van den Brink, 'Dirck van Baburen, Granida en Daifilo', *Het Gedroomde Land, Pastorale schilderkunst in de Gouden Eeuw* (Zwolle 1993), 87–90 and Dirk Faber, 1988, 142–49.
34. The Duke of Arundel asked him to paint an *'Aeneas flying out of Troy'*. Jos de Meyere, 'Utrecht als centrum van pastorale schilderkunst', *Het Gedroomde Land, Pastorale schilderkunst in de Gouden Eeuw* (Zwolle 1993), 23–32.
35. See for the most recent discussions of this painting and its provenance: Peter van den Brink, 'Gerard van Honthorst'. *Het Gedroomde Land, Pastorale schilderkunst in de Gouden Eeuw* (Zwolle 1993), 173–76.
36. See for references: Meyere, 1993, 23. This group was probably a birthday present.
37. G. van Honthorst, *Apollo and Diana*, 350 × 650 cm, 1628, Hampton Court, London.
38. G. van Honthorst, *Portrait of Frederick V of Paltz and his wife Elizabeth Stuart as Céladon and Astrée*, 1629, Collection of the Prince of Hannover, Hannover. The characters come from Honoré d'Urfé's novel *Astrée*, which was very fashionable after the first two parts appeared in 1610, followed by other parts in the succeeding years until 1627.
39. Jacob van Eyck, *Euterpe oft Speel-godinne* (Amsterdam 1644) was enlarged in 1649 and dedicated to C. Huygens as *Den Fluyten Lusthof*.
40. All four paintings are now in the Jagdschloss Grünewald, Berlin: Abraham Bloemaert, *The marriage of Amaryllis and Mirtillo*, canvas, 115.3 × 140.4 cm; Cornelis van Poelenburch, *Crowning of Mirtillo by Amaryllis*, canvas, 116.5 × 148.3 cm; Herman Saftleven, *Silvio and Dorinda*, canvas, 114 × 140 cm; Dirck van der Lisse, *Blindman's buff*, canvas, 117.3 × 142.5 cm.
41. E. Haverkamp-Begeman, *Rembrandt: The Nightwatch* (Princeton 1982).

A

C

Iᴀ. Utrecht. Tufa fragment of the archway to the *principia*. The largest part has a height of *c.* 0.85m. The width of the arch would have been between *c.* 3.20 and *c.* 3.80m
C. Schokker, Amsterdam

Iʙ. Utrecht. Excavations Domplein 1993. The *principia* showing the atrium surrounded by a portico. The bases are put on a foundation of tufa and cobblestones.
Fotodienst Gemeente Utrecht

Iᴄ. Utrecht. Fragment of a Roman rooftile with inscription of the second cohort of the Spanish infantry: COH II HISP PED PF
Rijksdienst Oudheidkundig Bodemonderzoek, Amersfoort

IIA. The chancel of
St Martin's/Holy Cross-chapel,
from the north
R. Rÿntjes, 1993

IIB. South annex with
rectangular niche, from the
south-east
R. Rÿntjes, 1993

IIc. Chancel and south annex,
from the north-east
R. Rÿntjes, 1993

IIIA. Detail of the junction of nave (right) and south annex (left) from the east
R. Rÿntjes, 1993

IIIB. The junction of south annex and nave; on the foreground: remains of the Roman *principia*
R. Rÿntjes, 1993

IIIC. Foundation of church at Elst

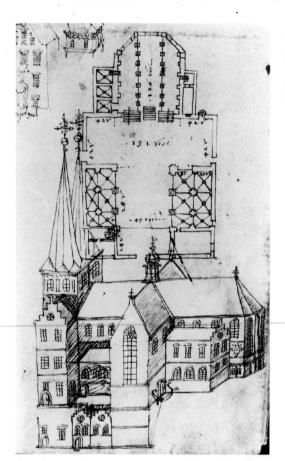

IVA. The church of the Saviour at Utrecht. Pen and ink drawings of groundplan by Arnout van Buchel in his historical work *Monumenta passim in templis ac monasteriis Trajectinae orbis*

IVB. Model of the early medieval group of churches at Eichstätt. The grand hall in the background was the cathedral, dedicated to the Saviour and Mana. Source: Arnold Angenendt. *Das Frühmittelalter. Die abendländische Christenheit von 400 bis 900* (Stuttgart, Berlin, Cologne, 1990) 278

VA. The discovery of the medieval Utrecht boat
Centraal Museum

VB. The Utrecht boat on arrival in the museum
Centraal Museum

VC. The Utrecht boat on display in the museum now
Centraal Museum

VIA. The funeral crown of emperor Conrad II, Speyer cathedral, from P. E. Schramm and F. Mütherich, *Denkmale der deutschen Könige und Kaiser* (München 1980), I, Pl. 149)

VIB. Emperor Henry III offers his patron saints, Simon and Jude, the 'Evangeliarium of Goslar' (Echternach, 1050–56), fol. 4ʳ (P. E. Schramm and F. Mütherich, *Denkmale der deutschen Könige und Kaiser* (München 1980), I, Pl. 155)

VIIA. Utrecht, Pieterskerk, from the south
(F. Delemarre, A. van Deijk, P. van Traa,
Middeleeuwse kerken in Utrecht (Zutphen 1988)
pl. 19)

VIIB. Utrecht, the 'procession route' between
the cathedral and the Mariakerk: Mariaplaats (146),
Zadelstraat (148), Maartensbrug (56),
Servetstraat (58). (N. van der Monde, *Geschied- en
Oudheidkundige Beschrijving van de pleinen,
straten etc. van de stad Utrecht* (Utrecht, 1846), III)

VIIIA. The exterior of the Klaaskerk.
The westwork (*c.* 1100–30) with its pair of
towers and the southern aisle of the
hall-church (*c.* 1470)
K. Emmens 1995

VIIIB. The interior of the Jacobikerk.
Looking through the northern aisle with its
low-placed disfunctional capitals (*c.* 1290),
the nave (partly *c.* 1290) into the southern
aisle (*c.* 1470)
K. Emmens 1995

VIIIC. A view through the northern arcade of the Buurkerk's nave
into the side-aisles. The cylindrical piers flanked by four columns
belong to the phase of the second half of the thirteenth century.
The vaulting, in the nave, a bit higher than in the side-aisles, took
place around 1445
K. Emmens 1995

IX. Pieter Saenredam, *The Mariakerk, Utrecht, Kunsthalle, Hamburg*
Hamburger Kunsthalle

Xᴀ. Pieterskerk, Utrecht. The angel on the empty tomb of Christ and the three Marys
Reproduced with the kind permission of the 'Administration de l'église Wallone d'Utrecht'

Xʙ. Pieterskerk, Utrecht. The Crucifixion and a seated ruler with his swordbearer
Reproduced with the kind permission of the 'Administration de l'église Wallone d'Utrecht'

XIA. Liège, University Library.
The Evangeliary of Averbode.
Cod. 363c, fol. 87ʳ. The Crucifixion

XIB. London, British Museum.
The Floreffe Bible. Add. MS 17738,
fol. 187. The Crucifixion

XIC. Moscow, Hist. Mus. Codex 129,
fol. 4ʳ. Cludov Psalter. King David
pointing at a cross with a portrait of
Christ in the centre

XIIB. Count Thierry II († 988) and his wife Hildegard († 990)
presenting a book to Egmond Abbey
The Hague, Royal Library, MS S76F1, fol. 214ᵛ

XIIA. Lebuin codex, bookbinding
Utrecht, Museum Catharijneconvent, ABM h1

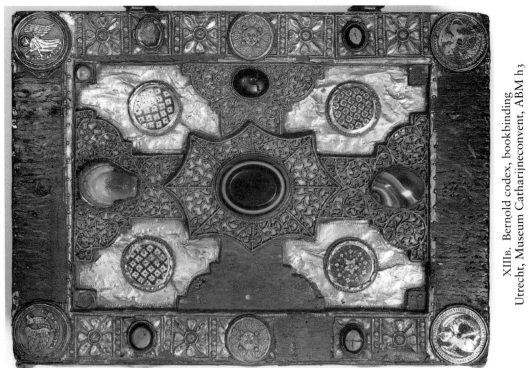

XIIIв. Bernold codex, bookbinding
Utrecht, Museum Catharijneconvent, ABM h3

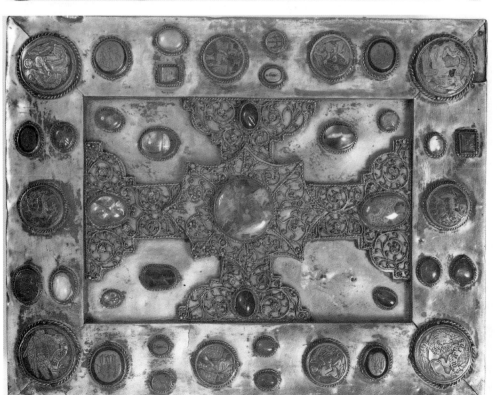

XIIIа. Ansfrid codex, bookbinding
Utrecht, Museum Catharijneconvent, ABM h2

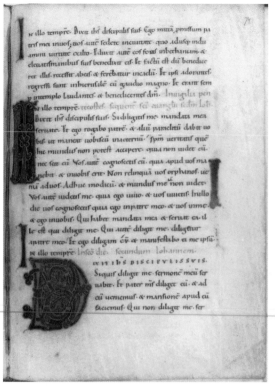

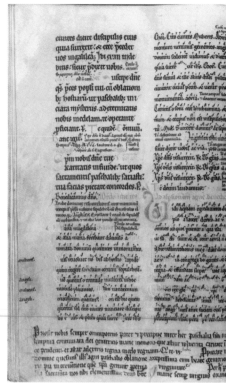

XIVA. The Evangelist St Mark and decorated page. Utrecht, Museum Catharijneconvent, ABM h3, fols 1ᵛ–2ʳ

XIVB. Evangelistary of St Mary's. Utrecht, Museum Catharijneconvent, BMH h9, fol. 74ʳ

XIVC. Text of Easter play in Missal of Hellum and/or Bedum. Utrecht, Museum Catharijneconvent, BMH h7, fol. 45ᵛ

XVA. Apeldoorn. Font, a Janus-head

XVB. Rijssen. Font

XVC. Baarn. Font, detail

XVD. Baarn. Font

Schönhank-van der Wal

XVIA. Aberdeen Cathedral, south-west crossing pier. (The walls to each side of the pier are post-medieval insertions; the slender 'shaft' at its centre is, of course, a drain pipe)
R. Fawcett

XVIB. Perth St John's Parish Church, as it was in 1806, from the north-west before restorations of the 1820s and 1920s (Cant's *Memorabilia of Perth*)

XVIIA. Haddington St Mary's Parish Church, from the west

XVIIB. Dordrecht Great Church,
south transept

XVIIc. Dundee St Mary's Parish Church, west tower
(Billing's *Baronial and ecclesiastical antiquities*)

XVIID. Utrecht Cathedral, west tower

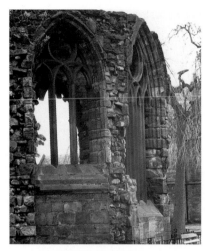

XVIIIA. St Andrews
Blackfriars' Church, south chapel

XVIIIB. Kapelle Parish Church, north chapel windows

XVIIIc. Aberdeen King's College Chapel,
west window

XVIIID. Utrecht Cathedral, Domproosten
Chapel window

XIXa. Utrecht Cathedral, Chapel of Guy d'Avesnes, Crucifixion with Mary, St John and St Margaret, mural

XIXb. Detail with Mary and St John

XIXc. Detail with St Margaret and the dragon

XXв. Master of St Bartholomew Altarpiece, *St Margaret*, detail, Münich, Alte Pinacothek
Bayerische Staatsgemäldesammlungen

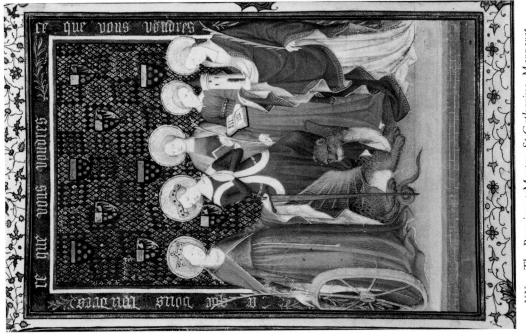

XXA. The Boucicaut Master, *St Catherine, Margaret, Martha, Christine and Barbara* from the Boucicaut Hours. Musée Jacquemart-André, Paris

XXIA. Nivelles. Collégiale Sainte
Gértrude, brass epitaph for
Marguerite de Gavres-Escornay

XXIB. Detail of XXIA

XXIIA. Oude Gracht 114, House Drakenburg. Remains of twelfth-century tufa wall and late thirteenth-century timbers
Fotodienst Gemeente Utrecht

XXIIB. Oude Gracht 306. Tiled roof in 1906. The roof was taken down in 1920
Photo W. G. Baer, Gemeentelijke Archiefdienst Utrecht, Topografische Atlas

XXIIIA. Oude Gracht 175. Early fourteenth-century timber frame with curved braces on
the first floor
Fotodienst Gemeente Utrecht

XXIIIB. Lijnmarkt. Row of back gables of narrow-fronted houses. During the
fourteenth century the houses were extended towards the canal (Oude Gracht), though
building on the wharfs was not allowed, hence the arches supporting the gables
Fotodienst Gemeente Utrecht

XXIVA. Voorstraat 27. Three-quarter house
in *c.* 1650
Drawing by Jan van der Heyden, *Gemeentelijke
Archiefdienst Utrecht, Topografische Atlas*

XXIVB. Hamburgerstraat 23/25. Wide-fronted,
fourteenth-century house. The façade in large
part belongs to the eighteenth century
Fotodienst Gemeente Utrecht

XXIVC. Lange Nieuwstraat 108–32. Beyerskameren, a row of *kameren* from 1597
Fotodienst Gemeente Utrecht

XXVA. Achter St Pieter 140. Double-aisled, wide-fronted house from the
middle of the seventeenth century, seen from the back
Fotodienst Gemeente Utrecht

XXVB. Janskerkhof 13. A square house built in 1648
Fotodienst Gemeente Utrecht

XXVIA. Achter de Dom 7. Freestanding composite
house from *c*. 1400. The crenellation and the
hipped roof are reconstructions from 1894
Fotodienst Gemeente Utrecht

XXVIB. Oude Gracht 53/55. Large house with side-
annex. House Cranestein was first mentioned in 1382.
The imitation stone front dates from the middle of
the eighteenth century
Fotodienst Gemeente Utrecht

XXVIC. Jeruzalemstraat 8/10. House with aisles on
both sides of a backyard from the first half of the
sixteenth century
Fotodienst Gemeente Utrecht

XXVID. Donkerstraat 15/19.
Multi-period, composite house.
Front of Belgian stone dating
from 1467/68
Fotodienst Gemeente Utrecht

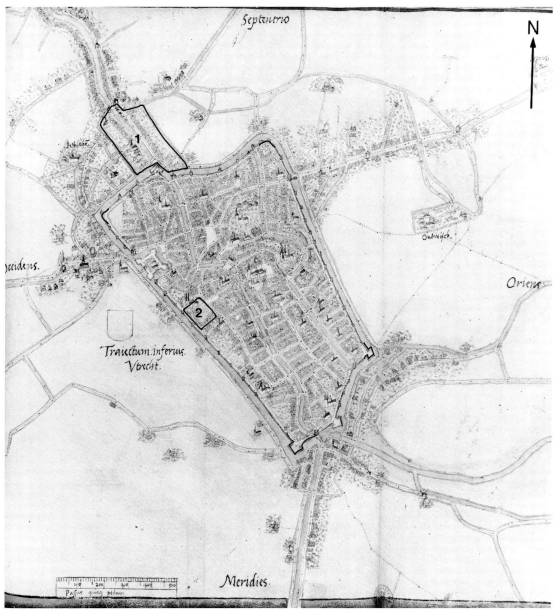

XXVII. Map of Utrecht by Jacob van Deventer (*c.* 1570). 1: the suburb of the Bemuurde Weerd; the number is placed in the area which was excavated in 1984. The Kaatstraat site is just north of the street. The chapel there is of fifteenth-century date. 2: St Mary's Close

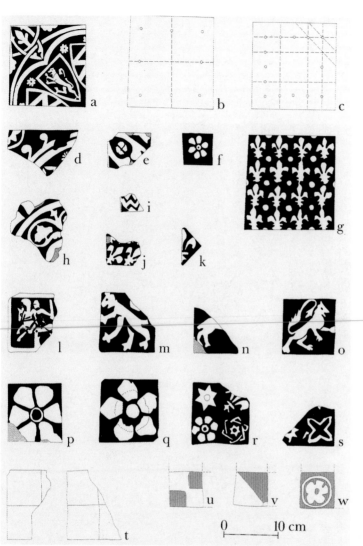

XXVIIIA. Utrecht decorated tiles.
Numbers t–w imported from the
Ardenne region
Drawings by C. A. M. van Rooijen

XXVIIIB. Drawing of part of a mosaic
tile floor and decorated tiles found in
1896 in the remains of the Abbey of
Oostbroek. Drawing by B. van
Beijnum 1896
*Rijksarchief in Utrecht, Topografische
Atlas, no. 1932*

XXIXA. Waster from the Bemuurde Weerd with the
head of a man; B. Tile fragment from Haskerdijken
with identical man's head; C. and D. Tin-glazed tiles
from the Bemuurde Weerd

A, C *and* D *Fotodienst Gemeente Utrecht;*
B: *H. De Jong, Tjalleberd;* C *and* D *are reproduced by
permission of the owner mr Thomas Kleij, Utrecht*

B

C

XXXA. Floor from house no. III;
B Floor from house no. V;
C Floor with a square of Essex-type
tiles from house no. II
Slides by C. A. M. van Rooijen

XXXI. Floor in the church of Heukelum. The 'English' tiles are in the uppermost border of
the pavement
Rijksdienst voor de Monumentenzorg, Zeist

XXXIIA. Norwich, Church of St Peter
Mancroft, *c.* 1450–55, Mocking of Christ
and Crowning with Thorns
National Monuments Record

XXXIIB. London, British Library, MS Add. 38527,
c. 1415, *Spieghel der Maeghden*, fol. 90ᵛ
British Library

XXXIIc. Amsterdam, Rijksmuseum, *c.* 1390, Epitaph of the Lords of Montfoort
Rijksmuseum

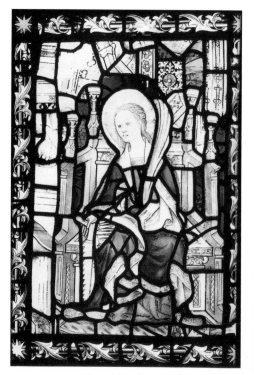

XXXIIIA. Norwich, church of St Peter
Mancroft, *c.* 1450–55, St Faith
National Monuments Record

XXXIIIB. Norwich, church of St Peter
Mancroft, *c.* 1453, Two scenes from the Life
of St Margaret
National Monuments Record

XXXIIIc. and D.
Norwich, church of
St Peter Mancroft,
c. 1453, St Elizabeth
from Visitation from
Name of Jesus window
and St Margaret
window
*National Monuments
Record*

XXXIVA. Chimney frieze with Christ as Man of Sorrows, Utrecht, Centraal Museum
Centraal Museum

XXXIVB. Chimney frieze with Virgin with Child, Utrecht, Centraal Museum
Centraal Museum

XXXIVC. Chimney frieze with Virgin with Child and St Anne, Utrecht, Centraal Museum
Centraal Museum

XXXVA. Chimney frieze with the temptation of St Antony, Utrecht, Museum Catharijneconvent
Catharijneconvent

XXXVB. Adriaen van Wesel, Altar of the
Brotherhood of our Lady at Bois-le-Duc, detail,
Amsterdam, Rijksmuseum
Rijksmuseum

XXXVC. Master of the Utrechse Stenen
Vrouwenkop, Head of the Virgin, Utrecht,
Museum Catharijneconvent
Catharijneconvent

XXXVIA. Workshop of Adriaen van Wesel, Console with cherubim, bearing a coat of arms, *c.* 1475–77, Centraal Museum Utrecht
Centraal Museum Utrecht

XXXVIB. Detail of XXXVIA
Jan W. Klinckaert

XXXVIC. Detail of XXXVIA
Jan W. Klinckaert

XXXVIIA. C. van Hardenbergh, Interior of the Mariakerk in Utrecht, *c.* 1790, Gemeentelijke Archiefdienst Utrecht, Topografische Atlas
Gemeentelijke Archiefdienst Utrecht

XXXVIIB. Coat of arms of Petrus Ramp, Canon of the Chapter of Our Lady in Utrecht from A. van Buchell, *Monumenta passim in templis ac monasteriis trajectinae urbis, c.* 1600
Gemeentelijke Archiefdienst Utrecht

XXXVIIIA. The first page of the sacristy
inventory of 1571, with on the left side the
annotation of 1578. (RAU, dom,
inv. no. 2505, fol. 1
Rijksarchief in Utrecht

XXXVIIIB. The entrance to the sacristy
complex in the northern choir aisle
Monumentendienst, Zeist

XXXVIIIC. The cermonial shoe once
belonging to the episcopal dress of bishop
Gwijde van Avesnes (Centraal Museum, inv.
no. 12354/A
Centraal Museum

XXXVIIID. View from the north at the *Dom* of
Utrecht in 1660. Engraving J. van Lamsweerde, 1660
Gemeentelijke Archiefdienst Utrecht

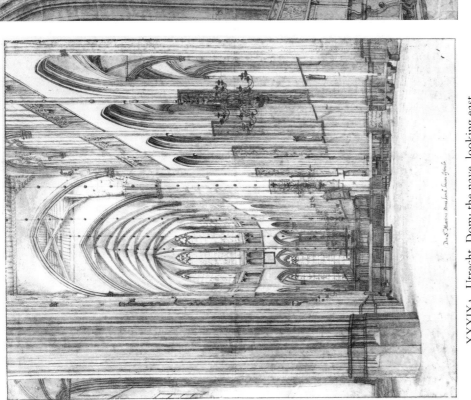

XXXIXB. Utrecht, Dom: the choir, looking north-east
Drawing by Pieter Saenredam, September 1636. *Koninklijk Huisarchief, The Hague cat. N. MCS/189) Royal Collections, reproduced with gracious permission of Her Royal Highness Princess Juliana of the Netherlands*

XXXIXA. Utrecht, Dom: the nave, looking east
Drawing by Pieter Saenredam, September 1636.
Gemeentelijke Archiefdienst Utrecht

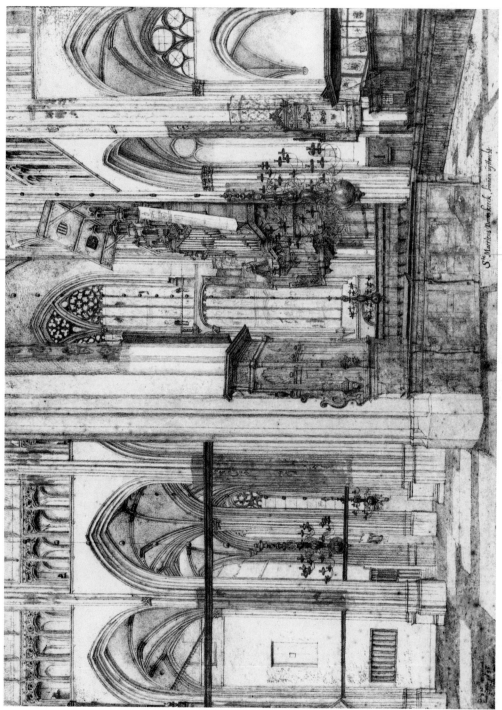

XL. Utrecht, Dom: the transepts, looking north
Drawing by Pieter Saenredam, September 1636.
Gemeentelijke Archiefdienst Utrecht

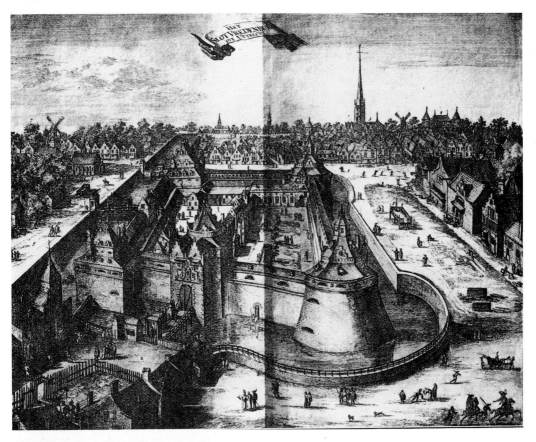

XLIA. Bastion Vredenburg, Utrecht
Engraving by C. Decker

XLIB. Jan Gossaert, *Neptune and Amphtrite*, 1516,
Berlin, Bode Museum

A

B

C

XLIIA. Jan van Scorel, *The Lokhorst Triptych*, Utrecht Centraal Museum. The inside of the left-hand panel with St Agnes, St Cornelius and St Anthony Major
Centraal Museum

XLIIB. idem. The inside of the right-hand panel with St Sebastian, Gertrude of Nijvel and St Christopher
Centraal Museum

XLIIc. Willem van Noort, Doorframe of former townhall, Utrecht, 1546, sandstone, Utrecht
Centraal Museum

XLIIIA. Dirck van Baburen, *Granida and Daifilo* Private collection

XLIIIB. Cornelis van Poelenburg, Banquet of the Gods, *c.* 1627,
Mauritshuis, The Hague
Mauritshuis